MIGRATION AND REMITTANCES
FACTBOOK 2011

MIGRATION AND REMITTANCES FACTBOOK 2011

2nd Edition

THE WORLD BANK

ISBN: 978-0-8213-8218-9
eISBN: 978-0-8213-8511-1
DOI: 10.1596/978-0-8213-8218-9

Library of Congress Cataloging-in-Publication data has been applied for.

Cover and interior design by Auras Design.

Contents

List of Figures

Foreword

There are more than 215 million international migrants in the world. Recorded remittances received by developing countries, estimated to be US$325 billion in 2010, far exceed the volume of official aid flows and constitute more than 10 percent of gross domestic product (GDP) in many developing countries. Cross-country analysis and evidence from household surveys suggest that migration and remittances reduce poverty in the origin communities. Remittances lead to increased investments in health, education, and small businesses. At the same time, the loss of skills associated with migration can hamper development and delivery of basic services in sending countries. The diaspora of developing countries can be a source of capital, trade, investment, knowledge, and technology transfers.

Migration and Remittances Factbook 2011 provides a comprehensive picture of emigration, skilled emigration, immigration, and remittance flows for 210 countries and 15 country groups, drawing on authoritative, publicly available data. The current edition of the *Factbook* updates the information in the popular 2008 edition with additional data for 71 countries collected from various sources, including national censuses, labor force surveys, population registers, and other national sources. In addition, it provides selected socioeconomic characteristics such as population, labor force, age dependency ratio, gross national income (GNI) per capita, and poverty headcount for each country and regional grouping.

More frequent and timely monitoring of migration and remittance trends can provide policy makers, researchers, and the development community with the tools to make informed decisions. The *Factbook* makes an important contribution to this effort by providing the latest available data and facts on migration and remittance trends worldwide in a comprehensive and readily accessible format.

The *Factbook* is part of a broader effort of the Development Prospects Group of the World Bank to monitor and analyze migration and remittances from a development perspective.

Hans Timmer
Director, Development Prospects Group
The World Bank

Highlights

Migration and Remittances Factbook 2011 presents numbers and facts behind the stories of international migration and remittances, drawing on authoritative, publicly available data. Some interesting facts:

- More than 215 million people, or 3 percent of the world population, live outside their countries of birth. Current migration flows, relative to population, are weaker than those of the last decades of the nineteenth century.

- The top migrant destination country is the United States, followed by the Russian Federation, Germany, Saudi Arabia, and Canada. The top immigration countries, relative to population, are Qatar (87 percent), Monaco (72 percent), the United Arab Emirates (70 percent), Kuwait (69 percent), and Andorra (64 percent).

- The United States has seen the largest inflows of migrants between 2005 and 2010. There was a surge of migrant flows to Spain, Italy, and the United Kingdom, mainly from Eastern Europe as well as Latin America and North Africa. The six Gulf Cooperation Council countries (Bahrain, Kuwait, Oman, Qatar, Saudi Arabia, and the United Arab Emirates) have also seen a significant increase in migrant flows in the past few years, mostly from South Asia and East Asia. However, new migration flows in all regions have weakened because of the global financial crisis.

- The volume of South–South migration (migration between developing countries) is larger than migration from the South to high-income countries belonging to the Organisation for Economic Co-operation and Development (OECD). High-income non-OECD countries such as the Gulf countries are also major destinations for migrants from the South. South–South migration is significantly larger than migration from the South to high-income OECD countries in Sub-Saharan Africa (73 percent) and Europe and Central Asia (61 percent).

- According to available official data, Mexico–United States is the largest migration corridor in the world, accounting for 11.6 million migrants in 2010. Migration corridors in the former Soviet Union—Russia–Ukraine and Ukraine–Russia—are the next largest, followed by Bangladesh–India; in these corridors, many natives became migrants without moving when new international boundaries were drawn.

- Smaller countries tend to have higher rates of skilled emigration. Almost all physicians trained in Grenada and Dominica have emigrated abroad. Cape Verde, Fiji, Liberia, São Tomé and Principe, and St. Lucia are also among the countries with very high emigration rates of physicians.

- Refugees and asylum seekers made up 16.3 million, or 8 percent, of international migrants in 2010. The share of refugees in the migrant population was 14.6 percent in low-income countries compared with 2.1 percent in high-income OECD countries. The Middle East and North Africa region had the largest share of refugees and asylum seekers among immigrants (65 percent), followed by South Asia (20 percent), Sub-Saharan Africa (17 percent), and East Asia and Pacific (8.8 percent).

- In 2010, worldwide remittance flows are estimated to have exceeded $440 billion. From that amount, developing countries received $325 billion, which represents an increase of 6 percent from the 2009 level. The true size, including unrecorded flows through formal and informal channels, is believed to be significantly larger. Recorded remittances in 2009 were nearly three times the amount of official aid and almost as large as foreign direct investment (FDI) flows to developing countries.

- In 2010, the top recipient countries of recorded remittances were India, China, Mexico, the Philippines, and France. As a share of GDP, however, smaller countries such as Tajikistan (35 percent), Tonga (28 percent), Lesotho (25 percent), Moldova (31 percent), and Nepal (23 percent) were the largest recipients in 2009.

- High-income countries are the main source of remittances. The United States is by far the largest, with $48 billion in recorded outward flows in 2009. Saudi Arabia ranks as the second largest, followed by Switzerland and Russia.

- Remittance flows to developing countries proved to be resilient during the recent global financial crisis—they fell only 5.5 percent in 2009 and registered a quick recovery in 2010. By contrast, there was a decline of 40 percent in FDI flows and a 46 percent decline in private debt and portfolio equity flows in 2009.

Migration and Remittances Factbook 2011 is also available online at http://www.worldbank.org/prospects/migrationandremittances. The Web site also provides updates of data and information on migration and remittances.

Acknowledgments

Migration and Remittances Factbook 2011 was compiled by Dilip Ratha, Sanket Mohapatra, and Ani Silwal of the Development Prospects Group at the World Bank. They gratefully acknowledge constructive comments and advice at various stages of publication from Susan Martin of Georgetown University; Jean-Christophe Dumont and Sarah Widmaier of the Organisation for Economic Co-operation and Development; Rakesh Kochhar and Mark Lopez of the Pew Hispanic Center; and Sonia Plaza, Neil Ruiz, Elina Scheja, and Hans Timmer of the World Bank.

Production of this volume (including design, editing, and layout) was coordinated by Stephen McGroarty and Susan Graham of the Office of the Publisher at the World Bank. The printing was managed by Andrés Meneses.

Data Notes

The data on migration, remittances, and other socioeconomic variables presented in *Migration and Remittances Factbook 2011* (*Factbook 2011*) are the latest available as of October 1, 2010. The reader is advised to note the pitfalls of using the data on international migration and remittances, which are often missing, lagging, or lacking in cross-country comparability. Capturing data on irregular movements of migrants and remittances remains a big challenge.

Changes to Country Classification since the 2008 Edition of the *Factbook*

The aggregate data on migration and remittances for different regions and income groups have changed since the publication of *Migration and Remittances Factbook 2008* (*Factbook 2008*) because of changes in country classification (see table 1). These changes, in particular the reclassification of Poland as a high-income country, reduce the total remittances received by developing countries to US$307 billion, reported in *Factbook 2011*, from US$316 billion, reported by Ratha, Mohapatra, and Silwal (2010) in April 2010.

The World Bank country classifications (World Bank 2010a) include any territory with population greater than 30,000 for which authorities report separate social and economic statistics. One exception is Palau, which has a population of less than 30,000 but appears in the classifications because it is a World Bank member state. These territories include American Samoa; Aruba; Bermuda; Cayman Islands; Faeroe Islands; French Polynesia; Greenland; Guam; Hong Kong SAR, China; Isle of Man; Macao SAR, China; Mayotte; Netherlands Antilles; New Caledonia; Northern Mariana Islands; Puerto Rico; and Virgin Islands (U.S.). Residents of some of these entities have access to citizenship rights of other entities (e.g., Puerto Ricans are U.S. citizens). However, to maintain consistency with the World Bank's country classification, migrants between these entities are considered international migrants in *Factbook 2011*.

Table 1 Changes to World Bank Income Classification between 2008 and 2011

Country	Income group (July 2007)	Income group (July 2010)
Antigua and Barbuda	. .	Middle
Channel Islands	. .	High
Côte d'Ivoire	Low	Middle
Croatia	Middle	High
Equatorial Guinea	Middle	High
Gibraltar[a]	. .	High
Hungary	Middle	High
India	Low	Middle
Isle of Man	. .	High
Kosovo	. .	Middle
Latvia	Middle	High
Mongolia	Low	Middle
Montenegro	. .	Middle
Nigeria	Low	Middle
Northern Mariana Islands	. .	High
Oman	Middle	High
Pakistan	Low	Middle
Papua New Guinea	Low	Middle
Poland	Middle	High
São Tomé and Principe	Low	Middle
Senegal	Low	Middle
Serbia	. .	Middle
Serbia and Montenegro[b]	Middle	. .
Slovak Republic	Middle	High
Sudan	Low	Middle
Timor-Leste	Low	Middle
Turks and Caicos Islands[a]	. .	High
Tuvalu[a]	. .	Middle
Uzbekistan	Low	Middle
Vietnam	Low	Middle
Yemen, Rep.	Low	Middle

Source: World Bank country classifications (World Bank 2010a).

a. These countries were added to the World Bank's country classifications in July 2010 but are not included in *Migration and Remittances Factbook 2011* because very little data are available on them.

b. Serbia and Montenegro are now separate countries.

. . indicates that these countries were not included in the World Bank's country classification.

Data on Migration

According to the "Recommendations on Statistics of International Migration" by the United Nations Statistics Division (1998), *long-term migrants* are persons who move to a country other than that of their usual residence for a period of at least one year, so that the country of destination effectively becomes their new country of usual residence. *Short-term migrants* are persons who move to a country other than that of their usual residence for a period of at least three months but less than one year except in cases where the movement to that country is for purposes of recreation, holiday, visits to friends and relatives, business, medical treatment, or religious pilgrimage (UN Statistics Division 1998).

The duration threshold that identifies migrants varies across countries (Lemaitre, Liebig, and Thoreau 2006). For example, under the United Nations

(UN) definition, international students who study in the receiving country for more than one year would be considered migrants. The *International Migration Outlook* (OECD 2006) made a first attempt to characterize migrants by "reasons for movement" and to harmonize statistics among Organisation for Economic Co-operation and Development (OECD) countries.

The database of the UN Population Division (UNPD) is the most comprehensive source of information on international migrant stocks for the period 1960–2010 for all 210 countries in this *Factbook* (UNPD 2009). The bilateral migrant stock data used here for 193 countries are based on statistics on foreign-born population for 109 countries, foreign nationality data for 75 countries, and migrant stock data that are estimated indirectly using various assumptions for 9 countries. Data on bilateral migration are not available for 17 countries.

Preliminary efforts to estimate bilateral migration data include data by Harrison (2004), the University of Sussex data originally constructed for the Global Trade Analysis Project trade modeling, and data by the Development Prospects Group of the World Bank used for estimating South–South migration and remittance flows (Ratha and Shaw 2007). Parsons et al. (2007) have created a "composite" matrix that contains estimates of bilateral migrant stocks for 226 x 226 countries. Because these data were constructed for modeling purposes, Parsons et al. use a variety of assumptions to make total immigrant stock add up to total emigrant stock.[1]

We have updated the bilateral migration matrix compiled by Ratha and Shaw (2007) using data from various sources. Bilateral migration data for the following 42 countries were updated using national censuses compiled by the UNPD (2010): Angola; Azerbaijan; Benin; Bhutan; Burkina Faso; Burundi; Cameroon; Cape Verde; Colombia; the Comoros; Côte d'Ivoire; Cuba; Djibouti; Dominica; the Arab Republic of Egypt; El Salvador; Faeroe Islands; Gabon; The Gambia; Guinea; Indonesia; Iraq; Jamaica; Jordan; Kenya; the Lao People's Democratic Republic; Liberia; Macao SAR, China; the former Yugoslav Republic of Macedonia; Malaysia; Mali; Malta; Niger; Puerto Rico; San Marino; Sierra Leone; St. Kitts and Nevis; Suriname; Tajikistan; Timor-Leste; the Republic of Yemen; and Zimbabwe.

The latest immigration data for the following countries belonging to the OECD were obtained from the International Migration Database (OECD 2010): Australia, Austria, Belgium, Canada, the Czech Republic, Denmark, Finland, France, Germany, Greece, Hungary, Ireland, Italy, Japan, the Republic of Korea, the Netherlands, New Zealand, Norway, Poland, the Slovak Republic, Spain, and Sweden. Data for most countries are for 2005 and 2007. The data collected from national-level labor force and population surveys are the best available data on immigrant stocks since the 2000 round of censuses, even though the coverage of migrants in this database is somewhat heterogeneous across countries.

Available bilateral migration data for the United States from the 2000 census were complemented with the nationally representative American Community Survey for 2008 (U.S. Census Bureau 2008). Census data on immigrants in the United Kingdom was complemented with more recent migration data from the UK Office of National Statistics (UK ONS 2009). Immigration data for the six Gulf Cooperation Council countries (Bahrain, Kuwait, Oman, Qatar, Saudi

---

[1] The resulting final bilateral migrant stock matrix, according to Parsons et al. (2007), "though the fullest, is arguably the least accurate set of data" (Parsons et al. 2007, 11).

Arabia, and United Arab Emirates) were obtained from Kapiszewski (2006). The quality of data on bilateral migration is as good (or poor) as the quality of the population censuses and other national-level sources in different countries, but in a number of countries, the data are simply missing.

The 2010 round of censuses are currently being conducted, but the data are not available as of October 2010. As discussed above, the census data from the 2000 round of censuses were supplemented with the latest available data from national-level sources to obtain the most recent picture of migrant stocks for 2010. Available data may not accurately reflect some recent trends, such as return of migrants from the United Kingdom to Poland or from the Russian Federation to Tajikistan because of the global financial crisis.

Even in the 2010 census round, a number of countries (including Japan, Mexico, Korea, the Philippines, and Egypt) do not plan to ask about the country of birth (Center for Global Development 2009). However, other important countries are starting to record foreign-born persons. China recently announced that it will ask questions about migrant workers in the 2010 census.[2] Although the UNPD estimates that there are 0.7 million immigrants in China in 2010 (the figure used in *Factbook 2011*), the Chinese authorities report 2.9 million registered foreign workers in 2007. The actual number, including the unregistered and illegal workers, is likely to be far higher.

Data on Remittances[3]

Migrant remittances are defined as the sum of workers' remittances, compensation of employees, and migrants' transfers.

Workers' remittances, as defined by the International Monetary Fund (IMF) in the *Balance of Payments Manual*, 6th edition (IMF 2010a), are current private transfers from migrant workers who are considered residents of the host country to recipients in the workers' country of origin.[4] If the migrants live in the host country for one year or longer, they are considered residents, regardless of their immigration status. If the migrants have lived in the host country for less than one year, their entire income in the host country should be classified as compensation of employees.

Although the residence guideline in the manual is clear, this rule is often not followed for various reasons. Many countries compile data based on the citizenship of the migrant worker rather than on their residency status. Further, data are shown entirely as either compensation of employees or worker remittances, although they should be split between the two categories if the guidelines were correctly followed.[5] The distinction between these two categories

---

[2] Eimer, David. 2010. "Beijing plans curbs on number of foreigners working in China." Telegraph.co.uk, May 23. http://www.telegraph.co.uk/news/worldnews/asia/china/7756638/Beijing-plans-curbs-on-number-of-foreigners-working-in-China.html.

[3] This part is based on *Global Economic Prospects 2006* (World Bank 2006). See also IMF (2009).

[4] Official statistics on remittances tend to underestimate the size of remittance flows. Following a request from the G7 nations in June 2004, the World Bank together with the IMF and the UN led an international working group to improve remittance statistics. Based on the recommendation of the Luxembourg Group, the new *Balance of Payments Manual*, 6th edition, includes three new items: personal remittances, total remittances, and total remittances and transfers to nonprofit institutions serving households.

[5] For example, India shows very little compensation of employees, but large workers' remittances, although it is well known that India supplies a large number of temporary information technology workers to the United States and to European countries. On the other hand, the Philippines shows large compensation of employees and very few migrants' transfers.

appears to be entirely arbitrary, depending on country preference, convenience, and tax laws or data availability.[6]

Migrants' transfers are the net worth of migrants' assets that are transferred from one country to another at the time of migration (for a period of at least one year). As the number of temporary workers increases, the importance of migrants' transfers may increase. Therefore, to gain a complete picture of the resource flow, one has to consider these three items together.

Some countries do not report data on remittances in the IMF Balance of Payments statistics. Several developing countries (for example, Afghanistan, Cuba, Turkmenistan, Uzbekistan, and Zimbabwe) do not report remittance inflows data to the IMF, even though it is known that emigration from those countries took place. Some high-income countries (notably Canada, Qatar, Singapore, and the United Arab Emirates) do not report data on remittance outflows, even though they are important destinations for migrants. A global survey of central banks reveals significant heterogeneity in the quality of remittance data compilation across countries (Irving, Mohapatra, and Ratha 2010). Some central banks use remittance data reported by commercial banks, but do not adequately capture flows through money transfer operators, post offices, and emerging channels such as mobile money transfers. Even when data are available and properly classified, in some cases, these data are out of date. The methodologies used by countries for remittance data compilation are not always publicly available. It is hoped that the increased awareness about the importance of remittances and the shortcomings in the data on both remittances and migrant workers will result in efforts to improve data collection. In some cases, such as China, Malaysia, and Nigeria, the sources for total remittances are different from data on workers' remittances, compensation of employees, and migrants' transfer. As a result, the total remittances figure does not match the sum of the components.

Perhaps the most difficult aspect of remittance data is estimating informal flows. One way to estimate the true size of remittances is to undertake surveys of remittance senders and recipients. Without new, adequately randomized and representative surveys of recipients and senders, evidence from existing household surveys will only be indicative rather than comprehensive.

Caveats on the Quality of Data

As discussed above, the authors have built on *Factbook 2008* by updating the latest migration data from the UN Population Division, national censuses, labor force surveys, population registers, and other national sources for 210 countries. The remittance data were obtained from Ratha, Mohapatra, and Silwal (2010), whose data were based on the IMF Balance of Payments database as well as data from central banks, national statistical agencies, and World Bank country desks. *Factbook 2011* has arguably the most comprehensive collection of data and facts on migration and remittances that is available.

However, the reader is advised to note the pitfalls of using currently available migration and remittance data. Remittance flows and the stock of migrants may

---

[6] Because of the difficulty in classifications, countries have often classified workers' remittances as either other current transfers or transfers from other sectors. In some countries, notably China, remittances may have been misclassified as foreign direct investment. In the case of India and many other countries, remittances may have been classified as nonresident deposits, especially those in local currency terms.

be underestimated due to the use of informal remittance channels, irregular migration, and ambiguity in the definition of migrants (foreign born versus foreigner, seasonal versus permanent). Considerably more effort is needed to improve the quality of data. The recommendations of a commission on improving migration data led by the Center for Global Development appear to be a step in the right direction (Center for Global Development 2009).

Sources of Data

Data on immigration and emigration are from UNPD (2009) and Ratha and Shaw (2007). Data on the emigration rate of the tertiary-educated population are from Docquier and Marfouk (2006). Data on emigration of physicians are from Bhargava, Docquier, and Moullan (2010), while supplementary data on physicians and data on nurses are from Clemens and Pettersson (2006) and are used for Sub-Saharan African countries. Data on remittances are from Ratha, Mohapatra, and Silwal (2010), and data on the components of remittances are from IMF (2010b). Bhargava, Docquier, and Moullan (2010) update the information in Docquier and Bhargava (2006) with additional destination countries and a harmonized definition of migrant physicians across countries.

Data on the following variables are from World Bank (2010b): Population, Population growth, Population density, Labor force, Unemployment rate, Urban population, Surface area, GNI (gross national income), GNI per capita, GDP (gross domestic product) growth, Poverty headcount ratio at national poverty line, and Age dependency ratio.

In the tables, "—" indicates the data are not available and "2010e" indicates 2010 estimate.

Bibliography

Bilsborrow, Richard E., Graeme Hugo, Amarjit S. Oberai, Hania Zlotnik. 1997. *International Migration Statistics, Guidelines for Improving Data Collection Systems*. Geneva: International Labour Office.

Bhargava, Alok, Frédéric Docquier, and Yasser Moullan. 2010. "Modeling the Effect of Physician Emigration on Human Development." Manuscript. http://ssrn.com/abstract=1555775.

Center for Global Development. 2009. *Migrants Count: Five Steps Toward Better Migration Data*. Report of the Commission on International Migration Data for Development Research and Policy, Washington, DC: Center for Global Development.

Clemens, Michael A., and Gunilla Pettersson. 2006. "New Data on African Health Professionals Abroad." Working Paper 95, Center for Global Development, Washington, DC.

Docquier, Frédéric, and Alok Bhargava. 2006. "The Medical Brain Drain: A New Panel Dataset on Physicians' Emigration Rates (1991–2004)." World Bank, Washington, DC.

Docquier, Frédéric, and Abdeslam Marfouk. 2006. "International Migration by Education Attainment 1990–2000." In *International Migration, Remittances, and the Brain Drain*, ed. Caglar Özden and Maurice Schiff, 151–99. Palgrave Macmillan: New York; and the World Bank: Washington, DC.

Harrison, Anne, assisted by Tolani Britton and Annika Swanson. 2004. "Working Abroad—The Benefits Flowing from Nationals Working in Other Countries." Paper prepared for the Organisation for Economic Co-operation and Development Round Table on Sustainable Development, Paris.

IMF (International Monetary Fund). 2009. *International Transactions in Remittances: Guide for Compilers and Users*. Washington, DC: IMF.

_____. 2010a. *Balance of Payments Manual*. 6th ed. Washington, DC: IMF.

_____. 2010b. Balance of Payments Statistics Database. Washington, DC. http://www2.imfstatistics.org/BOP/.

Irving, Jacqueline, Sanket Mohapatra, and Dilip Ratha. 2010. "Migrant Remittance Flows: Findings from a Global Survey of Central Banks." Working Paper 94, World Bank, Washington, DC.

Kapiszewski, Andrzej. 2006. "Arab Versus Asian Migrant Workers in the GCC Countries." Paper presented at the United Nations Expert Group Meeting on International Migration and Development in the Arab Region, Beirut, May 15–17. UN/POP/EGM/2006/02.

Lemaitre, George, Thomas Liebig, and Cécile Thoreau. 2006. "Harmonized Statistics on Immigrant Inflows—Preliminary Results, Sources and Methods." Report, Organisation for Economic Co-operation and Development, Paris.

OECD (Organisation for Economic Co-operation and Development). 2006. *International Migration Outlook*. Paris: OECD.

_____. 2010. International Migration Database. Paris. http://stats.oecd.org/Index.aspx?DataSetCode=MIG.

Parsons, Christopher R., Ronald Skeldon, Terrie L. Walmsley, and L. Alan Winters. 2007. "Quantifying International Migration: A Database of Bilateral Migrant Stocks." Policy Research Working Paper 4165, World Bank, Washington, DC.

Ratha, Dilip. 2003. "Worker's Remittances: An Important and Stable Source of External Development Finance." In *Global Development Finance: Striving for Stability in Development Finance*, 157–75. Washington, DC: World Bank.

Ratha, Dilip, Sanket Mohapatra, and Ani Silwal. 2010. Migration and Development Brief 12, World Bank, Washington, DC, April.

Ratha, Dilip, and William Shaw. 2007. "South–South Migration and Remittances." Working Paper 102, World Bank, Washington, DC.

Taylor, J. Edward. 2000. "Do Government Programs 'Crowd-in' Remittances?" Tomás Rivera Policy Institute, University of Southern California, and Inter-American Dialogue, Washington, DC.

UK ONS (United Kingdom Office of National Statistics). 2009.

UN (United Nations) Statistics Division. 1998. "Recommendations on Statistics of International Migration, Revision 1." Statistical Papers Series M, No. 58, United Nations, New York.

UNPD (United Nations Population Division). 2009. *Trends in Total Migrant Stock: The 2008 Revision*. New York: UN Department of Economic and Social Affairs.

_____. 2010. United Nations Global Migration Database v.0.3.6. New York. http://esa.un.org/unmigration/.

U.S. (United States) Census Bureau. 2008. American Community Survey.

World Bank. 1990. *World Devlopment Report 1990*. Washington, DC: World Bank.

_____. 2006. *Global Economic Prospects 2006: Economic Implications of Remittances and Migration*. Washington, DC: World Bank.

_____. 2010a. World Bank Country Classifications database. Washington, DC: World Bank. http://data.worldbank.org/about/country-classifications.

_____. 2010b. *World Development Indicators*. Washington, DC: World Bank.

Migration and Remittances: Top Countries

Top Immigration Countries[a], 2010
number of immigrants, millions

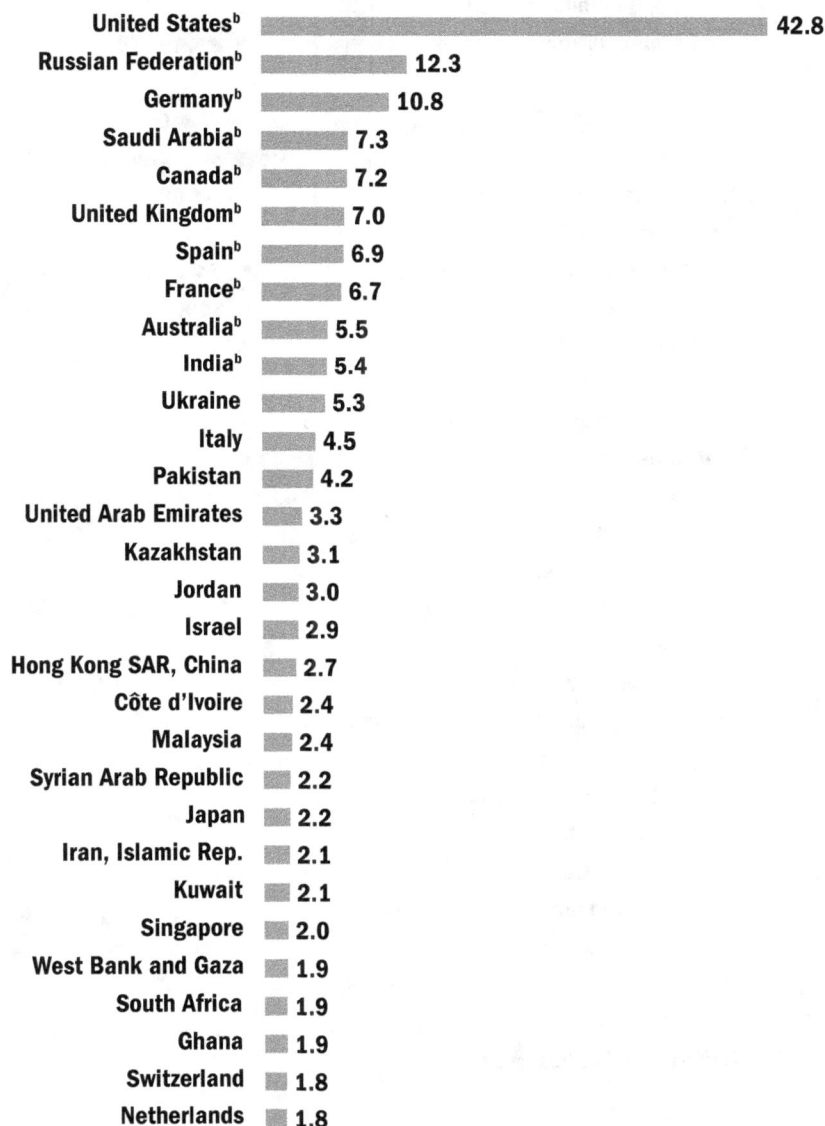

Country	Immigrants (millions)
United States[b]	42.8
Russian Federation[b]	12.3
Germany[b]	10.8
Saudi Arabia[b]	7.3
Canada[b]	7.2
United Kingdom[b]	7.0
Spain[b]	6.9
France[b]	6.7
Australia[b]	5.5
India[b]	5.4
Ukraine	5.3
Italy	4.5
Pakistan	4.2
United Arab Emirates	3.3
Kazakhstan	3.1
Jordan	3.0
Israel	2.9
Hong Kong SAR, China	2.7
Côte d'Ivoire	2.4
Malaysia	2.4
Syrian Arab Republic	2.2
Japan	2.2
Iran, Islamic Rep.	2.1
Kuwait	2.1
Singapore	2.0
West Bank and Gaza	1.9
South Africa	1.9
Ghana	1.9
Switzerland	1.8
Netherlands	1.8

Sources: Development Prospects Group, World Bank; UNPD 2009.
a. Includes countries and territories (see Data Notes, page xiii).
b. Top 10 country.

Top Immigration Countries[a], 2010

percentage of population

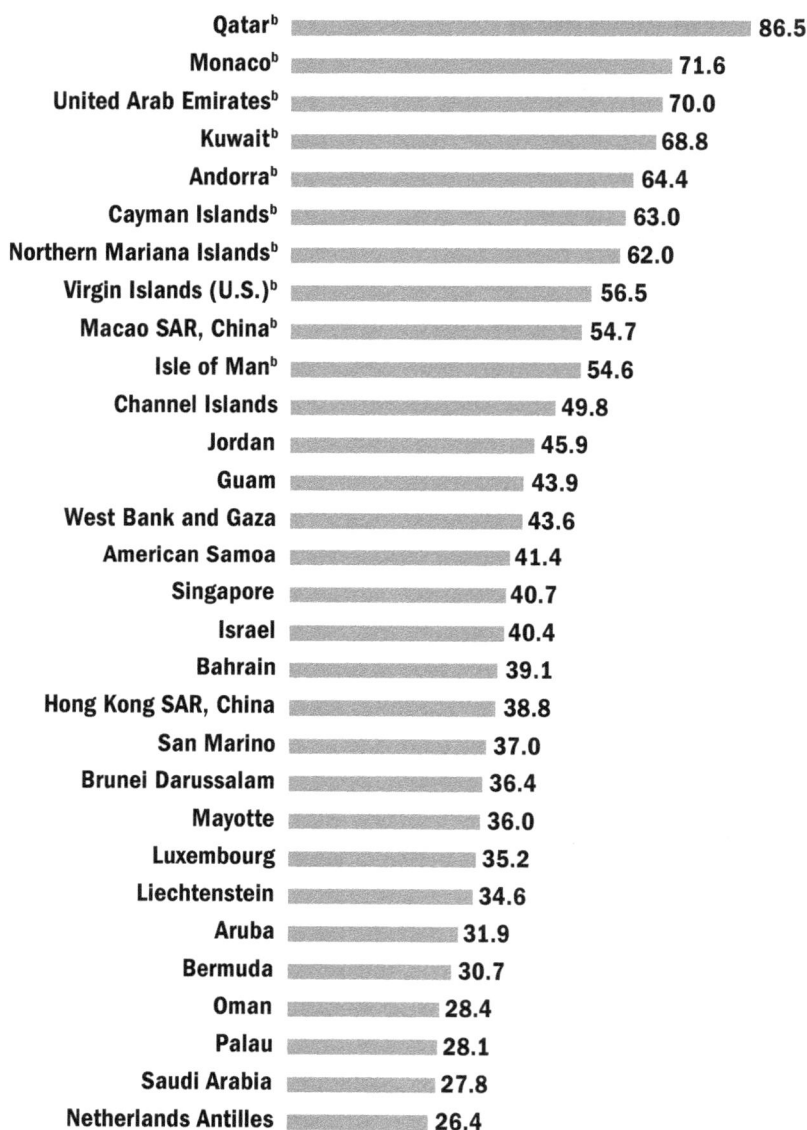

Country	Percentage
Qatar[b]	86.5
Monaco[b]	71.6
United Arab Emirates[b]	70.0
Kuwait[b]	68.8
Andorra[b]	64.4
Cayman Islands[b]	63.0
Northern Mariana Islands[b]	62.0
Virgin Islands (U.S.)[b]	56.5
Macao SAR, China[b]	54.7
Isle of Man[b]	54.6
Channel Islands	49.8
Jordan	45.9
Guam	43.9
West Bank and Gaza	43.6
American Samoa	41.4
Singapore	40.7
Israel	40.4
Bahrain	39.1
Hong Kong SAR, China	38.8
San Marino	37.0
Brunei Darussalam	36.4
Mayotte	36.0
Luxembourg	35.2
Liechtenstein	34.6
Aruba	31.9
Bermuda	30.7
Oman	28.4
Palau	28.1
Saudi Arabia	27.8
Netherlands Antilles	26.4

Sources: Development Prospects Group, World Bank; UNPD 2009.
a. Includes countries and territories (see Data Notes, page xiii).
b. Top 10 country.

Top Emigration Countries[a], 2010

number of emigrants, millions

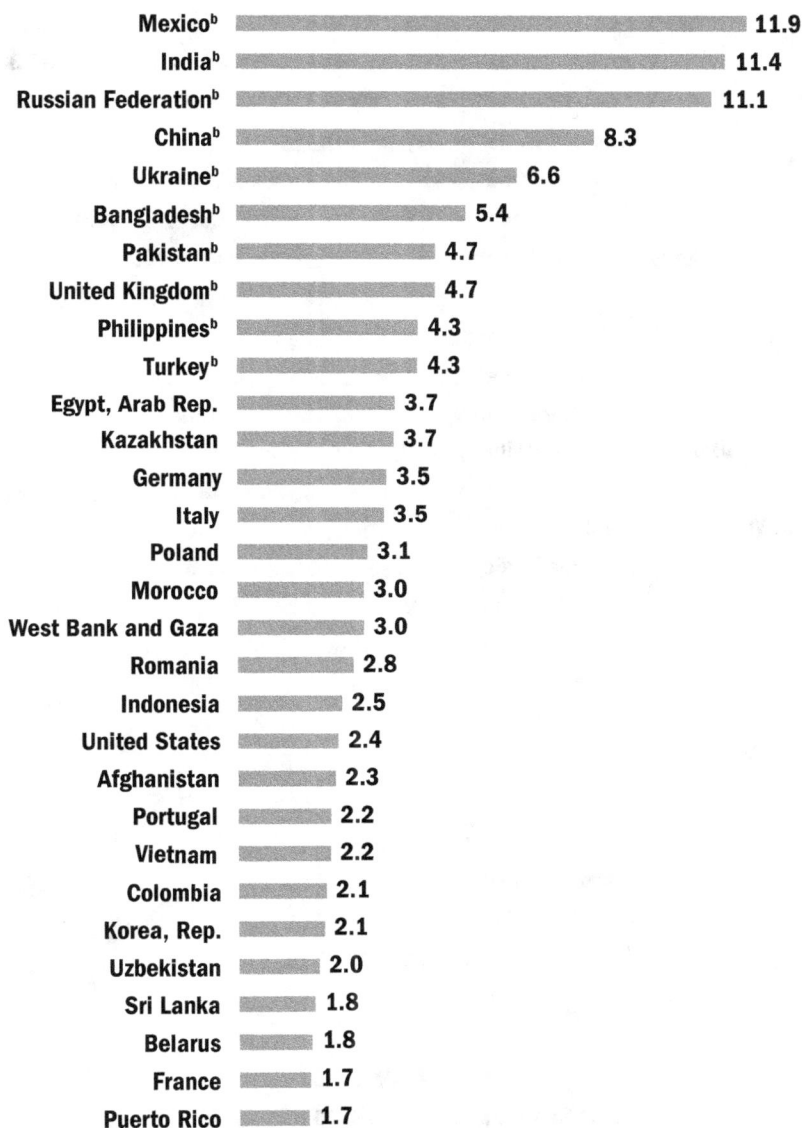

Mexico[b]	11.9
India[b]	11.4
Russian Federation[b]	11.1
China[b]	8.3
Ukraine[b]	6.6
Bangladesh[b]	5.4
Pakistan[b]	4.7
United Kingdom[b]	4.7
Philippines[b]	4.3
Turkey[b]	4.3
Egypt, Arab Rep.	3.7
Kazakhstan	3.7
Germany	3.5
Italy	3.5
Poland	3.1
Morocco	3.0
West Bank and Gaza	3.0
Romania	2.8
Indonesia	2.5
United States	2.4
Afghanistan	2.3
Portugal	2.2
Vietnam	2.2
Colombia	2.1
Korea, Rep.	2.1
Uzbekistan	2.0
Sri Lanka	1.8
Belarus	1.8
France	1.7
Puerto Rico	1.7

Sources: Development Prospects Group, World Bank; UNPD 2009.
a. Includes countries and territories (see Data Notes, page xiii).
b. Top 10 country.

Top Emigration Countries[a], 2010

percentage of population

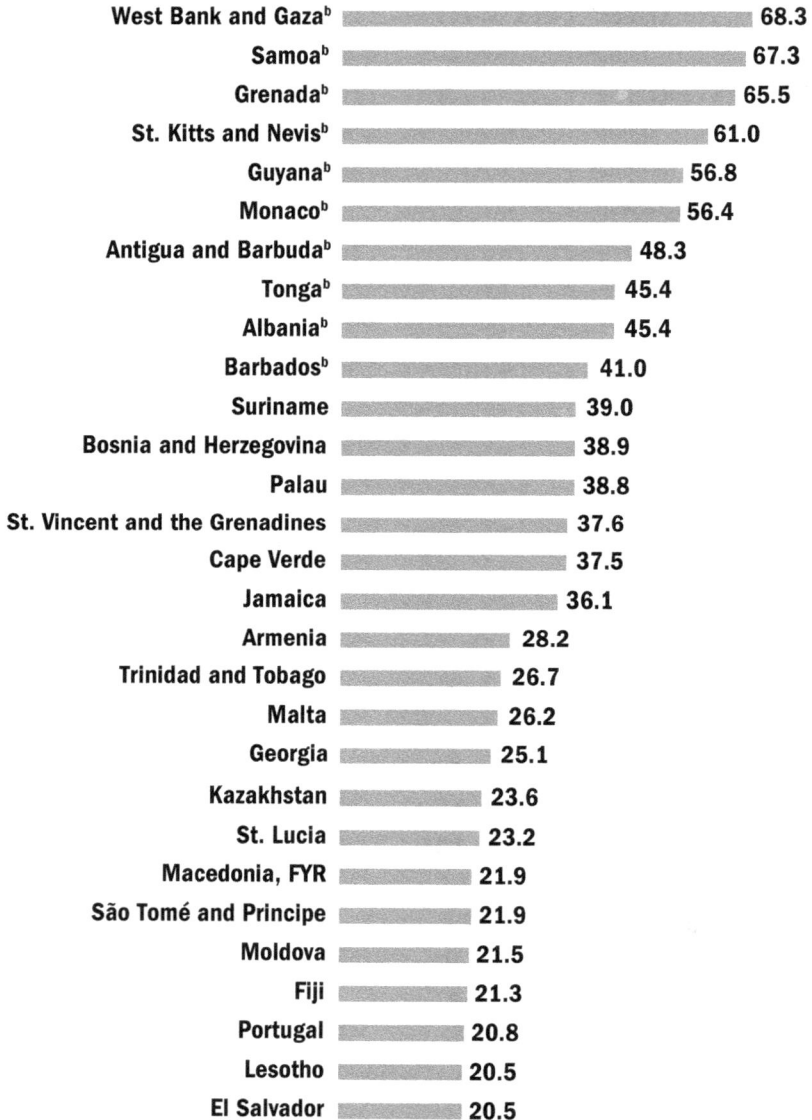

West Bank and Gaza[b]	68.3
Samoa[b]	67.3
Grenada[b]	65.5
St. Kitts and Nevis[b]	61.0
Guyana[b]	56.8
Monaco[b]	56.4
Antigua and Barbuda[b]	48.3
Tonga[b]	45.4
Albania[b]	45.4
Barbados[b]	41.0
Suriname	39.0
Bosnia and Herzegovina	38.9
Palau	38.8
St. Vincent and the Grenadines	37.6
Cape Verde	37.5
Jamaica	36.1
Armenia	28.2
Trinidad and Tobago	26.7
Malta	26.2
Georgia	25.1
Kazakhstan	23.6
St. Lucia	23.2
Macedonia, FYR	21.9
São Tomé and Principe	21.9
Moldova	21.5
Fiji	21.3
Portugal	20.8
Lesotho	20.5
El Salvador	20.5

Sources: Development Prospects Group, World Bank.

a. Includes countries and territories (see Data Notes, page xiii).

b. Top 10 country.

Top Migration Corridors, 2010
number of migrants, millions

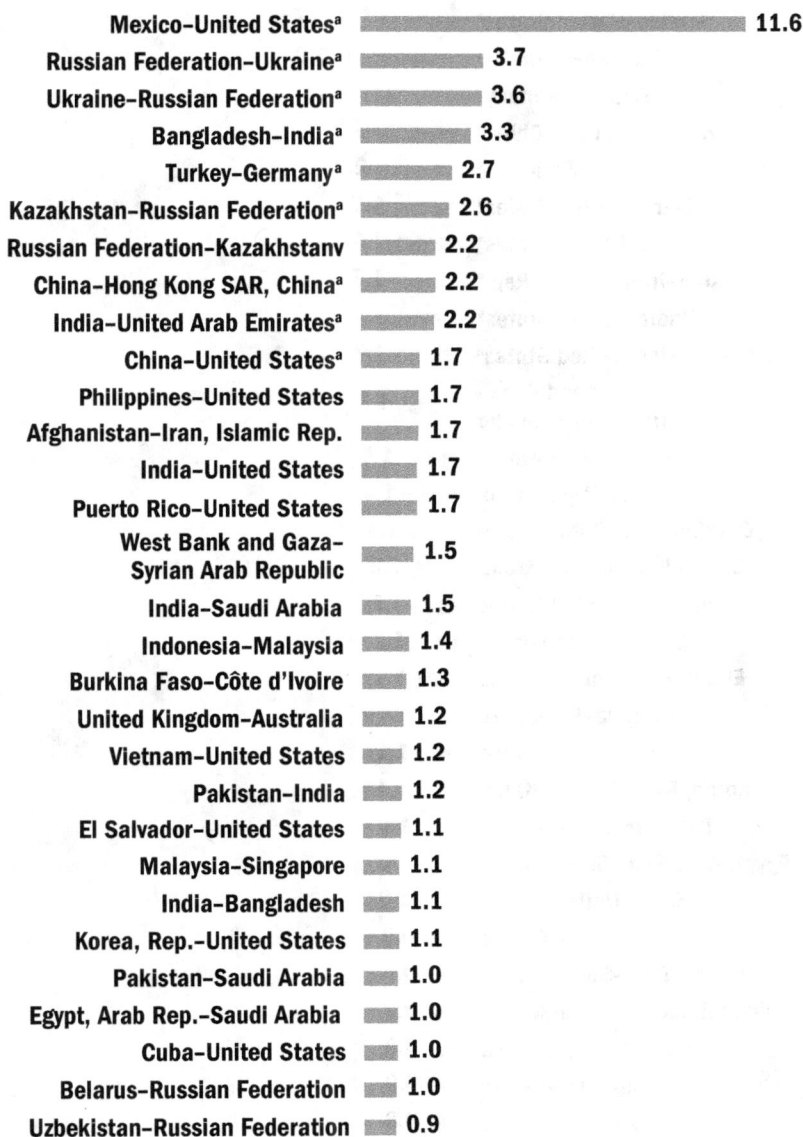

Corridor	Migrants
Mexico–United States[a]	11.6
Russian Federation–Ukraine[a]	3.7
Ukraine–Russian Federation[a]	3.6
Bangladesh–India[a]	3.3
Turkey–Germany[a]	2.7
Kazakhstan–Russian Federation[a]	2.6
Russian Federation–Kazakhstanv	2.2
China–Hong Kong SAR, China[a]	2.2
India–United Arab Emirates[a]	2.2
China–United States[a]	1.7
Philippines–United States	1.7
Afghanistan–Iran, Islamic Rep.	1.7
India–United States	1.7
Puerto Rico–United States	1.7
West Bank and Gaza–Syrian Arab Republic	1.5
India–Saudi Arabia	1.5
Indonesia–Malaysia	1.4
Burkina Faso–Côte d'Ivoire	1.3
United Kingdom–Australia	1.2
Vietnam–United States	1.2
Pakistan–India	1.2
El Salvador–United States	1.1
Malaysia–Singapore	1.1
India–Bangladesh	1.1
Korea, Rep.–United States	1.1
Pakistan–Saudi Arabia	1.0
Egypt, Arab Rep.–Saudi Arabia	1.0
Cuba–United States	1.0
Belarus–Russian Federation	1.0
Uzbekistan–Russian Federation	0.9

Source: Development Prospects Group, World Bank.
a. Top 10 country.

Top Migration Corridors (excluding the Former Soviet Union), 2010

number of migrants, millions

Mexico–United States[a]	11.6
Bangladesh–India[a]	3.3
Turkey–Germany[a]	2.7
China–Hong Kong SAR, China[a]	2.2
India–United Arab Emirates[a]	2.2
China–United States[a]	1.7
Philippines–United States[a]	1.7
Afghanistan–Iran, Islamic Rep.[a]	1.7
India–United States[a]	1.7
Puerto Rico–United States[a]	1.7
West Bank and Gaza–Syrian Arab Republic	1.5
India–Saudi Arabia	1.5
Indonesia–Malaysia	1.4
Burkina Faso–Côte d'Ivoire	1.3
United Kingdom–Australia	1.2
Vietnam–United States	1.2
Pakistan–India	1.2
El Salvador–United States	1.1
Malaysia–Singapore	1.1
India–Bangladesh	1.1
Korea, Rep.–United States	1.1
Pakistan–Saudi Arabia	1.0
Egypt, Arab Rep.–Saudi Arabia	1.0
Cuba–United States	1.0
Algeria–France	0.9
Yemen, Rep.–Saudi Arabia	0.9
West Bank and Gaza–Jordan	0.9
Zimbabwe–South Africa	0.9
Egypt, Arab Rep.–Jordan	0.9
Côte d'Ivoire–Burkina Faso	0.8

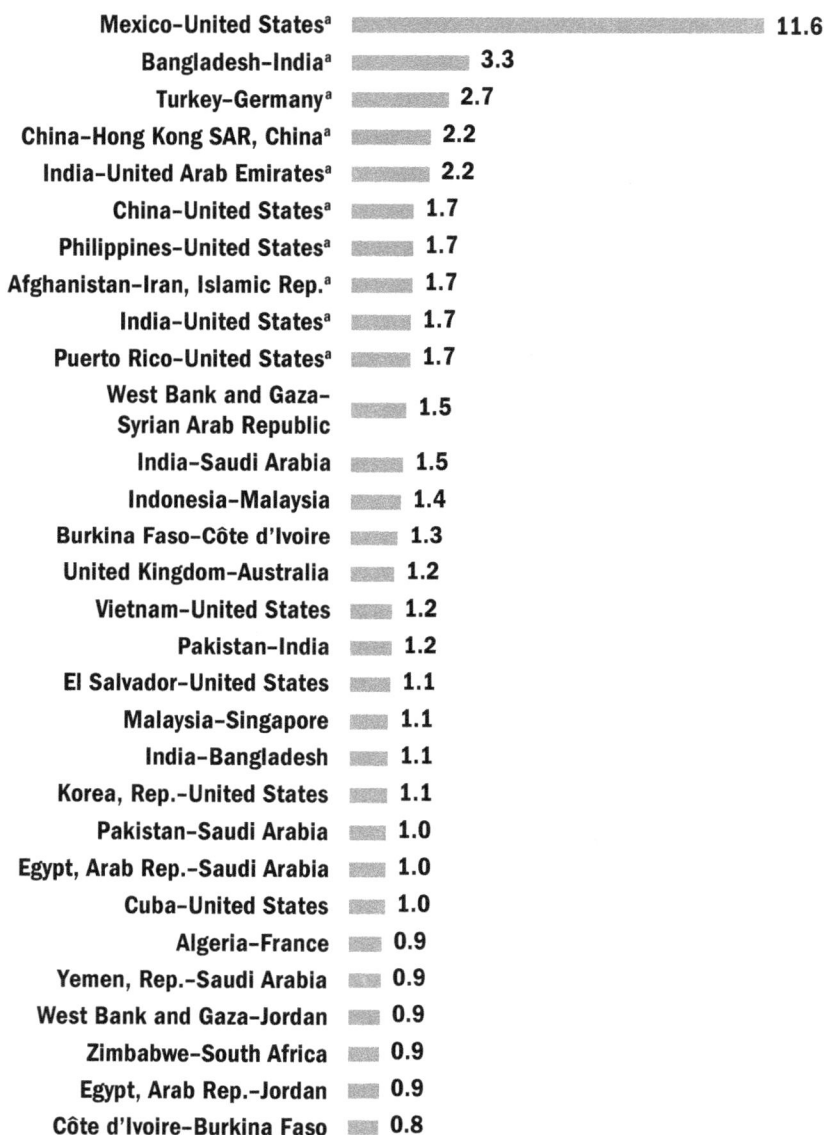

Source: Development Prospects Group, World Bank.
a. Top 10 country.

Top Destination Countries[a] for Refugees, 2010

number of migrants, millions

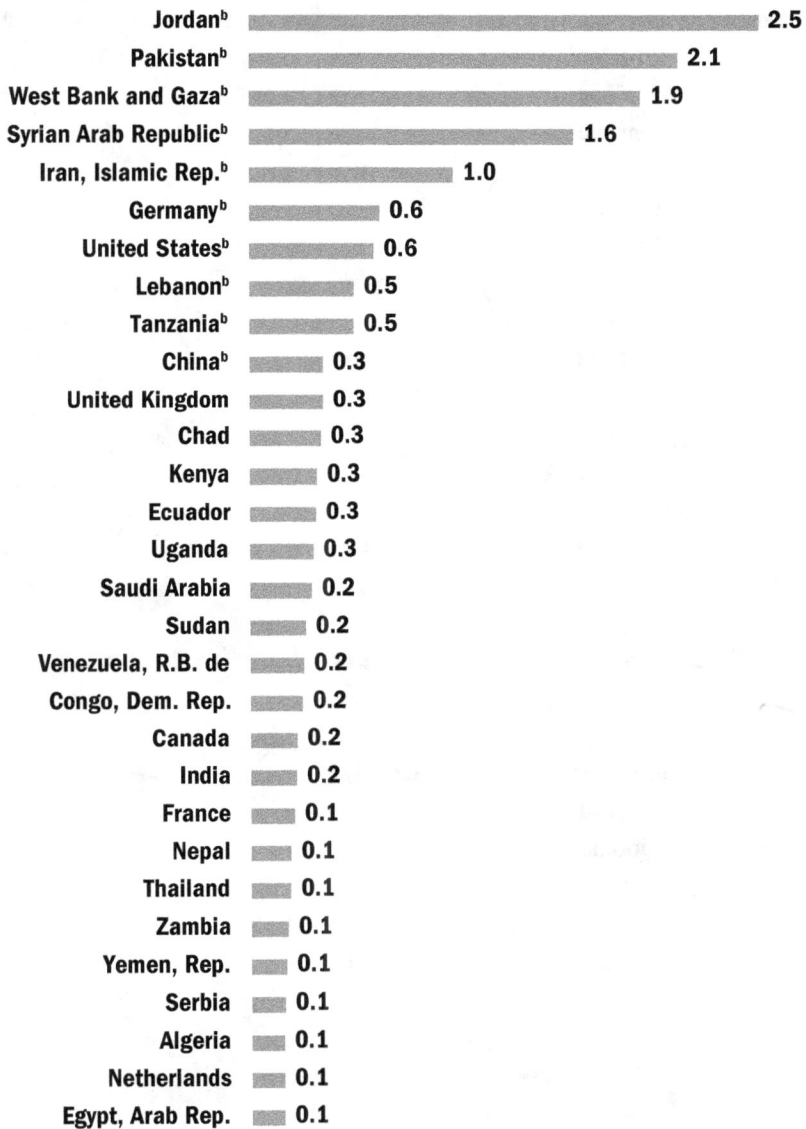

Jordan[b]	2.5
Pakistan[b]	2.1
West Bank and Gaza[b]	1.9
Syrian Arab Republic[b]	1.6
Iran, Islamic Rep.[b]	1.0
Germany[b]	0.6
United States[b]	0.6
Lebanon[b]	0.5
Tanzania[b]	0.5
China[b]	0.3
United Kingdom	0.3
Chad	0.3
Kenya	0.3
Ecuador	0.3
Uganda	0.3
Saudi Arabia	0.2
Sudan	0.2
Venezuela, R.B. de	0.2
Congo, Dem. Rep.	0.2
Canada	0.2
India	0.2
France	0.1
Nepal	0.1
Thailand	0.1
Zambia	0.1
Yemen, Rep.	0.1
Serbia	0.1
Algeria	0.1
Netherlands	0.1
Egypt, Arab Rep.	0.1

Source: United Nations Population Division based on United Nations High Commissioner for Refugees data.
a. Includes countries and territories (see Data Notes, page xiii).
b. Top 10 country.

Top Destination Countries[a] for Refugees, 2010

percentage of migrants

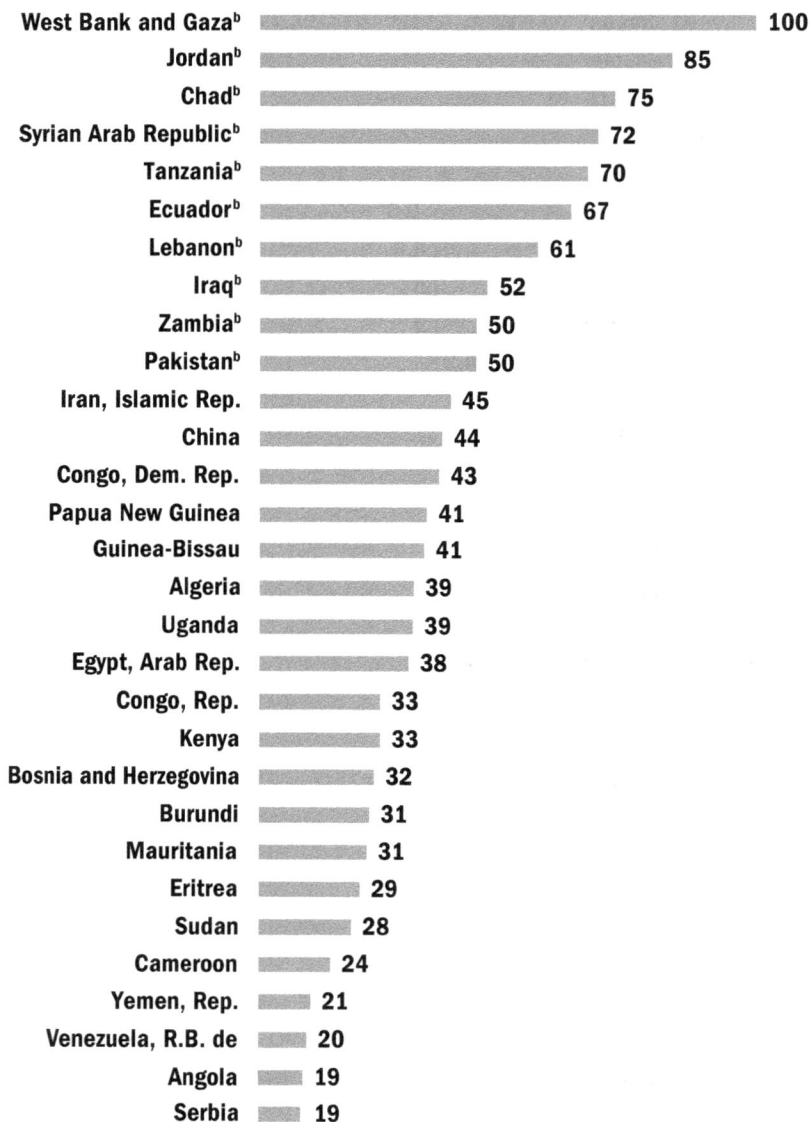

West Bank and Gaza[b]	100
Jordan[b]	85
Chad[b]	75
Syrian Arab Republic[b]	72
Tanzania[b]	70
Ecuador[b]	67
Lebanon[b]	61
Iraq[b]	52
Zambia[b]	50
Pakistan[b]	50
Iran, Islamic Rep.	45
China	44
Congo, Dem. Rep.	43
Papua New Guinea	41
Guinea-Bissau	41
Algeria	39
Uganda	39
Egypt, Arab Rep.	38
Congo, Rep.	33
Kenya	33
Bosnia and Herzegovina	32
Burundi	31
Mauritania	31
Eritrea	29
Sudan	28
Cameroon	24
Yemen, Rep.	21
Venezuela, R.B. de	20
Angola	19
Serbia	19

Source: United Nations Population Division based on United Nations High Commissioner for Refugees data.

a. Includes countries and territories (see Data Notes, page xiii).

b. Top 10 country.

Top Emigration Countries[a] of Tertiary-Educated, 2000
number of migrants, thousands

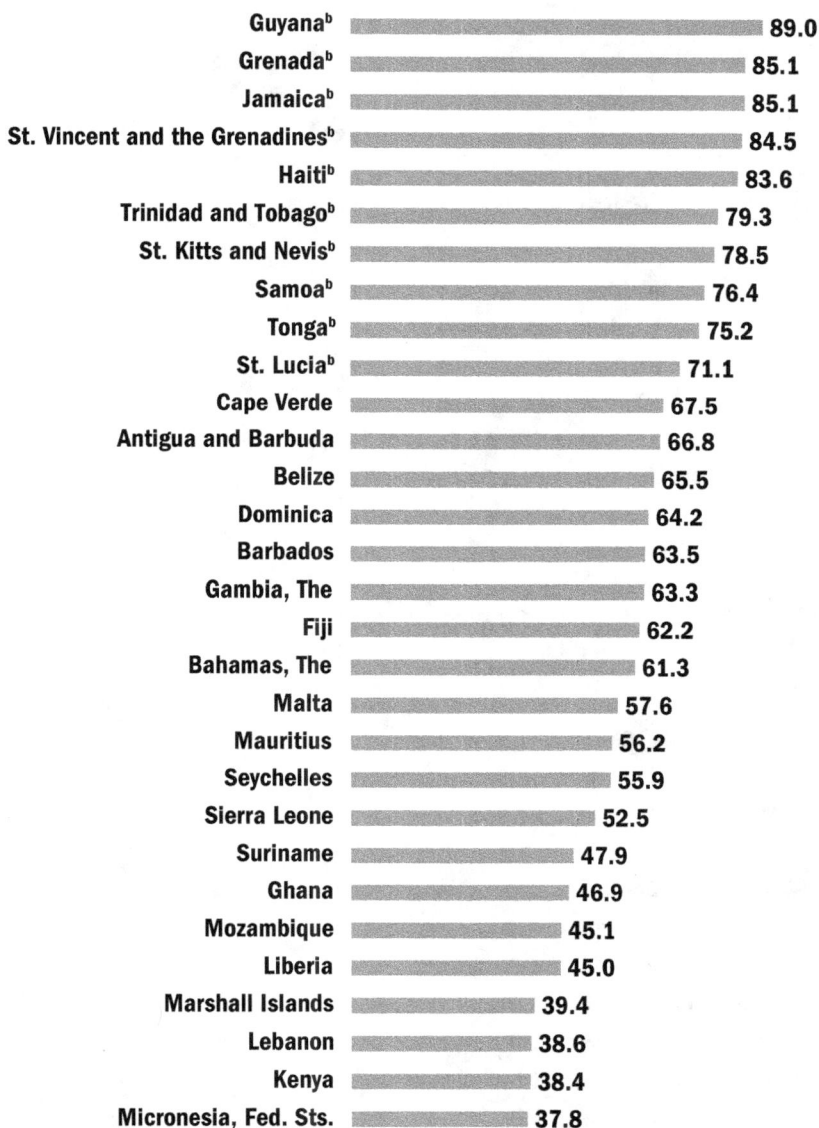

Guyana[b]	89.0
Grenada[b]	85.1
Jamaica[b]	85.1
St. Vincent and the Grenadines[b]	84.5
Haiti[b]	83.6
Trinidad and Tobago[b]	79.3
St. Kitts and Nevis[b]	78.5
Samoa[b]	76.4
Tonga[b]	75.2
St. Lucia[b]	71.1
Cape Verde	67.5
Antigua and Barbuda	66.8
Belize	65.5
Dominica	64.2
Barbados	63.5
Gambia, The	63.3
Fiji	62.2
Bahamas, The	61.3
Malta	57.6
Mauritius	56.2
Seychelles	55.9
Sierra Leone	52.5
Suriname	47.9
Ghana	46.9
Mozambique	45.1
Liberia	45.0
Marshall Islands	39.4
Lebanon	38.6
Kenya	38.4
Micronesia, Fed. Sts.	37.8

Source: Docquier and Marfouk 2006.
a. Includes countries and territories (see Data Notes, page xiii).
b. Top 10 country.

Top Emigration Countries[a] of Physicians, 2000

number of migrants, thousands

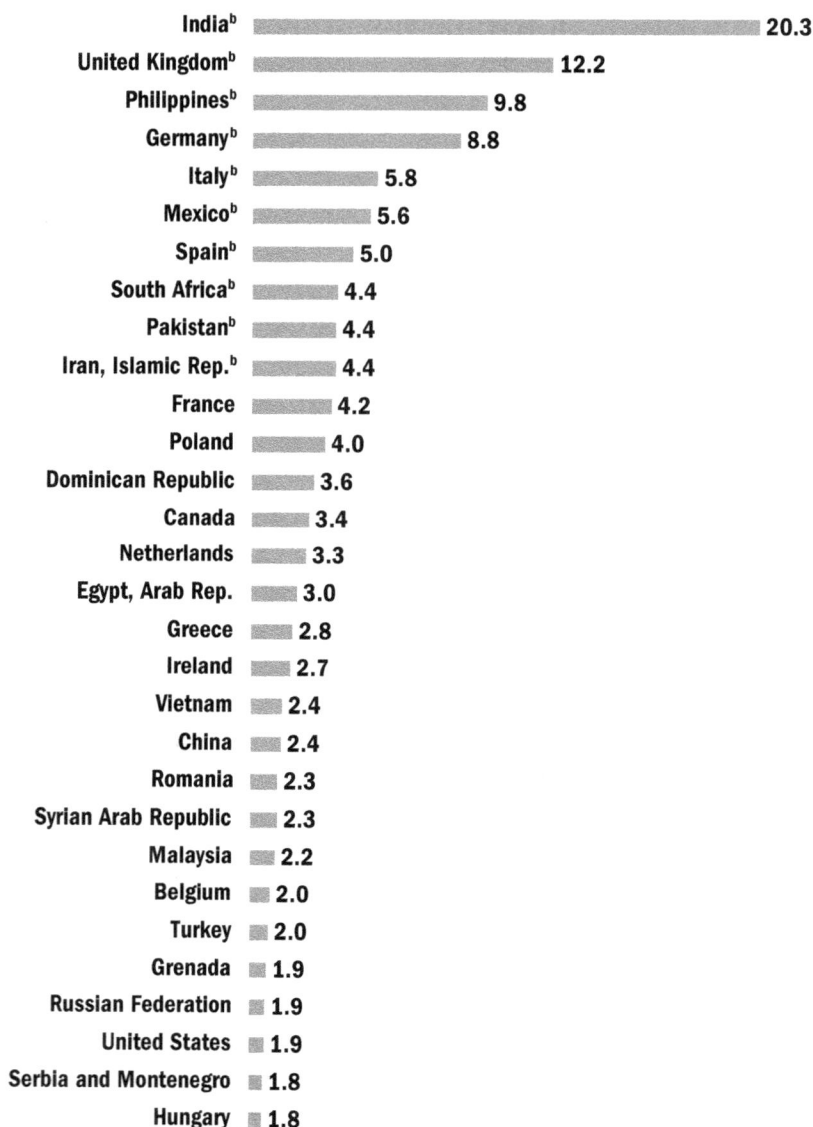

India[b]	20.3
United Kingdom[b]	12.2
Philippines[b]	9.8
Germany[b]	8.8
Italy[b]	5.8
Mexico[b]	5.6
Spain[b]	5.0
South Africa[b]	4.4
Pakistan[b]	4.4
Iran, Islamic Rep.[b]	4.4
France	4.2
Poland	4.0
Dominican Republic	3.6
Canada	3.4
Netherlands	3.3
Egypt, Arab Rep.	3.0
Greece	2.8
Ireland	2.7
Vietnam	2.4
China	2.4
Romania	2.3
Syrian Arab Republic	2.3
Malaysia	2.2
Belgium	2.0
Turkey	2.0
Grenada	1.9
Russian Federation	1.9
United States	1.9
Serbia and Montenegro	1.8
Hungary	1.8

Source: Bhargava, Docquier, and Moullan 2010.

a. Includes countries and territories (see Data Notes, page xiii).

b. Top 10 country.

Top Emigration Countries[a] of Physicians, 2000
percentage of total physicians trained in the country

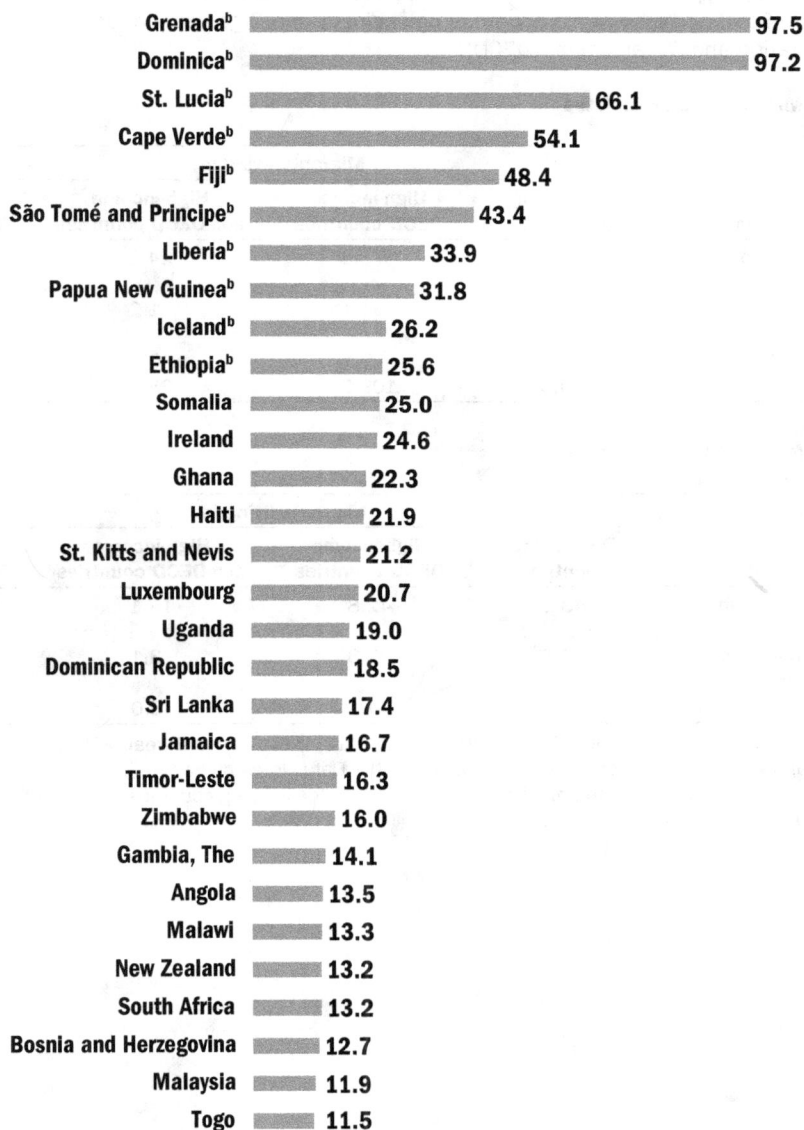

Country	Percentage
Grenada[b]	97.5
Dominica[b]	97.2
St. Lucia[b]	66.1
Cape Verde[b]	54.1
Fiji[b]	48.4
São Tomé and Principe[b]	43.4
Liberia[b]	33.9
Papua New Guinea[b]	31.8
Iceland[b]	26.2
Ethiopia[b]	25.6
Somalia	25.0
Ireland	24.6
Ghana	22.3
Haiti	21.9
St. Kitts and Nevis	21.2
Luxembourg	20.7
Uganda	19.0
Dominican Republic	18.5
Sri Lanka	17.4
Jamaica	16.7
Timor-Leste	16.3
Zimbabwe	16.0
Gambia, The	14.1
Angola	13.5
Malawi	13.3
New Zealand	13.2
South Africa	13.2
Bosnia and Herzegovina	12.7
Malaysia	11.9
Togo	11.5

Source: Bhargava, Docquier, and Moullan 2010.
a. Includes countries and territories (see Data Notes, page xiii).
b. Top 10 country.

South–South Migration versus South–North Migration

South–South migration (migration between developing countries) is larger than migration from the South to high-income countries belonging to the Organisation for Economic Co-operation and Development (OECD).

Global Migrant Stock Estimates
millions

	Migrants living in			
Migrants from	**Developing countries**	**High-income OECD countries**	**High-income non-OECD countries**	**Total**
Developing countries	74.0	73.3	24.2	171.6
High-income OECD countries	5.1	31.1	1.2	37.3
High-income non-OECD countries	1.4	5.1	0.3	6.9
Total	80.5	109.5	25.7	215.8

Global Migrant Stock Estimates
percentage of emigrants

	Migrants living in			
Migrants from	**Developing countries**	**High-income OECD countries**	**High-income non-OECD countries**	**Total**
Developing countries	43.1	42.8	14.1	100
High-income OECD countries	13.6	83.3	3.1	100
High-income non-OECD countries	20.9	74.1	5.0	100

Sources: Ratha and Shaw 2007; UNPD 2009; OECD 2010; U.S. Census Bureau 2008; UK ONS 2009; and various country sources. For details, see the Data Notes on page xiii.
Note: "South" refers to low- and middle-income countries ("developing countries") as defined by the World Bank's country classification.

Migration and Remittances Factbook 2011

Top Remittance-Receiving Countries[a], 2010e

US$ billions

India[b]	55.0
China[b]	51.0
Mexico[b]	22.6
Philippines[b]	21.3
France[b]	15.9
Germany[b]	11.6
Bangladesh[b]	11.1
Belgium[b]	10.4
Spain[b]	10.2
Nigeria[b]	10.0
Pakistan	9.4
Poland	9.1
Lebanon	8.2
Egypt, Arab Rep.	7.7
United Kingdom	7.4
Vietnam	7.2
Indonesia	7.1
Morocco	6.4
Russian Federation	5.6
Serbia	5.6
Ukraine	5.3
Romania	4.5
Australia	4.3
Brazil	4.3
Guatemala	4.3
Netherlands	4.1
Colombia	3.9
Jordan	3.8
Portugal	3.7
El Salvador	3.6

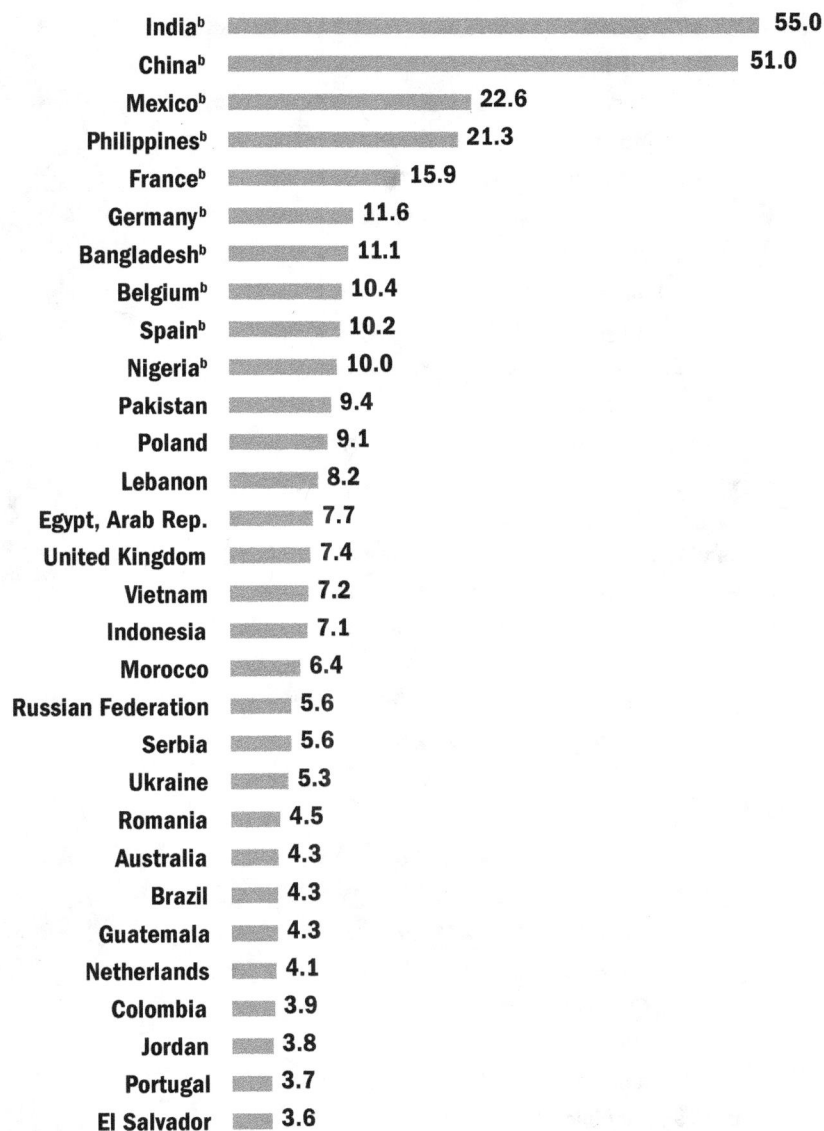

Source: Development Prospects Group, World Bank.
a. Includes countries and territories (see Data Notes, page xiii).
b. Top 10 country.

Top Remittance-Receiving Countries[a], 2009

percentage of GDP

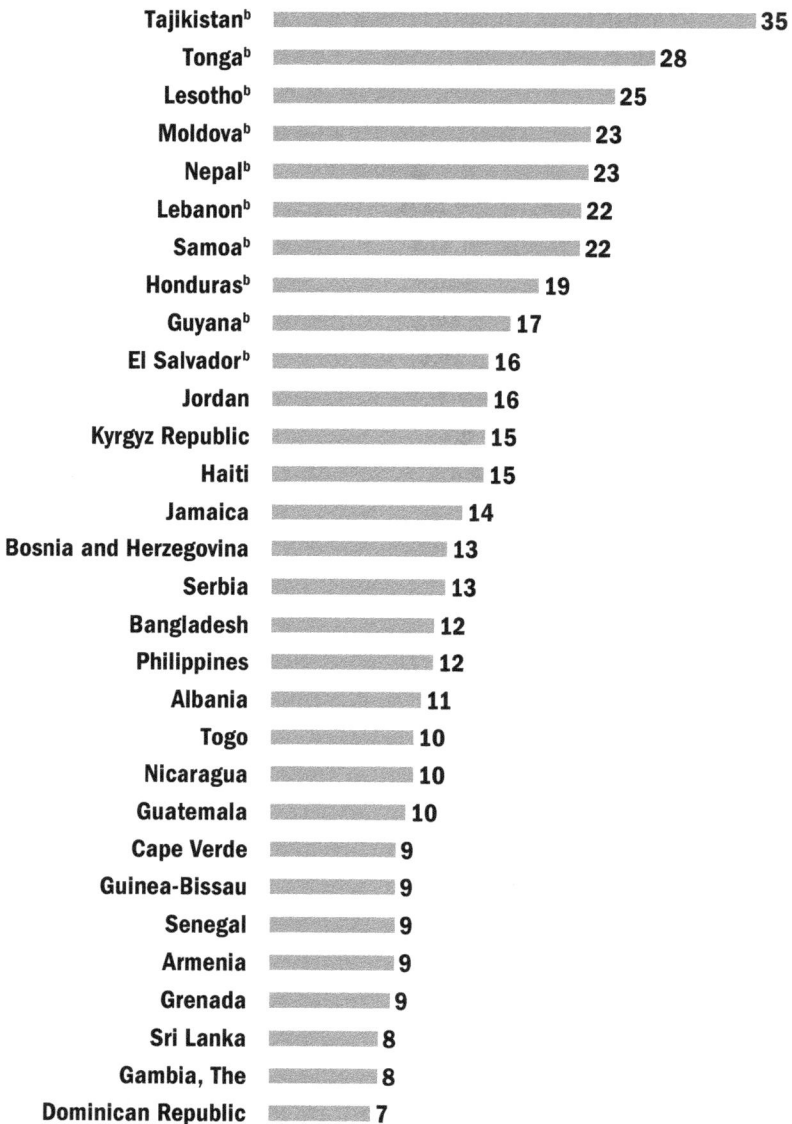

Country	Percentage
Tajikistan[b]	35
Tonga[b]	28
Lesotho[b]	25
Moldova[b]	23
Nepal[b]	23
Lebanon[b]	22
Samoa[b]	22
Honduras[b]	19
Guyana[b]	17
El Salvador[b]	16
Jordan	16
Kyrgyz Republic	15
Haiti	15
Jamaica	14
Bosnia and Herzegovina	13
Serbia	13
Bangladesh	12
Philippines	12
Albania	11
Togo	10
Nicaragua	10
Guatemala	10
Cape Verde	9
Guinea-Bissau	9
Senegal	9
Armenia	9
Grenada	9
Sri Lanka	8
Gambia, The	8
Dominican Republic	7

Source: Development Prospects Group, World Bank.

a. Includes countries and territories (see Data Notes, page xiii).

b. Top 10 country.

Top Remittance-Sending Countries[a], 2009
US$ billions

United States[b]	48.3
Saudi Arabia[b]	26.0
Switzerland[b]	19.6
Russian Federation[b]	18.6
Germany[b]	15.9
Italy[b]	13.0
Spain[b]	12.6
Luxembourg[b]	10.6
Kuwait[b]	9.9
Netherlands[b]	8.1
Malaysia	6.8
Lebanon	5.7
Oman	5.3
France	5.2
China	4.4
Belgium	4.3
Norway	4.1
Japan	4.1
India	4.0
United Kingdom	3.7
Denmark	3.4
Austria	3.3
Israel	3.3
Kazakhstan	3.1
Korea, Rep.	3.1
Australia	3.0
Indonesia	2.7
Czech Republic	2.6
Ireland	2.0
Greece	1.8

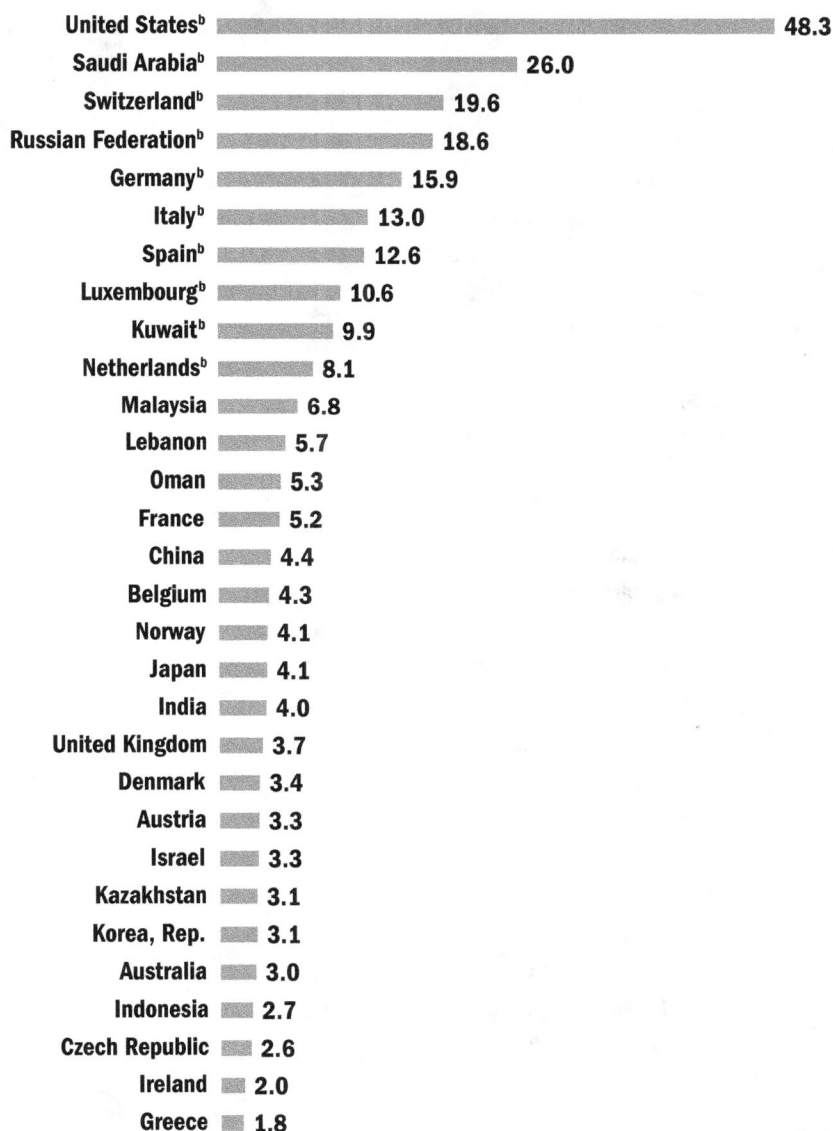

Source: Development Prospects Group, World Bank.
a. Includes countries and territories (see Data Notes, page xiii).
b. Top 10 country.

Top Remittance-Sending Countries[a], 2009

percentage of GDP

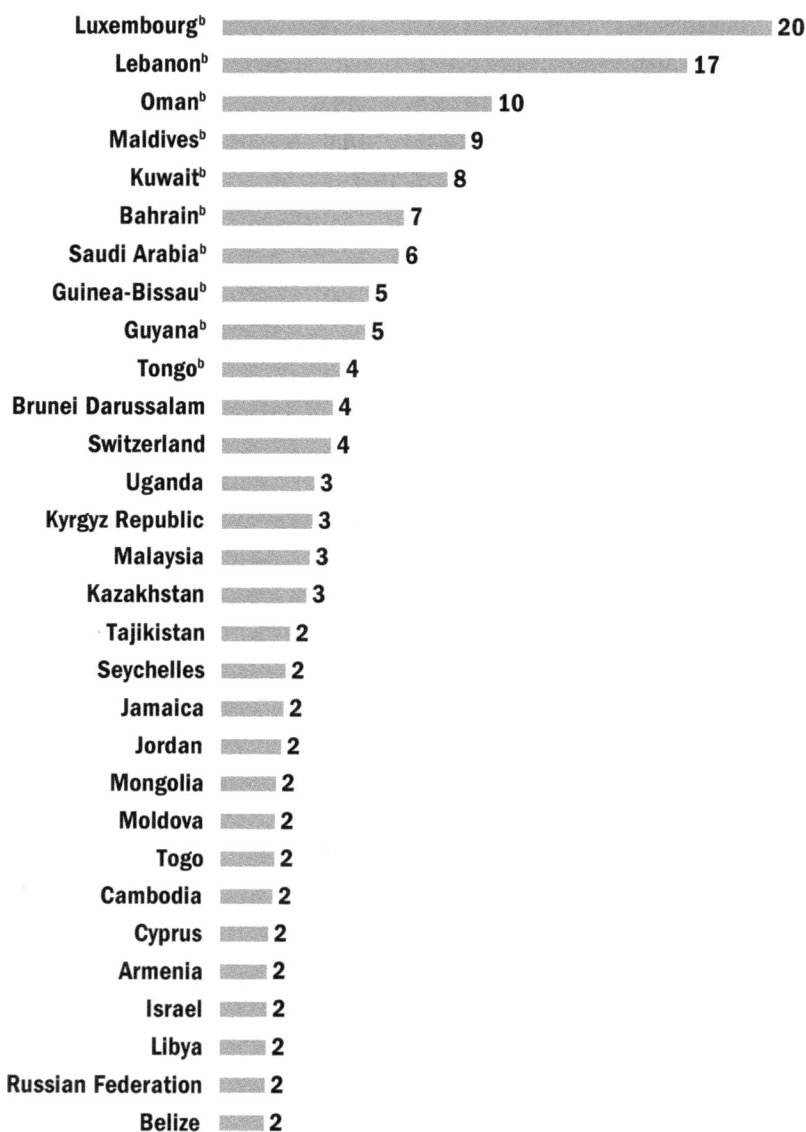

Luxembourg[b]	20
Lebanon[b]	17
Oman[b]	10
Maldives[b]	9
Kuwait[b]	8
Bahrain[b]	7
Saudi Arabia[b]	6
Guinea-Bissau[b]	5
Guyana[b]	5
Tongo[b]	4
Brunei Darussalam	4
Switzerland	4
Uganda	3
Kyrgyz Republic	3
Malaysia	3
Kazakhstan	3
Tajikistan	2
Seychelles	2
Jamaica	2
Jordan	2
Mongolia	2
Moldova	2
Togo	2
Cambodia	2
Cyprus	2
Armenia	2
Israel	2
Libya	2
Russian Federation	2
Belize	2

Source: Development Prospects Group, World Bank.

a. Includes countries and territories (see Data Notes, page xiii).

b. Top 10 country.

Remittances Compared with Other Resource Flows

Remittance Flows Are Large and Resilient
US$ billions

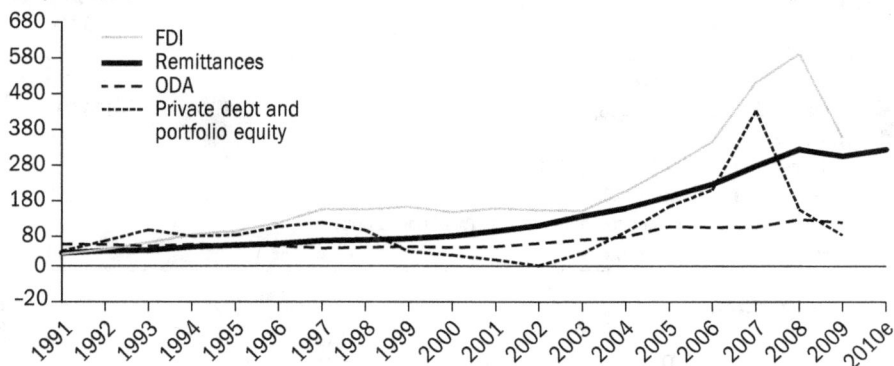

Legend:
- FDI
- **Remittances**
- ODA
- Private debt and portfolio equity

Resource Flows to Developing Countries
US$ billions

	1995	2000	2004	2005	2006	2007	2008	2009	2010e
FDI	95	149	208	276	346	514	593	359	–
Remittances	55	81	159	192	227	278	325	307	325
ODA	57	49	79	108	106	107	128	120	–
Private debt and portfolio equity	83	27	93	165	211	434	157	85	–

Sources: World Development Indicators database and World Bank Migration and Remittances Unit.
Note: Private debt includes only medium- and long-term debt. FDI = foreign direct investment; ODA = official development assistance; – = not available.

Resilience of Remittance Flows Relative to Other Types of Flows during the Global Financial Crisis

Despite a modest decline in remittance inflows to developing countries, these flows have remained more resilient compared with private debt and equity flows and foreign direct investment. There are several reasons for the resilience of remittances in the face of economic downturns in host countries:

1. Remittances are sent by the cumulated flows of migrants over the years, not only by the new migrants of the past year or two. This makes remittances persistent over time. If new migration stops, then over a period of a decade or so, remittances may stop growing. But they will continue to increase as long as migration flows continue.

2. Remittances are a small part of migrants' incomes, and migrants continue to send remittances when affected by income shocks.

3. Because of a rise in anti-immigration sentiments and tighter border controls in the United States and Europe, the duration of migration appears to have increased. Those migrants staying back are likely to continue to send remittances.

4. If migrants do indeed return, they are likely to take back accumulated savings. This may have been the case in India during the Gulf war of 1990–91, which forced a large number of Indian workers in the Gulf to return home (Ratha 2003, 163). Also the "safe haven" factor, or "home bias," can cause remittances for investment purposes to return home during an economic downturn in the host country.

World

Population (millions, 2009)	6,775
Population growth (avg. annual %, 2000-09)	1.2
Population density (people per km², 2008)	51.6
Labor force (millions, 2008)	3,100
Unemployment rate (% of labor force, 2008)	5.8
Urban population (% of pop., 2009)	50.3
Surface area (1,000 km², 2008)	134,095
GNI (US$ billions, 2009)	58,000
GNI per capita, Atlas method (US$, 2009)	8,740.5
GDP growth (avg. annual %, 2005-09)	2.3
Poverty headcount ratio at national poverty line (% of pop., 2005)	—
Age dependency ratio (2009)	54.4

Migration

MIGRATION, 2010

- Stock of immigrants: **215.8 million** or **3.2 percent** of population
- Females as percentage of immigrants: **48.4 percent**
- Refugees: **16.3 million** or **7.6 percent** of the total immigrants
- South–South migration is larger than migration from the South to the high-income OECD countries. Over **43 percent** of the migrants from developing countries are believed to be residing in other developing countries.
- Top 10 destination countries: the United States, the Russian Federation, Germany, Saudi Arabia, Canada, the United Kingdom, Spain, France, Australia, India. As a share of population, top immigration countries include Qatar (86.5 percent); Monaco (71.6 percent); the United Arab Emirates (70.0 percent); Kuwait (68.8 percent); Andorra (64.4 percent); Cayman Islands (63.0 percent); Northern Mariana Islands (62.0 percent); Virgin Islands (U.S.) (56.5 percent); Macao SAR, China (54.7 percent); Isle of Man (54.6 percent)
- Top 10 emigration countries: Mexico, India, the Russian Federation, China, Ukraine, Bangladesh, Pakistan, the United Kingdom, the Philippines, Turkey
- Top 10 migration corridors: Mexico–United States; the Russian Federation–Ukraine; Ukraine–Russian Federation; Bangladesh–India; Turkey–Germany; Kazakhstan–the Russian Federation; the Russian Federation–Kazakhstan; China–Hong Kong SAR, China; China–United States; the Philippines–United States

SKILLED EMIGRATION, 2000

- Emigration rate of tertiary-educated population (top 10 countries): Guyana (89.0 percent), Grenada (85.1 percent), Jamaica (85.1 percent), St. Vincent and the Grenadines (84.5 percent), Haiti (83.6 percent), Trinidad and Tobago (79.3 percent), St. Kitts and Nevis (78.5 percent), Samoa (76.4 percent), Tonga (75.2 percent), St. Lucia (71.1 percent)
- Emigration of physicians: **336,416** or **4.2 percent** of physicians trained in the world

Remittances

US$ billions	1995	2000	2004	2005	2006	2007	2008	2009	2010e
Inward									
remittance flows	**101.3**	**131.5**	**237.0**	**274.9**	**317.9**	**385.0**	**443.2**	**416.0**[a]	**440.1**
All developing									
countries	*55.2*	*81.3*	*159.3*	*192.1*	*226.7*	*278.5*	*324.8*	*307.1*	*325.5*
Outward									
remittance flows	**97.5**	**108.5**	**168.0**	**185.3**	**213.7**	**255.2**	**295.7**	**282.5**[b]	—
All developing									
countries	*10.4*	*9.5*	*28.5*	*33.0*	*41.0*	*52.7*	*67.3*	*58.7*	—

Note: This table reports officially recorded remittances. The true size of remittances, including unrecorded flows through formal and informal channels, is believed to be larger. 2010e = 2010 estimate.
a. 0.7% of GDP in 2009.
b. 0.5% of GDP in 2009.

REMITTANCES

- Top 10 remittance recipients in 2010 (billions): India ($55.0 bn), China ($51.0 bn), Mexico ($22.6 bn), Philippines ($21.3 bn), France ($15.9 bn), Germany ($11.6 bn), Bangladesh ($11.1 bn), Belgium ($10.4 bn), Spain ($10.2 bn), Nigeria ($10.0 bn)
- Top 10 remittance recipients in 2009 (percentage of GDP): Tajikistan (35.1 percent), Tonga (27.7 percent), Lesotho (24.8 percent), Moldova (23.1 percent), Nepal (22.9 percent), Lebanon (22.4 percent), Samoa (22.3 percent), Honduras (19.3 percent), Guyana (17.3 percent), El Salvador (15.7 percent)
- Top 10 remittance senders in 2009 (billions): the United States ($48.3 bn), Saudi Arabia ($26.0 bn), Switzerland ($19.6 bn), Russian Federation ($18.6 bn), Germany ($15.9 bn), Italy ($13.0 bn), Spain ($12.6 bn), Luxembourg ($10.6 bn), Kuwait ($9.9 bn), Netherlands ($8.1 bn)
- Top 10 remittance senders in 2009 (percentage of GDP): Luxembourg (20.1 percent), Lebanon (17.0 percent), Oman (9.9 percent), Maldives (8.9 percent), Kuwait (8.2 percent), Bahrain (6.6 percent), Saudi Arabia (6.5 percent), Guinea-Bissau (5.4 percent), Guyana (5.2 percent), Tonga (4.3 percent)

Developing Countries

Population (millions, 2009)	5,659
Population growth (avg. annual %, 2000–09)	1.3
Population density (people per km², 2008)	58.5
Labor force (millions, 2008)	2,582
Unemployment rate (% of labor force, 2008)	5.7
Urban population (% of pop., 2009)	45.1
Surface area (1,000 km², 2008)	98,795
GNI (US$ billions, 2009)	16,406
GNI per capita, Atlas method (US$, 2009)	2,946
GDP growth (avg. annual %, 2005–09)	6.5
Poverty headcount ratio at national poverty line (% of pop., 2005)	—
Age dependency ratio (2009)	42.9

Migration

EMIGRATION, 2010

- Stock of emigrants: **171.6 million** or **3.0 percent** of population
- Top 10 emigration countries: Mexico, India, the Russian Federation, China, Ukraine, Bangladesh, Pakistan, the Philippines, Turkey, the Arab Republic of Egypt
- Destinations: high-income OECD countries (42.8 percent), high-income non-OECD countries (14.1 percent), other developing countries (43.1 percent)
- Top 10 migration corridors: Mexico–the United States; the Russian Federation–Ukraine; Ukraine–the Russian Federation; Bangladesh–India; Turkey–Germany; Kazakhstan–the Russian Federation; the Russian Federation–Kazakhstan; China–Hong Kong SAR, China; China–the United States; India–the United Arab Emirates
- Top 10 migration corridors excluding the former Soviet Union: Mexico–the United States; Bangladesh–India; Turkey–Germany; China–Hong Kong SAR, China; China–the United States; the Philippines–the United States; Afghanistan–the Islamic Republic of Iran; India–the United States; Puerto Rico–the United States; India–the United Arab Emirates

SKILLED EMIGRATION, 2000

- Emigration rate of tertiary-educated population (top 10 countries): Guyana (89.0 percent), Grenada (85.1 percent), Jamaica (85.1 percent), St. Vincent and the Grenadines (84.5 percent), Haiti (83.6 percent), St. Kitts and Nevis (78.5 percent), Samoa (76.4 percent), Tonga (75.2 percent), St. Lucia (71.1 percent), Cape Verde (67.5 percent)
- Emigration of physicians: **220,150** or **3.9 percent** of physicians trained in the region

IMMIGRATION, 2010

- Stock of immigrants: **80.5 million** or **1.4 percent** of population (compared to 215.8 million or 3.2 percent for the world)
- Females as percentage of immigrants: **50.1 percent** (compared to 48.4 percent for the world)
- Refugees as percentage of immigrants: **13.8 percent** (compared to 7.6 percent for the world)

- Top 10 immigration countries: the Russian Federation, India, Ukraine, Pakistan, Kazakhstan, Jordan, Côte d'Ivoire, Malaysia, the Syrian Arab Republic, the Islamic Republic of Iran

Remittances

US$ billions	1995	2000	2004	2005	2006	2007	2008	2009	2010e
Inward									
remittance flows	**55.2**	**81.3**	**159.3**	**192.1**	**226.7**	**278.5**	**324.8**	**307.1**[a]	**325.5**
World	*101.3*	*131.5*	*237.0*	*274.9*	*317.9*	*385.0*	*443.2*	*416.0*	*440.1*
Outward									
remittance flows	**10.4**	**9.5**	**28.5**	**33.0**	**41.0**	**52.7**	**67.3**	**58.7**[b]	—
World	*97.5*	*108.5*	*168.0*	*185.3*	*213.7*	*255.2*	*295.7*	*282.5*	—
Memorandum items									
Developing countries									
FDI	95	149	208	276	346	514	593	359	—
ODA	57	49	79	108	106	107	128	120	—
Private debt and portfolio equity	83	27	93	165	211	434	157	85	—

Note: This table reports officially recorded remittances. The true size of remittances, including unrecorded flows through formal and informal channels, is believed to be larger. Private debt includes only medium- and long-term debt. FDI = foreign direct investment; ODA = official development assistance.
a. 2.0% of GDP in 2009.
b. 0.4% of GDP in 2009.

REMITTANCES

- Top 10 remittance recipients in 2010 (billions): India ($55.0 bn), China ($51.0 bn), Mexico ($22.6 bn), Philippines ($21.3 bn), Bangladesh ($11.1 bn), Nigeria ($10.0 bn), Pakistan ($9.4 bn), Lebanon ($8.2 bn), the Arab Republic of Egypt ($7.7 bn), Vietnam ($7.2 bn)
- Top 10 remittance recipients in 2009 (percentage of GDP): Tajikistan (35.1 percent), Tonga (27.7 percent), Lesotho (24.8 percent), Moldova (23.1 percent), Nepal (22.9 percent), Lebanon (22.4 percent), Samoa (22.3 percent), Honduras (19.3 percent), Guyana (17.3 percent), El Salvador (15.7 percent)
- Top 10 remittance senders in 2009 (billions): Russian Federation ($18.6 bn), Malaysia ($6.8 bn), Lebanon ($5.7 bn), China ($4.4 bn), India ($4.0 bn), Kazakhstan ($3.1 bn), Indonesia ($2.7 bn), South Africa ($1.2 bn), Brazil ($1.0 bn), Libya ($1.0 bn)
- Top 10 remittance senders in 2009 (percentage of GDP): Luxembourg (20.1 percent), Lebanon (17.0 percent), Oman (9.9 percent), Maldives (8.9 percent), Kuwait (8.2 percent), Bahrain (6.6 percent), Saudi Arabia (6.5 percent), Guinea-Bissau (5.4 percent), Guyana (5.2 percent), Tonga (4.3 percent)

Regional Tables

The country composition of regions[1] is based on the World Bank's analytical regions and may differ from common geographic usage.

East Asia and Pacific (developing only: 23)

American Samoa, Cambodia, China, Fiji, Indonesia, Kiribati, the Democratic People's Republic of Korea, the Lao People's Democratic Republic, Malaysia, the Marshall Islands, the Federated States of Micronesia, Mongolia, Myanmar, Palau, Papua New Guinea, the Philippines, Samoa, the Solomon Islands, Thailand, Timor-Leste, Tonga, Vanuatu, Vietnam

Europe and Central Asia (developing only: 22)

Albania, Armenia, Azerbaijan, Belarus, Bosnia and Herzegovina, Bulgaria, Georgia, Kazakhstan, Kosovo, the Kyrgyz Republic, Lithuania, the former Yugoslav Republic of Macedonia, Moldova, Montenegro, Romania, the Russian Federation, Serbia, Tajikistan, Turkey, Turkmenistan, Ukraine, Uzbekistan

Latin America and the Caribbean (developing only: 30)

Antigua and Barbuda, Argentina, Belize, Bolivia, Brazil, Chile, Colombia, Costa Rica, Cuba, Dominica, Dominican Republic, Ecuador, El Salvador, Grenada, Guatemala, Guyana, Haiti, Honduras, Jamaica, Mexico, Nicaragua, Panama, Paraguay, Peru, St. Kitts and Nevis, St. Lucia, St. Vincent and the Grenadines, Suriname, Uruguay, República Bolivariana de Venezuela

Middle East and North Africa (developing only: 13)

Algeria, Djibouti, the Arab Republic of Egypt, the Islamic Republic of Iran, Iraq, Jordan, Lebanon, Libya, Morocco, the Syrian Arab Republic, Tunisia, West Bank and Gaza, the Republic of Yemen

South Asia (8)

Afghanistan, Bangladesh, Bhutan, India, Maldives, Nepal, Pakistan, Sri Lanka

Sub-Saharan Africa (47)

Angola, Benin, Botswana, Burkina Faso, Burundi, Cameroon, Cape Verde, the Central African Republic, Chad, the Comoros, the Democratic Republic of Congo, the Republic of Congo, Côte d'Ivoire, Eritrea, Ethiopia, Gabon, The Gambia, Ghana, Guinea, Guinea-Bissau, Kenya, Lesotho, Liberia, Madagascar, Malawi, Mali, Mauritania, Mauritius, Mayotte, Mozambique, Namibia, Niger, Nigeria, Rwanda, São Tomé and Principe, Senegal, the Seychelles, Sierra Leone, Somalia, South Africa, Sudan, Swaziland, Tanzania, Togo, Uganda, Zambia, Zimbabwe

---

1. See the Data Notes on page xiii for the definitions of regional groups that have changed since *Migration and Remittances Factbook 2008* was published.

East Asia and Pacific

East Asia and Pacific	
Population (millions, 2009)	1,944
Population growth (avg. annual %, 2000–09)	0.8
Population density (people per km², 2008)	121.7
Labor force (millions, 2008)	1,081
Unemployment rate (% of labor force, 2008)	4.7
Urban population (% of pop., 2009)	45.0
Surface area (1,000 km², 2008)	16,299
GNI (US$ billions, 2009)	6,259
GNI per capita, Atlas method (US$, 2009)	3,143
GDP growth (avg. annual %, 2005–09)	9.8
Poverty headcount ratio at national poverty line (% of pop., 2005)	–
Age dependency ratio (2009)	42.9

Migration

EMIGRATION, 2010

- Stock of emigrants: **21.7 million** or **1.1 percent** of population
- Top 10 emigration countries: China, the Philippines, Indonesia, Vietnam, Malaysia, Thailand, Myanmar, the Lao People's Democratic Republic, Cambodia, the Democratic People's Republic of Korea
- Destinations: high-income OECD countries (54.9 percent), high-income non-OECD countries (26.0 percent), intra-regional (15.1 percent), other developing countries (2.1 percent), unidentified (0.3 percent)
- Top 10 migration corridors: China–Hong Kong SAR, China; China–the United States; the Philippines–the United States; Indonesia–Malaysia; Vietnam–the United States; Malaysia–Singapore; China–Japan; the Philippines–Saudi Arabia; China–Canada; China–Singapore

SKILLED EMIGRATION, 2000

- Emigration rate of tertiary-educated population (top 10 countries): Samoa (76.4 percent), Tonga (75.2 percent), Fiji (62.2 percent), the Marshall Islands (39.4 percent), the Federated States of Micronesia (37.8 percent), the Lao People's Democratic Republic (37.4 percent), Papua New Guinea (28.5 percent), Vietnam (27.1 percent), Palau (26.1 percent), Kiribati (23.1 percent)
- Emigration of physicians: **33,178** or **1.4 percent** of physicians trained in the region

IMMIGRATION, 2010

- Stock of immigrants: **5.4 million** or **0.3 percent** of population (compared to 215.8 million or 3.2 percent for the world)
- Females as percentage of immigrants: **47.4 percent** (compared to 48.4 percent for the world)
- Refugees as percentage of immigrants: **8.8 percent** (compared to 7.6 percent for the world)
- Top 10 immigration countries: Malaysia, Thailand, China, the Philippines, Cambodia, Indonesia, Myanmar, Vietnam, the Democratic People's Republic of Korea, American Samoa

Remittances

US$ billions	1995	2000	2004	2005	2006	2007	2008	2009	2010e
Inward									
remittance flows	**8.9**	**15.8**	**40.0**	**50.3**	**57.4**	**71.1**	**85.5**	**85.7**[a]	**91.2**
All developing									
countries	*55.2*	*81.3*	*159.3*	*192.1*	*226.7*	*278.5*	*324.8*	*307.1*	*325.5*
Outward									
remittance flows	**1.6**	**1.7**	**8.4**	**9.9**	**10.3**	**12.8**	**15.0**	**14.4**[b]	−
All developing									
countries	*10.4*	*9.5*	*28.5*	*33.0*	*41.0*	*52.7*	*67.3*	*58.7*	*−*

Note: This table reports officially recorded remittances. The true size of remittances, including unrecorded flows through formal and informal channels, is believed to be larger.

a. 1.9% of GDP in 2009.
b. 0.3% of GDP in 2009.

REMITTANCES

- Top 10 remittance recipients in 2010 (billions): China ($51.0 bn), Philippines ($21.3 bn), Vietnam ($7.2 bn), Indonesia ($7.1 bn), Thailand ($1.8 bn), Malaysia ($1.6 bn), Cambodia ($0.4 bn), Mongolia ($0.2 bn), Myanmar ($0.2 bn), Samoa ($0.1 bn)
- Top 10 remittance recipients in 2009 (percentage of GDP): Tonga (27.7 percent), Samoa (22.3 percent), Philippines (11.7 percent), Vietnam (7.0 percent), Kiribati (6.3 percent), Mongolia (4.6 percent), Fiji (3.4 percent), Cambodia (3.0 percent), Indonesia (1.3 percent), China (1.0 percent)

Europe and Central Asia

Population (millions, 2009)	404
Population growth (avg. annual %, 2000–09)	0.1
Population density (people per km², 2008)	19.1
Labor force (millions, 2008)	206
Unemployment rate (% of labor force, 2008)	6.9
Urban population (% of pop., 2009)	64.0
Surface area (1,000 km², 2008)	23,916
GNI (US$ billions, 2009)	2,519
GNI per capita, Atlas method (US$, 2009)	6,793
GDP growth (avg. annual %, 2005–09)	4.0
Poverty headcount ratio at national poverty line (% of pop., 2005)	–
Age dependency ratio (2009)	43.8

Migration

EMIGRATION, 2010

- Stock of emigrants: **43.1 million** or **10.7 percent** of population
- Top 10 emigration countries: the Russian Federation, Ukraine, Turkey, Kazakhstan, Romania, Uzbekistan, Belarus, Bosnia and Herzegovina, Albania, Azerbaijan
- Destinations: high-income OECD countries (31.3 percent), high-income non-OECD countries (6.7 percent), intra-regional (55.1 percent), other developing countries (0.2 percent), unidentified (6.7 percent)
- Top 10 migration corridors: the Russian Federation–Ukraine, Ukraine–the Russian Federation, Turkey–Germany, Kazakhstan–the Russian Federation, the Russian Federation–Kazakhstan, Belarus–the Russian Federation, Uzbekistan–the Russian Federation, Azerbaijan–the Russian Federation, Romania–Italy, Romania–Spain

SKILLED EMIGRATION, 2000

- Emigration rate of tertiary-educated population (top 10 countries): the former Yugoslav Republic of Macedonia (29.1 percent), Bosnia and Herzegovina (23.9 percent), Romania (11.8 percent), Albania (9.0 percent), Armenia (8.8 percent), Lithuania (8.6 percent), Bulgaria (8.6 percent), Turkey (5.8 percent), Ukraine (3.5 percent), Moldova (3.4 percent)
- Emigration of physicians: **15,687** or **1.2 percent** of physicians trained in the region

IMMIGRATION, 2010

- Stock of immigrants: **27.3 million** or **6.8 percent** of population (compared to 215.8 million or 3.2 percent for the world)
- Females as percentage of immigrants: **56.7 percent** (compared to 48.4 percent for the world)
- Refugees as percentage of immigrants: **0.8 percent** (compared to 7.6 percent for the world)
- Top 10 immigration countries: the Russian Federation, Ukraine, Kazakhstan, Turkey, Uzbekistan, Belarus, Serbia, Moldova, Armenia, Tajikistan

Remittances

US$ billions	1995	2000	2004	2005	2006	2007	2008	2009	2010e
Inward									
remittance flows	**6.5**	**10.4**	**16.0**	**23.3**	**28.4**	**39.3**	**45.8**	**35.4ᵃ**	**36.7**
All developing									
countries	*55.2*	*81.3*	*159.3*	*192.1*	*226.7*	*278.5*	*324.8*	*307.1*	*325.5*
Outward									
remittance flows	**4.5**	**1.9**	**7.4**	**10.2**	**16.5**	**24.7**	**33.0**	**24.5ᵇ**	—
All developing									
countries	*10.4*	*9.5*	*28.5*	*33.0*	*41.0*	*52.7*	*67.3*	*58.7*	—

Note: This table reports officially recorded remittances. The true size of remittances, including unrecorded flows through formal and informal channels, is believed to be larger.

a. 1.3% of GDP in 2009.

b. 1.2% of GDP in 2009.

REMITTANCES

- Top 10 remittance recipients in 2010 (billions): Russian Federation ($5.6 bn), Serbia ($5.6 bn), Ukraine ($5.3 bn), Romania ($4.5 bn), Bosnia and Herzegovina ($2.2 bn), Tajikistan ($2.1 bn), Bulgaria ($1.6 bn), Azerbaijan ($1.5 bn), Moldova ($1.3 bn), Albania ($1.3 bn)
- Top 10 remittance recipients in 2009 (percentage of GDP): Tajikistan (35.1 percent), Moldova (23.1 percent), Kyrgyz Republic (15.4 percent), Bosnia and Herzegovina (12.7 percent), Serbia (12.6 percent), Albania (10.9 percent), Armenia (9.0 percent), Georgia (6.4 percent), FYR Macedonia FYR (4.5 percent), Romania (4.4 percent)

Latin America and the Caribbean

Population (millions, 2009)	572.5
Population growth (avg. annual %, 2000–09)	1.3
Population density (people per km², 2008)	28
Labor force (millions, 2008)	262.1
Unemployment rate (% of labor force, 2008)	7.3
Urban population (% of pop., 2009)	79.0
Surface area (1,000 km², 2008)	20,421
GNI (US$ billions, 2009)	3,891.0
GNI per capita, Atlas method (US$, 2009)	6,936.5
GDP growth (avg. annual %, 2005–09)	3.8
Poverty headcount ratio at national poverty line (% of pop., 2005)	—
Age dependency ratio (2009)	53.9

Migration

EMIGRATION, 2010

- Stock of emigrants: **30.2 million** or **5.2 percent** of population
- Top 10 emigration countries: Mexico, Colombia, Brazil, El Salvador, Cuba, Ecuador, Peru, the Dominican Republic, Haiti, Jamaica
- Destinations: high-income OECD countries (84.8 percent), high-income non-OECD countries (0.7 percent), intra-regional (12.9 percent), other developing countries (0.1 percent), unidentified (1.6 percent)
- Top 10 migration corridors: Mexico–the United States, El Salvador–the United States, Cuba–the United States, the Dominican Republic–the United States, Guatemala–the United States, Jamaica–the United States, Colombia–the United States, Colombia–República Bolivariana de Venezuela, Haiti–the United States, Ecuador–Spain

SKILLED EMIGRATION, 2000

- Emigration rate of tertiary-educated population (top 10 countries): Guyana (89.0 percent), Grenada (85.1 percent), Jamaica (85.1 percent), St. Vincent and the Grenadines (84.5 percent), Haiti (83.6 percent), St. Kitts and Nevis (78.5 percent), St. Lucia (71.1 percent), Antigua and Barbuda (66.8 percent), Belize (65.5 percent), Dominica (64.2 percent)
- Emigration of physicians: **45,988** or **5.0 percent** of physicians trained in the region

IMMIGRATION, 2010

- Stock of immigrants: **6.6 million** or **1.1 percent** of population (compared to 215.8 million or 3.2 percent for the world)
- Females as percentage of immigrants: **49.7 percent** (compared to 48.4 percent for the world)
- Refugees as percentage of immigrants: **8.1 percent** (compared to 7.6 percent for the world)
- Top 10 immigration countries: Argentina, República Bolivariana de Venezuela, Mexico, Brazil, Costa Rica, the Dominican Republic, Ecuador, Chile, Paraguay, Bolivia

Remittances

US$ billions	1995	2000	2004	2005	2006	2007	2008	2009	2010e
Inward									
remittance flows	**13.3**	**20.2**	**43.4**	**50.1**	**59.2**	**63.3**	**64.6**	**56.9**[a]	**58.1**
All developing									
countries	*55.2*	*81.3*	*159.3*	*192.1*	*226.7*	*278.5*	*324.8*	*307.1*	*325.5*
Outward									
remittance flows	**1.1**	**2.0**	**2.1**	**2.3**	**2.7**	**3.6**	**4.3**	**3.8**[b]	—
All developing									
countries	*10.4*	*9.5*	*28.5*	*33.0*	*41.0*	*52.7*	*67.3*	*58.7*	—

Note: This table reports officially recorded remittances. The true size of remittances, including unrecorded flows through formal and informal channels, is believed to be larger.

a. 1.5% of GDP in 2009.

b. 0.1% of GDP in 2009.

REMITTANCES

- Top 10 remittance recipients in 2010 (billions): Mexico ($22.6 bn), Brazil ($4.3 bn), Guatemala ($4.3 bn), Colombia ($3.9 bn), El Salvador ($3.6 bn), the Dominican Republic ($3.4 bn), Honduras ($2.7 bn), Ecuador ($2.5 bn), Peru ($2.5 bn), Jamaica ($2.0 bn)
- Top 10 remittance recipients in 2009 (percentage of GDP): Honduras (19.3 percent), Guyana (17.3 percent), El Salvador (15.7 percent), Haiti (15.4 percent), Jamaica (13.8 percent), Nicaragua (10.3 percent), Guatemala (9.8 percent), Grenada (8.7 percent), the Dominican Republic (7.3 percent), St. Kitts and Nevis (7.3 percent)

Middle East and North Africa

Population (millions, 2009)	330.9
Population growth (avg. annual %, 2000–09)	1.9
Population density (people per km², 2008)	37.6
Labor force (millions, 2008)	108.7
Unemployment rate (% of labor force, 2008)	9.5
Urban population (% of pop., 2009)	57.6
Surface area (1,000 km², 2008)	8,778
GNI (US$ billions, 2009)	1,190.5
GNI per capita, Atlas method (US$, 2009)	3,594
GDP growth (avg. annual %, 2005–09)	4.8
Poverty headcount ratio at national poverty line (% of pop., 2005)	–
Age dependency ratio (2009)	56.5

Migration

EMIGRATION, 2010

- Stock of emigrants: **18.1 million** or **5.3 percent** of population
- Top 10 emigration countries: the Arab Republic of Egypt, Morocco, West Bank and Gaza, Iraq, the Islamic Republic of Iran, Algeria, the Republic of Yemen, the Syrian Arab Republic, Jordan, Lebanon
- Destinations: high-income OECD countries (40.2 percent), high-income non-OECD countries (23.2 percent), intra-regional (31.5 percent), other developing countries (1.2 percent), unidentified (4.0 percent)
- Top 10 migration corridors: West Bank and Gaza–the Syrian Arab Republic, the Arab Republic of Egypt–Saudi Arabia, Algeria–France, the Republic of Yemen–Saudi Arabia, West Bank and Gaza–Jordan, the Arab Republic of Egypt–Jordan, Morocco–France, Morocco–Spain, Morocco–Italy, the Arab Republic of Egypt–Libya

SKILLED EMIGRATION, 2000

- Emigration rate of tertiary-educated population (top 10 countries): Lebanon (38.6 percent), Morocco (17.0 percent), the Islamic Republic of Iran (14.5 percent), Tunisia (12.5 percent), Iraq (11.1 percent), Djibouti (11.0 percent), Algeria (9.4 percent), Jordan (7.2 percent), West Bank and Gaza (7.2 percent), the Syrian Arab Republic (6.1 percent)
- Emigration of physicians: **27,265** or **7.8 percent** of physicians trained in the region

IMMIGRATION, 2010

- Stock of immigrants: **12.0 million** or **3.5 percent** of population (compared to 215.8 million or 3.2 percent for the world)
- Females as percentage of immigrants: **45.7 percent** (compared to 48.4 percent for the world)
- Refugees as percentage of immigrants: **65.3 percent** (compared to 7.6 percent for the world)
- Top 10 immigration countries: Jordan, the Syrian Arab Republic, the Islamic Republic of Iran, West Bank and Gaza, Lebanon, Libya, the Republic of Yemen, the Arab Republic of Egypt, Algeria, Djibouti

Remittances

US$ billions	1995	2000	2004	2005	2006	2007	2008	2009	2010e
Inward									
remittance flows	**13.3**	**13.1**	**23.2**	**25.1**	**26.5**	**32.1**	**35.9**	**33.7**[a]	**35.4**
All developing									
countries	*55.2*	*81.3*	*159.3*	*192.1*	*226.7*	*278.5*	*324.8*	*307.1*	*325.5*
Outward									
remittance flows	**0.7**	**0.8**	**5.7**	**5.6**	**6.1**	**5.1**	**6.7**	**8.1**[b]	**—**
All developing									
countries	*10.4*	*9.5*	*28.5*	*33.0*	*41.0*	*52.7*	*67.3*	*58.7*	*—*

Note: This table reports officially recorded remittances. The true size of remittances, including unre-corded flows through formal and informal channels, is believed to be larger.

a. 3.1% of GDP in 2009.
b. 0.6% of GDP in 2009.

REMITTANCES

- Top 10 remittance recipients in 2010 (billions): Lebanon ($8.2 bn), the Arab Republic of Egypt ($7.7 bn), Morocco ($6.4 bn), Jordan ($3.8 bn), Algeria ($2.0 bn), Tunisia ($2.0 bn), the Republic of Yemen ($1.5 bn), Syrian Arab Republic ($1.4 bn), West Bank and Gaza ($1.3 bn), the Islamic Republic of Iran ($1.1 bn)
- Top 10 remittance recipients in 2009 (percentage of GDP): Lebanon (22.4 percent), Jordan (15.6 percent), Morocco (6.6 percent), Tunisia (5.3 percent), the Republic of Yemen (5.2 percent), the Arab Republic of Egypt (4.0 percent), Djibouti (2.7 percent), Syrian Arab Republic (2.4 percent), Algeria (1.4 percent), the Islamic Republic of Iran (0.3 percent)

South Asia

Population (millions, 2009)	1,568
Population growth (avg. annual %, 2000–09)	1.6
Population density (people per km², 2008)	322.7
Labor force (millions, 2008)	606.6
Unemployment rate (% of labor force, 2008)	5.2
Urban population (% of pop., 2009)	29.8
Surface area (1,000 km², 2008)	5,140
GNI (US$ billions, 2009)	1,644
GNI per capita, Atlas method (US$, 2009)	1,096
GDP growth (avg. annual %, 2005–09)	7.6
Poverty headcount ratio at national poverty line (% of pop., 2005)	–
Age dependency ratio (2009)	58.5

Migration

EMIGRATION, 2010

- Stock of emigrants: **26.7 million** or **1.6 percent** of population
- Top 5 emigration countries: India, Bangladesh, Pakistan, Afghanistan, Sri Lanka
- Destinations: high-income OECD countries (23.6 percent), high-income non-OECD countries (34.2 percent), intra-regional (28.2 percent), other developing countries (9.4 percent), unidentified (4.6 percent)
- Top 5 migration corridors: Bangladesh–India, Afghanistan–the Islamic Republic of Iran, India–the United States, India–Saudi Arabia, India–United Arab Emirates

SKILLED EMIGRATION, 2000

- Emigration rate of tertiary-educated population (top 5 countries): Sri Lanka (29.7 percent), Afghanistan (23.3 percent), Pakistan (12.6 percent), Nepal (5.3 percent), Bangladesh (4.3 percent)
- Emigration of physicians: **76,517** or **10.6 percent** of physicians trained in the region

IMMIGRATION, 2010

- Stock of immigrants: **12.2 million** or **0.7 percent** of population (compared to 215.8 million or 3.2 percent for the world)
- Females as percentage of immigrants: **45.6 percent** (compared to 48.4 percent for the world)
- Refugees as percentage of immigrants: **20.0 percent** (compared to 7.6 percent for the world)
- Top 5 immigration countries: India, Pakistan, Bangladesh, Nepal, Sri Lanka

Remittances

US$ billions	1995	2000	2004	2005	2006	2007	2008	2009	2010e
Inward									
remittance flows	**10.0**	**17.2**	**28.7**	**33.9**	**42.5**	**54.0**	**71.6**	**74.9**[a]	**82.6**
All developing									
countries	*55.2*	*81.3*	*159.3*	*192.1*	*226.7*	*278.5*	*324.8*	*307.1*	*325.5*
Outward									
remittance flows	**0.5**	**0.6**	**2.0**	**1.7**	**2.0**	**2.5**	**4.3**	**4.6**[b]	–
All developing									
countries	*10.4*	*9.5*	*28.5*	*33.0*	*41.0*	*52.7*	*67.3*	*58.7*	–

Note: This table reports officially recorded remittances. The true size of remittances, including unrecorded flows through formal and informal channels, is believed to be larger.
a. 4.8% of GDP in 2009.
b. 0.3% of GDP in 2009.

REMITTANCES

- Top 5 remittance recipients in 2010 (billions): India ($55.0 bn), Bangladesh ($11.1 bn), Pakistan ($9.4 bn), Sri Lanka ($3.6 bn), Nepal ($3.5 bn), Maldives ($0.0 bn)
- Top 5 remittance recipients in 2009 (percentage of GDP): Nepal (22.9 percent), Bangladesh (11.8 percent), Sri Lanka (7.9 percent), Pakistan (6.0 percent), India (3.9 percent), Maldives (0.2 percent)

Sub-Saharan Africa

Sub-Saharan Africa

Population (millions, 2009)	840
Population growth (avg. annual %, 2000–09)	2.5
Population density (people per km², 2008)	34.7
Labor force (millions, 2008)	317.4
Unemployment rate (% of labor force, 2008)	22.5
Urban population (% of pop., 2009)	36.9
Surface area (1,000 km², 2008)	24,242
GNI (US$ billions, 2009)	879.6
GNI per capita, Atlas method (US$, 2009)	1,096
GDP growth (avg. annual %, 2005–09)	5.0
Poverty headcount ratio at national poverty line (% of pop., 2005)	—
Age dependency ratio (2009)	84.9

Migration

EMIGRATION, 2010

- Stock of emigrants: **21.8 million** or **2.5 percent** of population
- Top 10 emigration countries: Burkina Faso, Zimbabwe, Mozambique, Côte d'Ivoire, Mali, Nigeria, Sudan, Eritrea, the Democratic Republic of Congo, South Africa
- Destinations: high-income OECD countries (24.8 percent), high-income non-OECD countries (2.5 percent), intra-regional (63.0 percent), other developing countries (1.8 percent), unidentified (7.8 percent)
- Top 10 migration corridors: Burkina Faso–Côte d'Ivoire, Zimbabwe–South Africa, Côte d'Ivoire–Burkina Faso, Uganda–Kenya, Eritrea–Sudan, Mozambique–South Africa, Mali–Côte d'Ivoire, the Democratic Republic of Congo–Rwanda, Lesotho–South Africa, Eritrea–Ethiopia

SKILLED EMIGRATION, 2000

- Emigration rate of tertiary-educated population (top 10 countries): Cape Verde (67.5 percent), The Gambia (63.3 percent), Mauritius (56.2 percent), the Seychelles (55.9 percent), Sierra Leone (52.5 percent), Ghana (46.9 percent), Mozambique (45.1 percent), Liberia (45.0 percent), Kenya (38.4 percent), Uganda (35.6 percent)
- Emigration of physicians:
  (a) **21,516** or **18.4 percent** of physicians trained in the region *(Source: Bhargava, Docquier, and Moullan 2010)*
  (b) **36,653** or **28 percent** of physicians trained in the region *(Source: Clemens and Pettersson 2006)*
- Emigration of nurses: **53,298** or **11 percent** of nurses trained in the region

IMMIGRATION, 2010

- Stock of immigrants: **17.7 million** or **2.1 percent** of population (compared to 215.8 million or 3.2 percent for the world)
- Females as percentage of immigrants: **47.2 percent** (compared to 48.4 percent for the world)
- Refugees as percentage of immigrants: **13.4 percent** (compared to 7.6 percent for the world)
- Top 10 immigration countries: Côte d'Ivoire, South Africa, Ghana, Nigeria, Burkina Faso, Kenya, Sudan, Tanzania, Uganda, Ethiopia

Remittances

US$ billions	1995	2000	2004	2005	2006	2007	2008	2009	2010e
Inward									
remittance flows	**3.2**	**4.6**	**8.0**	**9.4**	**12.7**	**18.6**	**21.4**	**20.6**[a]	**21.5**
All developing									
countries	*55.2*	*81.3*	*159.3*	*192.1*	*226.7*	*278.5*	*324.8*	*307.1*	*325.5*
Outward									
remittance flows	**2.0**	**2.5**	**2.9**	**3.2**	**3.4**	**4.0**	**4.0**	**3.3**[b]	**–**
All developing									
countries	*10.4*	*9.5*	*28.5*	*33.0*	*41.0*	*52.7*	*67.3*	*58.7*	*–*

Note: This table reports officially recorded remittances. The true size of remittances, including unrecorded flows through formal and informal channels, is believed to be larger.

a. 2.2% of GDP in 2009.

b. 0.4% of GDP in 2009.

REMITTANCES

- Top 10 remittance recipients in 2010: Nigeria ($10.0 bn), Sudan ($3.2 bn), Kenya ($1.8 bn), Senegal ($1.2 bn), South Africa ($1.0 bn), Uganda ($0.8 bn), Lesotho ($0.5 bn), Ethiopia ($0.4 bn), Mali ($0.4 bn), Togo ($0.3 bn)
- Top 10 remittance recipients in 2009 (percentage of GDP): Lesotho (24.8 percent), Togo (10.3 percent), Cape Verde (9.1 percent), Guinea-Bissau (9.1 percent), Senegal (9.1 percent), the Gambia (7.9 percent), Liberia (6.2 percent), Sudan (5.6 percent), Nigeria (5.6 percent), Kenya (5.4 percent)

Income-Group Tables

Low-Income Countries (40)

Afghanistan, Bangladesh, Benin, Burkina Faso, Burundi, Cambodia, the Central African Republic, Chad, the Comoros, the Democratic Republic of Congo, Eritrea, Ethiopia, The Gambia, Ghana, Guinea, Guinea-Bissau, Haiti, Kenya, the Democratic People's Republic of Korea, the Kyrgyz Republic, the Lao People's Democratic Republic, Liberia, Madagascar, Malawi, Mali, Mauritania, Mozambique, Myanmar, Nepal, Niger, Rwanda, Sierra Leone, the Solomon Islands, Somalia, Tajikistan, Tanzania, Togo, Uganda, Zambia, Zimbabwe

Middle-Income Countries (103)

Albania, Algeria, American Samoa, Angola, Antigua and Barbuda, Argentina, Armenia, Azerbaijan, Belarus, Belize, Bhutan, Bolivia, Bosnia and Herzegovina, Botswana, Brazil, Bulgaria, Cameroon, Cape Verde, Chile, China, Colombia, the Republic of Congo, Costa Rica, Côte d'Ivoire, Cuba, Djibouti, Dominica, Dominican Republic, Ecuador, the Arab Republic of Egypt, El Salvador, Fiji, Gabon, Georgia, Grenada, Guatemala, Guyana, Honduras, India, Indonesia, the Islamic Republic of Iran, Iraq, Jamaica, Jordan, Kazakhstan, Kiribati, Kosovo, Lebanon, Lesotho, Libya, Lithuania, the former Yugoslav Republic of Macedonia, Malaysia, Maldives, the Marshall Islands, Mauritius, Mayotte, Mexico, the Federated States of Micronesia, Moldova, Mongolia, Montenegro, Morocco, Namibia, Nicaragua, Nigeria, Pakistan, Palau, Panama, Papua New Guinea, Paraguay, Peru, the Philippines, Romania, the Russian Federation, Samoa, São Tomé and Principe, Senegal, Serbia, the Seychelles, South Africa, Sri Lanka, St. Kitts and Nevis, St. Lucia, St. Vincent and the Grenadines, Sudan, Suriname, Swaziland, the Syrian Arab Republic, Thailand, Timor-Leste, Tonga, Tunisia, Turkey, Turkmenistan, Ukraine, Uruguay, Uzbekistan, Vanuatu, República Bolivariana de Venezuela, Vietnam, West Bank and Gaza, the Republic of Yemen

High-Income OECD Countries (28)

Australia, Austria, Belgium, Canada, the Czech Republic, Denmark, Finland, France, Germany, Greece, Hungary, Iceland, Ireland, Italy, Japan, the Republic of Korea, Luxembourg, the Netherlands, New Zealand, Norway, Poland, Portugal, the Slovak Republic, Spain, Sweden, Switzerland, the United Kingdom, the United States

High-Income Non-OECD Countries (39)

Andorra; Aruba; The Bahamas; Bahrain; Barbados; Bermuda; Brunei Darussalam; Cayman Islands; Channel Islands; Croatia; Cyprus; Equatorial Guinea; Estonia; Faeroe Islands; French Polynesia; Greenland; Guam; Hong Kong SAR, China; Isle of Man; Israel; Kuwait; Latvia; Liechtenstein; Macao SAR, China; Malta; Monaco; Netherlands Antilles; New Caledonia; Northern Mariana Islands; Oman; Puerto Rico; Qatar; San Marino; Saudi Arabia; Singapore; Slovenia; Trinidad and Tobago; the United Arab Emirates; Virgin Islands (U.S.)

Note: See the chapter titled "Data Notes" in this book for changes to the definitions of regional groups since *Migration and Remittances Factbook 2008.*

Low-Income Countries

Population (millions, 2009)	846.1
Population growth (avg. annual %, 2000–09)	2.2
Population density (people per km², 2008)	51.9
Labor force (millions, 2008)	430.4
Unemployment rate (% of labor force, 2008)	–
Urban population (% of pop., 2009)	28.7
Surface area (1,000 km², 2008)	19,311
GNI (US$ billions, 2009)	428.8
GNI per capita, Atlas method (US$, 2009)	503.1
GDP growth (avg. annual %, 2005–09)	6.0
Poverty headcount ratio at national poverty line (% of pop., 2005)	–
Age dependency ratio (2009)	77.2

Migration

EMIGRATION, 2010

- Stock of emigrants: **27.7 million** or **3.2 percent** of population
- Top 10 emigration countries: Bangladesh, Afghanistan, Burkina Faso, Zimbabwe, Mozambique, Mali, Haiti, Nepal, Eritrea, the Democratic Republic of Congo
- Destinations: high-income OECD countries (19.9 percent); high-income non-OECD countries (5.1 percent); developing countries, of which identified low-income countries (17.7 percent) and identified middle-income countries (49.2 percent), unidentified (8.1 percent)
- Top 10 migration corridors: Bangladesh–India, Afghanistan–the Islamic Republic of Iran, Burkina Faso–Côte d'Ivoire, Zimbabwe–South Africa, Nepal–India, Haiti–the United States, Uganda–Kenya, the Kyrgyz Republic–the Russian Federation, Eritrea–Sudan, Mozambique–South Africa

SKILLED EMIGRATION, 2000

- Emigration rate of tertiary-educated population (top 10 countries): Haiti (83.6 percent), The Gambia (63.3 percent), Sierra Leone (52.5 percent), Ghana (46.9 percent), Mozambique (45.1 percent), Liberia (45.0 percent), Kenya (38.4 percent), the Lao People's Democratic Republic (37.4 percent), Uganda (35.6 percent), Eritrea (34.0 percent)
- Emigration of physicians: **9,220** or **8.3 percent** of physicians trained in the region

IMMIGRATION, 2010

- Stock of immigrants: **13.4 million** or **1.5 percent** of population (compared to 215.8 million or 3.2 percent for the world)
- Females as percentage of immigrants: **47.3 percent** (compared to 48.4 percent for the world)
- Refugees as percentage of immigrants: **15.7 percent** (compared to 7.6 percent for the world)
- Top 10 immigration countries: Ghana, Bangladesh, Burkina Faso, Nepal, Kenya, Tanzania, Uganda, Ethiopia, Rwanda, Mozambique

Remittances

US$ billions	1995	2000	2004	2005	2006	2007	2008	2009	2010e
Inward									
remittance flows	**2.2**	**4.1**	**8.1**	**10.1**	**13.0**	**16.6**	**22.0**	**22.5ᵃ**	**24.3**
All developing									
countries	*55.2*	*81.3*	*159.3*	*192.1*	*226.7*	*278.5*	*324.8*	*307.1*	*325.5*
Outward									
remittance flows	**0.3**	**0.9**	**1.1**	**1.3**	**1.6**	**1.6**	**1.8**	**1.8ᵇ**	—
All developing									
countries	*10.4*	*9.5*	*28.5*	*33.0*	*41.0*	*52.7*	*67.3*	*58.7*	—

Note: This table reports officially recorded remittances. The true size of remittances, including unrecorded flows through formal and informal channels, is believed to be larger.
a. 5.4% of GDP in 2009.
b. 0.5% of GDP in 2009.

REMITTANCES

- Top 10 remittance recipients in 2010 (billions): Bangladesh ($11.1 bn), Nepal ($3.5 bn), Tajikistan ($2.1 bn), Kenya ($1.8 bn), Haiti ($1.5 bn), Kyrgyz Republic ($1.0 bn), Uganda ($0.8 bn), Ethiopia ($0.4 bn), Mali ($0.4 bn), Cambodia ($0.4 bn)
- Top 10 remittance recipients in 2009 (percentage of GDP): Tajikistan (35.1 percent), Nepal (22.9 percent), Kyrgyz Republic (15.4 percent), Haiti (15.4 percent), Bangladesh (11.8 percent), Togo (10.3 percent), Guinea-Bissau (9.1 percent), the Gambia (7.9 percent), Liberia (6.2 percent), Kenya (5.4 percent)

Middle-Income Countries

	MIDDLE INCOME
Population (millions, 2009)	4,813
Population growth (avg. annual %, 2000–09)	1.2
Population density (people per km², 2008)	60.1
Labor force (millions, 2008)	2,151
Unemployment rate (% of labor force, 2008)	5.7
Urban population (% of pop., 2009)	48.0
Surface area (1,000 km², 2008)	79,485
GNI (US$ billions, 2009)	15,966
GNI per capita, Atlas method (US$, 2009)	3,373
GDP growth (avg. annual %, 2005–09)	6.5
Poverty headcount ratio at national poverty line (% of pop., 2005)	—
Age dependency ratio (2009)	51.6

Migration

EMIGRATION, 2010

- Stock of emigrants: **133.8 million** or **2.7 percent** of population
- Top 10 emigration countries: Mexico, India, the Russian Federation, China, Ukraine, Pakistan, the Philippines, Turkey, the Arab Republic of Egypt, Kazakhstan
- Destinations: high-income OECD countries (48.2 percent); high-income non-OECD countries (15.8 percent); developing countries, of which identified low-income countries (3.8 percent) and identified middle-income countries (28.3 percent); unidentified (3.9 percent)
- Top 10 migration corridors: Mexico–the United States; the Russian Federation–Ukraine; Ukraine–the Russian Federation; Turkey–Germany; Kazakhstan–the Russian Federation; the Russian Federation–Kazakhstan; China–Hong Kong SAR, China; China–the United States; the Philippines–the United States; India–the United States
- Top 10 migration corridors excluding the former Soviet Union: Mexico–the United States; Turkey–Germany; China–Hong Kong SAR, China; China–the United States; the Philippines–the United States; India–the United States; India–Saudi Arabia; West Bank and Gaza–the Syrian Arab Republic; Indonesia–Malaysia; India–the United Arab Emirates

SKILLED EMIGRATION, 2000

- Emigration rate of tertiary-educated population (top 10 countries): Guyana (89.0 percent), Grenada (85.1 percent), Jamaica (85.1 percent), St. Vincent and the Grenadines (84.5 percent), St. Kitts and Nevis (78.5 percent), Samoa (76.4 percent), Tonga (75.2 percent), St. Lucia (71.1 percent), Cape Verde (67.5 percent), Antigua and Barbuda (66.8 percent)
- Emigration of physicians: **210,930** or **3.8 percent** of physicians trained in the region

IMMIGRATION, 2010

- Stock of immigrants: **68.7 million** or **1.4 percent** of population (compared to 215.8 million or 3.2 percent for the world)
- Females as percentage of immigrants: **50.7 percent** (compared to 48.4 percent for the world)

- Refugees as percentage of immigrants: **17.3 percent** (compared to 7.6 percent for the world)
- Top 10 immigration countries: the Russian Federation, India, Ukraine, Pakistan, Kazakhstan, Jordan, Côte d'Ivoire, Malaysia, the Syrian Arab Republic, the Islamic Republic of Iran

Remittances

US$ billions	1995	2000	2004	2005	2006	2007	2008	2009	2010e
Inward remittance flows	**53.0**	**77.1**	**151.2**	**182.1**	**213.7**	**261.9**	**302.9**	**284.6**[a]	**301.1**
All developing countries	*55.2*	*81.3*	*159.3*	*192.1*	*226.7*	*278.5*	*324.8*	*307.1*	*325.5*
Outward remittance flows	**10.1**	**8.6**	**27.5**	**31.7**	**39.5**	**51.1**	**65.5**	**57.0**[b]	—
All developing countries	*10.4*	*9.5*	*28.5*	*33.0*	*41.0*	*52.7*	*67.3*	*58.7*	—

Note: This table reports officially recorded remittances. The true size of remittances, including unrecorded flows through formal and informal channels, is believed to be larger.

a. 1.8% of GDP in 2009.
b. 0.4% of GDP in 2009.

REMITTANCES

- Top 10 remittance recipients in 2010 (billions): India ($55.0 bn), China ($51.0 bn), Mexico ($22.6 bn), Philippines ($21.3 bn), Nigeria ($10.0 bn), Pakistan ($9.4 bn), Lebanon ($8.2 bn), the Arab Republic of Egypt ($7.7 bn), Vietnam ($7.2 bn), Indonesia ($7.1 bn)
- Top 10 remittance recipients in 2009 (percentage of GDP): Tonga (27.7 percent), Lesotho (24.8 percent), Moldova (23.1 percent), Lebanon (22.4 percent), Samoa (22.3 percent), Honduras (19.3 percent), Guyana (17.3 percent), El Salvador (15.7 percent), Jordan (15.6 percent), Jamaica (13.8 percent)

High-Income OECD Countries

Population (millions, 2009)	1,025
Population growth (avg. annual %, 2000–09)	0.6
Population density (people per km², 2008)	31.9
Labor force (millions, 2008)	486.3
Unemployment rate (% of labor force, 2008)	5.9
Urban population (% of pop., 2009)	77.0
Surface area (1,000 km², 2008)	32,035
GNI (US$ billions, 2009)	39,729
GNI per capita, Atlas method (US$, 2009)	39,654
GDP growth (avg. annual %, 2005–09)	1.0
Poverty headcount ratio at national poverty line (% of pop., 2005)	–
Age dependency ratio (2009)	49.4

Migration

IMMIGRATION, 2010

- Stock of immigrants: **109.5 million** or **10.7 percent** of population (compared to 215.8 million or 3.2 percent for the world)
- Females as percentage of immigrants: **49.3 percent** (compared to 48.4 percent for the world)
- Refugees as percentage of immigrants: **2.1 percent** (compared to 7.6 percent for the world)
- Top 10 immigration countries: the United States, Germany, Canada, the United Kingdom, Spain, France, Australia, Italy, Japan, Switzerland
- Sources: high-income OECD countries (26.5 percent); high-income non-OECD countries (4.6 percent); developing countries, of which identified low-income countries (5.1 percent) and identified middle-income countries (59.3 percent); unidentified (4.5 percent)
- Top 10 migration corridors: the United Kingdom–Australia, the Republic of Korea–the United States, Italy–Germany, Canada–the United States, Portugal–France, the United Kingdom–the United States, the United Kingdom–Canada, Germany–the United States, Poland–Germany, the Republic of Korea–Japan

EMIGRATION, 2010

- Stock of emigrants: **37.3 million** or **3.6 percent** of population
- Top 10 emigration countries: the United Kingdom, Germany, Italy, Poland, the United States, Portugal, the Republic of Korea, France, Spain, Greece

SKILLED EMIGRATION, 2000

- Emigration rate of tertiary-educated population (top 10 countries): Ireland (29.5 percent), New Zealand (20.7 percent), Iceland (19.7 percent), Portugal (19.5 percent), the Slovak Republic (16.7 percent), the United Kingdom (16.7 percent), Poland (14.1 percent), Austria (13.5 percent), Hungary (13.2 percent), Greece (12.0 percent)
- Emigration of physicians: **135,749** or **4.6 percent** of physicians trained in the group

Remittances

US$ billions	1995	2000	2004	2005	2006	2007	2008	2009	2010e
Inward remittance flows	**44.3**	**48.4**	**72.9**	**77.2**	**85.2**	**100.1**	**110.8**	**102.1**[a]	**107.2**
All developing countries	*55.2*	*81.3*	*159.3*	*192.1*	*226.7*	*278.5*	*324.8*	*307.1*	*325.5*
Outward remittance flows	**65.5**	**75.5**	**116.8**	**127.9**	**144.3**	**165.3**	**182.3**	**175.1**[b]	—
All developing countries	*10.4*	*9.5*	*28.5*	*33.0*	*41.0*	*52.7*	*67.3*	*58.7*	—

Note: This table reports officially recorded remittances. The true size of remittances, including unrecorded flows through formal and informal channels, is believed to be larger.
a. 0.3% of GDP in 2009.
b. 0.4% of GDP in 2009.

REMITTANCES

- Top 10 remittance recipients in 2010 (billions): France ($15.9 bn), Germany ($11.6 bn), Belgium ($10.4 bn), Spain ($10.2 bn), Poland ($9.1 bn), the United Kingdom ($7.4 bn), Australia ($4.3 bn), Netherlands ($4.1 bn), Portugal ($3.7 bn), Italy ($3.4 bn)
- Top 10 remittance recipients in 2009 (percentage of GDP): Luxembourg (3.3 percent), Belgium (2.2 percent), Poland (2.0 percent), the Slovak Republic (1.9 percent), Hungary (1.7 percent), Portugal (1.5 percent), Austria (0.8 percent), Greece (0.7 percent), Spain (0.7 percent), the Czech Republic (0.6 percent)
- Top 10 remittance senders in 2009 (billions): the United States ($48.3 bn), Switzerland ($19.6 bn), Germany ($15.9 bn), Italy ($13.0 bn), Spain ($12.6 bn), Luxembourg ($10.6 bn), Netherlands ($8.1 bn), France ($5.2 bn), Belgium ($4.3 bn), Norway ($4.1 bn)
- Top 10 remittance senders in 2009 (percentage of GDP): Luxembourg (20.1 percent), Switzerland (4.0 percent), the Czech Republic (1.4 percent), Norway (1.1 percent), Denmark (1.1 percent), Hungary (1.0 percent), Netherlands (1.0 percent), Belgium (0.9 percent), Ireland (0.9 percent), Austria (0.9 percent)

High-Income Non-OECD Countries

Population (millions, 2009)	91.6
Population growth (avg. annual %, 2000–09)	1.4
Population density (people per km², 2008)	29.9
Labor force (millions, 2008)	31.9
Unemployment rate (% of labor force, 2008)	5.6
Urban population (% of pop., 2009)	82.1
Surface area (1,000 km², 2008)	3,265
GNI (US$ billions, 2009)	–
GNI per capita, Atlas method (US$, 2009)	–
GDP growth (avg. annual %, 2005–09)	–
Poverty headcount ratio at national poverty line (% of pop., 2005)	–
Age dependency ratio (2009)	45.2

Migration

IMMIGRATION, 2010

- Stock of immigrants: **25.7 million** or **32.5 percent** of population (compared to 215.8 million or 3.2 percent for the world)
- Females as percentage of immigrants: **39.5 percent** (compared to 48.4 percent for the world)
- Refugees as percentage of immigrants: **1.1 percent** (compared to 7.6 percent for the world)
- Top 10 immigration countries: Saudi Arabia; the United Arab Emirates; Israel; Hong Kong SAR, China; Kuwait; Singapore; Qatar; Oman; Croatia; Latvia
- Sources: high-income OECD countries (3.6 percent); high-income non-OECD countries (1.3 percent); developing countries, of which identified low-income countries (5.5 percent) and identified middle-income countries (81.8 percent); unidentified (7.7 percent)
- Top 10 migration corridors: Puerto Rico–the United States; Israel–West Bank and Gaza; Croatia–Germany; Hong Kong SAR, China–Canada; Trinidad and Tobago–the United States; Hong Kong SAR, China–the United States; Israel–the United States; Kuwait–Saudi Arabia; Latvia–the Russian Federation; Singapore–Malaysia

EMIGRATION, 2010

- Stock of emigrants: **6.9 million** or **8.7 percent** of population
- Top 10 emigration countries: Puerto Rico; Israel; Croatia; Hong Kong SAR, China; Trinidad and Tobago; Singapore; Latvia; Kuwait; Saudi Arabia; Estonia

SKILLED EMIGRATION, 2000

- Emigration rate of tertiary-educated population (top 10 countries): Trinidad and Tobago (79.3 percent); Barbados (63.5 percent); The Bahamas (61.3 percent); Malta (57.6 percent); Cyprus (31.2 percent); Hong Kong SAR, China (28.8 percent); Croatia (24.1 percent); San Marino (17.1 percent); Liechtenstein (17.0 percent); Monaco (15.9 percent)
- Emigration of physicians: **10,517** or **8.7 percent** of physicians trained in the group

Remittances

US$ billions	1995	2000	2004	2005	2006	2007	2008	2009	2010e
Inward									
remittance flows	**1.7**	**1.8**	**4.8**	**5.5**	**5.9**	**6.4**	**7.5**	**6.8ᵃ**	**7.4**
All developing									
countries	*55.2*	*81.3*	*159.3*	*192.1*	*226.7*	*278.5*	*324.8*	*307.1*	*325.5*
Outward									
remittance flows	**21.6**	**23.4**	**22.7**	**24.5**	**28.3**	**37.2**	**46.1**	**48.7ᵇ**	**—**
All developing									
countries	*10.4*	*9.5*	*28.5*	*33.0*	*41.0*	*52.7*	*67.3*	*58.7*	*—*

Note: This table reports officially recorded remittances. The true size of remittances, including unrecorded flows through formal and informal channels, is believed to be larger.

a. 0.4% of GDP in 2009.
b. 2.4% of GDP in 2009.

REMITTANCES

- Top 5 remittance recipients in 2010 (billions): Croatia ($1.5 bn), Israel ($1.4 bn), French Polynesia ($0.8 bn), New Caledonia ($0.7 bn), Latvia ($0.6 bn)
- Top 5 remittance recipients in 2009 (percentage of GDP): Barbados (3.8 percent), Croatia (2.4 percent), Latvia (2.2 percent), Estonia (1.6 percent), Israel (0.7 percent)
- Top 5 remittance senders in 2009 (billions): Saudi Arabia ($26.0 bn), Kuwait ($9.9 bn), Oman ($5.3 bn), Israel ($3.3 bn), Bahrain ($1.4 bn)
- Top 5 remittance senders in 2009 (percentage of GDP): Oman (9.9 percent), Kuwait (8.2 percent), Bahrain (6.6 percent), Saudi Arabia (6.5 percent), Brunei Darussalam (4.0 percent)

Other Country Group Tables

Least Developed Countries, United Nations Classification (49)

Afghanistan, Angola, Bangladesh, Benin, Bhutan, Burkina Faso, Burundi, Cambodia, the Central African Republic, Chad, Comoros, the Democratic Republic of Congo, Djibouti, Equatorial Guinea, Eritrea, Ethiopia, The Gambia, Guinea, Guinea-Bissau, Haiti, Kiribati, the Lao People's Democratic Republic, Lesotho, Liberia, Madagascar, Malawi, Maldives, Mali, Mauritania, Mozambique, Myanmar, Nepal, Niger, Rwanda, Samoa, São Tomé and Principe, Senegal, Sierra Leone, the Solomon Islands, Somalia, Sudan, Tanzania, Timor-Leste, Togo, Tuvalu, Uganda, Vanuatu, the Republic of Yemen, Zambia

Fragile States (32)

Afghanistan, Angola, Burundi, Cameroon, the Central African Republic, Chad, Comoros, the Democratic Republic of Congo, the Republic of Congo, Côte d'Ivoire, Djibouti, Eritrea, The Gambia, Guinea, Guinea-Bissau, Haiti, Kiribati, Kosovo, Liberia, Myanmar, São Tomé and Principe, Sierra Leone, the Solomon Islands, Somalia, Sudan, Tajikistan, Timor-Leste, Togo, Tonga, West Bank and Gaza, the Republic of Yemen, Zimbabwe

Small States (46)

Antigua and Barbuda, The Bahamas, Bahrain, Barbados, Belize, Bhutan, Botswana, Brunei Darussalam, Cape Verde, the Comoros, Cook Islands, Cyprus, Djibouti, Dominica, Equatorial Guinea, Estonia, Fiji, Gabon, The Gambia, Grenada, Guinea-Bissau, Guyana, Jamaica, Kiribati, Lesotho, Maldives, Malta, the Marshall Islands, Mauritius, the Federated States of Micronesia, Namibia, Nauru, Niue, Palau, Qatar, Samoa, São Tomé and Principe, the Seychelles, the Solomon Islands, St. Kitts and Nevis, St. Lucia, St. Vincent and the Grenadines, Suriname, Swaziland, Timor-Leste, Tonga, Trinidad and Tobago, Tuvalu, Vanuatu

Least Developed Countries, United Nations Classification

Population (millions, 2009)	837.1
Population growth (avg. annual %, 2000–09)	2.3
Population density (people per km², 2008)	40.4
Labor force (millions, 2008)	346.7
Unemployment rate (% of labor force, 2008)	–
Urban population (% of pop., 2009)	29.0
Surface area (1,000 km², 2008)	20,803
GNI (US$ billions, 2009)	528
GNI per capita, Atlas method (US$, 2009)	639
GDP growth (avg. annual %, 2005–09)	6.8
Poverty headcount ratio at national poverty line (% of pop., 2005)	–
Age dependency ratio (2009)	78.7

Migration

EMIGRATION, 2010

- Stock of emigrants: **27.5 million** or **3.2 percent** of population
- Top 10 emigration countries: Bangladesh, Afghanistan, Burkina Faso, Mozambique, the Republic of Yemen, Mali, Haiti, Nepal, Sudan, Eritrea
- Destinations: high-income OECD countries (19.2 percent); high-income non-OECD countries (9.8 percent); developing countries, of which identified low-income countries (19.3 percent) and identified middle-income countries (44.0 percent); unidentified (7.6 percent)
- Top 10 migration corridors: Bangladesh–India, Afghanistan–the Islamic Republic of Iran, Burkina Faso–Côte d'Ivoire, the Republic of Yemen–Saudi Arabia, Nepal–India, Haiti–the United States, Uganda–Kenya, Eritrea–Sudan, Mozambique–South Africa, Bangladesh–Saudi Arabia

SKILLED EMIGRATION, 2000

- Emigration rate of tertiary-educated population (top 10 countries): Haiti (83.6 percent), Samoa (76.4 percent), The Gambia (63.3 percent), Sierra Leone (52.5 percent), Mozambique (45.1 percent), Liberia (45.0 percent), the Lao People's Democratic Republic (37.4 percent), Uganda (35.6 percent), Eritrea (34.0 percent), Angola (33.0 percent)
- Emigration of physicians: **8,792** or **10 percent** of physicians trained in the group

IMMIGRATION, 2010

- Stock of immigrants: **11.5 million** or **1.3 percent** of population (compared to 215.8 million or 3.2 percent for the world)
- Females as percentage of immigrants: **47.4 percent** (compared to 48.4 percent for the world)
- Refugees as percentage of immigrants: **18.6 percent** (compared to 7.6 percent for the world)
- Top 10 immigration countries: Bangladesh, Burkina Faso, Nepal, Sudan, Tanzania, Uganda, Ethiopia, the Republic of Yemen, Rwanda, Mozambique

Remittances

US$ billions	1995	2000	2004	2005	2006	2007	2008	2009	2010e
Inward									
remittance flows	**3.9**	**6.1**	**10.8**	**11.9**	**14.2**	**17.4**	**22.9**	**24.2**[a]	**25.9**
All developing									
countries	*55.2*	*81.3*	*159.3*	*192.1*	*226.7*	*278.5*	*324.8*	*307.1*	*325.5*
Outward									
remittance flows	**0.7**	**1.4**	**1.4**	**1.5**	**1.7**	**2.4**	**2.5**	**2.6**[b]	**–**
All developing									
countries	*10.4*	*9.5*	*28.5*	*33.0*	*41.0*	*52.7*	*67.3*	*58.7*	*–*

Note: This table reports officially recorded remittances. The true size of remittances, including unrecorded flows through formal and informal channels, is believed to be larger.

a. 4.5% of GDP in 2009.

b. 0.5% of GDP in 2009.

REMITTANCES

- Top 10 remittance recipients in 2010 (billions): Bangladesh ($11.1 bn), Nepal ($3.5 bn), Sudan ($3.2 bn), Haiti ($1.5 bn), the Republic of Yemen ($1.5 bn), Senegal ($1.2 bn), Uganda ($0.8 bn), Lesotho ($0.5 bn), Ethiopia ($0.4 bn), Mali ($0.4 bn)
- Top 10 remittance recipients in 2009 (percentage of GDP): Lesotho (24.8 percent), Nepal (22.9 percent), Samoa (22.3 percent), Haiti (15.4 percent), Bangladesh (11.8 percent), Togo (10.3 percent), Guinea-Bissau (9.1 percent), Senegal (9.1 percent), the Gambia (7.9 percent), Kiribati (6.3 percent)

Fragile States

Population (millions, 2009)	381.2
Population growth (avg. annual %, 2000–09)	2.3
Population density (people per km², 2008)	104.8
Labor force (millions, 2008)	141.6
Unemployment rate (% of labor force, 2008)	–
Urban population (% of pop., 2009)	40.9
Surface area (1,000 km², 2008)	13,137
GNI (US$ billions, 2009)	222.4
GNI per capita, Atlas method (US$, 2009)	1,176
GDP growth (avg. annual %, 2005–09)	4.6
Poverty headcount ratio at national poverty line (% of pop., 2005)	–
Age dependency ratio (2009)	80.1

Migration

EMIGRATION, 2010

- Stock of emigrants: **18.6 million** or **4.8 percent** of population
- Top 10 emigration countries: West Bank and Gaza, Afghanistan, Zimbabwe, Côte d'Ivoire, the Republic of Yemen, Haiti, Sudan, Eritrea, the Democratic Republic of Congo, Somalia
- Destinations: high-income OECD countries (19.4 percent); high-income non-OECD countries (8.5 percent); developing countries, of which identified low-income countries (23.2 percent) and identified middle-income countries (41.1 percent); unidentified (7.8 percent)
- Top 10 migration corridors: Afghanistan–the Islamic Republic of Iran, West Bank and Gaza–the Syrian Arab Republic, the Republic of Yemen–Saudi Arabia, West Bank and Gaza–Jordan, Zimbabwe–South Africa, Côte d'Ivoire–Burkina Faso, Haiti–the United States, Eritrea–Sudan, Tajikistan–the Russian Federation, the Democratic Republic of Congo–Rwanda

SKILLED EMIGRATION, 2000

- Emigration rate of tertiary-educated population (top 10 countries): Haiti (83.6 percent), Tonga (75.2 percent), The Gambia (63.3 percent), Sierra Leone (52.5 percent), Liberia (45.0 percent), Eritrea (34.0 percent), Angola (33.0 percent), Somalia (32.7 percent), Guinea-Bissau (24.4 percent), Afghanistan (23.3 percent)
- Emigration of physicians: **5,897** or **9.3 percent** of physicians trained in the group

IMMIGRATION, 2010

- Stock of immigrants: **9.1 million** or **2.4 percent** of population (compared to 215.8 million or 3.2 percent for the world)
- Females as percentage of immigrants: **47.3 percent** (compared to 48.4 percent for the world)
- Refugees as percentage of immigrants: **32.7 percent** (compared to 7.6 percent for the world)
- Top 10 immigration countries: Côte d'Ivoire, West Bank and Gaza, Sudan, the Republic of Yemen, the Democratic Republic of Congo, Guinea, Chad, Zimbabwe, The Gambia, Tajikistan

Remittances

US$ billions	1995	2000	2004	2005	2006	2007	2008	2009	2010e
Inward									
remittance flows	**1.9**	**2.1**	**4.1**	**4.4**	**4.8**	**5.3**	**5.3**	**4.8**[a]	**5.1**
All developing									
countries	*55.2*	*81.3*	*159.3*	*192.1*	*226.7*	*278.5*	*324.8*	*307.1*	*325.5*
Outward									
remittance flows	**1.2**	**1.9**	**2.9**	**1.5**	**1.7**	**2.4**	**2.5**	**2.6**[b]	**—**
All developing									
countries	*10.4*	*9.5*	*28.5*	*33.0*	*41.0*	*52.7*	*67.3*	*58.7*	*—*

Note: This table reports officially recorded remittances. The true size of remittances, including unrecorded flows through formal and informal channels, is believed to be larger.
a. 3.1% of GDP in 2009.
b. 0.5% of GDP in 2009.

REMITTANCES

- Top 10 remittance recipients in 2010 (billions): Sudan ($3.2 bn), Tajikistan ($2.1 bn), Haiti ($1.5 bn), the Republic of Yemen ($1.5 bn), West Bank and Gaza ($1.3 bn), Togo ($0.3 bn), Côte d'Ivoire ($0.2 bn), Myanmar ($0.2 bn), Cameroon ($0.1 bn), Tonga ($0.1 bn)
- Top 10 remittance recipients in 2009 (percentage of GDP): Tajikistan (35.1 percent), Tonga (27.7 percent), Haiti (15.4 percent), Togo (10.3 percent), Guinea-Bissau (9.1 percent), the Gambia (7.9 percent), Kiribati (6.3 percent), Liberia (6.2 percent), Sudan (5.6 percent), the Republic of Yemen (5.2 percent)

Small States

Population (millions, 2009)	32.8
Population growth (avg. annual %, 2000–09)	1.5
Population density (people per km², 2008)	206.3
Labor force (millions, 2008)	13.5
Unemployment rate (% of labor force, 2008)	10.2
Urban population (% of pop., 2009)	49.9
Surface area (1,000 km², 2008)	2,478
GNI (US$ billions, 2009)	120.6
GNI per capita, Atlas method (US$, 2009)	5,156
GDP growth (avg. annual %, 2005–09)	3.5
Poverty headcount ratio at national poverty line (% of pop., 2005)	–
Age dependency ratio (2009)	60.2

Migration

EMIGRATION, 2010

- Stock of emigrants: **4.8 million** or **14.5 percent** of population
- Top 10 emigration countries: Jamaica, Guyana, Lesotho, Trinidad and Tobago, Suriname, Cape Verde, Fiji, Estonia, Swaziland, Cyprus
- Destinations: high-income OECD countries (72.5 percent); high-income non-OECD countries (2.6 percent); developing countries, of which identified low-income countries (3.2 percent) and identified middle-income countries (18.8 percent); unidentified (3.0 percent)
- Top 10 migration corridors: Jamaica–the United States, Lesotho–South Africa, Guyana–the United States, Trinidad and Tobago–the United States, Suriname–the Netherlands, Jamaica–the United Kingdom, Jamaica–Canada, Swaziland–South Africa, Guyana–Canada, Trinidad and Tobago–Canada

SKILLED EMIGRATION, 2000

- Emigration rate of tertiary-educated population (top 10 countries): Guyana (89.0 percent), Grenada (85.1 percent), Jamaica (85.1 percent), St. Vincent and the Grenadines (84.5 percent), Trinidad and Tobago (79.3 percent), St. Kitts and Nevis (78.5 percent), Samoa (76.4 percent), Tonga (75.2 percent), St. Lucia (71.1 percent), Cape Verde (67.5 percent)
- Emigration of physicians: **8,890** or **39.4 percent** of physicians trained in the group

IMMIGRATION, 2010

- Stock of immigrants: **3.6 million** or **10.8 percent** of population (compared to 215.8 million or 3.2 percent for the world)
- Females as percentage of immigrants: **39.3 percent** (compared to 48.4 percent for the world)
- Refugees as percentage of immigrants: **1.5 percent** (compared to 7.6 percent for the world)
- Top 10 immigration countries: Qatar, Bahrain, The Gambia, Gabon, Estonia, Cyprus, Brunei Darussalam, Namibia, Botswana, Djibouti

Remittances

US$ billions	1995	2000	2004	2005	2006	2007	2008	2009	2010e
Inward									
remittance flows	**2.3**	**3.9**	**5.4**	**5.4**	**6.6**	**8.4**	**11.9**	**9.9**[a]	**10.7**
All developing									
countries	*55.2*	*81.3*	*159.3*	*192.1*	*226.7*	*278.5*	*324.8*	*307.1*	*325.5*
Outward									
remittance flows	**0.8**	**0.9**	**1.4**	**1.3**	**1.9**	**2.3**	**2.3**	**1.6**[b]	**—**
All developing									
countries	*10.4*	*9.5*	*28.5*	*33.0*	*41.0*	*52.7*	*67.3*	*58.7*	*—*

Note: This table reports officially recorded remittances. The true size of remittances, including unrecorded flows through formal and informal channels, is believed to be larger.

a. 1.5% of GDP in 2009.

b. 1.4% of GDP in 2009.

REMITTANCES

- Top 10 remittance recipients in 2010 (billions): Jamaica ($2.0 bn), Lesotho ($0.5 bn), Estonia ($0.3 bn), Guyana ($0.3 bn), Mauritius ($0.2 bn), Barbados ($0.2 bn), Cyprus ($0.1 bn), Cape Verde ($0.1 bn), Samoa ($0.1 bn), Fiji ($0.1 bn)
- Top 10 remittance recipients in 2009 (percentage of GDP): Tonga (27.7 percent), Lesotho (24.8 percent), Samoa (22.3 percent), Guyana (17.3 percent), Jamaica (13.8 percent), Cape Verde (9.1 percent), Guinea-Bissau (9.1 percent), Grenada (8.7 percent), the Gambia (7.9 percent), St. Kitts and Nevis (7.3 percent)

Country Tables

Afghanistan

Population (millions, 2009)	29.8
Population growth (avg. annual %, 2000–09)	2.6
Population density (people per km², 2008)	—
Labor force (millions, 2008)	—
Unemployment rate (% of labor force, 2008)	—
Urban population (% of pop., 2009)	24.4
Surface area (1,000 km², 2008)	652.1
GNI (US$ billions, 2009)	—
GNI per capita, Atlas method (US$, 2009)	—
GDP growth (avg. annual %, 2005–09)	11.0
Poverty headcount ratio at national poverty line (% of pop., 2005)	—
Age dependency ratio (2009)	93.5

Migration

EMIGRATION, 2010

- Stock of emigrants: **2,348.7 thousands**
- Stock of emigrants as percentage of population: **8.1%**
- Top destination countries: the Islamic Republic of Iran, Germany, the United States, the United Kingdom, Tajikistan, Canada, the Netherlands, Australia, Saudi Arabia, Denmark

SKILLED EMIGRATION, 2000

- Emigration rate of tertiary-educated population: **23.3%**
- Emigration of physicians: **449** or **9.1%** of physicians trained in the country *(Source: Bhargava, Docquier, and Moullan 2010)*

IMMIGRATION, 2010

- Stock of immigrants: **90.9 thousands**
- Stock of immigrants as percentage of population: **0.3%**
- Females as percentage of immigrants: **43.6%**
- Refugees as percentage of immigrants: **0.0%**

Remittances

Remittance data are currently not available for this country.

Albania

　　　　　　　　　　　　　　UPPER MIDDLE INCOME

Population (millions, 2009)	3.2
Population growth (avg. annual %, 2000–09)	0.3
Population density (people per km², 2008)	114.7
Labor force (millions, 2008)	1.4
Unemployment rate (% of labor force, 2008)	–
Urban population (% of pop., 2009)	47.4
Surface area (1,000 km², 2008)	28.8
GNI (US$ billions, 2009)	12.7
GNI per capita, Atlas method (US$, 2009)	3,950
GDP growth (avg. annual %, 2005–09)	5.0
Poverty headcount ratio at national poverty line (% of pop., 2005)	0.9
Age dependency ratio (2009)	49.4

Migration

EMIGRATION, 2010

- Stock of emigrants: **1,438.3 thousands**
- Stock of emigrants as percentage of population: **45.4%**
- Top destination countries: Greece, Italy, the former Yugoslav Republic of Macedonia, the United States, Germany, Canada, Turkey, the United Kingdom, France, Australia

SKILLED EMIGRATION, 2000

- Emigration rate of tertiary-educated population: **9.0%**
- Emigration of physicians: **46** or **1.0%** of physicians trained in the country *(Source: Bhargava, Docquier, and Moullan 2010)*

IMMIGRATION, 2010

- Stock of immigrants: **89.1 thousands**
- Stock of immigrants as percentage of population: **2.8%**
- Females as percentage of immigrants: **53.1%**
- Refugees as percentage of immigrants: **0.1%**
- Top source countries: Greece, the former Yugoslav Republic of Macedonia, the Czech Republic, Israel, Italy, the Russian Federation

Remittances

US$ millions	2003	2004	2005	2006	2007	2008	2009	2010e
Inward remittance flows[a]	**889**	**1,161**	**1,290**	**1,359**	**1,468**	**1,495**	**1,317**	**1,285**
of which								
Workers' remittances	778	1,028	1,161	1,176	1,305	1,226	1,090	–
Compensation of employees	111	132	129	184	163	270	227	–
Migrants' transfers	–	–	–	–	–	–	–	–
Outward remittance flows	**4**	**5**	**7**	**27**	**10**	**16**	**10**	–
of which								
Workers' remittances	0	0	–	0	–	–	1	–
Compensation of employees	4	5	7	27	10	16	9	–
Migrants' transfers	–	–	–	–	–	–	–	–

a. **For comparison: net FDI inflows US$0.9 bn, net ODA received US$0.4 bn, total international reserves US$2.4 bn, exports of goods and services US$3.8 bn in 2008.**

Algeria

Population (millions, 2009)	34.9
Population growth (avg. annual %, 2000–09)	1.5
Population density (people per km², 2008)	14.4
Labor force (millions, 2008)	13.9
Unemployment rate (% of labor force, 2008)	–
Urban population (% of pop., 2009)	65.9
Surface area (1,000 km², 2008)	2,381.7
GNI (US$ billions, 2009)	139.6
GNI per capita, Atlas method (US$, 2009)	4,420
GDP growth (avg. annual %, 2005–09)	3.7
Poverty headcount ratio at national poverty line (% of pop., 2005)	4.3
Age dependency ratio (2009)	46.9

Migration

EMIGRATION, 2010

- Stock of emigrants: **1,211.1 thousands**
- Stock of emigrants as percentage of population: **3.4%**
- Top destination countries: France, Spain, Israel, Canada, Italy, Belgium, Germany, the United Kingdom, Tunisia, the United States

SKILLED EMIGRATION, 2000

- Emigration rate of tertiary-educated population: **9.4%**
- Emigration of physicians:
  - (a) **879** or **2.8%** of physicians trained in the country *(Source: Bhargava, Docquier, and Moullan 2010)*
  - (b) **10,860** or **44.3%** of physicians born in the country *(Source: Clemens and Pettersson 2006)*
- Emigration of nurses: **8,245** or **9.0%** of nurses born in the country

IMMIGRATION, 2010

- Stock of immigrants: **242.3 thousands**
- Stock of immigrants as percentage of population: **0.7%**
- Females as percentage of immigrants: **45.2%**
- Refugees as percentage of immigrants: **38.9%**

Remittances

US$ millions	2003	2004	2005	2006	2007	2008	2009	2010e
Inward remittance flows[a]	**1,750**	**2,460**	**2,060**	**1,610**	**2,120**	**2,202**	**2,059**	**2,031**
of which								
Workers' remittances	–	–	–	–	–	–	–	–
Compensation of employees	–	–	–	–	–	–	–	–
Migrants' transfers	–	–	–	–	–	–	–	–
Outward remittance flows	–	–	–	–	–	–	–	–
of which								
Workers' remittances	–	–	–	–	–	–	–	–
Compensation of employees	–	–	–	–	–	–	–	–
Migrants' transfers	–	–	–	–	–	–	–	–

a. For comparison: net FDI inflows US$2.6 bn, net ODA received US$0.3 bn, total international reserves US$148.1 bn, exports of goods and services US$79.1 bn in 2008.

American Samoa

Population (thousands, 2009)	67.2
Population growth (avg. annual %, 2000–09)	1.7
Population density (people per km², 2008)	330.5
Labor force (millions, 2008)	–
Unemployment rate (% of labor force, 2008)	–
Urban population (% of pop., 2009)	92.7
Surface area (1,000 km², 2008)	0.2
GNI (US$ billions, 2009)	–
GNI per capita, Atlas method (US$, 2009)	–
GDP growth (avg. annual %, 2005-09)	–
Poverty headcount ratio at national poverty line (% of pop., 2005)	–
Age dependency ratio (2009)	–

Migration

EMIGRATION, 2010

- Stock of emigrants: **45.7 thousands**
- Stock of emigrants as percentage of population: **66.7%**
- Top destination countries: the United States, Samoa, New Zealand, Australia, Fiji, Kiribati, Canada, the United Kingdom, the Czech Republic, the Slovak Republic

SKILLED EMIGRATION, 2000

- Skilled emigration data are currently not available for this country.

IMMIGRATION, 2010

- Stock of immigrants: **28.4 thousands**
- Stock of immigrants as percentage of population: **41.4%**
- Females as percentage of immigrants: **49.0%**
- Refugees as percentage of immigrants: **0.0%**
- Top source countries: Samoa, the United States, Tonga, the Philippines, New Zealand, Vietnam, the Republic of Korea, China, Fiji

Remittances

Remittance data are currently not available for this country.

Andorra

HIGH-INCOME NON-OECD

Population (thousands, 2009)	85.2
Population growth (avg. annual %, 2000–09)	3.3
Population density (people per km², 2008)	178.3
Labor force (millions, 2008)	–
Unemployment rate (% of labor force, 2008)	–
Urban population (% of pop., 2009)	88.5
Surface area (1,000 km², 2008)	0.5
GNI (US$ billions, 2009)	–
GNI per capita, Atlas method (US$, 2009)	–
GDP growth (avg. annual %, 2005–09)	4.4
Poverty headcount ratio at national poverty line (% of pop., 2005)	–
Age dependency ratio (2009)	–

Migration

EMIGRATION, 2010

- Stock of emigrants: **9.3 thousands**
- Stock of emigrants as percentage of population: **10.7%**
- Top destination countries: Spain, France, Portugal, Tanzania, the United States, Germany, the United Kingdom, Belgium, Switzerland, Canada

SKILLED EMIGRATION, 2000

- Emigration rate of tertiary-educated population: **6.9%**
- Emigration of physicians: **1** or **0.6%** of physicians trained in the country
  (Source: Bhargava, Docquier, and Moullan 2010)

IMMIGRATION, 2010

- Stock of immigrants: **55.8 thousands**
- Stock of immigrants as percentage of population: **64.4%**
- Females as percentage of immigrants: **47.3%**
- Refugees as percentage of immigrants: **0.0%**
- Top source countries: Spain, Portugal, France, the United Kingdom, Morocco, Germany, the Philippines, Belgium, the Netherlands, Argentina

Remittances

Remittance data are currently not available for this country.

Angola

Population (millions, 2009)	18.5
Population growth (avg. annual %, 2000–09)	2.9
Population density (people per km², 2008)	14.5
Labor force (millions, 2008)	7.8
Unemployment rate (% of labor force, 2008)	–
Urban population (% of pop., 2009)	57.6
Surface area (1,000 km², 2008)	1,246.7
GNI (US$ billions, 2009)	59.3
GNI per capita, Atlas method (US$, 2009)	3,490
GDP growth (avg. annual %, 2005–09)	14.6
Poverty headcount ratio at national poverty line (% of pop., 2005)	42.5
Age dependency ratio (2009)	90.2

Migration

EMIGRATION, 2010

- Stock of emigrants: **533.3 thousands**
- Stock of emigrants as percentage of population: **2.8%**
- Top destination countries: Portugal, Zambia, Namibia, France, Germany, the United Kingdom, the Republic of Congo, the Netherlands, Brazil, the United States

SKILLED EMIGRATION, 2000

- Emigration rate of tertiary-educated population: **33.0%**
- Emigration of physicians:
  - (a) **110** or **10.0%** of physicians trained in the country *(Source: Bhargava, Docquier, and Moullan 2010)*
  - (b) **2,102** or **70.5%** of physicians born in the country *(Source: Clemens and Pettersson 2006)*
- Emigration of nurses: **1,841** or **12.3%** of nurses born in the country

IMMIGRATION, 2010

- Stock of immigrants: **65.4 thousands**
- Stock of immigrants as percentage of population: **0.3%**
- Females as percentage of immigrants: **53.0%**
- Refugees as percentage of immigrants: **19.2%**
- Top source countries: Portugal, Cape Verde, São Tomé and Principe, the Democratic Republic of Congo, the Republic of Congo, Guinea, Zambia

Remittances

US$ millions	2003	2004	2005	2006	2007	2008	2009	2010e
Inward remittance flows[a]	–	–	–	–	–	**82**	–	–
of which								
Workers' remittances	–	–	–	–	–	71	–	–
Compensation of employees	–	–	–	–	–	11	–	–
Migrants' transfers	–	–	–	–	–	–	–	–
Outward remittance flows	**230**	**296**	**215**	**413**	**603**	**669**	–	**716**
of which								
Workers' remittances	88	117	117	172	228	222	–	395
Compensation of employees	142	179	98	241	374	447	–	321
Migrants' transfers	–	–	–	–	–	–	–	–

a. For comparison: net FDI inflows US$1.7 bn, net ODA received US$0.4 bn, total international reserves US$17.9 bn, exports of goods and services US$64.2 bn in 2008.

Antigua and Barbuda

Latin America and the Caribbean	UPPER MIDDLE INCOME

Population (thousands, 2009)	87.6
Population growth (avg. annual %, 2000–09)	1.5
Population density (people per km², 2008)	194.4
Labor force (millions, 2008)	–
Unemployment rate (% of labor force, 2008)	–
Urban population (% of pop., 2009)	30.4
Surface area (1,000 km², 2008)	0.4
GNI (US$ billions, 2009)	1.1
GNI per capita, Atlas method (US$, 2009)	12,070
GDP growth (avg. annual %, 2005–09)	3.6
Poverty headcount ratio at national poverty line (% of pop., 2005)	–
Age dependency ratio (2009)	–

Migration

EMIGRATION, 2010

- Stock of emigrants: **42.8 thousands**
- Stock of emigrants as percentage of population: **48.3%**
- Top destination countries: the United States, the Philippines, Virgin Islands (U.S.), the United Kingdom, Canada, Netherlands Antilles, Dominica, the Dominican Republic, St. Lucia, St. Kitts and Nevis

SKILLED EMIGRATION, 2000

- Emigration rate of tertiary-educated population: **66.8%**
- Emigration of physicians: **34** or **37.6%** of physicians trained in the country *(Source: Bhargava, Docquier, and Moullan 2010)*

IMMIGRATION, 2010

- Stock of immigrants: **20.9 thousands**
- Stock of immigrants as percentage of population: **23.6%**
- Females as percentage of immigrants: **56.2%**
- Refugees as percentage of immigrants: **0.0%**
- Top source countries: Guyana, Dominica, Jamaica, the United States, the Dominican Republic, the United Kingdom, St. Vincent and the Grenadines, Virgin Islands (U.S.), Trinidad and Tobago, St. Lucia

Remittances

US$ millions	2003	2004	2005	2006	2007	2008	2009	2010e
Inward remittance flows[a]	**20**	**21**	**22**	**23**	**24**	**26**	**24**	**27**
of which								
Workers' remittances	11	11	12	12	12	13	12	–
Compensation of employees	5	6	7	7	8	9	9	–
Migrants' transfers	3	3	4	4	4	4	3	–
Outward remittance flows	**1**	**2**	**2**	**2**	**2**	**2**	**2**	**–**
of which								
Workers' remittances	1	2	2	2	2	2	2	–
Compensation of employees	–	–	–	–	–	–	–	–
Migrants' transfers	–	–	–	–	–	–	–	–

a. For comparison: net FDI inflows US$0.3 bn, total international reserves US$0.1 bn, exports of goods and services US$0.6 bn in 2008.

Argentina

Latin America and the Caribbean	UPPER MIDDLE INCOME
Population (millions, 2009)	40.3
Population growth (avg. annual %, 2000-09)	1.0
Population density (people per km², 2008)	14.6
Labor force (millions, 2008)	18.3
Unemployment rate (% of labor force, 2008)	7.3
Urban population (% of pop., 2009)	92.2
Surface area (1,000 km², 2008)	2,780.4
GNI (US$ billions, 2009)	299.5
GNI per capita, Atlas method (US$, 2009)	7,570
GDP growth (avg. annual %, 2005-09)	6.8
Poverty headcount ratio at national poverty line (% of pop., 2005)	–
Age dependency ratio (2009)	55.6

Migration

EMIGRATION, 2010

- Stock of emigrants: **956.8 thousands**
- Stock of emigrants as percentage of population: **2.4%**
- Top destination countries: Spain, the United States, Chile, Paraguay, Israel, Bolivia, Brazil, Uruguay, Canada, Italy

SKILLED EMIGRATION, 2000

- Emigration rate of tertiary-educated population: **2.5%**
- Emigration of physicians: **3,232** or **2.9%** of physicians trained in the country *(Source: Bhargava, Docquier, and Moullan 2010)*

IMMIGRATION, 2010

- Stock of immigrants: **1,449.3 thousands**
- Stock of immigrants as percentage of population: **3.6%**
- Females as percentage of immigrants: **53.4%**
- Refugees as percentage of immigrants: **0.2%**
- Top source countries: Paraguay, Bolivia, Italy, Chile, Spain, Uruguay, Peru, Brazil, Poland, Germany

Remittances

US$ millions	2003	2004	2005	2006	2007	2008	2009	2010e
Inward remittance flows[a]	**273**	**312**	**432**	**541**	**606**	**698**	**660**	**682**
of which								
Workers' remittances	236	270	381	486	541	606	567	–
Compensation of employees	38	42	51	56	65	92	93	–
Migrants' transfers	–	–	–	–	–	–	–	–
Outward remittance flows	**180**	**234**	**314**	**356**	**463**	**609**	**701**	–
of which								
Workers' remittances	117	154	212	240	325	460	544	–
Compensation of employees	63	81	102	115	137	150	157	–
Migrants' transfers	–	–	–	–	–	–	–	–

a. **For comparison: net FDI inflows US$9.8 bn, net ODA received US$0.1 bn, total international reserves US$46.4 bn, exports of goods and services US$80.4 bn in 2008.**

Armenia

Population (millions, 2009)	3.1
Population growth (avg. annual %, 2000–09)	0.0
Population density (people per km², 2008)	109.1
Labor force (millions, 2008)	1.5
Unemployment rate (% of labor force, 2008)	–
Urban population (% of pop., 2009)	63.8
Surface area (1,000 km², 2008)	29.8
GNI (US$ billions, 2009)	8.9
GNI per capita, Atlas method (US$, 2009)	3,100
GDP growth (avg. annual %, 2005–09)	6.6
Poverty headcount ratio at national poverty line (% of pop., 2005)	4.7
Age dependency ratio (2009)	46.2

Migration

EMIGRATION, 2010

- Stock of emigrants: **870.2 thousands**
- Stock of emigrants as percentage of population: **28.2%**
- Top destination countries: the Russian Federation, the United States, Ukraine, Azerbaijan, Georgia, Israel, Germany, France, Spain, Greece

SKILLED EMIGRATION, 2000

- Emigration rate of tertiary-educated population: **8.8%**
- Emigration of physicians: **211** or **2.2%** of physicians trained in the country
  (Source: Bhargava, Docquier, and Moullan 2010)

IMMIGRATION, 2010

- Stock of immigrants: **324.2 thousands**
- Stock of immigrants as percentage of population: **10.5%**
- Females as percentage of immigrants: **58.9%**
- Refugees as percentage of immigrants: **18.2%**
- Top source countries: Azerbaijan, Georgia, the Russian Federation, the Islamic Republic of Iran, the Syrian Arab Republic, Ukraine, Turkey, Greece, Uzbekistan, Lebanon

Remittances

US$ millions	2003	2004	2005	2006	2007	2008	2009	2010e
Inward remittance flows[a]	**168**	**435**	**498**	**658**	**846**	**1,062**	**769**	**824**
of which								
Workers' remittances	9	43	58	74	94	124	86	–
Compensation of employees	153	382	429	576	743	929	677	–
Migrants' transfers	6	10	11	8	9	9	7	–
Outward remittance flows	**27**	**138**	**152**	**154**	**176**	**185**	**145**	**–**
of which								
Workers' remittances	6	10	16	19	5	11	11	–
Compensation of employees	19	122	133	130	166	169	130	–
Migrants' transfers	2	6	3	6	5	5	4	–

a. For comparison: net FDI inflows US$0.9 bn, net ODA received US$0.3 bn, total international reserves US$1.4 bn, exports of goods and services US$1.8 bn in 2008.

Aruba

Population (millions, 2009)	0.1
Population growth (avg. annual %, 2000–09)	1.8
Population density (people per km², 2008)	585.9
Labor force (millions, 2008)	–
Unemployment rate (% of labor force, 2008)	–
Urban population (% of pop., 2009)	46.8
Surface area (1,000 km², 2008)	0.2
GNI (US$ billions, 2009)	–
GNI per capita, Atlas method (US$, 2009)	–
GDP growth (avg. annual %, 2005–09)	–
Poverty headcount ratio at national poverty line (% of pop., 2005)	–
Age dependency ratio (2009)	40.5

Migration

EMIGRATION, 2010

- Stock of emigrants: **13.7 thousands**
- Stock of emigrants as percentage of population: **12.8%**
- Top destination countries: the United States, Netherlands Antilles, the Netherlands, Canada, the Dominican Republic, República Bolivariana de Venezuela, Colombia, the Philippines, Australia, Greece

SKILLED EMIGRATION, 2000

- Skilled emigration data are currently not available for this country.

IMMIGRATION, 2010

- Stock of immigrants: **34.3 thousands**
- Stock of immigrants as percentage of population: **31.9%**
- Females as percentage of immigrants: **55.4%**
- Refugees as percentage of immigrants: **0.0%**
- Top source countries: Colombia, República Bolivariana de Venezuela, the Dominican Republic, the United States, Portugal, Dominica

Remittances

US$ millions	2003	2004	2005	2006	2007	2008	2009	2010e
Inward remittance flows[a]	**10**	**13**	**12**	**12**	**14**	**15**	**19**	**20**
of which								
Workers' remittances	–	1	–	–	0	2	5	–
Compensation of employees	0	1	1	1	5	5	3	–
Migrants' transfers	10	12	11	11	9	8	12	–
Outward remittance flows	**60**	**61**	**70**	**80**	**82**	**86**	**77**	**–**
of which								
Workers' remittances	47	48	59	63	63	70	69	–
Compensation of employees	1	1	3	9	10	5	1	–
Migrants' transfers	13	12	8	8	9	10	6	–

a. For comparison: net FDI inflows US$0.2 bn, total international reserves US$0.7 bn in 2008.

Australia

Population (millions, 2009)	21.9
Population growth (avg. annual %, 2000–09)	1.4
Population density (people per km², 2008)	2.8
Labor force (millions, 2008)	10.9
Unemployment rate (% of labor force, 2008)	4.2
Urban population (% of pop., 2009)	88.9
Surface area (1,000 km², 2008)	7,741.2
GNI (US$ billions, 2009)	900.7
GNI per capita, Atlas method (US$, 2009)	43,770
GDP growth (avg. annual %, 2005–09)	2.9
Poverty headcount ratio at national poverty line (% of pop., 2005)	—
Age dependency ratio (2009)	48.5

Migration

EMIGRATION, 2010

- Stock of emigrants: **442.8 thousands**
- Stock of emigrants as percentage of population: **2.1%**
- Top destination countries: the United Kingdom, the United States, New Zealand, Canada, Papua New Guinea, Germany, Japan, the Netherlands, Ireland, Malaysia

SKILLED EMIGRATION, 2000

- Emigration rate of tertiary-educated population: **2.7%**
- Emigration of physicians: **7,194** or **12.6%** of physicians trained in the country *(Source: Bhargava, Docquier, and Moullan 2010)*

IMMIGRATION, 2010

- Stock of immigrants: **5,522.4 thousands**
- Stock of immigrants as percentage of population: **25.7%**
- Females as percentage of immigrants: **43.8%**
- Refugees as percentage of immigrants: **0.8%**
- Top source countries: the United Kingdom, New Zealand, China, Italy, India, Vietnam, the Philippines, Greece, South Africa, Germany

Remittances

US$ millions	2003	2004	2005	2006	2007	2008	2009	2010e
Inward remittance flows[a]	**2,326**	**2,837**	**2,990**	**3,131**	**3,826**	**4,713**	**4,089**	**4,335**
of which								
Workers' remittances	—	—	—	—	—	—	—	—
Compensation of employees	695	868	982	1,018	1,213	1,475	—	—
Migrants' transfers	1,631	1,969	2,008	2,112	2,613	3,238	—	—
Outward remittance flows	**1,779**	**2,254**	**2,375**	**2,815**	**3,024**	**3,049**	**3,000**	**—**
of which								
Workers' remittances	—	—	—	—	—	—	—	—
Compensation of employees	1,192	1,530	1,686	2,190	2,225	2,170	—	—
Migrants' transfers	587	723	689	625	799	879	—	—

a. For comparison: net FDI inflows US$47.3 bn, total international reserves US$32.9 bn, exports of goods and services US$209.7 bn in 2008.

Austria

Population (millions, 2009)	8.4
Population growth (avg. annual %, 2000–09)	0.4
Population density (people per km², 2008)	101.2
Labor force (millions, 2008)	4.2
Unemployment rate (% of labor force, 2008)	3.8
Urban population (% of pop., 2009)	67.4
Surface area (1,000 km², 2008)	83.9
GNI (US$ billions, 2009)	383.0
GNI per capita, Atlas method (US$, 2009)	46,850
GDP growth (avg. annual %, 2005–09)	1.6
Poverty headcount ratio at national poverty line (% of pop., 2005)	—
Age dependency ratio (2009)	47.6

Migration

EMIGRATION, 2010

- Stock of emigrants: **598.3 thousands**
- Stock of emigrants as percentage of population: **7.1%**
- Top destination countries: Germany, Switzerland, the United States, Canada, Australia, the United Kingdom, Turkey, France, Spain, Italy

SKILLED EMIGRATION, 2000

- Emigration rate of tertiary-educated population: **13.5%**
- Emigration of physicians: **1,586** or **6.0%** of physicians trained in the country *(Source: Bhargava, Docquier, and Moullan 2010)*

IMMIGRATION, 2010

- Stock of immigrants: **1,310.2 thousands**
- Stock of immigrants as percentage of population: **15.6%**
- Females as percentage of immigrants: **52.0%**
- Refugees as percentage of immigrants: **2.2%**
- Top source countries: Germany, Bosnia and Herzegovina, Turkey, Serbia, Poland, Romania, Croatia, the Czech Republic, Hungary, Italy

Remittances

US$ millions	2003	2004	2005	2006	2007	2008	2009	2010e
Inward remittance flows[a]	**2,496**	**2,521**	**2,608**	**2,639**	**3,012**	**3,239**	**3,201**	**3,340**
of which								
Workers' remittances	340	383	398	418	467	519	508	—
Compensation of employees	1,608	1,865	1,917	1,880	2,172	2,320	2,291	—
Migrants' transfers	548	273	294	341	373	400	402	—
Outward remittance flows	**1,874**	**2,228**	**2,567**	**2,575**	**3,008**	**3,446**	**3,339**	**—**
of which								
Workers' remittances	694	789	804	839	1,058	1,220	1,156	—
Compensation of employees	856	1,121	1,316	1,406	1,594	1,844	1,801	—
Migrants' transfers	324	317	447	330	356	382	382	—

a. **For comparison: net FDI inflows US$14.4 bn, total international reserves US$16.7 bn, exports of goods and services US$243.2 bn in 2008.**

Azerbaijan

Population (millions, 2009)	8.8
Population growth (avg. annual %, 2000–09)	1.0
Population density (people per km², 2008)	105.0
Labor force (millions, 2008)	4.2
Unemployment rate (% of labor force, 2008)	—
Urban population (% of pop., 2009)	52.1
Surface area (1,000 km², 2008)	86.6
GNI (US$ billions, 2009)	40.3
GNI per capita, Atlas method (US$, 2009)	4,840
GDP growth (avg. annual %, 2005–09)	21.2
Poverty headcount ratio at national poverty line (% of pop., 2005)	0.0
Age dependency ratio (2009)	44.7

Migration

EMIGRATION, 2010

- Stock of emigrants: **1,432.6 thousands**
- Stock of emigrants as percentage of population: **16.0%**
- Top destination countries: the Russian Federation, Armenia, Ukraine, Kazakhstan, Israel, Germany, Turkey, the United States, Turkmenistan, Georgia

SKILLED EMIGRATION, 2000

- Emigration rate of tertiary-educated population: **2.0%**
- Emigration of physicians: **86** or **0.3%** of physicians trained in the country *(Source: Bhargava, Docquier, and Moullan 2010)*

IMMIGRATION, 2010

- Stock of immigrants: **263.9 thousands**
- Stock of immigrants as percentage of population: **3.0%**
- Females as percentage of immigrants: **57.1%**
- Refugees as percentage of immigrants: **0.9%**
- Top source countries: the Russian Federation, Armenia, Ukraine, Georgia

Remittances

US$ millions	2003	2004	2005	2006	2007	2008	2009	2010e
Inward remittance flows[a]	**171**	**228**	**693**	**813**	**1,287**	**1,554**	**1,274**	**1,472**
of which								
Workers' remittances	154	191	490	662	1,192	1,416	1,182	—
Compensation of employees	2	12	133	128	76	102	73	—
Migrants' transfers	15	24	70	22	20	36	19	—
Outward remittance flows	**169**	**200**	**269**	**301**	**435**	**593**	**652**	—
of which								
Workers' remittances	78	65	127	149	273	399	522	—
Compensation of employees	54	108	112	125	131	168	116	—
Migrants' transfers	38	28	29	26	31	25	14	—

a. **For comparison: net ODA received US$0.2 bn, total international reserves US$6.5 bn, exports of goods and services US$32.0 bn in 2008.**

Bahamas, The

HIGH-INCOME NON-OECD

Population (millions, 2009)	0.3
Population growth (avg. annual %, 2000–09)	1.3
Population density (people per km², 2008)	33.5
Labor force (millions, 2008)	0.2
Unemployment rate (% of labor force, 2008)	–
Urban population (% of pop., 2009)	83.9
Surface area (1,000 km², 2008)	13.9
GNI (US$ billions, 2009)	–
GNI per capita, Atlas method (US$, 2009)	–
GDP growth (avg. annual %, 2005–09)	3.6
Poverty headcount ratio at national poverty line (% of pop., 2005)	
Age dependency ratio (2009)	47.7

Migration

EMIGRATION, 2010

- Stock of emigrants: **44.1 thousands**
- Stock of emigrants as percentage of population: **12.8%**
- Top destination countries: the United States, the United Kingdom, Canada, Australia, Cayman Islands, Netherlands Antilles, the Dominican Republic, Spain, Japan, Switzerland

SKILLED EMIGRATION, 2000

- Emigration rate of tertiary-educated population: **61.3%**

IMMIGRATION, 2010

- Stock of immigrants: **33.4 thousands**
- Stock of immigrants as percentage of population: **9.7%**
- Females as percentage of immigrants: **48.5%**
- Refugees as percentage of immigrants: **0.0%**
- Top source countries: Haiti, the United States, Jamaica, the United Kingdom, Canada, Guyana, Trinidad and Tobago, India, Germany, Switzerland

Remittances

US$ millions	2003	2004	2005	2006	2007	2008	2009	2010e
Inward remittance flows[a]	–	–	–	–	–	–	–	–
of which								
Workers' remittances	–	–	–	–	–	–	–	–
Compensation of employees	–	–	–	–	–	–	–	–
Migrants' transfers	–	–	–	–	–	–	–	–
Outward remittance flows	100	119	144	164	171	143	96	–
of which								
Workers' remittances	6	8	11	7	10	8	7	–
Compensation of employees	56	63	73	93	85	59	57	–
Migrants' transfers	37	48	60	64	76	76	32	–

a. **For comparison: net FDI inflows US$0.8 bn, total international reserves US$0.6 bn in 2008.**

Bahrain

Population (millions, 2009)	0.8
Population growth (avg. annual %, 2000–09)	2.2
Population density (people per km², 2008)	1,080.2
Labor force (millions, 2008)	0.3
Unemployment rate (% of labor force, 2008)	–
Urban population (% of pop., 2009)	88.6
Surface area (1,000 km², 2008)	0.7
GNI (US$ billions, 2009)	–
GNI per capita, Atlas method (US$, 2009)	–
GDP growth (avg. annual %, 2005–09)	7.3
Poverty headcount ratio at national poverty line (% of pop., 2005)	–
Age dependency ratio (2009)	40.1

Migration

EMIGRATION, 2010

- Stock of emigrants: **30.0 thousands**
- Stock of emigrants as percentage of population: **3.7%**
- Top destination countries: the Philippines, the United Kingdom, Jordan, the United States, Canada, Australia, Ireland, the Arab Republic of Egypt, New Zealand, Sudan

SKILLED EMIGRATION, 2000

- Emigration rate of tertiary-educated population: **4.9%**
- Emigration of physicians: **29** or **2.8%** of physicians trained in the country (*Source: Bhargava, Docquier, and Moullan 2010*)

IMMIGRATION, 2010

- Stock of immigrants: **315.4 thousands**
- Stock of immigrants as percentage of population: **39.1%**
- Females as percentage of immigrants: **32.9%**
- Refugees as percentage of immigrants: **0.0%**
- Top source countries: India, Pakistan, the Arab Republic of Egypt, the Islamic Republic of Iran, the Philippines, Saudi Arabia, Sudan, Algeria, Morocco, Iraq

Remittances

US$ millions	2003	2004	2005	2006	2007	2008	2009	2010e
Inward remittance flows[a]	–	–	–	–	–	–	–	–
of which								
Workers' remittances	–	–	–	–	–	–	–	–
Compensation of employees	–	–	–	–	–	–	–	–
Migrants' transfers	–	–	–	–	–	–	–	–
Outward remittance flows	1,082	1,120	1,223	1,531	1,483	1,774	1,391	–
of which								
Workers' remittances	1,082	1,120	1,223	1,531	1,483	1,774	1,391	–
Compensation of employees	–	–	–	–	–	–	–	–
Migrants' transfers	–	–	–	–	–	–	–	–

a. For comparison: net FDI inflows US$1.8 bn, exports of goods and services US$21.2 bn in 2008.

Bangladesh

South Asia | **LOW INCOME**

Population (millions, 2009)	162.2
Population growth (avg. annual %, 2000-09)	1.6
Population density (people per km², 2008)	1,229.2
Labor force (millions, 2008)	75.7
Unemployment rate (% of labor force, 2008)	–
Urban population (% of pop., 2009)	27.6
Surface area (1,000 km², 2008)	144.0
GNI (US$ billions, 2009)	99.4
GNI per capita, Atlas method (US$, 2009)	590
GDP growth (avg. annual %, 2005-09)	6.2
Poverty headcount ratio at national poverty line (% of pop., 2005)	50.5
Age dependency ratio (2009)	54.7

Migration

EMIGRATION, 2010

- Stock of emigrants: **5,380.2 thousands**
- Stock of emigrants as percentage of population: **3.3%**
- Top destination countries: India, Saudi Arabia, the United Kingdom, Kuwait, Oman, the United States, Malaysia, the United Arab Emirates, Italy, Jordan

SKILLED EMIGRATION, 2000

- Emigration rate of tertiary-educated population: **4.3%**
- Emigration of physicians: **1,912** or **6.5%** of physicians trained in the country *(Source: Bhargava, Docquier, and Moullan 2010)*

IMMIGRATION, 2010

- Stock of immigrants: **1,085.3 thousands**
- Stock of immigrants as percentage of population: **0.7%**
- Females as percentage of immigrants: **13.9%**
- Refugees as percentage of immigrants: **2.5%**
- Top source countries: India, Pakistan

Remittances

US$ millions	2003	2004	2005	2006	2007	2008	2009	2010e
Inward remittance flows[a]	**3,192**	**3,584**	**4,315**	**5,428**	**6,562**	**8,995**	**10,523**	**11,050**
of which								
Workers' remittances	3,180	3,572	4,302	5,418	6,553	8,981	10,510	–
Compensation of employees	12	12	12	10	9	14	13	–
Migrants' transfers	–	–	–	–	–	–	–	–
Outward remittance flows	**7**	**8**	**5**	**3**	**3**	**14**	**8**	**–**
of which								
Workers' remittances	4	5	3	2	2	6	6	–
Compensation of employees	3	3	3	1	1	9	2	–
Migrants' transfers	–	–	–	–	–	–	–	–

a. For comparison: net FDI inflows US$1.0 bn, net ODA received US$2.1 bn, total international reserves US$5.8 bn, exports of goods and services US$16.2 bn in 2008.

Barbados

HIGH-INCOME NON-OECD

Population (millions, 2009)	0.3
Population growth (avg. annual %, 2000–09)	0.1
Population density (people per km², 2008)	593.5
Labor force (millions, 2008)	0.2
Unemployment rate (% of labor force, 2008)	–
Urban population (% of pop., 2009)	40.3
Surface area (1,000 km², 2008)	0.4
GNI (US$ billions, 2009)	–
GNI per capita, Atlas method (US$, 2009)	–
GDP growth (avg. annual %, 2005–09)	–
Poverty headcount ratio at national poverty line (% of pop., 2005)	–
Age dependency ratio (2009)	38.0

Migration

EMIGRATION, 2010

- Stock of emigrants: **105,200**
- Stock of emigrants as percentage of population: **41.0%**
- Top destination countries: the United States, the United Kingdom, Canada, Trinidad and Tobago, St. Lucia, Netherlands Antilles, St. Vincent and the Grenadines, Australia, Guyana, Germany

SKILLED EMIGRATION, 2000

- Emigration rate of tertiary-educated population: **63.5%**
- Emigration of physicians: **6** or **1.9%** of physicians trained in the country
  (Source: Bhargava, Docquier, and Moullan 2010)

IMMIGRATION, 2010

- Stock of immigrants: **28.1 thousands**
- Stock of immigrants as percentage of population: **10.9%**
- Females as percentage of immigrants: **60.7%**
- Refugees as percentage of immigrants: **0.0%**
- Top source countries: St. Vincent and the Grenadines, St. Lucia, the United Kingdom, Guyana, Trinidad and Tobago, the United States, Canada, Jamaica, Grenada, Dominica

Remittances

US$ millions	2003	2004	2005	2006	2007	2008	2009	2010e
Inward remittance flows[a]	131	131	135	139	141	168	149	161
of which								
Workers' remittances	97	100	103	106	90	–	–	–
Compensation of employees	34	31	32	32	51	–	–	–
Migrants' transfers	–	–	–	–	–	–	–	–
Outward remittance flows	22	18	43	33	54	54	–	–
of which								
Workers' remittances	16	16	37	28	49	–	–	–
Compensation of employees	6	3	7	5	5	–	–	–
Migrants' transfers	–	–	–	–	–	–	–	–

a. For comparison: total international reserves US$0.7 bn, exports of goods and services US$2.2 bn in 2008.

Belarus

Europe and Central Asia	UPPER MIDDLE INCOME
Population (millions, 2009)	9.7
Population growth (avg. annual %, 2000–09)	-0.4
Population density (people per km², 2008)	46.7
Labor force (millions, 2008)	4.9
Unemployment rate (% of labor force, 2008)	—
Urban population (% of pop., 2009)	73.9
Surface area (1,000 km², 2008)	207.6
GNI (US$ billions, 2009)	59.8
GNI per capita, Atlas method (US$, 2009)	5,540
GDP growth (avg. annual %, 2005–09)	7.7
Poverty headcount ratio at national poverty line (% of pop., 2005)	0.0
Age dependency ratio (2009)	39.5

Migration

EMIGRATION, 2010

- Stock of emigrants: **1,778.9 thousands**
- Stock of emigrants as percentage of population: **18.6%**
- Top destination countries: the Russian Federation, Ukraine, Poland, Kazakhstan, Israel, Lithuania, the United States, Germany, Latvia, Estonia

SKILLED EMIGRATION, 2000

- Emigration rate of tertiary-educated population: **3.2%**
- Emigration of physicians: **165** or **0.4%** of physicians trained in the country *(Source: Bhargava, Docquier, and Moullan 2010)*

IMMIGRATION, 2010

- Stock of immigrants: **1,090.4 thousands**
- Stock of immigrants as percentage of population: **11.4%**
- Females as percentage of immigrants: **54.2%**
- Refugees as percentage of immigrants: **0.1%**
- Top source countries: the Russian Federation, Poland, Ukraine, Armenia, Lithuania, Azerbaijan, Germany, Moldova, Georgia, Latvia

Remittances

US$ millions	2003	2004	2005	2006	2007	2008	2009	2010e
Inward remittance flows[a]	**222**	**257**	**255**	**340**	**354**	**443**	**352**	**387**
of which								
Workers' remittances	—	—	—	—	—	—	—	—
Compensation of employees	89	126	120	175	157	177	103	—
Migrants' transfers	133	130	135	164	198	266	255	—
Outward remittance flows	**65**	**82**	**95**	**93**	**109**	**141**	**112**	**—**
of which								
Workers' remittances	—	—	—	—	—	—	—	—
Compensation of employees	1	1	0	3	5	11	10	—
Migrants' transfers	64	81	94	90	104	130	102	—

a. **For comparison: net FDI inflows US$2.2 bn, net ODA received US$0.1 bn, total international reserves US$3.1 bn, exports of goods and services US$37.3 bn in 2008.**

Belgium

Population (millions, 2009)	10.8
Population growth (avg. annual %, 2000–09)	0.5
Population density (people per km², 2008)	354.1
Labor force (millions, 2008)	4.6
Unemployment rate (% of labor force, 2008)	7.0
Urban population (% of pop., 2009)	97.4
Surface area (1,000 km², 2008)	30.5
GNI (US$ billions, 2009)	474.7
GNI per capita, Atlas method (US$, 2009)	45,310
GDP growth (avg. annual %, 2005–09)	1.1
Poverty headcount ratio at national poverty line (% of pop., 2005)	–
Age dependency ratio (2009)	51.7

Migration

EMIGRATION, 2010

- Stock of emigrants: **455.0 thousands**
- Stock of emigrants as percentage of population: **4.3%**
- Top destination countries: France, Spain, the Netherlands, Germany, the United States, Canada, the United Kingdom, Luxembourg, Switzerland, Turkey

SKILLED EMIGRATION, 2000

- Emigration rate of tertiary-educated population: **4.9%**
- Emigration of physicians: **3,302** or **7.3%** of physicians trained in the country *(Source: Bhargava, Docquier, and Moullan 2010)*

IMMIGRATION, 2010

- Stock of immigrants: **1,465.7 thousands**
- Stock of immigrants as percentage of population: **13.7%**
- Females as percentage of immigrants: **32.8%**
- Refugees as percentage of immigrants: **1.2%**
- Top source countries: France, Morocco, Italy, the Netherlands, Turkey, Germany, the Democratic Republic of Congo, Poland, Spain, Russia

Remittances

US$ millions	2003	2004	2005	2006	2007	2008	2009	2010e
Inward remittance flows[a]	**5,990**	**6,863**	**7,242**	**7,488**	**9,098**	**10,255**	**10,360**	**10,466**
of which								
Workers' remittances	20	19	20	27	114	139	137	–
Compensation of employees	5,754	6,536	6,868	7,239	8,984	10,116	10,223	–
Migrants' transfers	216	308	354	222	–	–	–	–
Outward remittance flows	**2,329**	**2,617**	**2,754**	**2,698**	**3,204**	**4,057**	**4,278**	–
of which								
Workers' remittances	333	343	416	429	476	585	613	–
Compensation of employees	1,763	1,997	2,012	2,134	2,728	3,471	3,665	–
Migrants' transfers	233	277	327	136	–	–	–	–

a. For comparison: net FDI inflows US$99.7 bn, total international reserves US$15.7 bn, exports of goods and services US$464.2 bn in 2008.

Belize

Latin America and the Caribbean	LOWER MIDDLE INCOME
Population (millions, 2009)	0.3
Population growth (avg. annual %, 2000-09)	3.2
Population density (people per km², 2008)	13.6
Labor force (millions, 2008)	0.1
Unemployment rate (% of labor force, 2008)	8.2
Urban population (% of pop., 2009)	52.2
Surface area (1,000 km², 2008)	23.0
GNI (US$ billions, 2009)	1.2
GNI per capita, Atlas method (US$, 2008)	3,820
GDP growth (avg. annual %, 2004-08)	3.3
Poverty headcount ratio at national poverty line (% of pop., 2005)	—
Age dependency ratio (2009)	64.6

Migration

EMIGRATION, 2010

- Stock of emigrants: **50.2 thousands**
- Stock of emigrants as percentage of population: **16.1%**
- Top destination countries: the United States, Canada, the United Kingdom, Mexico, Bolivia, Guatemala, Cayman Islands, El Salvador, Honduras, Costa Rica

SKILLED EMIGRATION, 2000

- Emigration rate of tertiary-educated population: **65.5%**
- Emigration of physicians: **10** or **3.7%** of physicians trained in the country
  (Source: Bhargava, Docquier, and Moullan 2010)

IMMIGRATION, 2010

- Stock of immigrants: **46.8 thousands**
- Stock of immigrants as percentage of population: **15.0%**
- Females as percentage of immigrants: **52.1%**
- Refugees as percentage of immigrants: **0.9%**
- Top source countries: Guatemala, El Salvador, Honduras, Mexico, the United States, China, Canada, Jamaica, Nicaragua, India

Remittances

US$ millions	2003	2004	2005	2006	2007	2008	2009	2010e
Inward remittance flows[a]	**34**	**35**	**46**	**65**	**75**	**78**	**80**	**88**
of which								
Workers' remittances	30	31	41	58	71	74	76	—
Compensation of employees	2	2	4	6	2	2	2	—
Migrants' transfers	2	1	1	2	2	2	2	—
Outward remittance flows	**21**	**19**	**20**	**22**	**22**	**29**	**23**	**—**
of which								
Workers' remittances	14	12	13	15	16	22	17	—
Compensation of employees	5	6	6	6	5	6	6	—
Migrants' transfers	1	1	1	1	1	1	0	—

a. **For comparison: net FDI inflows US$0.2 bn, total international reserves US$0.2 bn, exports of goods and services US$0.8 bn in 2008.**

Benin

Sub-Saharan Africa **LOW INCOME**

Population (millions, 2009)	8.9
Population growth (avg. annual %, 2000–09)	3.3
Population density (people per km², 2008)	78.3
Labor force (millions, 2008)	3.4
Unemployment rate (% of labor force, 2008)	–
Urban population (% of pop., 2009)	41.6
Surface area (1,000 km², 2008)	112.6
GNI (US$ billions, 2009)	6.6
GNI per capita, Atlas method (US$, 2009)	750
GDP growth (avg. annual %, 2005–09)	4.1
Poverty headcount ratio at national poverty line (% of pop., 2005)	50.0
Age dependency ratio (2009)	86.2

Migration

EMIGRATION, 2010

- Stock of emigrants: **531.6 thousands**
- Stock of emigrants as percentage of population: **5.8%**
- Top destination countries: Nigeria, Togo, Côte d'Ivoire, Gabon, Niger, France, Burkina Faso, the Republic of Congo, Italy, Guinea

SKILLED EMIGRATION, 2000

- Emigration rate of tertiary-educated population: **11.3%**
- Emigration of physicians:
  - (a) **20** or **5.3%** of physicians trained in the country (Source: Bhargava, Docquier, and Moullan 2010)
  - (b) **224** or **35.6%** of physicians born in the country (Source: Clemens and Pettersson 2006)
- Emigration of nurses: **187** or **12.5%** of nurses born in the country

IMMIGRATION, 2010

- Stock of immigrants: **232.0 thousands**
- Stock of immigrants as percentage of population: **2.5%**
- Females as percentage of immigrants: **45.5%**
- Refugees as percentage of immigrants: **4.0%**
- Top source countries: Niger, Togo, Nigeria, Burkina Faso, France

Remittances

US$ millions	2003	2004	2005	2006	2007	2008	2009	2010e
Inward remittance flows[a]	**55**	**63**	**173**	**224**	**282**	**271**	**243**	**236**
of which								
Workers' remittances	49	54	137	186	234	–	–	–
Compensation of employees	6	9	10	9	6	–	–	–
Migrants' transfers	0	0	26	29	41	–	–	–
Outward remittance flows	**6**	**6**	**40**	**67**	**115**	**115**	**–**	**–**
of which								
Workers' remittances	4	3	30	52	102	–	–	–
Compensation of employees	1	3	3	9	5	–	–	–
Migrants' transfers	0	1	6	6	7	–	–	–

a. For comparison: net FDI inflows US$0.1 bn, net ODA received US$0.6 bn, total international reserves US$1.3 bn, exports of goods and services US$1.0 bn in 2008.

Bermuda

HIGH-INCOME NON-OECD

Population (thousands, 2009)	64.4
Population growth (avg. annual %, 2000–09)	0.4
Population density (people per km², 2008)	1,284.0
Labor force (millions, 2008)	—
Unemployment rate (% of labor force, 2008)	—
Urban population (% of pop., 2009)	100.0
Surface area (1,000 km², 2008)	0.1
GNI (US$ billions, 2009)	—
GNI per capita, Atlas method (US$, 2009)	—
GDP growth (avg. annual %, 2005–09)	—
Poverty headcount ratio at national poverty line (% of pop., 2005)	—
Age dependency ratio (2009)	—

Migration

EMIGRATION, 2010

- Stock of emigrants: **15.7 thousands**
- Stock of emigrants as percentage of population: **24.1%**
- Top destination countries: the United States, the United Kingdom, Canada, Australia, Portugal, New Zealand, Ireland, France, Cayman Islands, the Netherlands

SKILLED EMIGRATION, 2000

- Skilled emigration data are currently not available for this country.

IMMIGRATION, 2010

- Stock of immigrants: **19.9 thousands**
- Stock of immigrants as percentage of population: **30.7%**
- Females as percentage of immigrants: **51.7%**
- Refugees as percentage of immigrants: **0.0%**
- Top source countries: the United Kingdom, the United States, Canada, Portugal

Remittances

Remittance data are currently not available for this country.

Bhutan

South Asia | **LOWER MIDDLE INCOME**

Population (millions, 2009)	0.7
Population growth (avg. annual %, 2000–09)	2.5
Population density (people per km², 2008)	14.6
Labor force (millions, 2008)	0.3
Unemployment rate (% of labor force, 2008)	—
Urban population (% of pop., 2009)	35.6
Surface area (1,000 km², 2008)	47.0
GNI (US$ billions, 2009)	1.3
GNI per capita, Atlas method (US$, 2009)	2,020
GDP growth (avg. annual %, 2005–09)	9.1
Poverty headcount ratio at national poverty line (% of pop., 2005)	26.8
Age dependency ratio (2009)	54.7

Migration

EMIGRATION, 2010

- Stock of emigrants: **44.6 thousands**
- Stock of emigrants as percentage of population: **6.3%**
- Top destination countries: Nepal, India, Germany, the United States, France, Australia, the United Kingdom, Belgium, the Netherlands, Switzerland

SKILLED EMIGRATION, 2000

- Emigration rate of tertiary-educated population: **0.6%**

IMMIGRATION, 2010

- Stock of immigrants: **40.2 thousands**
- Stock of immigrants as percentage of population: **5.7%**
- Females as percentage of immigrants: **18.5%**
- Refugees as percentage of immigrants: **0.0%**
- Top source countries: India, China, Nepal, the United States, Japan

Remittances

Remittance data are currently not available for this country.

Bolivia, Plurinational State of

Latin America and the Caribbean	LOWER MIDDLE INCOME
Population (millions, 2009)	9.9
Population growth (avg. annual %, 2000–09)	1.9
Population density (people per km², 2008)	8.9
Labor force (millions, 2008)	4.4
Unemployment rate (% of labor force, 2008)	—
Urban population (% of pop., 2009)	66.0
Surface area (1,000 km², 2008)	1,098.6
GNI (US$ billions, 2009)	16.7
GNI per capita, Atlas method (US$, 2009)	1,620
GDP growth (avg. annual %, 2005–09)	4.7
Poverty headcount ratio at national poverty line (% of pop., 2005)	19.6
Age dependency ratio (2009)	69.4

Migration

EMIGRATION, 2010

- Stock of emigrants: **684.6 thousands**
- Stock of emigrants as percentage of population: **6.8%**
- Top destination countries: Spain, Argentina, the United States, Brazil, Chile, Italy, Japan, Canada, Sweden, Germany

SKILLED EMIGRATION, 2000

- Emigration rate of tertiary-educated population: **5.8%**
- Emigration of physicians: **383** or **5.1%** of physicians trained in the country *(Source: Bhargava, Docquier, and Moullan 2010)*

IMMIGRATION, 2010

- Stock of immigrants: **145.8 thousands**
- Stock of immigrants as percentage of population: **1.5%**
- Females as percentage of immigrants: **47.7%**
- Refugees as percentage of immigrants: **0.4%**
- Top source countries: Argentina, Brazil, Mexico, Peru, Chile, the United States, Paraguay, Canada, Spain, Japan

Remittances

US$ millions	2003	2004	2005	2006	2007	2008	2009	2010e
Inward remittance flows[a]	**158**	**211**	**346**	**612**	**1,065**	**1,144**	**1,061**	**1,064**
of which								
Workers' remittances	127	178	304	569	1,020	1,097	–	–
Compensation of employees	32	32	34	33	35	37	–	–
Migrants' transfers	–	–	9	9	9	10	–	–
Outward remittance flows	**46**	**51**	**67**	**73**	**79**	**106**	**106**	**–**
of which								
Workers' remittances	39	43	59	66	72	98	–	–
Compensation of employees	7	7	7	7	7	7	–	–
Migrants' transfers	–	–	–	–	–	–	–	–

a. For comparison: net FDI inflows US$0.5 bn, net ODA received US$0.6 bn, total international reserves US$7.7 bn, exports of goods and services US$7.5 bn in 2008.

Bosnia and Herzegovina

Europe and Central Asia	UPPER MIDDLE INCOME
Population (millions, 2009)	3.8
Population growth (avg. annual %, 2000–09)	0.8
Population density (people per km², 2008)	73.7
Labor force (millions, 2008)	1.9
Unemployment rate (% of labor force, 2008)	–
Urban population (% of pop., 2009)	48.0
Surface area (1,000 km², 2008)	51.2
GNI (US$ billions, 2009)	17.6
GNI per capita, Atlas method (US$, 2009)	4,700
GDP growth (avg. annual %, 2005–09)	4.0
Poverty headcount ratio at national poverty line (% of pop., 2005)	0.2
Age dependency ratio (2009)	41.3

Migration

EMIGRATION, 2010

- Stock of emigrants: **1,461.0 thousands**
- Stock of emigrants as percentage of population: **38.9%**
- Top destination countries: Croatia, Germany, Austria, the United States, Slovenia, Sweden, Switzerland, Australia, Italy, Canada

SKILLED EMIGRATION, 2000

- Emigration rate of tertiary-educated population: **23.9%**
- Emigration of physicians: **705** or **11.1%** of physicians trained in the country (*Source: Bhargava, Docquier, and Moullan 2010*)

IMMIGRATION, 2010

- Stock of immigrants: **27.8 thousands**
- Stock of immigrants as percentage of population: **0.7%**
- Females as percentage of immigrants: **50.3%**
- Refugees as percentage of immigrants: **31.8%**
- Top source countries: Croatia, Albania, Ukraine, Slovenia, the former Yugoslav Republic of Macedonia, Hungary, Italy, the Czech Republic, Poland, Germany

Remittances

US$ millions	2003	2004	2005	2006	2007	2008	2009	2010e
Inward remittance flows[a]	**1,749**	**2,072**	**2,043**	**2,157**	**2,700**	**2,735**	**2,167**	**2,228**
of which								
Workers' remittances	1,143	1,474	1,467	1,589	1,947	1,899	1,432	–
Compensation of employees	595	579	570	560	739	828	643	–
Migrants' transfers	11	19	5	8	13	8	6	–
Outward remittance flows	**20**	**62**	**40**	**55**	**65**	**70**	**61**	**–**
of which								
Workers' remittances	10	49	28	41	50	53	46	–
Compensation of employees	11	13	12	14	15	17	15	–
Migrants' transfers	–	–	–	–	–	–	–	–

a. For comparison: net FDI inflows US$1.1 bn, net ODA received US$0.5 bn, total international reserves US$3.5 bn, exports of goods and services US$6.8 bn in 2008.

Botswana

Population (millions, 2009)	1.9
Population growth (avg. annual %, 2000–09)	1.4
Population density (people per km², 2008)	3.4
Labor force (millions, 2008)	0.7
Unemployment rate (% of labor force, 2008)	–
Urban population (% of pop., 2009)	60.3
Surface area (1,000 km², 2008)	581.7
GNI (US$ billions, 2009)	11.4
GNI per capita, Atlas method (US$, 2009)	6,240
GDP growth (avg. annual %, 2005–09)	1.7
Poverty headcount ratio at national poverty line (% of pop., 2005)	23.1
Age dependency ratio (2009)	58.9

Migration

EMIGRATION, 2010

- Stock of emigrants: **63.0 thousands**
- Stock of emigrants as percentage of population: **3.2%**
- Top destination countries: South Africa, Zimbabwe, Namibia, the United Kingdom, the United States, Australia, Tanzania, Zambia, Ireland, Canada

SKILLED EMIGRATION, 2000

- Emigration rate of tertiary-educated population: **3.6%**
- Emigration of physicians: **68** or **11.4%** of physicians born in the country *(Source: Clemens and Pettersson 2006)*
- Emigration of nurses: 80 or 2.2% of nurses born in the country

IMMIGRATION, 2010

- Stock of immigrants: **114.8 thousands**
- Stock of immigrants as percentage of population: **5.8%**
- Females as percentage of immigrants: **46.3%**
- Refugees as percentage of immigrants: **2.4%**

Remittances

US$ millions	2003	2004	2005	2006	2007	2008	2009	2010e
Inward remittance flows[a]	**39**	**93**	**127**	**117**	**105**	**114**	**111**	**124**
of which								
Workers' remittances	0	51	82	79	80	81	–	–
Compensation of employees	27	29	31	26	12	20	–	–
Migrants' transfers	12	13	13	13	13	13	–	–
Outward remittance flows	**206**	**120**	**129**	**118**	**120**	**145**	**145**	**–**
of which								
Workers' remittances	103	10	17	10	10	41	–	–
Compensation of employees	82	89	91	87	89	82	–	–
Migrants' transfers	20	21	22	21	21	23	–	–

a. For comparison: net FDI inflows US$0.1 bn, net ODA received US$0.7 bn, total international reserves US$9.1 bn, exports of goods and services US$6.2 bn in 2008.

Brazil

Latin America and the Caribbean	UPPER MIDDLE INCOME
Population (millions, 2009)	193.7
Population growth (avg. annual %, 2000–09)	1.2
Population density (people per km², 2008)	22.7
Labor force (millions, 2008)	97.7
Unemployment rate (% of labor force, 2008)	7.9
Urban population (% of pop., 2009)	86.0
Surface area (1,000 km², 2008)	8,514.9
GNI (US$ billions, 2009)	1,547.1
GNI per capita, Atlas method (US$, 2009)	8,040
GDP growth (avg. annual %, 2005–09)	3.6
Poverty headcount ratio at national poverty line (% of pop., 2005)	7.8
Age dependency ratio (2009)	48.5

Migration

EMIGRATION, 2010

- Stock of emigrants: **1,367.1 thousands**
- Stock of emigrants as percentage of population: **0.7%**
- Top destination countries: the United States, Japan, Spain, Paraguay, Portugal, the United Kingdom, Italy, Germany, Argentina, France

SKILLED EMIGRATION, 2000

- Emigration rate of tertiary-educated population: **2.2%**
- Emigration of physicians: **2,090** or **0.6%** of physicians trained in the country (Source: Bhargava, Docquier, and Moullan 2010)

IMMIGRATION, 2010

- Stock of immigrants: **688.0 thousands**
- Stock of immigrants as percentage of population: **0.4%**
- Females as percentage of immigrants: **46.3%**
- Refugees as percentage of immigrants: **3.0%**
- Top source countries: Portugal, Japan, Italy, Spain, Paraguay, Argentina, Uruguay, Bolivia, Germany, Chile

Remittances

US$ millions	2003	2004	2005	2006	2007	2008	2009	2010e
Inward remittance flows[a]	**2,821**	**3,575**	**3,540**	**4,253**	**4,382**	**5,089**	**4,234**	**4,277**
of which								
Workers' remittances	2,018	2,459	2,480	2,890	2,809	2,913	2,224	–
Compensation of employees	269	354	325	397	497	730	665	–
Migrants' transfers	535	763	735	966	1,077	1,446	1,345	–
Outward remittance flows	**333**	**401**	**498**	**691**	**896**	**1,191**	**1,003**	**–**
of which								
Workers' remittances	136	167	263	309	514	628	669	–
Compensation of employees	160	173	111	220	49	185	62	–
Migrants' transfers	37	61	124	161	333	378	272	–

a. For comparison: net FDI inflows US$45.1 bn, net ODA received US$0.5 bn, total international reserves US$193.8 bn, exports of goods and services US$225.8 bn in 2008.

Brunei Darussalam

Population (millions, 2009)	0.4
Population growth (avg. annual %, 2000-09)	2.2
Population density (people per km², 2008)	75.3
Labor force (millions, 2008)	0.2
Unemployment rate (% of labor force, 2008)	—
Urban population (% of pop., 2009)	75.3
Surface area (1,000 km², 2008)	5.8
GNI (US$ billions, 2009)	—
GNI per capita, Atlas method (US$, 2009)	—
GDP growth (avg. annual %, 2005-09)	—
Poverty headcount ratio at national poverty line (% of pop., 2005)	—
Age dependency ratio (2009)	43.2

Migration

EMIGRATION, 2010

- Stock of emigrants: **24.3 thousands**
- Stock of emigrants as percentage of population: **6.0%**
- Top destination countries: Malaysia, Canada, the United Kingdom, Australia, the Philippines, the United States, the Netherlands, New Zealand, Germany, Ireland

SKILLED EMIGRATION, 2000

- Emigration rate of tertiary-educated population: **15.6%**

IMMIGRATION, 2010

- Stock of immigrants: **148.1 thousands**
- Stock of immigrants as percentage of population: **36.4%**
- Females as percentage of immigrants: **45.5%**
- Refugees as percentage of immigrants: **0.0%**
- Top source countries: Malaysia, the Philippines, Thailand, Nepal, Indonesia, India, the United Kingdom, China, Singapore, Sri Lanka

Remittances

US$ millions	2003	2004	2005	2006	2007	2008	2009	2010e
Inward remittance flows[a]	—	—	—	—	—	—	—	—
of which								
Workers' remittances	—	—	—	—	—	—	—	—
Compensation of employees	—	—	—	—	—	—	—	—
Migrants' transfers	—	—	—	—	—	—	—	—
Outward remittance flows	303	323	376	405	430	420	420	—
of which								
Workers' remittances	—	—	—	—	—	—	—	—
Compensation of employees	—	—	—	—	—	—	—	—
Migrants' transfers	—	—	—	—	—	—	—	—

a. For comparison: net FDI inflows US$0.2 bn, total international reserves US$0.8 bn in 2008.

Bulgaria

Population (millions, 2009)	7.6
Population growth (avg. annual %, 2000–09)	-0.8
Population density (people per km², 2008)	70.2
Labor force (millions, 2008)	3.4
Unemployment rate (% of labor force, 2008)	5.7
Urban population (% of pop., 2009)	71.4
Surface area (1,000 km², 2008)	111.0
GNI (US$ billions, 2009)	44.9
GNI per capita, Atlas method (US$, 2009)	5,770
GDP growth (avg. annual %, 2005–09)	4.0
Poverty headcount ratio at national poverty line (% of pop., 2005)	0.0
Age dependency ratio (2009)	44.6

Migration

EMIGRATION, 2010

- Stock of emigrants: **1,200.6 thousands**
- Stock of emigrants as percentage of population: **16.0%**
- Top destination countries: Turkey, Spain, Germany, Greece, Italy, Moldova, the United Kingdom, the United States, Romania, Canada

SKILLED EMIGRATION, 2000

- Emigration rate of tertiary-educated population: **6.6%**
- Emigration of physicians: **814** or **2.9%** of physicians trained in the country
  (Source: Bhargava, Docquier, and Moullan 2010)

IMMIGRATION, 2010

- Stock of immigrants: **107.2 thousands**
- Stock of immigrants as percentage of population: **1.4%**
- Females as percentage of immigrants: **57.9%**
- Refugees as percentage of immigrants: **4.4%**
- Top source country: Turkey

Remittances

US$ millions	2003	2004	2005	2006	2007	2008	2009	2010e
Inward remittance flows[a]	**1,718**	**1,723**	**1,613**	**1,716**	**1,694**	**1,874**	**1,558**	**1,602**
of which								
Workers' remittances	681	436	462	420	905	981	965	–
Compensation of employees	1,037	1,286	1,151	1,297	788	894	593	–
Migrants' transfers	–	–	–	–	–	–	–	–
Outward remittance flows	**13**	**29**	**35**	**50**	**103**	**162**	**101**	–
of which								
Workers' remittances	–	18	22	21	33	33	14	–
Compensation of employees	113	11	14	29	69	128	88	–
Migrants' transfers	–	–	–	–	–	–	–	–

a. For comparison: net FDI inflows US$9.2 bn, total international reserves US$17.9 bn, exports of goods and services US$30.2 bn in 2008.

Burkina Faso

Population (millions, 2009)	15.8
Population growth (avg. annual %, 2000–09)	3.3
Population density (people per km², 2008)	55.6
Labor force (millions, 2008)	6.6
Unemployment rate (% of labor force, 2008)	–
Urban population (% of pop., 2009)	20.0
Surface area (1,000 km², 2008)	274.0
GNI (US$ billions, 2009)	8.0
GNI per capita, Atlas method (US$, 2009)	510
GDP growth (avg. annual %, 2005–09)	4.8
Poverty headcount ratio at national poverty line (% of pop., 2005)	55.0
Age dependency ratio (2009)	93.5

Migration

EMIGRATION, 2010

- Stock of emigrants: **1,576.4 thousands**
- Stock of emigrants as percentage of population: **9.7%**
- Top destination countries: Côte d'Ivoire, Niger, Mali, Italy, Benin, Nigeria, France, Gabon, Germany, the United States

SKILLED EMIGRATION, 2000

- Emigration rate of tertiary-educated population: **2.6%**
- Emigration of physicians:
  - (a) **1** or **0.2%** of physicians trained in the country *(Source: Bhargava, Docquier, and Moullan 2010)*
  - (b) **78** or **19.9%** of physicians born in the country *(Source: Clemens and Pettersson 2006)*
- Emigration of nurses: **76** or **2.4%** of nurses born in the country

IMMIGRATION, 2010

- Stock of immigrants: **1,043.0 thousands**
- Stock of immigrants as percentage of population: **6.4%**
- Females as percentage of immigrants: **50.8%**
- Refugees as percentage of immigrants: **0.1%**
- Top source countries: Côte d'Ivoire, Mali, Ghana, Togo, Niger, Benin

Remittances

US$ millions	2003	2004	2005	2006	2007	2008	2009	2010e
Inward remittance flows[a]	**50**	**50**	**50**	**50**	**50**	**50**	**49**	**43**
of which								
Workers' remittances	–	–	–	–	–	–	–	–
Compensation of employees	–	–	–	–	–	–	–	–
Migrants' transfers	–	–	–	–	–	–	–	–
Outward remittance flows	**–**	**–**	**–**	**–**	**–**	**–**	**–**	**–**
of which								
Workers' remittances	–	–	–	–	–	–	–	–
Compensation of employees	–	–	–	–	–	–	–	–
Migrants' transfers	–	–	–	–	–	–	–	–

a. For comparison: net FDI inflows US$0.1 bn, net ODA received US$1.0 bn, total international reserves US$0.9 bn in 2008.

Burundi

Sub-Saharan Africa | **LOW INCOME**

Population (millions, 2009)	8.3
Population growth (avg. annual %, 2000–09)	2.6
Population density (people per km², 2008)	314.4
Labor force (millions, 2008)	4.2
Unemployment rate (% of labor force, 2008)	—
Urban population (% of pop., 2009)	10.7
Surface area (1,000 km², 2008)	27.8
GNI (US$ billions, 2009)	1.3
GNI per capita, Atlas method (US$, 2009)	150
GDP growth (avg. annual %, 2005–09)	3.5
Poverty headcount ratio at national poverty line (% of pop., 2005)	81.3
Age dependency ratio (2009)	70.0

Migration

EMIGRATION, 2010

- Stock of emigrants: **356.0 thousands**
- Stock of emigrants as percentage of population: **4.2%**
- Top destination countries: Tanzania, Uganda, Rwanda, Belgium, Canada, the Netherlands, the United Kingdom, France, Australia, the United States

SKILLED EMIGRATION, 2000

- Emigration rate of tertiary-educated population: **8.5%**
- Emigration of physicians:
  - (a) **19** or **5.2%** of physicians trained in the country *(Source: Bhargava, Docquier, and Moullan 2010)*
  - (b) **136** or **37.2%** of physicians born in the country *(Source: Clemens and Pettersson 2006)*
- Emigration of nurses: **134** or **77.9%** of nurses born in the country

IMMIGRATION, 2010

- Stock of immigrants: **60.8 thousands**
- Stock of immigrants as percentage of population: **0.7%**
- Females as percentage of immigrants: **54.6%**
- Refugees as percentage of immigrants: **31.0%**
- Top source countries: Rwanda, the Democratic Republic of Congo, Tanzania

Remittances

US$ millions	2003	2004	2005	2006	2007	2008	2009	2010e
Inward remittance flows[a]	—	0	0	0	0	4	3	3
of which								
Workers' remittances	—	0	0	0	0	4	—	—
Compensation of employees	—	—	—	—	—	—	—	—
Migrants' transfers	—	—	—	—	—	—	—	—
Outward remittance flows	4	1	0	0	0	0	0	—
of which								
Workers' remittances	—	0	0	0	0	0	—	—
Compensation of employees	3	—	—	—	—	—	—	—
Migrants' transfers	1	1	0	0	0	0	—	—

a. For comparison: net ODA received US$0.5 bn, total international reserves US$0.3 bn in 2008.

Cambodia

| East Asia and Pacific | LOW INCOME |

Population (millions, 2009)	14.8
Population growth (avg. annual %, 2000–09)	1.7
Population density (people per km², 2008)	83.3
Labor force (millions, 2008)	7.5
Unemployment rate (% of labor force, 2008)	—
Urban population (% of pop., 2009)	22.2
Surface area (1,000 km², 2008)	181.0
GNI (US$ billions, 2009)	9.7
GNI per capita, Atlas method (US$, 2009)	650
GDP growth (avg. annual %, 2005–09)	7.8
Poverty headcount ratio at national poverty line (% of pop., 2005)	40.2
Age dependency ratio (2009)	58.1

Migration

EMIGRATION, 2010

- Stock of emigrants: **350.4 thousands**
- Stock of emigrants as percentage of population: **2.3%**
- Top destination countries: the United States, France, Thailand, Australia, Canada, New Zealand, the Republic of Korea, Japan, Switzerland, Belgium

SKILLED EMIGRATION, 2000

- Emigration rate of tertiary-educated population: **18.3%**
- Emigration of physicians: **71** or **3.5%** of physicians trained in the country *(Source: Bhargava, Docquier, and Moullan 2010)*

IMMIGRATION, 2010

- Stock of immigrants: **335.8 thousands**
- Stock of immigrants as percentage of population: **2.2%**
- Females as percentage of immigrants: **51.7%**
- Refugees as percentage of immigrants: **0.0%**
- Top source countries: Vietnam, Thailand, China, France, the Lao People's Democratic Republic, the United States, Malaysia, the Philippines, Japan, Singapore

Remittances

US$ millions	2003	2004	2005	2006	2007	2008	2009	2010e
Inward remittance flows[a]	**138**	**177**	**200**	**297**	**353**	**325**	**338**	**364**
of which								
Workers' remittances	125	144	160	180	184	187	140	—
Compensation of employees	3	3	4	4	4	5	5	—
Migrants' transfers	10	30	36	114	165	133	193	—
Outward remittance flows	**109**	**129**	**184**	**173**	**186**	**230**	**215**	**—**
of which								
Workers' remittances	10	12	16	20	24	24	19	—
Compensation of employees	46	44	113	100	94	147	140	—
Migrants' transfers	53	73	56	53	67	60	56	—

a. For comparison: net FDI inflows US$0.8 bn, net ODA received US$0.7 bn, total international reserves US$2.6 bn in 2008.

Cameroon

Population (millions, 2009)	19.5
Population growth (avg. annual %, 2000–09)	2.3
Population density (people per km², 2008)	40.6
Labor force (millions, 2008)	6.9
Unemployment rate (% of labor force, 2008)	–
Urban population (% of pop., 2009)	57.6
Surface area (1,000 km², 2008)	475.4
GNI (US$ billions, 2009)	21.6
GNI per capita, Atlas method (US$, 2009)	1,170
GDP growth (avg. annual %, 2005–09)	3.0
Poverty headcount ratio at national poverty line (% of pop., 2005)	27.5
Age dependency ratio (2009)	80.1

Migration

EMIGRATION, 2010

- Stock of emigrants: **279.2 thousands**
- Stock of emigrants as percentage of population: **1.4%**
- Top destination countries: France, Chad, Gabon, the United States, Nigeria, Germany, Italy, the Central African Republic, Spain, the United Kingdom

SKILLED EMIGRATION, 2000

- Emigration rate of tertiary-educated population: **17.2%**
- Emigration of physicians:
  - (a) **106** or **8.0%** of physicians trained in the country *(Source: Bhargava, Docquier, and Moullan 2010)*
  - (b) **845** or **45.6%** of physicians born in the country *(Source: Clemens and Pettersson 2006)*
- Emigration of nurses: 1,163 or 18.9% of nurses born in the country

IMMIGRATION, 2010

- Stock of immigrants: **196.6 thousands**
- Stock of immigrants as percentage of population: **1.0%**
- Females as percentage of immigrants: **45.7%**
- Refugees as percentage of immigrants: **24.2%**
- Top source countries: Nigeria, Chad, France

Remittances

US$ millions	2003	2004	2005	2006	2007	2008	2009	2010e
Inward remittance flows[a]	**76**	**103**	**77**	**130**	**167**	**162**	**148**	**148**
of which								
Workers' remittances	61	98	67	118	152	129	129	–
Compensation of employees	15	5	10	12	15	15	18	–
Migrants' transfers	0	–	0	–	–	0	–	–
Outward remittance flows	**57**	**42**	**56**	**92**	**90**	**56**	**94**	**–**
of which								
Workers' remittances	29	23	20	48	42	20	58	–
Compensation of employees	28	20	36	44	48	36	37	–
Migrants' transfers	0	–	0	–	–	–	–	–

a. For comparison: net ODA received US$0.5 bn, total international reserves US$3.1 bn, exports of goods and services US$6.9 bn in 2008.

Canada

Population (millions, 2009)	33.7
Population growth (avg. annual %, 2000–09)	1.0
Population density (people per km², 2008)	3.7
Labor force (millions, 2008)	18.5
Unemployment rate (% of labor force, 2008)	6.1
Urban population (% of pop., 2009)	80.5
Surface area (1,000 km², 2008)	9,984.7
GNI (US$ billions, 2009)	1,323.5
GNI per capita, Atlas method (US$, 2009)	42,170
GDP growth (avg. annual %, 2005–09)	1.2
Poverty headcount ratio at national poverty line (% of pop., 2005)	—
Age dependency ratio (2009)	43.6

Migration

EMIGRATION, 2010

- Stock of emigrants: **1,186.0 thousands**
- Stock of emigrants as percentage of population: **3.5%**
- Top destination countries: the United States, the United Kingdom, Australia, Germany, France, Japan, Portugal, New Zealand, the Netherlands, the Republic of Korea

SKILLED EMIGRATION, 2000

- Emigration rate of tertiary-educated population: **4.6%**
- Emigration of physicians: **18,375** or **22.2%** of physicians trained in the country *(Source: Bhargava, Docquier, and Moullan 2010)*

IMMIGRATION, 2010

- Stock of immigrants: **7,202.3 thousands**
- Stock of immigrants as percentage of population: **21.3%**
- Females as percentage of immigrants: **52.2%**
- Refugees as percentage of immigrants: **2.3%**
- Top source countries: the United Kingdom; China; India; the Philippines; Italy; the United States; Hong Kong SAR, China; Germany; Poland; Vietnam

Remittances

Remittance data are currently not available for this country.

Cape Verde

Population (millions, 2009)	0.5
Population growth (avg. annual %, 2000–09)	1.6
Population density (people per km², 2008)	123.7
Labor force (millions, 2008)	0.2
Unemployment rate (% of labor force, 2008)	–
Urban population (% of pop., 2009)	60.4
Surface area (1,000 km², 2008)	4.0
GNI (US$ billions, 2009)	1.5
GNI per capita, Atlas method (US$, 2009)	3,010
GDP growth (avg. annual %, 2005–09)	8.0
Poverty headcount ratio at national poverty line (% of pop., 2005)	18.4
Age dependency ratio (2009)	67.8

Migration

EMIGRATION, 2010

- Stock of emigrants: **192.5 thousands**
- Stock of emigrants as percentage of population: **37.5%**
- Top destination countries: Portugal, France, the United States, Mozambique, Angola, the Netherlands, Senegal, Italy, Spain, Nigeria

SKILLED EMIGRATION, 2000

- Emigration rate of tertiary-educated population: **67.5%**
- Emigration of physicians: **211** or **51.1%** of physicians born in the country *(Source: Clemens and Pettersson 2006)*
- Emigration of nurses: **244** or **40.7%** of nurses born in the country

IMMIGRATION, 2010

- Stock of immigrants: **12.1 thousands**
- Stock of immigrants as percentage of population: **2.4%**
- Females as percentage of immigrants: **50.4%**
- Refugees as percentage of immigrants: **0.0%**
- Top source countries: São Tomé and Principe, Angola, Guinea-Bissau, Portugal, Senegal, Italy, the United States, France, Nigeria, Brazil

Remittances

US$ millions	2003	2004	2005	2006	2007	2008	2009	2010e
Inward remittance flows[a]	**109**	**113**	**137**	**137**	**139**	**155**	**145**	**144**
of which								
Workers' remittances	108	113	137	136	138	154	154	–
Compensation of employees	0	0	0	1	0	1	1	–
Migrants' transfers	–	–	–	–	–	–	–	–
Outward remittance flows	**7**	**12**	**5**	**6**	**6**	**10**	**10**	**–**
of which								
Workers' remittances	7	11	4	5	5	8	–	–
Compensation of employees	1	1	1	1	1	2	–	–
Migrants' transfers	–	–	–	–	–	–	–	–

a. For comparison: net FDI inflows US$0.2 bn, net ODA received US$0.2 bn, total international reserves US$0.3 bn, exports of goods and services US$0.3 bn in 2008.

Cayman Islands

HIGH-INCOME NON-OECD

Population (thousands, 2009)	55.0
Population growth (avg. annual %, 2000–09)	3.4
Population density (people per km², 2008)	208.6
Labor force (millions, 2008)	—
Unemployment rate (% of labor force, 2008)	—
Urban population (% of pop., 2009)	100.0
Surface area (1,000 km², 2008)	0.3
GNI (US$ billions, 2009)	—
GNI per capita, Atlas method (US$, 2009)	—
GDP growth (avg. annual %, 2005–09)	—
Poverty headcount ratio at national poverty line (% of pop., 2005)	—
Age dependency ratio (2009)	—

Migration

EMIGRATION, 2010

- Stock of emigrants: **3.9 thousands**
- Stock of emigrants as percentage of population: **7.0%**
- Top destination countries: the United States, the United Kingdom, Canada, Virgin Islands (U.S.), Ireland, Honduras, the Dominican Republic, Mexico, Greece, Australia

SKILLED EMIGRATION, 2000

- Skilled emigration data are currently not available for this country.

IMMIGRATION, 2010

- Stock of immigrants: **35.7 thousands**
- Stock of immigrants as percentage of population: **63.0%**
- Females as percentage of immigrants: **48.4%**
- Refugees as percentage of immigrants: **0.0%**
- Top source countries: Jamaica, the United States, the United Kingdom, Honduras, Canada, Nicaragua, Cuba, Trinidad and Tobago, Belize, Costa Rica

Remittances

Remittance data are currently not available for this country.

Central African Republic

Sub-Saharan Africa **LOW INCOME**

Population (millions, 2009)	4.4
Population growth (avg. annual %, 2000–09)	1.9
Population density (people per km², 2008)	7.1
Labor force (millions, 2008)	2.0
Unemployment rate (% of labor force, 2008)	—
Urban population (% of pop., 2009)	38.7
Surface area (1,000 km², 2008)	623.0
GNI (US$ billions, 2009)	2.0
GNI per capita, Atlas method (US$, 2009)	450
GDP growth (avg. annual %, 2005–09)	2.9
Poverty headcount ratio at national poverty line (% of pop., 2005)	64.4
Age dependency ratio (2009)	80.2

Migration

EMIGRATION, 2010

- Stock of emigrants: **129.3 thousands**
- Stock of emigrants as percentage of population: **2.9%**
- Top destination countries: Chad, France, the Republic of Congo, the Netherlands, the United Kingdom, the United States, Mali, Canada, Italy, Belgium

SKILLED EMIGRATION, 2000

- Emigration rate of tertiary-educated population: **7.1%**
- Emigration of physicians:
  - (a) **5** or **3.6%** of physicians trained in the country *(Source: Bhargava, Docquier, and Moullan 2010)*
  - (b) **87** or **42.0%** of physicians born in the country *(Source: Clemens and Pettersson 2006)*
- Emigration of nurses: **99** or **24.8%** of nurses born in the country

IMMIGRATION, 2010

- Stock of immigrants: **80.5 thousands**
- Stock of immigrants as percentage of population: **1.8%**
- Females as percentage of immigrants: **46.6%**
- Refugees as percentage of immigrants: **12.4%**
- Top source countries: Chad, the Democratic Republic of Congo, Cameroon, France, Sudan, Senegal, Nigeria, the Republic of Congo, Mali, Niger

Remittances

Remittance data are currently not available for this country.

Chad

Population (millions, 2009)	11.2
Population growth (avg. annual %, 2000–09)	3.2
Population density (people per km^2, 2008)	8.8
Labor force (millions, 2008)	4.3
Unemployment rate (% of labor force, 2008)	—
Urban population (% of pop., 2009)	27.1
Surface area (1,000 km^2, 2008)	1,284.0
GNI (US$ billions, 2009)	6.1
GNI per capita, Atlas method (US$, 2009)	610
GDP growth (avg. annual %, 2005–09)	3.8
Poverty headcount ratio at national poverty line (% of pop., 2005)	58.7
Age dependency ratio (2009)	94.4

Migration

EMIGRATION, 2010

- Stock of emigrants: **243.3 thousands**
- Stock of emigrants as percentage of population: **2.1%**
- Top destination countries: Cameroon, Sudan, the Central African Republic, Nigeria, Saudi Arabia, France, the Republic of Congo, Canada, the United States, Germany

SKILLED EMIGRATION, 2000

- Emigration rate of tertiary-educated population: **2.4%**
- Emigration of physicians:
  - (a) **1** or **0.4%** of physicians trained in the country *(Source: Bhargava, Docquier, and Moullan 2010)*
  - (b) **70** or **22.0%** of physicians born in the country *(Source: Clemens and Pettersson 2006)*
- Emigration of nurses: **131** or **11.1%** of nurses born in the country

IMMIGRATION, 2010

- Stock of immigrants: **388.3 thousands**
- Stock of immigrants as percentage of population: **3.4%**
- Females as percentage of immigrants: **48.0%**
- Refugees as percentage of immigrants: **74.8%**
- Top source countries: Nigeria, the Central African Republic, Cameroon, Sudan, Niger, Libya, the Republic of Congo, Gabon

Remittances

Remittance data are currently not available for this country.

Channel Islands

Population (millions, 2009)	0.1
Population growth (avg. annual %, 2000–09)	0.2
Population density (people per km², 2008)	786.7
Labor force (millions, 2008)	—
Unemployment rate (% of labor force, 2008)	—
Urban population (% of pop., 2009)	31.3
Surface area (1,000 km², 2008)	0.2
GNI (US$ billions, 2009)	—
GNI per capita, Atlas method (US$, 2009)	—
GDP growth (avg. annual %, 2005–09)	—
Poverty headcount ratio at national poverty line (% of pop., 2005)	—
Age dependency ratio (2009)	44.5

Migration

EMIGRATION, 2010

- Stock of emigrants: **0.0 thousands**
- Stock of emigrants as percentage of population: **0.0%**

SKILLED EMIGRATION, 2000

- Skilled emigration data are currently not available for this country.

IMMIGRATION, 2010

- Stock of immigrants: **74.8 thousands**
- Stock of immigrants as percentage of population: **49.8%**
- Females as percentage of immigrants: **53.0%**
- Refugees as percentage of immigrants: **0.0%**

Remittances

Remittance data are currently not available for this country.

Chile

Latin America and the Caribbean	UPPER MIDDLE INCOME
Population (millions, 2009)	17.0
Population growth (avg. annual %, 2000–09)	1.1
Population density (people per km², 2008)	22.4
Labor force (millions, 2008)	7.0
Unemployment rate (% of labor force, 2008)	7.8
Urban population (% of pop., 2009)	88.7
Surface area (1,000 km², 2008)	756.6
GNI (US$ billions, 2009)	153.4
GNI per capita, Atlas method (US$, 2009)	9,420
GDP growth (avg. annual %, 2005–09)	3.4
Poverty headcount ratio at national poverty line (% of pop., 2005)	0.7
Age dependency ratio (2009)	46.4

Migration

EMIGRATION, 2010

- Stock of emigrants: **633.6 thousands**
- Stock of emigrants as percentage of population: **3.7%**
- Top destination countries: Argentina, the United States, Spain, Canada, Sweden, Australia, Brazil, Ecuador, República Bolivariana de Venezuela, France

SKILLED EMIGRATION, 2000

- Emigration rate of tertiary-educated population: **6.1%**
- Emigration of physicians: **917** or **5.1%** of physicians trained in the country *(Source: Bhargava, Docquier, and Moullan 2010)*

IMMIGRATION, 2010

- Stock of immigrants: **320.4 thousands**
- Stock of immigrants as percentage of population: **1.9%**
- Females as percentage of immigrants: **53.5%**
- Refugees as percentage of immigrants: **0.4%**
- Top source countries: Argentina, Peru, Bolivia, Ecuador, Spain, the United States, Brazil, Germany, República Bolivariana de Venezuela, Colombia

Remittances

US$ millions	2003	2004	2005	2006	2007	2008	2009	2010e
Inward remittance flows[a]	**12**	**12**	**13**	**3**	**3**	**3**	**4**	**5**
of which								
Workers' remittances	–	–	–	–	–	–	–	–
Compensation of employees	12	12	13	3	3	3	–	–
Migrants' transfers	–	–	–	–	–	–	–	–
Outward remittance flows	**15**	**15**	**16**	**6**	**6**	**6**	**6**	**–**
of which								
Workers' remittances	–	–	–	–	–	–	–	–
Compensation of employees	15	15	16	6	6	6	–	–
Migrants' transfers	–	–	–	–	–	–	–	–

a. For comparison: net FDI inflows US$16.8 bn, net ODA received US$0.1 bn, total international reserves US$23.1 bn, exports of goods and services US$76.5 bn in 2008.

China

Population (millions, 2009)	1,331.5
Population growth (avg. annual %, 2000–09)	0.6
Population density (people per km², 2008)	142.1
Labor force (millions, 2008)	782.8
Unemployment rate (% of labor force, 2008)	4.2
Urban population (% of pop., 2009)	44.0
Surface area (1,000 km², 2008)	9,598.1
GNI (US$ billions, 2009)	4,938.0
GNI per capita, Atlas method (US$, 2009)	3,590
GDP growth (avg. annual %, 2005–09)	11.4
Poverty headcount ratio at national poverty line (% of pop., 2005)	—
Age dependency ratio (2009)	39.4

Migration

EMIGRATION, 2010

- Stock of emigrants: **8,343.6 thousands**
- Stock of emigrants as percentage of population: **0.6%**
- Top destination countries: Hong Kong SAR, China; the United States; Japan; Canada; Singapore; Thailand; Australia; the Republic of Korea; Macao SAR, China; Italy

SKILLED EMIGRATION, 2000

- Emigration rate of tertiary-educated population: **3.8%**
- Emigration of physicians: **4,459** or **0.2%** of physicians trained in the country *(Source: Bhargava, Docquier, and Moullan 2010)*

IMMIGRATION, 2010

- Stock of immigrants: **685.8 thousands**
- Stock of immigrants as percentage of population: **0.1%**
- Females as percentage of immigrants: **50.0%**
- Refugees as percentage of immigrants: **43.9%**

Remittances

US$ million	2003	2004	2005	2006	2007	2008	2009	2010e
Inward remittance flows[a]	**15,059**	**20,186**	**24,102**	**27,954**	**38,791**	**48,524**	**48,729**	**51,000**
of which								
Workers' remittances	3,343	4,627	5,495	6,830	10,679	13,557	13,693	—
Compensation of employees	1,283	2,014	3,337	4,319	6,833	9,137	9,209	—
Migrants' transfers	—	—	—	—	—	—	—	—
Outward remittance flows	**1,597**	**1,998**	**2,550**	**3,025**	**4,372**	**5,737**	**4,444**	—
of which								
Workers' remittances	477	616	732	695	1,879	3,000	2,393	—
Compensation of employees	1,120	1,382	1,817	2,330	2,493	2,736	2,052	—
Migrants' transfers	—	—	—	—	—	—	—	—

a. For comparison: net FDI inflows US$147.8 bn, net ODA received US$1.5 bn, total international reserves US$1,966.0 bn, exports of goods and services US$1,581.7 bn in 2008.

Colombia

Latin America and the Caribbean	UPPER MIDDLE INCOME
Population (millions, 2009)	45.7
Population growth (avg. annual %, 2000–09)	1.5
Population density (people per km², 2008)	40.1
Labor force (millions, 2008)	21.8
Unemployment rate (% of labor force, 2008)	11.7
Urban population (% of pop., 2009)	74.8
Surface area (1,000 km², 2008)	1,141.8
GNI (US$ billions, 2009)	221.2
GNI per capita, Atlas method (US$, 2009)	4,930
GDP growth (avg. annual %, 2005–09)	4.6
Poverty headcount ratio at national poverty line (% of pop., 2005)	13.9
Age dependency ratio (2009)	53.0

Migration

EMIGRATION, 2010

- Stock of emigrants: **2,122.1 thousands**
- Stock of emigrants as percentage of population: **4.6%**
- Top destination countries: the United States, República Bolivariana de Venezuela, Spain, Ecuador, Canada, Panama, France, Italy, the United Kingdom, Germany

SKILLED EMIGRATION, 2000

- Emigration rate of tertiary-educated population: **10.4%**
- Emigration of physicians: **2,820** or **5.7%** of physicians trained in the country (Source: Bhargava, Docquier, and Moullan 2010)

IMMIGRATION, 2010

- Stock of immigrants: **110.3 thousands**
- Stock of immigrants as percentage of population: **0.2%**
- Females as percentage of immigrants: **47.9%**
- Refugees as percentage of immigrants: **0.1%**
- Top source countries: República Bolivariana de Venezuela, the United States, Ecuador, Spain, Peru, Argentina, Mexico, Italy, Germany, Brazil

Remittances

US$ millions	2003	2004	2005	2006	2007	2008	2009	2010e
Inward remittance flows[a]	**3,076**	**3,190**	**3,346**	**3,928**	**4,523**	**4,884**	**4,180**	**3,942**
of which								
Workers' remittances	3,060	3,170	3,314	3,890	4,493	4,842	4,145	–
Compensation of employees	16	20	32	38	30	42	35	–
Migrants' transfers	–	–	–	–	–	–	–	–
Outward remittance flows	**65**	**51**	**56**	**66**	**95**	**88**	**92**	**–**
of which								
Workers' remittances	52	31	37	47	66	59	60	–
Compensation of employees	12	19	19	19	29	29	33	–
Migrants' transfers	–	–	–	–	–	–	–	–

a. For comparison: net FDI inflows US$10.6 bn, net ODA received US$1.0 bn, total international reserves US$23.7 bn, exports of goods and services US$44.3 bn in 2008.

Comoros

Sub-Saharan Africa **LOW INCOME**

Population (millions, 2009)	0.7
Population growth (avg. annual %, 2000–09)	2.2
Population density (people per km², 2008)	345.8
Labor force (millions, 2008)	0.3
Unemployment rate (% of labor force, 2008)	–
Urban population (% of pop., 2009)	28.1
Surface area (1,000 km², 2008)	1.9
GNI (US$ billions, 2009)	0.5
GNI per capita, Atlas method (US$, 2009)	870
GDP growth (avg. annual %, 2005–09)	3.8
Poverty headcount ratio at national poverty line (% of pop., 2005)	46.1
Age dependency ratio (2009)	70.1

Migration

EMIGRATION, 2010

- Stock of emigrants: **38.6 thousands**
- Stock of emigrants as percentage of population: **5.6%**
- Top destination countries: France, Madagascar, Tanzania, the Arab Republic of Egypt, the United States, the United Kingdom, Germany, Belgium, Canada, Bahrain

SKILLED EMIGRATION, 2000

- Emigration rate of tertiary-educated population: **21.2%**
- Emigration of physicians:
  - (a) **1** or **2.4%** of physicians trained in the country *(Source: Bhargava, Docquier, and Moullan 2010)*
  - (b) **24** or **32.4%** of physicians born in the country *(Source: Clemens and Pettersson 2006)*
- Emigration of nurses: **70** or **23.3%** of nurses born in the country

IMMIGRATION, 2010

- Stock of immigrants: **13.5 thousands**
- Stock of immigrants as percentage of population: **2.0%**
- Females as percentage of immigrants: **53.3%**
- Refugees as percentage of immigrants: **0.0%**
- Top source countries: Madagascar, Mayotte, France, Tanzania

Remittances

US$ millions	2003	2004	2005	2006	2007	2008	2009	2010e
Inward remittance flows[a]	**12**	**12**	**12**	**12**	**12**	**12**	**11**	**11**
of which								
Workers' remittances	–	–	–	–	–	–	–	–
Compensation of employees	–	–	–	–	–	–	–	–
Migrants' transfers	–	–	–	–	–	–	–	–
Outward remittance flows	**–**	**–**	**–**	**–**	**–**	**–**	**–**	**–**
of which								
Workers' remittances	–	–	–	–	–	–	–	–
Compensation of employees	–	–	–	–	–	–	–	–
Migrants' transfers	–	–	–	–	–	–	–	–

a. **For comparison: total international reserves US$0.1 bn, exports of goods and services US$0.1 bn in 2008.**

Congo, Democratic Republic of

Sub-Saharan Africa	LOW INCOME
Population (millions, 2009)	66.0
Population growth (avg. annual %, 2000–09)	2.2
Population density (people per km², 2008)	28.3
Labor force (millions, 2008)	23.6
Unemployment rate (% of labor force, 2008)	–
Urban population (% of pop., 2009)	34.6
Surface area (1,000 km², 2008)	2,344.9
GNI (US$ billions, 2009)	10.0
GNI per capita, Atlas method (US$, 2009)	160
GDP growth (avg. annual %, 2005–09)	5.3
Poverty headcount ratio at national poverty line (% of pop., 2005)	59.2
Age dependency ratio (2009)	97.3

Migration

EMIGRATION, 2010

- Stock of emigrants: **913.9 thousands**
- Stock of emigrants as percentage of population: **1.3%**
- Top destination countries: Rwanda, Uganda, the Republic of Congo, Belgium, France, Zambia, Germany, the Central African Republic, Canada, Burundi

SKILLED EMIGRATION, 2000

- Emigration rate of tertiary-educated population: **13.7%**
- Emigration of physicians:
  - (a) **403** or **10.7%** of physicians trained in the country *(Source: Bhargava, Docquier, and Moullan 2010)*
  - (b) **552** or **8.9%** of physicians born in the country *(Source: Clemens and Pettersson 2006)*
- Emigration of nurses: 2,288 or 11.9% of nurses born in the country

IMMIGRATION, 2010

- Stock of immigrants: **444.7 thousands**
- Stock of immigrants as percentage of population: **0.7%**
- Females as percentage of immigrants: **53.1%**
- Refugees as percentage of immigrants: **43.4%**

Remittances

Remittance data are currently not available for this country.

Congo, Republic of

Population (millions, 2009)	3.7
Population growth (avg. annual %, 2000–09)	2.1
Population density (people per km², 2008)	10.6
Labor force (millions, 2008)	1.5
Unemployment rate (% of labor force, 2008)	–
Urban population (% of pop., 2009)	61.7
Surface area (1,000 km², 2008)	342.0
GNI (US$ billions, 2009)	6.0
GNI per capita, Atlas method (US$, 2009)	1,830
GDP growth (avg. annual %, 2005–09)	5.1
Poverty headcount ratio at national poverty line (% of pop., 2005)	54.1
Age dependency ratio (2009)	79.5

Migration

EMIGRATION, 2010

- Stock of emigrants: **208.6 thousands**
- Stock of emigrants as percentage of population: **5.6%**
- Top destination countries: Tanzania, France, Gabon, the United States, the Netherlands, Zambia, Italy, the United Kingdom, Belgium, Mali

SKILLED EMIGRATION, 2000

- Emigration rate of tertiary-educated population: **22.2%**
- Emigration of physicians:
  - (a) **62** or **6.7%** of physicians trained in the country *(Source: Bhargava, Docquier, and Moullan 2010)*
  - (b) **747** or **52.7%** of physicians born in the country *(Source: Clemens and Pettersson 2006)*
- Emigration of nurses: 660 or 11.8% of nurses born in the country

IMMIGRATION, 2010

- Stock of immigrants: **143.2 thousands**
- Stock of immigrants as percentage of population: **3.8%**
- Females as percentage of immigrants: **49.4%**
- Refugees as percentage of immigrants: **32.9%**
- Top source countries: the Democratic Republic of Congo, France, Angola, the Central African Republic, Mali, Benin, Senegal, Chad, Cameroon, Mauritania

Remittances

US$ millions	2003	2004	2005	2006	2007	2008	2009	2010e
Inward remittance flows[a]	12	15	11	13	15	15	14	13
of which								
Workers' remittances	5	6	–	–	–	–	–	–
Compensation of employees	8	9	11	13	15	–	–	–
Migrants' transfers	–	–	–	–	–	–	–	–
Outward remittance flows	39	49	66	81	102	102	–	–
of which								
Workers' remittances	6	7	7	8	9	–	–	–
Compensation of employees	34	43	59	73	93	–	–	–
Migrants' transfers	–	–	–	–	–	–	–	–

a. For comparison: net FDI inflows US$2.6 bn, net ODA received US$0.5 bn, total international reserves US$3.9 bn, exports of goods and services US$8.4 bn in 2008.

Costa Rica

Latin America and the Caribbean	UPPER MIDDLE INCOME
Population (millions, 2009)	4.6
Population growth (avg. annual %, 2000–09)	1.8
Population density (people per km², 2008)	88.7
Labor force (millions, 2008)	2.0
Unemployment rate (% of labor force, 2008)	–
Urban population (% of pop., 2009)	63.8
Surface area (1,000 km², 2008)	51.1
GNI (US$ billions, 2009)	28.8
GNI per capita, Atlas method (US$, 2009)	6,230
GDP growth (avg. annual %, 2005–09)	4.7
Poverty headcount ratio at national poverty line (% of pop., 2005)	2.4
Age dependency ratio (2009)	47.4

Migration

EMIGRATION, 2010

- Stock of emigrants: **125.3 thousands**
- Stock of emigrants as percentage of population: **2.7%**
- Top destination countries: the United States, Nicaragua, Panama, Canada, Spain, Mexico, the Dominican Republic, Ecuador, Germany, República Bolivariana de Venezuela

SKILLED EMIGRATION, 2000

- Emigration rate of tertiary-educated population: **7.2%**
- Emigration of physicians: **313** or **4.6%** of physicians trained in the country *(Source: Bhargava, Docquier, and Moullan 2010)*

IMMIGRATION, 2010

- Stock of immigrants: **489.2 thousands**
- Stock of immigrants as percentage of population: **10.5%**
- Females as percentage of immigrants: **50.0%**
- Refugees as percentage of immigrants: **3.5%**
- Top source countries: Nicaragua, Panama, El Salvador, Honduras, Guatemala, Belize

Remittances

US$ millions	2003	2004	2005	2006	2007	2008	2009	2010e
Inward remittance flows[a]	**321**	**320**	**420**	**513**	**618**	**605**	**574**	**622**
of which								
Workers' remittances	306	302	400	490	596	584	489	–
Compensation of employees	15	17	21	23	22	21	25	–
Migrants' transfers	–	–	–	–	–	–	–	–
Outward remittance flows	**192**	**192**	**209**	**246**	**271**	**269**	**239**	–
of which								
Workers' remittances	156	155	196	233	258	254	224	–
Compensation of employees	36	37	13	13	14	14	15	–
Migrants' transfers	–	–	–	–	–	–	–	–

a. For comparison: net FDI inflows US$2.0 bn, net ODA received US$0.1 bn, total international reserves US$3.8 bn, exports of goods and services US$13.6 bn in 2008.

Côte d'Ivoire

Sub-Saharan Africa | **LOWER MIDDLE INCOME**

Population (millions, 2009)	21.1
Population growth (avg. annual %, 2000–09)	2.2
Population density (people per km², 2008)	64.8
Labor force (millions, 2008)	7.4
Unemployment rate (% of labor force, 2008)	–
Urban population (% of pop., 2009)	49.4
Surface area (1,000 km², 2008)	322.5
GNI (US$ billions, 2009)	22.1
GNI per capita, Atlas method (US$, 2009)	1,060
GDP growth (avg. annual %, 2005–09)	1.9
Poverty headcount ratio at national poverty line (% of pop., 2005)	20.4
Age dependency ratio (2009)	80.2

Migration

EMIGRATION, 2010

- Stock of emigrants: **1,170.9 thousands**
- Stock of emigrants as percentage of population: **5.4%**
- Top destination countries: Burkina Faso, Mali, France, Italy, the United States, Nigeria, Germany, the United Kingdom, Gabon, Liberia

SKILLED EMIGRATION, 2000

- Emigration rate of tertiary-educated population: **5.7%**
- Emigration of physicians:
  - (a) **9** or **0.6%** of physicians trained in the country *(Source: Bhargava, Docquier, and Moullan 2010)*
  - (b) **284** or **13.9%** of physicians born in the country *(Source: Clemens and Pettersson 2006)*
- Emigration of nurses: **509** or **6.6%** of nurses born in the country

IMMIGRATION, 2010

- Stock of immigrants: **2,406.7 thousands**
- Stock of immigrants as percentage of population: **11.2%**
- Females as percentage of immigrants: **45.1%**
- Refugees as percentage of immigrants: **1.1%**
- Top source countries: Burkina Faso, Mali, Guinea, Ghana, Niger, Liberia, Benin, Togo, Nigeria, Senegal

Remittances

US$ millions	2003	2004	2005	2006	2007	2008	2009	2010e
Inward remittance flows[a]	142	159	163	167	185	199	185	177
of which								
Workers' remittances	–	1	2	2	2	–	–	–
Compensation of employees	142	158	161	165	182	195	–	–
Migrants' transfers	–	–	–	–	–	–	–	–
Outward remittance flows	628	591	597	660	698	756	120	–
of which								
Workers' remittances	613	575	580	643	679	–	–	–
Compensation of employees	15	16	17	17	19	–	–	–
Migrants' transfers	–	–	–	–	–	–	–	–

a. For comparison: net FDI inflows US$0.4 bn, net ODA received US$0.6 bn, total international reserves US$2.3 bn, exports of goods and services US$10.9 bn in 2008.

Croatia

Population (millions, 2009)	4.4
Population growth (avg. annual %, 2000–09)	-0.3
Population density (people per km², 2008)	79.3
Labor force (millions, 2008)	2.0
Unemployment rate (% of labor force, 2008)	8.4
Urban population (% of pop., 2009)	57.5
Surface area (1,000 km², 2008)	56.5
GNI (US$ billions, 2009)	61.0
GNI per capita, Atlas method (US$, 2009)	13,810
GDP growth (avg. annual %, 2005–09)	2.2
Poverty headcount ratio at national poverty line (% of pop., 2005)	0.0
Age dependency ratio (2009)	47.8

Migration

EMIGRATION, 2010

- Stock of emigrants: **753.9 thousands**
- Stock of emigrants as percentage of population: **17.1%**
- Top destination countries: Germany, Australia, Austria, the United States, Canada, France, Italy, Switzerland, Slovenia, Bosnia and Herzegovina

SKILLED EMIGRATION, 2000

- Emigration rate of tertiary-educated population: **24.1%**
- Emigration of physicians: **707** or **6.3%** of physicians trained in the country *(Source: Bhargava, Docquier, and Moullan 2010)*

IMMIGRATION, 2010

- Stock of immigrants: **699.9 thousands**
- Stock of immigrants as percentage of population: **15.9%**
- Females as percentage of immigrants: **53.0%**
- Refugees as percentage of immigrants: **0.3%**
- Top source countries: Bosnia and Herzegovina, Slovenia, the former Yugoslav Republic of Macedonia, Germany, Italy, Austria, the United States, Australia, Switzerland, Canada

Remittances

US$ millions	2003	2004	2005	2006	2007	2008	2009	2010e
Inward remittance flows[a]	**1,085**	**1,222**	**1,222**	**1,234**	**1,394**	**1,602**	**1,476**	**1,545**
of which								
Workers' remittances	797	851	845	689	611	664	544	–
Compensation of employees	247	333	359	510	724	880	870	–
Migrants' transfers	41	37	18	34	59	58	62	–
Outward remittance flows	**67**	**69**	**62**	**274**	**86**	**116**	**99**	**–**
of which								
Workers' remittances	17	17	21	27	31	42	33	–
Compensation of employees	38	43	36	39	46	52	52	–
Migrants' transfers	12	9	5	208	8	22	14	–

a. For comparison: net FDI inflows US$4.8 bn, net ODA received US$0.4 bn, total international reserves US$13.0 bn, exports of goods and services US$29.1 bn in 2008.

Cuba

Population (millions, 2009)	11.2
Population growth (avg. annual %, 2000–09)	0.1
Population density (people per km², 2008)	102.4
Labor force (millions, 2008)	5.2
Unemployment rate (% of labor force, 2008)	–
Urban population (% of pop., 2009)	75.7
Surface area (1,000 km², 2008)	110.9
GNI (US$ billions, 2009)	–
GNI per capita, Atlas method (US$, 2009)	–
GDP growth (avg. annual %, 2005–09)	5.4
Poverty headcount ratio at national poverty line (% of pop., 2005)	–
Age dependency ratio (2009)	42.1

Migration

EMIGRATION, 2010

- Stock of emigrants: **1,219.2 thousands**
- Stock of emigrants as percentage of population: **10.9%**
- Top destination countries: the United States, Spain, Italy, Germany, Canada, the Dominican Republic, Mexico, República Bolivariana de Venezuela, Haiti, Chile

SKILLED EMIGRATION, 2000

- Emigration rate of tertiary-educated population: **28.7%**
- Emigration of physicians: **2,592** or **3.8%** of physicians trained in the country (Source: Bhargava, Docquier, and Moullan 2010)

IMMIGRATION, 2010

- Stock of immigrants: **15.3 thousands**
- Stock of immigrants as percentage of population: **0.1%**
- Females as percentage of immigrants: **28.9%**
- Refugees as percentage of immigrants: **4.2%**
- Top source countries: Spain, the Russian Federation, Haiti, Ukraine, the United States, Mexico, Germany, China, Jamaica, Nicaragua

Remittances

Remittance data are currently not available for this country.

Cyprus

Population (millions, 2009)	0.9
Population growth (avg. annual %, 2000-09)	1.2
Population density (people per km², 2008)	93.5
Labor force (millions, 2008)	0.4
Unemployment rate (% of labor force, 2008)	3.7
Urban population (% of pop., 2009)	70.1
Surface area (1,000 km², 2008)	9.3
GNI (US$ billions, 2009)	—
GNI per capita, Atlas method (US$, 2009)	—
GDP growth (avg. annual %, 2005-09)	4.0
Poverty headcount ratio at national poverty line (% of pop., 2005)	—
Age dependency ratio (2009)	44.5

Migration

EMIGRATION, 2010

- Stock of emigrants: **149.6 thousands**
- Stock of emigrants as percentage of population: **17.0%**
- Top destination countries: the United Kingdom, Australia, Greece, Turkey, the United States, Canada, Germany, France, Jordan, Sweden

SKILLED EMIGRATION, 2000

- Emigration rate of tertiary-educated population: **31.2%**

IMMIGRATION, 2010

- Stock of immigrants: **154.3 thousands**
- Stock of immigrants as percentage of population: **17.5%**
- Females as percentage of immigrants: **57.2%**
- Refugees as percentage of immigrants: **0.7%**
- Top source countries: the United Kingdom, Greece, Georgia, the Russian Federation, Sri Lanka, the Philippines, Bulgaria, Romania, the Arab Republic of Egypt, South Africa

Remittances

US$ millions	2003	2004	2005	2006	2007	2008	2009	2010e
Inward remittance flows[a]	**84**	**245**	**189**	**169**	**172**	**279**	**153**	**146**
of which								
Workers' remittances	6	44	51	70	99	170	91	—
Compensation of employees	25	33	54	35	44	88	39	—
Migrants' transfers	52	168	85	65	30	21	23	—
Outward remittance flows	**202**	**255**	**273**	**279**	**370**	**577**	**409**	**—**
of which								
Workers' remittances	47	54	55	55	81	115	120	—
Compensation of employees	137	159	185	184	223	408	241	—
Migrants' transfers	18	42	33	39	66	54	48	—

a. For comparison: net FDI inflows US$3.9 bn, total international reserves US$1.0 bn, exports of goods and services US$11.7 bn in 2008.

Czech Republic

Population (millions, 2009)	10.5
Population growth (avg. annual %, 2000–09)	0.2
Population density (people per km², 2008)	135.0
Labor force (millions, 2008)	5.2
Unemployment rate (% of labor force, 2008)	4.4
Urban population (% of pop., 2009)	73.5
Surface area (1,000 km², 2008)	78.9
GNI (US$ billions, 2009)	178.1
GNI per capita, Atlas method (US$, 2009)	17,310
GDP growth (avg. annual %, 2005–09)	3.5
Poverty headcount ratio at national poverty line (% of pop., 2005)	0.0
Age dependency ratio (2009)	40.9

Migration

EMIGRATION, 2010

- Stock of emigrants: **370.6 thousands**
- Stock of emigrants as percentage of population: **3.6%**
- Top destination countries: the Slovak Republic, Germany, Austria, the United States, Canada, the United Kingdom, Israel, Australia, Switzerland, Spain

SKILLED EMIGRATION, 2000

- Emigration rate of tertiary-educated population: **10.4%**
- Emigration of physicians: **1,921** or **5.2%** of physicians trained in the country *(Source: Bhargava, Docquier, and Moullan 2010)*

IMMIGRATION, 2010

- Stock of immigrants: **453.0 thousands**
- Stock of immigrants as percentage of population: **4.4%**
- Females as percentage of immigrants: **53.2%**
- Refugees as percentage of immigrants: **0.4%**
- Top source countries: the Slovak Republic, Ukraine, Poland, Vietnam, the Russian Federation, Romania, Germany, Austria, Hungary, Bulgaria

Remittances

US$ millions	2003	2004	2005	2006	2007	2008	2009	2010e
Inward remittance flows[a]	**498**	**815**	**1,026**	**1,190**	**1,332**	**1,360**	**1,201**	**1,263**
of which								
Workers' remittances	–	–	100	128	150	168	96	–
Compensation of employees	494	805	917	1,054	1,174	1,234	1,094	–
Migrants' transfers	5	9	9	8	9	13	10	–
Outward remittance flows	**1,102**	**1,431**	**1,677**	**1,481**	**2,069**	**2,948**	**2,562**	–
of which								
Workers' remittances	–	–	291	462	630	590	747	–
Compensation of employees	1,100	1,426	1,384	1,016	1,437	2,355	1,799	–
Migrants' transfers	3	5	2	3	2	3	16	–

a. For comparison: net FDI inflows US$10.9 bn, total international reserves US$37.0 bn, exports of goods and services US$166.1 bn in 2008.

Denmark

Population (millions, 2009)	5.5
Population growth (avg. annual %, 2000–09)	0.4
Population density (people per km², 2008)	129.6
Labor force (millions, 2008)	2.9
Unemployment rate (% of labor force, 2008)	3.3
Urban population (% of pop., 2009)	86.9
Surface area (1,000 km², 2008)	43.1
GNI (US$ billions, 2009)	317.6
GNI per capita, Atlas method (US$, 2009)	58,930
GDP growth (avg. annual %, 2005–09)	0.4
Poverty headcount ratio at national poverty line (% of pop., 2005)	—
Age dependency ratio (2009)	52.7

Migration

EMIGRATION, 2010

- Stock of emigrants: **259.6 thousands**
- Stock of emigrants as percentage of population: **4.7%**
- Top destination countries: Sweden, the United States, Germany, Norway, Canada, the United Kingdom, Spain, Australia, France, Iceland

SKILLED EMIGRATION, 2000

- Emigration rate of tertiary-educated population: **7.7%**
- Emigration of physicians: **955** or **5.0%** of physicians trained in the country *(Source: Bhargava, Docquier, and Moullan 2010)*

IMMIGRATION, 2010

- Stock of immigrants: **483.7 thousands**
- Stock of immigrants as percentage of population: **8.8%**
- Females as percentage of immigrants: **59.9%**
- Refugees as percentage of immigrants: **7.7%**
- Top source countries: Turkey, Germany, Iraq, Poland, Bosnia and Herzegovina, Norway, Sweden, Lebanon, the Islamic Republic of Iran, the United Kingdom

Remittances

US$ millions	2003	2004	2005	2006	2007	2008	2009	2010e
Inward remittance flows[a]	**941**	**1,075**	**867**	**982**	**819**	**903**	**926**	**952**
of which								
Workers' remittances	—	—	—	—	—	—	—	—
Compensation of employees	941	1,075	867	982	819	903	926	—
Migrants' transfers	—	—	—	—	—	—	—	—
Outward remittance flows	**1,029**	**1,226**	**1,488**	**1,766**	**3,019**	**3,994**	**3,417**	**—**
of which								
Workers' remittances	—	—	—	—	—	—	—	—
Compensation of employees	1,029	1,226	1,488	1,766	3,019	3,222	—	—
Migrants' transfers	—	—	—	—	—	—	—	—

a. For comparison: net FDI inflows US$3.1 bn, total international reserves US$42.3 bn, exports of goods and services US$186.5 bn in 2008.

Djibouti

Population (millions, 2009)	0.9
Population growth (avg. annual %, 2000–09)	2.0
Population density (people per km², 2008)	36.6
Labor force (millions, 2008)	0.4
Unemployment rate (% of labor force, 2008)	—
Urban population (% of pop., 2009)	87.7
Surface area (1,000 km², 2008)	23.2
GNI (US$ billions, 2009)	1.1
GNI per capita, Atlas method (US$, 2009)	1,280
GDP growth (avg. annual %, 2005–09)	4.8
Poverty headcount ratio at national poverty line (% of pop., 2005)	18.6
Age dependency ratio (2009)	64.8

Migration

EMIGRATION, 2010

- Stock of emigrants: **13.5 thousands**
- Stock of emigrants as percentage of population: **1.5%**
- Top destination countries: France, Ethiopia, Canada, the Arab Republic of Egypt, the United Kingdom, the United States, Belgium, Germany, Australia, Italy

SKILLED EMIGRATION, 2000

- Emigration rate of tertiary-educated population: **11.0%**
- Emigration of physicians: **26** or **23.2%** of physicians born in the country *(Source: Clemens and Pettersson 2006)*
- Emigration of nurses: **9** or **2.1%** of nurses born in the country

IMMIGRATION, 2010

- Stock of immigrants: **114.1 thousands**
- Stock of immigrants as percentage of population: **13.0%**
- Females as percentage of immigrants: **45.9%**
- Refugees as percentage of immigrants: **7.0%**
- Top source countries: Somalia, Ethiopia, the Republic of Yemen

Remittances

US$ millions	2003	2004	2005	2006	2007	2008	2009	2010e
Inward remittance flows[a]	**25**	**25**	**26**	**28**	**29**	**30**	**28**	**28**
of which								
Workers' remittances	3	3	3	4	4	4	—	—
Compensation of employees	22	22	23	25	25	26	—	—
Migrants' transfers	—	—	—	—	—	—	—	—
Outward remittance flows	**5**	**5**	**5**	**5**	**5**	**5**	**5**	**—**
of which								
Workers' remittances	5	5	5	5	5	5	—	—
Compensation of employees	—	—	—	—	—	—	—	—
Migrants' transfers	—	—	—	—	—	—	—	—

a. For comparison: net FDI inflows US$0.3 bn, net ODA received US$0.1 bn, total international reserves US$0.2 bn in 2008.

Dominica

Population (thousands, 2009)	73.6
Population growth (avg. annual %, 2000–09)	0.3
Population density (people per km², 2008)	97.6
Labor force (millions, 2008)	—
Unemployment rate (% of labor force, 2008)	—
Urban population (% of pop., 2009)	74.3
Surface area (1,000 km², 2008)	0.8
GNI (US$ billions, 2009)	0.4
GNI per capita, Atlas method (US$, 2009)	4,870
GDP growth (avg. annual %, 2005–09)	3.4
Poverty headcount ratio at national poverty line (% of pop., 2005)	—
Age dependency ratio (2009)	—

Migration

EMIGRATION, 2010

- Stock of emigrants: **69.3 thousands**
- Stock of emigrants as percentage of population: **104.1%**[1]
- Top destination countries: the United States, the United Kingdom, Virgin Islands (U.S.), Antigua and Barbuda, Canada, Spain, Italy, France, Barbados, Greece

SKILLED EMIGRATION, 2000

- Emigration rate of tertiary-educated population: **64.2%**
- Emigration of physicians: **2,105** or **98.4%** of physicians trained in the country *(Source: Bhargava, Docquier, and Moullan 2010)*

IMMIGRATION, 2010

- Stock of immigrants: **5.5 thousands**
- Stock of immigrants as percentage of population: **8.3%**
- Females as percentage of immigrants: **45.6%**
- Refugees as percentage of immigrants: **0.0%**
- Top source countries: the United Kingdom, the United States, Antigua and Barbuda, Trinidad and Tobago, St. Lucia

Remittances

US$ millions	2003	2004	2005	2006	2007	2008	2009	2010e
Inward remittance flows[a]	**18**	**23**	**25**	**25**	**26**	**26**	**23**	**25**
of which								
Workers' remittances	—	—	—	—	—	—	—	—
Compensation of employees	14	18	20	21	22	22	19	—
Migrants' transfers	3	3	3	3	3	3	3	—
Outward remittance flows	**0**	**0**	**0**	**0**	**0**	**0**	**0**	—
of which								
Workers' remittances	—	—	—	—	—	—	—	—
Compensation of employees	—	—	—	—	—	—	—	—
Migrants' transfers	0	0	0	0	0	0	0	—

a. **For comparison: net FDI inflows US$0.1 bn, total international reserves US$0.1 bn, exports of goods and services US$0.1 bn in 2008.**

---

1. The stock of emigrants as percentage of population is defined as the ratio of emigrants of a country to the population—not the sum of population and migrants. Because of this definition, this ratio may exceed 100 percent in certain cases (e.g., Dominica.)

Dominican Republic

Latin America and the Caribbean	UPPER MIDDLE INCOME
Population (millions, 2009)	10.1
Population growth (avg. annual %, 2000–09)	1.5
Population density (people per km², 2008)	203.3
Labor force (millions, 2008)	4.3
Unemployment rate (% of labor force, 2008)	–
Urban population (% of pop., 2009)	69.8
Surface area (1,000 km², 2008)	48.7
GNI (US$ billions, 2009)	44.7
GNI per capita, Atlas method (US$, 2009)	4,510
GDP growth (avg. annual %, 2005–09)	7.4
Poverty headcount ratio at national poverty line (% of pop., 2005)	5.0
Age dependency ratio (2009)	59.9

Migration

EMIGRATION, 2010

- Stock of emigrants: **1,035.8 thousands**
- Stock of emigrants as percentage of population: **10.1%**
- Top destination countries: the United States, Spain, Italy, República Bolivariana de Venezuela, Netherlands Antilles, Haiti, Panama, Germany, Canada, the Netherlands

SKILLED EMIGRATION, 2000

- Emigration rate of tertiary-educated population: **21.6%**
- Emigration of physicians: **6,725** or **30.0%** of physicians trained in the country *(Source: Bhargava, Docquier, and Moullan 2010)*

IMMIGRATION, 2010

- Stock of immigrants: **434.3 thousands**
- Stock of immigrants as percentage of population: **4.2%**
- Females as percentage of immigrants: **41.0%**
- Refugees as percentage of immigrants: **0.0%**
- Top source countries: Haiti, República Bolivariana de Venezuela, the United States, Puerto Rico, Spain, Italy, Cuba, Germany, Colombia, Canada

Remittances

US$ millions	2003	2004	2005	2006	2007	2008	2009	2010e
Inward remittance flows[a]	**2,325**	**2,501**	**2,719**	**3,084**	**3,427**	**3,556**	**3,477**	**3,373**
of which								
Workers' remittances	2,061	2,230	2,430	2,738	3,046	3,111	3,042	–
Compensation of employees	265	271	289	316	351	384	373	–
Migrants' transfers	–	–	–	31	30	61	52	–
Outward remittance flows	**23**	**24**	**25**	**27**	**28**	**35**	**29**	**–**
of which								
Workers' remittances	–	–	–	–	–	–	–	–
Compensation of employees	23	24	25	27	28	35	29	–
Migrants' transfers	–	–	–	–	–	–	–	–

a. For comparison: net FDI inflows US$2.9 bn, net ODA received US$0.2 bn, total international reserves US$2.3 bn, exports of goods and services US$11.8 bn in 2008.

Ecuador

Latin America and the Caribbean	LOWER MIDDLE INCOME
Population (millions, 2009)	13.6
Population growth (avg. annual %, 2000–09)	1.1
Population density (people per km², 2008)	48.7
Labor force (millions, 2008)	5.9
Unemployment rate (% of labor force, 2008)	6.9
Urban population (% of pop., 2009)	66.2
Surface area (1,000 km², 2008)	283.6
GNI (US$ billions, 2009)	55.6
GNI per capita, Atlas method (US$, 2009)	3,920
GDP growth (avg. annual %, 2005–09)	4.3
Poverty headcount ratio at national poverty line (% of pop., 2005)	9.8
Age dependency ratio (2009)	60.2

Migration

EMIGRATION, 2010

- Stock of emigrants: **1,147.8 thousands**
- Stock of emigrants as percentage of population: **8.3%**
- Top destination countries: Spain, the United States, Italy, República Bolivariana de Venezuela, Chile, Canada, Colombia, Germany, the United Kingdom, Panama

SKILLED EMIGRATION, 2000

- Emigration rate of tertiary-educated population: **9.5%**
- Emigration of physicians: **508** or **2.7%** of physicians trained in the country *(Source: Bhargava, Docquier, and Moullan 2010)*

IMMIGRATION, 2010

- Stock of immigrants: **393.6 thousands**
- Stock of immigrants as percentage of population: **2.9%**
- Females as percentage of immigrants: **48.4%**
- Refugees as percentage of immigrants: **66.9%**
- Top source countries: Colombia, the United States, Peru, Chile, República Bolivariana de Venezuela, Spain, Argentina, Germany, Italy, Cuba

Remittances

US$ millions	2003	2004	2005	2006	2007	2008	2009	2010e
Inward remittance flows[a]	**1,633**	**1,838**	**2,460**	**2,934**	**3,094**	**2,828**	**2,502**	**2,548**
of which								
Workers' remittances	1,627	1,832	2,454	2,928	3,088	2,822	2,495	–
Compensation of employees	6	6	7	6	6	6	7	–
Migrants' transfers	–	–	–	–	–	–	–	–
Outward remittance flows	**7**	**7**	**54**	**62**	**83**	**66**	**81**	**–**
of which								
Workers' remittances	–	–	48	57	78	60	–	–
Compensation of employees	7	7	6	5	5	6	–	–
Migrants' transfers	–	–	–	–	–	–	–	–

a. For comparison: net FDI inflows US$1.0 bn, net ODA received US$0.2 bn, total international reserves US$4.5 bn, exports of goods and services US$20.7 bn in 2008.

Egypt, Arab Republic of

Population (millions, 2009)	83.0
Population growth (avg. annual %, 2000–09)	1.9
Population density (people per km², 2008)	81.9
Labor force (millions, 2008)	25.5
Unemployment rate (% of labor force, 2008)	8.7
Urban population (% of pop., 2009)	42.6
Surface area (1,000 km², 2008)	1,001.5
GNI (US$ billions, 2009)	188.5
GNI per capita, Atlas method (US$, 2009)	2,070
GDP growth (avg. annual %, 2005–09)	6,0
Poverty headcount ratio at national poverty line (% of pop., 2005)	2.0
Age dependency ratio (2009)	58.4

Migration

EMIGRATION, 2010

- Stock of emigrants: **3,739.1 thousands**
- Stock of emigrants as percentage of population: **4.4%**
- Top destination countries: Saudi Arabia, Jordan, Libya, Kuwait, the United Arab Emirates, the United States, West Bank and Gaza, Italy, Qatar, the Republic of Yemen

SKILLED EMIGRATION, 2000

- Emigration rate of tertiary-educated population: **4.6%**
- Emigration of physicians:
  - (a) **7,791** or **5.4%** of physicians trained in the country *(Source: Bhargava, Docquier, and Moullan 2010)*
  - (b) **7,119** or **4.7%** of physicians born in the country *(Source: Clemens and Pettersson 2006)*
- Emigration of nurses: **992** or **0.5%** of nurses born in the country

IMMIGRATION, 2010

- Stock of immigrants: **244.7 thousands**
- Stock of immigrants as percentage of population: **0.3%**
- Females as percentage of immigrants: **46.6%**
- Refugees as percentage of immigrants: **37.9%**
- Top source countries: West Bank and Gaza, Somalia, Iraq, Saudi Arabia, Libya, Jordan, Sudan, Indonesia, Lebanon, Kuwait

Remittances

US$ millions	2003	2004	2005	2006	2007	2008	2009	2010e
Inward remittance flows[a]	**2,961**	**3,341**	**5,017**	**5,330**	**7,656**	**8,694**	**7,150**	**7,681**
of which								
Workers' remittances	2,961	3,341	5,017	5,330	7,656	8,694	7,150	–
Compensation of employees	–	–	–	–	–	–	–	–
Migrants' transfers	–	–	–	–	–	–	–	–
Outward remittance flows	**79**	**13**	**57**	**135**	**180**	**241**	**255**	**–**
of which								
Workers' remittances	79	13	57	135	180	241	255	–
Compensation of employees	–	–	–	–	–	–	–	–
Migrants' transfers	–	–	–	–	–	–	–	–

a. **For comparison: net FDI inflows US$9.5 bn, net ODA received US$1.3 bn, total international reserves US$34.3 bn, exports of goods and services US$53.8 bn in 2008.**

El Salvador

Population (millions, 2009)	6.2
Population growth (avg. annual %, 2000–09)	0.4
Population density (people per km², 2008)	296.0
Labor force (millions, 2008)	2.5
Unemployment rate (% of labor force, 2008)	–
Urban population (% of pop., 2009)	61.0
Surface area (1,000 km², 2008)	21.0
GNI (US$ billions, 2009)	21.0
GNI per capita, Atlas method (US$, 2009)	3,370
GDP growth (avg. annual %, 2005–09)	2.4
Poverty headcount ratio at national poverty line (% of pop., 2005)	13.5
Age dependency ratio (2009)	65.2

Migration

EMIGRATION, 2010

- Stock of emigrants: **1,269.1 thousands**
- Stock of emigrants as percentage of population: **20.5%**
- Top destination countries: the United States, Canada, Guatemala, Costa Rica, Australia, Belize, Spain, Italy, Mexico, Honduras

SKILLED EMIGRATION, 2000

- Emigration rate of tertiary-educated population: **31.0%**
- Emigration of physicians: **368** or **4.7%** of physicians trained in the country *(Source: Bhargava, Docquier, and Moullan 2010)*

IMMIGRATION, 2010

- Stock of immigrants: **40.3 thousands**
- Stock of immigrants as percentage of population: **0.7%**
- Females as percentage of immigrants: **52.5%**
- Refugees as percentage of immigrants: **0.1%**
- Top source countries: Honduras, Guatemala, Nicaragua, the United States, Mexico, Costa Rica, Colombia, Spain, Panama, Belize

Remittances

US$ millions	2003	2004	2005	2006	2007	2008	2009	2010e
Inward remittance flows[a]	**2,122**	**2,564**	**3,030**	**3,485**	**3,712**	**3,804**	**3,531**	**3,648**
of which								
Workers' remittances	2,105	2,548	3,017	3,471	3,695	3,788	–	–
Compensation of employees	16	15	11	12	14	13	–	–
Migrants' transfers	1	1	1	2	3	3	–	–
Outward remittance flows	**25**	**33**	**24**	**28**	**29**	**19**	**19**	**–**
of which								
Workers' remittances	–	–	–	–	–	–	–	–
Compensation of employees	24	32	24	28	28	19	–	–
Migrants' transfers	1	1	0	1	1	1	–	–

a. **For comparison: net FDI inflows US$0.8 bn, net ODA received US$0.2 bn, total international reserves US$2.6 bn, exports of goods and services US$6.1 bn in 2008.**

Equatorial Guinea

Population (millions, 2009)	0.7
Population growth (avg. annual %, 2000–09)	2.8
Population density (people per km², 2008)	23.5
Labor force (millions, 2008)	0.3
Unemployment rate (% of labor force, 2008)	–
Urban population (% of pop., 2009)	39.5
Surface area (1,000 km², 2008)	28.1
GNI (US$ billions, 2009)	6.3
GNI per capita, Atlas method (US$, 2009)	12,420
GDP growth (avg. annual %, 2005–09)	7.7
Poverty headcount ratio at national poverty line (% of pop., 2005)	–
Age dependency ratio (2009)	78.2

Migration

EMIGRATION, 2010

- Stock of emigrants: **103.1 thousands**
- Stock of emigrants as percentage of population: **14.9%**
- Top destination countries: Gabon, Spain, Nigeria, the Republic of Congo, the United States, São Tomé and Principe, Germany, the Central African Republic, France, Portugal

SKILLED EMIGRATION, 2000

- Emigration rate of tertiary-educated population: **13.0%**
- Emigration of physicians:
  - (a) **1** or **0.9%** of physicians trained in the country *(Source: Bhargava, Docquier, and Moullan 2010)*
  - (b) **81** or **63.3%** of physicians born in the country *(Source: Clemens and Pettersson 2006)*
- Emigration of nurses: **98** or **37.7%** of nurses born in the country

IMMIGRATION, 2010

- Stock of immigrants: **7.4 thousands**
- Stock of immigrants as percentage of population: **1.1%**
- Females as percentage of immigrants: **47.0%**
- Refugees as percentage of immigrants: **0.0%**
- Top source countries: Cameroon, Nigeria, Spain, France

Remittances

Remittance data are currently not available for this country.

Eritrea

Sub-Saharan Africa	LOW INCOME
Population (millions, 2009)	5.1
Population growth (avg. annual %, 2000–09)	3.6
Population density (people per km², 2008)	49.5
Labor force (millions, 2008)	2.0
Unemployment rate (% of labor force, 2008)	–
Urban population (% of pop., 2009)	21.2
Surface area (1,000 km², 2008)	117.6
GNI (US$ billions, 2009)	1.6
GNI per capita, Atlas method (US$, 2009)	–
GDP growth (avg. annual %, 2005–09)	–
Poverty headcount ratio at national poverty line (% of pop., 2005)	–
Age dependency ratio (2009)	78.5

Migration

EMIGRATION, 2010

- Stock of emigrants: **941.2 thousands**
- Stock of emigrants as percentage of population: **18.0%**
- Top destination countries: Sudan, Ethiopia, Saudi Arabia, Italy, the United States, the United Kingdom, Canada, Germany, Sweden, Australia

SKILLED EMIGRATION, 2000

- Emigration rate of tertiary-educated population: **34.0%**
- Emigration of physicians: 98 or 36.2% of physicians born in the country *(Source: Clemens and Pettersson 2006)*
- Emigration of nurses: **497** or **38.0%** of nurses born in the country

IMMIGRATION, 2010

- Stock of immigrants: **16.5 thousands**
- Stock of immigrants as percentage of population: **0.3%**
- Females as percentage of immigrants: **45.9%**
- Refugees as percentage of immigrants: **29.3%**

Remittances

Remittance data are currently not available for this country.

Estonia

Population (millions, 2009)	1.3
Population growth (avg. annual %, 2000–09)	-0.3
Population density (people per km², 2008)	31.6
Labor force (millions, 2008)	0.7
Unemployment rate (% of labor force, 2008)	5.5
Urban population (% of pop., 2009)	69.5
Surface area (1,000 km², 2008)	45.2
GNI (US$ billions, 2009)	18.5
GNI per capita, Atlas method (US$, 2009)	14,060
GDP growth (avg. annual %, 2005–09)	1.8
Poverty headcount ratio at national poverty line (% of pop., 2005)	0.0
Age dependency ratio (2009)	47.3

Migration

EMIGRATION, 2010

- Stock of emigrants: **169.5 thousands**
- Stock of emigrants as percentage of population: **12.7%**
- Top destination countries: the Russian Federation, Finland, Sweden, the United States, Israel, Canada, Germany, Latvia, Ireland, the United Kingdom

SKILLED EMIGRATION, 2000

- Emigration rate of tertiary-educated population: **11.5%**
- Emigration of physicians: **222** or **4.8%** of physicians trained in the country
  (Source: Bhargava, Docquier, and Moullan 2010)

IMMIGRATION, 2010

- Stock of immigrants: **182.5 thousands**
- Stock of immigrants as percentage of population: **13.6%**
- Females as percentage of immigrants: **59.6%**
- Refugees as percentage of immigrants: **0.0%**
- Top source countries: the Russian Federation, Ukraine, Belarus, Latvia, Lithuania, Finland

Remittances

US$ millions	2003	2004	2005	2006	2007	2008	2009	2010e
Inward remittance flows[a]	**51**	**167**	**264**	**402**	**426**	**398**	**325**	**342**
of which								
Workers' remittances	9	12	10	10	30	60	57	–
Compensation of employees	42	155	255	392	396	338	268	–
Migrants' transfers	–	–	–	–	–	–	–	–
Outward remittance flows	**19**	**26**	**50**	**75**	**96**	**105**	**81**	**–**
of which								
Workers' remittances	2	1	1	2	2	2	2	–
Compensation of employees	16	25	49	74	94	103	78	–
Migrants' transfers	–	–	–	–	–	–	–	–

a. For comparison: net FDI inflows US$1.9 bn, total international reserves US$4.0 bn, exports of goods and services US$17.7 bn in 2008.

Ethiopia

Population (millions, 2009)	82.8
Population growth (avg. annual %, 2000–09)	2.6
Population density (people per km², 2008)	80.7
Labor force (millions, 2008)	37.4
Unemployment rate (% of labor force, 2008)	–
Urban population (% of pop., 2009)	17.3
Surface area (1,000 km², 2008)	1,104.3
GNI (US$ billions, 2009)	28.5
GNI per capita, Atlas method (US$, 2009)	330
GDP growth (avg. annual %, 2005–09)	10.7
Poverty headcount ratio at national poverty line (% of pop., 2005)	39.0
Age dependency ratio (2009)	87.6

Migration

EMIGRATION, 2010

- Stock of emigrants: **620.1 thousands**
- Stock of emigrants as percentage of population: **0.7%**
- Top destination countries: Sudan, the United States, Israel, Djibouti, Kenya, Saudi Arabia, Canada, Germany, Italy, Sweden

SKILLED EMIGRATION, 2000

- Emigration rate of tertiary-educated population: **10.1%**
- Emigration of physicians:
  - (a) **478** or **26.4%** of physicians trained in the country *(Source: Bhargava, Docquier, and Moullan 2010)*
  - (b) **553** or **29.7%** of physicians born in the country *(Source: Clemens and Pettersson 2006)*
- Emigration of nurses: **1,077** or **16.8%** of nurses born in the country

IMMIGRATION, 2010

- Stock of immigrants: **548.0 thousands**
- Stock of immigrants as percentage of population: **0.6%**
- Females as percentage of immigrants: **47.1%**
- Refugees as percentage of immigrants: **16.6%**
- Top source countries: Eritrea, Somalia, Sudan, Djibouti, Kenya

Remittances

US$ millions	2003	2004	2005	2006	2007	2008	2009	2010e
Inward remittance flows[a]	**46**	**134**	**174**	**172**	**358**	**387**	**353**	**387**
of which								
Workers' remittances	46	134	174	169	356	387	–	–
Compensation of employees	–	–	–	3	2	0	–	–
Migrants' transfers	–	–	–	–	–	–	–	–
Outward remittance flows	**17**	**9**	**16**	**14**	**15**	**21**	**21**	**–**
of which								
Workers' remittances	17	9	16	14	15	21	–	–
Compensation of employees	1	–	–	–	–	0	–	–
Migrants' transfers	–	–	–	–	–	–	–	–

a. For comparison: net FDI inflows US$0.1 bn, net ODA received US$3.3 bn, total international reserves US$0.9 bn, exports of goods and services US$2.9 bn in 2008.

Faeroe Islands

Population (thousands, 2009)	48.6
Population growth (avg. annual %, 2000–09)	0.8
Population density (people per km², 2008)	34.7
Labor force (millions, 2008)	—
Unemployment rate (% of labor force, 2008)	—
Urban population (% of pop., 2009)	42.0
Surface area (1,000 km², 2008)	1.4
GNI (US$ billions, 2009)	—
GNI per capita, Atlas method (US$, 2009)	—
GDP growth (avg. annual %, 2005–09)	—
Poverty headcount ratio at national poverty line (% of pop., 2005)	—
Age dependency ratio (2009)	—

Migration

EMIGRATION, 2010

- Stock of emigrants: **0.8 thousands**
- Stock of emigrants as percentage of population: **1.5%**
- Top destination countries: Iceland, Australia, Panama, New Zealand, Ecuador, the Netherlands, Greece, Mexico, Uruguay

SKILLED EMIGRATION, 2000

- Skilled emigration data are currently not available for this country.

IMMIGRATION, 2010

- Stock of immigrants: **3.3 thousands**
- Stock of immigrants as percentage of population: **6.5%**
- Females as percentage of immigrants: **43.8%**
- Refugees as percentage of immigrants: **0.0%**
- Top source countries: Denmark, Iceland

Remittances

Remittance data are currently not available for this country.

Fiji

Population (millions, 2009)	0.8
Population growth (avg. annual %, 2000–09)	0.6
Population density (people per km², 2008)	45.9
Labor force (millions, 2008)	0.3
Unemployment rate (% of labor force, 2008)	–
Urban population (% of pop., 2009)	52.9
Surface area (1,000 km², 2008)	18.3
GNI (US$ billions, 2009)	3.0
GNI per capita, Atlas method (US$, 2009)	3,950
GDP growth (avg. annual %, 2005–09)	-0.1
Poverty headcount ratio at national poverty line (% of pop., 2005)	–
Age dependency ratio (2009)	56.6

Migration

EMIGRATION, 2010

- Stock of emigrants: **182.2 thousands**
- Stock of emigrants as percentage of population: **21.3%**
- Top destination countries: Australia, the United States, New Zealand, Canada, the United Kingdom, New Caledonia, the Solomon Islands, Samoa, Japan, India

SKILLED EMIGRATION, 2000

- Emigration rate of tertiary-educated population: **62.2%**
- Emigration of physicians: **190** or **41.0%** of physicians trained in the country *(Source: Bhargava, Docquier, and Moullan 2010)*

IMMIGRATION, 2010

- Stock of immigrants: **18.5 thousands**
- Stock of immigrants as percentage of population: **2.2%**
- Females as percentage of immigrants: **47.8%**
- Refugees as percentage of immigrants: **0.0%**
- Top source countries: India, Australia, New Zealand, the United Kingdom, Papua New Guinea, French Polynesia, Samoa, Guam, Pakistan, Bangladesh

Remittances

US$ millions	2003	2004	2005	2006	2007	2008	2009	2010e
Inward remittance flows[a]	**124**	**173**	**185**	**185**	**160**	**123**	**113**	**128**
of which								
Workers' remittances	54	55	134	144	115	73	–	–
Compensation of employees	70	117	49	39	45	50	–	–
Migrants' transfers	1	1	2	1	0	1	–	–
Outward remittance flows	**26**	**42**	**34**	**32**	**31**	**44**	**44**	**–**
of which								
Workers' remittances	2	14	5	5	4	5	–	–
Compensation of employees	2	2	3	5	5	8	–	–
Migrants' transfers	22	26	26	22	22	31	–	–

a. For comparison: net FDI inflows US$0.3 bn in 2008.

Finland

Population (millions, 2009)	5.3
Population growth (avg. annual %, 2000–09)	0.3
Population density (people per km², 2008)	17.4
Labor force (millions, 2008)	2.7
Unemployment rate (% of labor force, 2008)	6.4
Urban population (% of pop., 2009)	63.6
Surface area (1,000 km², 2008)	338.2
GNI (US$ billions, 2009)	236.0
GNI per capita, Atlas method (US$, 2009)	45,680
GDP growth (avg. annual %, 2005–09)	1.1
Poverty headcount ratio at national poverty line (% of pop., 2005)	—
Age dependency ratio (2009)	50.3

Migration

EMIGRATION, 2010

- Stock of emigrants: **329.5 thousands**
- Stock of emigrants as percentage of population: **6.2%**
- Top destination countries: Sweden, Germany, the United Kingdom, Canada, the United States, Spain, Norway, Australia, Switzerland, Denmark

SKILLED EMIGRATION, 2000

- Emigration rate of tertiary-educated population: **7.5%**
- Emigration of physicians: **816** or **4.9%** of physicians trained in the country
  (Source: Bhargava, Docquier, and Moullan 2010)

IMMIGRATION, 2010

- Stock of immigrants: **225.6 thousands**
- Stock of immigrants as percentage of population: **4.2%**
- Females as percentage of immigrants: **47.7%**
- Refugees as percentage of immigrants: **3.8%**
- Top source countries: Sweden, Estonia, the Russian Federation, Somalia, Germany, China, Iraq, Thailand, Turkey, the United Kingdom

Remittances

US$ millions	2003	2004	2005	2006	2007	2008	2009	2010e
Inward remittance flows[a]	**526**	**666**	**693**	**698**	**762**	**818**	**797**	**872**
of which								
Workers' remittances	—	—	—	—	—	—	—	—
Compensation of employees	526	666	693	698	762	818	797	—
Migrants' transfers	—	—	—	—	—	—	—	—
Outward remittance flows	**149**	**225**	**266**	**331**	**391**	**457**	**436**	**—**
of which								
Workers' remittances	—	—	17	22	24	30	25	—
Compensation of employees	149	225	249	309	367	428	411	—
Migrants' transfers	—	—	—	—	—	—	—	—

a. For comparison: net FDI inflows US$−7.8 bn, total international reserves US$8.4 bn, exports of goods and services US$120.4 bn in 2008.

France

	HIGH-INCOME OECD
Population (millions, 2009)	62.6
Population growth (avg. annual %, 2000–09)	0.7
Population density (people per km², 2008)	112.8
Labor force (millions, 2008)	28.0
Unemployment rate (% of labor force, 2008)	7.4
Urban population (% of pop., 2009)	77.6
Surface area (1,000 km², 2008)	551.5
GNI (US$ billions, 2009)	2,674.8
GNI per capita, Atlas method (US$, 2009)	42,680
GDP growth (avg. annual %, 2005–09)	0.8
Poverty headcount ratio at national poverty line (% of pop., 2005)	—
Age dependency ratio (2009)	54.2

Migration

EMIGRATION, 2010

- Stock of emigrants: **1,742.1 thousands**
- Stock of emigrants as percentage of population: **2.8%**
- Top destination countries: Spain, Belgium, Germany, the United States, Portugal, the United Kingdom, Switzerland, Canada, Israel, Italy

SKILLED EMIGRATION, 2000

- Emigration rate of tertiary-educated population: **3.4%**
- Emigration of physicians: **4,039** or **2.0%** of physicians trained in the country *(Source: Bhargava, Docquier, and Moullan 2010)*

IMMIGRATION, 2010

- Stock of immigrants: **6,684.8 thousands**
- Stock of immigrants as percentage of population: **10.7%**
- Females as percentage of immigrants: **51.3%**
- Refugees as percentage of immigrants: **2.2%**
- Top source countries: Algeria, Morocco, Portugal, Italy, Spain, Tunisia, Turkey, the United Kingdom, Germany, Belgium

Remittances

US$ millions	2003	2004	2005	2006	2007	2008	2009	2010e
Inward remittance flows[a]	**11,311**	**12,277**	**11,945**	**13,031**	**14,445**	**16,408**	**15,551**	**15,939**
of which								
Workers' remittances	451	460	512	1,143	1,220	1,205	1,085	—
Compensation of employees	10,860	11,817	11,434	11,888	13,225	15,203	14,466	—
Migrants' transfers	—	—	—	—	—	—	—	—
Outward remittance flows	**4,388**	**4,262**	**4,182**	**5,511**	**5,998**	**6,334**	**5,224**	—
of which								
Workers' remittances	2,851	3,093	3,110	4,383	4,712	5,011	3,973	—
Compensation of employees	1,537	1,169	1,072	1,128	1,286	1,323	1,251	—
Migrants' transfers	—	—	—	—	—	—	—	—

a. For comparison: net FDI inflows US$100.4 bn, total international reserves US$103.3 bn, exports of goods and services US$755.3 bn in 2008.

French Polynesia

Population (millions, 2009)	0.3
Population growth (avg. annual %, 2000–09)	1.5
Population density (people per km², 2008)	72.7
Labor force (millions, 2008)	0.1
Unemployment rate (% of labor force, 2008)	–
Urban population (% of pop., 2009)	51.6
Surface area (1,000 km², 2008)	4.0
GNI (US$ billions, 2009)	–
GNI per capita, Atlas method (US$, 2009)	–
GDP growth (avg. annual %, 2005–09)	–
Poverty headcount ratio at national poverty line (% of pop., 2005)	–
Age dependency ratio (2009)	47.1

Migration

EMIGRATION, 2010

- Stock of emigrants: **4.2 thousands**
- Stock of emigrants as percentage of population: **1.5%**
- Top destination countries: New Caledonia, Fiji, New Zealand, Kiribati, Australia, Greece, the Netherlands, Chile, Mexico

SKILLED EMIGRATION, 2000

- Skilled emigration data are currently not available for this country.

IMMIGRATION, 2010

- Stock of immigrants: **34.8 thousands**
- Stock of immigrants as percentage of population: **12.8%**
- Females as percentage of immigrants: **45.4%**
- Refugees as percentage of immigrants: **0.0%**
- Top source countries: France, New Caledonia

Remittances

US$ millions	2003	2004	2005	2006	2007	2008	2009	2010e
Inward remittance flows	**509**	**598**	**557**	**622**	**689**	**751**	**690**	**771**
of which								
Workers' remittances	12	15	11	14	14	11	–	–
Compensation of employees	496	583	546	607	675	740	–	–
Migrants' transfers	–	–	–	–	–	–	–	–
Outward remittance flows	**51**	**46**	**47**	**51**	**56**	**69**	**69**	**–**
of which								
Workers' remittances	27	32	33	36	40	42	–	–
Compensation of employees	25	14	14	15	16	28	–	–
Migrants' transfers	–	–	–	–	–	–	–	–

Gabon

Population (millions, 2009)	1.5
Population growth (avg. annual %, 2000–09)	2.0
Population density (people per km², 2008)	5.6
Labor force (millions, 2008)	0.6
Unemployment rate (% of labor force, 2008)	–
Urban population (% of pop., 2009)	85.5
Surface area (1,000 km², 2008)	267.7
GNI (US$ billions, 2009)	9.5
GNI per capita, Atlas method (US$, 2009)	7,370
GDP growth (avg. annual %, 2005–09)	2.2
Poverty headcount ratio at national poverty line (% of pop., 2005)	4.8
Age dependency ratio (2009)	68.0

Migration

EMIGRATION, 2010

- Stock of emigrants: **25.2 thousands**
- Stock of emigrants as percentage of population: **1.7%**
- Top destination countries: France, Mali, the Republic of Congo, the United States, Canada, São Tomé and Principe, Germany, Belgium, Spain, Chad

SKILLED EMIGRATION, 2000

- Emigration rate of tertiary-educated population: **14.6%**
- Emigration of physicians:
  - (a) **4** or **1.1%** of physicians trained in the country *(Source: Bhargava, Docquier, and Moullan 2010)*
  - (b) **65** or **15.0%** of physicians born in the country *(Source: Clemens and Pettersson 2006)*
- Emigration of nurses: **107** or **6.4%** of nurses born in the country

IMMIGRATION, 2010

- Stock of immigrants: **284.1 thousands**
- Stock of immigrants as percentage of population: **18.9%**
- Females as percentage of immigrants: **43.0%**
- Refugees as percentage of immigrants: **3.0%**
- Top source countries: Equatorial Guinea, Cameroon, Benin, Mali, Senegal, Nigeria, the Republic of Congo, France, Togo, Burkina Faso

Remittances

US$ millions	2003	2004	2005	2006	2007	2008	2009	2010e
Inward remittance flows[a]	6	7	11	11	11	11	10	10
of which								
Workers' remittances	4	1	1	–	–	–	–	–
Compensation of employees	2	5	10	–	–	–	–	–
Migrants' transfers	–	–	–	–	–	–	–	–
Outward remittance flows	115	110	186	–	–	–	–	–
of which								
Workers' remittances	109	91	163	–	–	–	–	–
Compensation of employees	6	19	22	–	–	–	–	–
Migrants' transfers	–	–	–	–	–	–	–	–

a. For comparison: net ODA received US$0.1 bn, total international reserves US$1.9 bn, exports of goods and services US$9.7 bn in 2008.

Gambia, The

LOW INCOME

Population (millions, 2009)	1.7
Population growth (avg. annual %, 2000–09)	3.0
Population density (people per km², 2008)	166.0
Labor force (millions, 2008)	0.7
Unemployment rate (% of labor force, 2008)	–
Urban population (% of pop., 2009)	57.3
Surface area (1,000 km², 2008)	11.3
GNI (US$ billions, 2009)	0.7
GNI per capita, Atlas method (US$, 2009)	440
GDP growth (avg. annual %, 2005–09)	5.7
Poverty headcount ratio at national poverty line (% of pop., 2005)	31.3
Age dependency ratio (2009)	82.2

Migration

EMIGRATION, 2010

- Stock of emigrants: **64.9 thousands**
- Stock of emigrants as percentage of population: **3.7%**
- Top destination countries: Spain, the United States, Nigeria, Senegal, the United Kingdom, Germany, Sweden, Sierra Leone, Norway, France

SKILLED EMIGRATION, 2000

- Emigration rate of tertiary-educated population: **63.3%**
- Emigration of physicians: **46** or **53.5%** of physicians born in the country *(Source: Clemens and Pettersson 2006)*
- Emigration of nurses: **282** or **66.2%** of nurses born in the country

IMMIGRATION, 2010

- Stock of immigrants: **290.1 thousands**
- Stock of immigrants as percentage of population: **16.6%**
- Females as percentage of immigrants: **50.5%**
- Refugees as percentage of immigrants: **4.9%**
- Top source countries: Senegal, Guinea, Guinea-Bissau, Mali, Mauritania, Sierra Leone

Remittances

US$ millions	2003	2004	2005	2006	2007	2008	2009	2010e
Inward remittance flows[a]	65	62	57	64	63	67	60	61
of which								
Workers' remittances	64	61	57	63	61	57	–	–
Compensation of employees	1	1	1	1	2	9	–	–
Migrants' transfers	–	–	–	–	–	–	–	–
Outward remittance flows	1	1	1	1	1	3	3	–
of which								
Workers' remittances	–	–	–	–	–	2	–	–
Compensation of employees	1	1	1	1	1	1	–	–
Migrants' transfers	–	–	–	–	–	–	–	–

a. For comparison: net FDI inflows US$0.1 bn, net ODA received US$0.1 bn, total international reserves US$0.1 bn, exports of goods and services US$0.2 bn in 2008.

Georgia

Europe and Central Asia	LOWER MIDDLE INCOME
Population (millions, 2009)	4.3
Population growth (avg. annual %, 2000–09)	-1.2
Population density (people per km², 2008)	62.8
Labor force (millions, 2008)	2.3
Unemployment rate (% of labor force, 2008)	—
Urban population (% of pop., 2009)	52.8
Surface area (1,000 km², 2008)	69.7
GNI (US$ billions, 2009)	10.6
GNI per capita, Atlas method (US$, 2009)	2,530
GDP growth (avg. annual %, 2005–09)	5.9
Poverty headcount ratio at national poverty line (% of pop., 2005)	13.4
Age dependency ratio (2009)	45.3

Migration

EMIGRATION, 2010

- Stock of emigrants: **1,057.7 thousands**
- Stock of emigrants as percentage of population: **25.1%**
- Top destination countries: the Russian Federation, Armenia, Ukraine, Greece, Israel, the United States, Germany, Cyprus, Spain, Turkey

SKILLED EMIGRATION, 2000

- Emigration rate of tertiary-educated population: **1.6%**
- Emigration of physicians: **132** or **0.5%** of physicians trained in the country *(Source: Bhargava, Docquier, and Moullan 2010)*

IMMIGRATION, 2010

- Stock of immigrants: **167.3 thousands**
- Stock of immigrants as percentage of population: **4.0%**
- Females as percentage of immigrants: **57.1%**
- Refugees as percentage of immigrants: **0.7%**
- Top source countries: the Russian Federation, Armenia, Azerbaijan, Ukraine, Turkey, Germany, Pakistan, the United States, Greece, Bulgaria

Remittances

US$ millions	2003	2004	2005	2006	2007	2008	2009	2010e
Inward remittance flows[a]	**236**	**303**	**346**	**485**	**695**	**732**	**714**	**824**
of which								
Workers' remittances	64	64	94	153	245	305	317	—
Compensation of employees	168	236	247	315	406	419	391	—
Migrants' transfers	3	3	5	17	45	8	5	—
Outward remittance flows	**29**	**26**	**29**	**25**	**28**	**47**	**32**	**—**
of which								
Workers' remittances	6	7	8	4	2	2	2	—
Compensation of employees	16	15	18	20	26	44	30	—
Migrants' transfers	8	3	3	1	0	0	0	—

a. **For comparison: net FDI inflows US$1.6 bn, net ODA received US$0.9 bn, total international reserves US$1.5 bn, exports of goods and services US$3.7 bn in 2008.**

Germany

Population (millions, 2009)	81.9
Population growth (avg. annual %, 2000–09)	0.0
Population density (people per km², 2008)	235.5
Labor force (millions, 2008)	41.4
Unemployment rate (% of labor force, 2008)	7.5
Urban population (% of pop., 2009)	73.7
Surface area (1,000 km², 2008)	357.1
GNI (US$ billions, 2009)	3,394.1
GNI per capita, Atlas method (US$, 2009)	42,560
GDP growth (avg. annual %, 2005–09)	0.5
Poverty headcount ratio at national poverty line (% of pop., 2005)	—
Age dependency ratio (2009)	51.0

Migration

EMIGRATION, 2010

- Stock of emigrants: **3,540.6 thousands**
- Stock of emigrants as percentage of population: **4.3%**
- Top destination countries: the United States, Turkey, the United Kingdom, Spain, Switzerland, Austria, Canada, Kazakhstan, France, Australia

SKILLED EMIGRATION, 2000

- Emigration rate of tertiary-educated population: **5.2%**
- Emigration of physicians: **13,047** or **4.6%** of physicians trained in the country *(Source: Bhargava, Docquier, and Moullan 2010)*

IMMIGRATION, 2010

- Stock of immigrants: **10,758.1 thousands**
- Stock of immigrants as percentage of population: **13.1%**
- Females as percentage of immigrants: **46.7%**
- Refugees as percentage of immigrants: **5.5%**
- Top source countries: Turkey, Italy, Poland, Greece, Croatia, the Russian Federation, Austria, Bosnia and Herzegovina, the Netherlands, Ukraine

Remittances

US$ millions	2003	2004	2005	2006	2007	2008	2009	2010e
Inward remittance flows[a]	**5,783**	**6,581**	**6,933**	**7,567**	**9,898**	**10,908**	**10,879**	**11,559**
of which								
Workers' remittances	—	—	—	—	—	—	—	—
Compensation of employees	5,744	6,510	6,867	7,481	9,775	10,711	10,728	—
Migrants' transfers	40	71	66	86	124	198	151	—
Outward remittance flows	**11,190**	**12,069**	**12,499**	**12,546**	**13,882**	**14,951**	**15,924**	—
of which								
Workers' remittances	3,766	3,951	3,646	3,676	4,106	4,530	4,172	—
Compensation of employees	7,098	7,715	8,414	8,489	9,337	9,954	11,352	—
Migrants' transfers	326	403	438	382	439	468	400	—

a. For comparison: net FDI inflows US$21.2 bn, total international reserves US$138.6 bn, exports of goods and services US$1,724.2 bn in 2008.

Ghana

Sub-Saharan Africa	LOW INCOME
Population (millions, 2009)	23.8
Population growth (avg. annual %, 2000–09)	2.2
Population density (people per km², 2008)	102.6
Labor force (millions, 2008)	10.1
Unemployment rate (% of labor force, 2008)	–
Urban population (% of pop., 2009)	50.8
Surface area (1,000 km², 2008)	238.5
GNI (US$ billions, 2009)	15.3
GNI per capita, Atlas method (US$, 2009)	700
GDP growth (avg. annual %, 2005–09)	5.8
Poverty headcount ratio at national poverty line (% of pop., 2005)	30.0
Age dependency ratio (2009)	72.5

Migration

EMIGRATION, 2010

- Stock of emigrants: **824.9 thousands**
- Stock of emigrants as percentage of population: **3.4%**
- Top destination countries: Nigeria, Côte d'Ivoire, the United States, the United Kingdom, Burkina Faso, Italy, Togo, Germany, Canada, Liberia

SKILLED EMIGRATION, 2000

- Emigration rate of tertiary-educated population: **46.9%**
- Emigration of physicians:
  - (a) **924** or **37.1%** of physicians trained in the country *(Source: Bhargava, Docquier, and Moullan 2010)*
  - (b) **1,639** or **55.9%** of physicians born in the country *(Source: Clemens and Pettersson 2006)*
- Emigration of nurses: **4,766** or **24.1%** of nurses born in the country

IMMIGRATION, 2010

- Stock of immigrants: **1,851.8 thousands**
- Stock of immigrants as percentage of population: **7.6%**
- Females as percentage of immigrants: **41.8%**
- Refugees as percentage of immigrants: **2.2%**

Remittances

US$ millions	2003	2004	2005	2006	2007	2008	2009	2010e
Inward remittance flows[a]	**65**	**82**	**99**	**105**	**117**	**126**	**114**	**119**
of which								
Workers' remittances	65	82	99	105	117	126	114	–
Compensation of employees	–	–	–	–	–	–	–	–
Migrants' transfers	–	–	–	–	–	–	–	–
Outward remittance flows	**–**	**–**	**–**	**–**	**–**	**–**	**–**	**–**
of which								
Workers' remittances	–	–	–	–	–	–	–	–
Compensation of employees	–	–	–	–	–	–	–	–
Migrants' transfers	–	–	–	–	–	–	–	–

a. **For comparison: net FDI inflows US$2.1 bn, net ODA received US$1.3 bn, exports of goods and services US$7.1 bn in 2008.**

Greece

Population (millions, 2009)	11.3
Population growth (avg. annual %, 2000–09)	0.4
Population density (people per km², 2008)	87.2
Labor force (millions, 2008)	5.2
Unemployment rate (% of labor force, 2008)	7.7
Urban population (% of pop., 2009)	61.2
Surface area (1,000 km², 2008)	132.0
GNI (US$ billions, 2009)	316.3
GNI per capita, Atlas method (US$, 2009)	28,630
GDP growth (avg. annual %, 2005–09)	2.3
Poverty headcount ratio at national poverty line (% of pop., 2005)	–
Age dependency ratio (2009)	48.0

Migration

EMIGRATION, 2010

- Stock of emigrants: **1,210.3 thousands**
- Stock of emigrants as percentage of population: **10.8%**
- Top destination countries: Germany, the United States, Australia, Canada, Albania, Turkey, the United Kingdom, Cyprus, Israel, Belgium

SKILLED EMIGRATION, 2000

- Emigration rate of tertiary-educated population: **12.0%**
- Emigration of physicians: **4,886** or **9.4%** of physicians trained in the country *(Source: Bhargava, Docquier, and Moullan 2010)*

IMMIGRATION, 2010

- Stock of immigrants: **1,132.8 thousands**
- Stock of immigrants as percentage of population: **10.1%**
- Females as percentage of immigrants: **44.6%**
- Refugees as percentage of immigrants: **0.2%**
- Top source countries: Albania, Bulgaria, Romania, Georgia, the Russian Federation, Poland, Ukraine, Pakistan, Cyprus, the United Kingdom

Remittances

US$ millions	2003	2004	2005	2006	2007	2008	2009	2010e
Inward remittance flows[a]	**1,564**	**1,242**	**1,220**	**1,543**	**2,484**	**2,687**	**2,020**	**2,107**
of which								
Workers' remittances	1,183	894	863	1,143	1,980	2,178	1,609	–
Compensation of employees	381	348	357	400	504	509	411	–
Migrants' transfers	–	–	–	–	–	–	–	–
Outward remittance flows	**379**	**497**	**902**	**982**	**1,460**	**1,912**	**1,843**	**–**
of which								
Workers' remittances	187	262	630	629	1,003	1,316	1,268	–
Compensation of employees	193	235	273	353	457	596	575	–
Migrants' transfers	–	–	–	–	–	–	–	–

a. For comparison: net FDI inflows US$5.3 bn, total international reserves US$3.5 bn, exports of goods and services US$82.2 bn in 2008.

Greenland

HIGH-INCOME NON-OECD

Population (thousands, 2009)	56.1
Population growth (avg. annual %, 2000–09)	0.0
Population density (people per km², 2008)	0.1
Labor force (millions, 2008)	—
Unemployment rate (% of labor force, 2008)	—
Urban population (% of pop., 2009)	83.8
Surface area (1,000 km², 2008)	410.5
GNI (US$ billions, 2009)	—
GNI per capita, Atlas method (US$, 2009)	—
GDP growth (avg. annual %, 2005–09)	—
Poverty headcount ratio at national poverty line (% of pop., 2005)	—
Age dependency ratio (2009)	—

Migration

EMIGRATION, 2010

- Stock of emigrants: **5.8 thousands**
- Stock of emigrants as percentage of population: **10.1%**
- Top destination countries: Norway, Guatemala, Iceland, Australia, the Netherlands, Panama, Greece, Mexico, New Zealand

SKILLED EMIGRATION, 2000

- Skilled emigration data are currently not available for this country.

IMMIGRATION, 2010

- Stock of immigrants: **5.8 thousands**
- Stock of immigrants as percentage of population: **10.2%**
- Females as percentage of immigrants: **32.9%**
- Refugees as percentage of immigrants: **0.0%**

Remittances

Remittance data are currently not available for this country.

Grenada

Population (millions, 2009)	0.1
Population growth (avg. annual %, 2000–09)	0.3
Population density (people per km², 2008)	310.4
Labor force (millions, 2008)	–
Unemployment rate (% of labor force, 2008)	–
Urban population (% of pop., 2009)	30.9
Surface area (1,000 km², 2008)	0.3
GNI (US$ billions, 2009)	0.6
GNI per capita, Atlas method (US$, 2009)	5,550
GDP growth (avg. annual %, 2005–09)	1.8
Poverty headcount ratio at national poverty line (% of pop., 2005)	–
Age dependency ratio (2009)	53.4

Migration

EMIGRATION, 2010

- Stock of emigrants: **68.3 thousands**
- Stock of emigrants as percentage of population: **65.5%**
- Top destination countries: the United States, the United Kingdom, Canada, Trinidad and Tobago, Barbados, St. Vincent and the Grenadines, Mexico, Antigua and Barbuda, República Bolivariana de Venezuela, Australia

SKILLED EMIGRATION, 2000

- Emigration rate of tertiary-educated population: **85.1%**
- Emigration of physicians: **3,433** or **98.6%** of physicians trained in the country *(Source: Bhargava, Docquier, and Moullan 2010)*

IMMIGRATION, 2010

- Stock of immigrants: **12.6 thousands**
- Stock of immigrants as percentage of population: **12.1%**
- Females as percentage of immigrants: **54.2%**
- Refugees as percentage of immigrants: **0.0%**

Remittances

US$ millions	2003	2004	2005	2006	2007	2008	2009	2010e
Inward remittance flows[a]	**49**	**72**	**52**	**54**	**55**	**55**	**54**	**59**
of which								
Workers' remittances	25	48	27	28	28	29	26	–
Compensation of employees	0	0	0	1	0	0	–	–
Migrants' transfers	23	24	25	25	26	27	27	–
Outward remittance flows	**3**	**3**	**3**	**4**	**4**	**4**	**4**	–
of which								
Workers' remittances	1	1	1	1	2	2	2	–
Compensation of employees	–	–	–	–	–	–	–	–
Migrants' transfers	2	2	2	2	2	2	2	–

a. **For comparison: net FDI inflows US$0.2 bn, total international reserves US$0.1 bn, exports of goods and services US$0.2 bn in 2008.**

Guam

Population (millions, 2009)	0.2
Population growth (avg. annual %, 2000–09)	1.5
Population density (people per km², 2008)	324.9
Labor force (millions, 2008)	0.1
Unemployment rate (% of labor force, 2008)	–
Urban population (% of pop., 2009)	93.2
Surface area (1,000 km², 2008)	0.5
GNI (US$ billions, 2009)	–
GNI per capita, Atlas method (US$, 2009)	–
GDP growth (avg. annual %, 2005-09)	–
Poverty headcount ratio at national poverty line (% of pop., 2005)	–
Age dependency ratio (2009)	53.2

Migration

EMIGRATION, 2010

- Stock of emigrants: **48.7 thousands**
- Stock of emigrants as percentage of population: **27.1%**
- Top destination countries: the United States, Northern Mariana Islands, the Philippines, Fiji, Mexico, Palau, Australia, Canada, the United Kingdom, New Zealand

SKILLED EMIGRATION, 2000

- Skilled emigration data are currently not available for this country.

IMMIGRATION, 2010

- Stock of immigrants: **78.9 thousands**
- Stock of immigrants as percentage of population: **43.9%**
- Females as percentage of immigrants: **43.6%**
- Refugees as percentage of immigrants: **0.0%**
- Top source countries: the Philippines, the United States, the Federated States of Micronesia, the Republic of Korea, China, Japan, Northern Mariana Islands, Palau, the Marshall Islands, Puerto Rico

Remittances

Remittance data are currently not available for this country.

Guatemala

LOWER MIDDLE INCOME

Population (millions, 2009)	14.0
Population growth (avg. annual %, 2000–09)	2.5
Population density (people per km², 2008)	126.1
Labor force (millions, 2008)	4.9
Unemployment rate (% of labor force, 2008)	–
Urban population (% of pop., 2009)	49.0
Surface area (1,000 km², 2008)	108.9
GNI (US$ billions, 2009)	35.6
GNI per capita, Atlas method (US$, 2009)	2,620
GDP growth (avg. annual %, 2005–09)	3.9
Poverty headcount ratio at national poverty line (% of pop., 2005)	13.1
Age dependency ratio (2009)	86.1

Migration

EMIGRATION, 2010

- Stock of emigrants: **871.9 thousands**
- Stock of emigrants as percentage of population: **6.1%**
- Top destination countries: the United States, Mexico, Belize, Canada, El Salvador, Spain, Costa Rica, Honduras, France, Nicaragua

SKILLED EMIGRATION, 2000

- Emigration rate of tertiary-educated population: **24.2%**
- Emigration of physicians: **606** or **5.6%** of physicians trained in the country (Source: Bhargava, Docquier, and Moullan 2010)

IMMIGRATION, 2010

- Stock of immigrants: **59.5 thousands**
- Stock of immigrants as percentage of population: **0.4%**
- Females as percentage of immigrants: **54.4%**
- Refugees as percentage of immigrants: **0.6%**
- Top source countries: El Salvador, Mexico, Nicaragua, Honduras, the United States, the Republic of Korea, Spain, Costa Rica, Colombia, Belize

Remittances

US$ millions	2003	2004	2005	2006	2007	2008	2009	2010e
Inward remittance flows[a]	**2,147**	**2,628**	**3,067**	**3,700**	**4,236**	**4,460**	**4,026**	**4,255**
of which								
Workers' remittances	2,107	2,616	3,045	3,680	4,207	4,419	3,993	–
Compensation of employees	40	12	22	20	29	40	34	–
Migrants' transfers	–	–	–	–	–	–	–	–
Outward remittance flows	**86**	**34**	**42**	**46**	**17**	**26**	**23**	**–**
of which								
Workers' remittances	80	32	33	35	7	16	15	–
Compensation of employees	6	1	9	11	10	10	8	–
Migrants' transfers	–	–	–	–	–	–	–	–

a. For comparison: net FDI inflows US$0.8 bn, net ODA received US$0.5 bn, total international reserves US$4.7 bn, exports of goods and services US$9.6 bn in 2008.

Guinea

Population (millions, 2009)	10.1
Population growth (avg. annual %, 2000–09)	2.0
Population density (people per km², 2008)	40.0
Labor force (millions, 2008)	4.6
Unemployment rate (% of labor force, 2008)	–
Urban population (% of pop., 2009)	34.9
Surface area (1,000 km², 2008)	245.9
GNI (US$ billions, 2009)	4.2
GNI per capita, Atlas method (US$, 2009)	–
GDP growth (avg. annual %, 2005–09)	3.0
Poverty headcount ratio at national poverty line (% of pop., 2005)	69.8
Age dependency ratio (2009)	85.3

Migration

EMIGRATION, 2010

- Stock of emigrants: **532.7 thousands**
- Stock of emigrants as percentage of population: **5.2%**
- Top destination countries: Côte d'Ivoire, Senegal, Sierra Leone, The Gambia, Liberia, France, Mali, Spain, the United States, Nigeria

SKILLED EMIGRATION, 2000

- Emigration rate of tertiary-educated population: **11.3%**
- Emigration of physicians:
  - (a) **58** or **7.7%** of physicians trained in the country (Source: Bhargava, Docquier, and Moullan 2010)
  - (b) **115** or **11.4%** of physicians born in the country (Source: Clemens and Pettersson 2006)
- Emigration of nurses: **267** or **6.5%** of nurses born in the country

IMMIGRATION, 2010

- Stock of immigrants: **394.6 thousands**
- Stock of immigrants as percentage of population: **3.8%**
- Females as percentage of immigrants: **53.1%**
- Refugees as percentage of immigrants: **7.2%**
- Top source countries: Liberia, Sierra Leone, Mali, Senegal, Guinea-Bissau, Côte d'Ivoire, Benin, France, Togo, Niger

Remittances

US$ millions	2003	2004	2005	2006	2007	2008	2009	2010e
Inward remittance flows[a]	**111**	**42**	**–**	**–**	**151**	**72**	**68**	**66**
of which								
Workers' remittances	111	42	–	–	15	60	–	–
Compensation of employees	–	–	–	–	–	2	–	–
Migrants' transfers	–	–	–	–	136	10	–	–
Outward remittance flows	**46**	**48**	**48**	**48**	**119**	**56**	**56**	**–**
of which								
Workers' remittances	42	46	–	–	34	36	–	–
Compensation of employees	4	2	–	–	5	20	–	–
Migrants' transfers	–	–	–	–	80	–	–	–

a. **For comparison: net FDI inflows US$0.4 bn, net ODA received US$0.3 bn, exports of goods and services US$1.3 bn in 2008.**

Guinea-Bissau

Population (millions, 2009)	1.6
Population growth (avg. annual %, 2000–09)	2.3
Population density (people per km², 2008)	56.0
Labor force (millions, 2008)	0.6
Unemployment rate (% of labor force, 2008)	—
Urban population (% of pop., 2009)	29.9
Surface area (1,000 km², 2008)	36.1
GNI (US$ billions, 2009)	0.4
GNI per capita, Atlas method (US$, 2009)	—
GDP growth (avg. annual %, 2005–09)	—
Poverty headcount ratio at national poverty line (% of pop., 2005)	42.5
Age dependency ratio (2009)	85.5

Migration

EMIGRATION, 2010

- Stock of emigrants: **111.3 thousands**
- Stock of emigrants as percentage of population: **6.8%**
- Top destination countries: Portugal, Senegal, The Gambia, France, Spain, Nigeria, Guinea, Mauritania, Cape Verde, Germany

SKILLED EMIGRATION, 2000

- Emigration rate of tertiary-educated population: **24.4%**
- Emigration of physicians: **251** or **70.9%** of physicians born in the country
  (Source: Clemens and Pettersson 2006)
- Emigration of nurses: **262** or **24.7%** of nurses born in the country

IMMIGRATION, 2010

- Stock of immigrants: **19.2 thousands**
- Stock of immigrants as percentage of population: **1.2%**
- Females as percentage of immigrants: **50.0%**
- Refugees as percentage of immigrants: **40.7%**
- Top source countries: Senegal, Guinea, The Gambia, Portugal, Mauritania, Cape Verde, France

Remittances

US$ millions	2003	2004	2005	2006	2007	2008	2009	2010e
Inward remittance flows[a]	**23**	**28**	**28**	**28**	**29**	**30**	**28**	**27**
of which								
Workers' remittances	21	27	—	—	—	—	—	—
Compensation of employees	2	1	—	—	—	—	—	—
Migrants' transfers	—	—	—	—	—	—	—	—
Outward remittance flows	**6**	**5**	**5**	**4**	**4**	**17**	**17**	**—**
of which								
Workers' remittances	6	5	—	—	—	—	—	—
Compensation of employees	0	0	—	—	—	—	—	—
Migrants' transfers	—	—	—	—	—	—	—	—

a. For comparison: net ODA received US$0.1 bn, total international reserves US$0.1 bn, exports of goods and services US$0.1 bn in 2008.

Guyana

Latin America and the Caribbean	LOWER MIDDLE INCOME
Population (millions, 2009)	0.8
Population growth (avg. annual %, 2000–09)	0.1
Population density (people per km², 2008)	3.9
Labor force (millions, 2008)	0.3
Unemployment rate (% of labor force, 2008)	–
Urban population (% of pop., 2009)	28.4
Surface area (1,000 km², 2008)	215.0
GNI (US$ billions, 2009)	1.1
GNI per capita, Atlas method (US$, 2009)	–
GDP growth (avg. annual %, 2005–09)	–
Poverty headcount ratio at national poverty line (% of pop., 2005)	7.3
Age dependency ratio (2009)	55.5

Migration

EMIGRATION, 2010

- Stock of emigrants: **432.9 thousands**
- Stock of emigrants as percentage of population: **56.8%**
- Top destination countries: the United States, Canada, the United Kingdom, Suriname, República Bolivariana de Venezuela, Antigua and Barbuda, Trinidad and Tobago, Barbados, the Netherlands, Brazil

SKILLED EMIGRATION, 2000

- Emigration rate of tertiary-educated population: **89.0%**
- Emigration of physicians: **7** or **1.8%** of physicians trained in the country *(Source: Bhargava, Docquier, and Moullan 2010)*

IMMIGRATION, 2010

- Stock of immigrants: **11.6 thousands**
- Stock of immigrants as percentage of population: **1.5%**
- Females as percentage of immigrants: **46.5%**
- Refugees as percentage of immigrants: **0.0%**
- Top source countries: Suriname, Brazil, República Bolivariana de Venezuela, the United States, China, Trinidad and Tobago, the United Kingdom, St. Lucia, Barbados, Canada

Remittances

US$ millions	2003	2004	2005	2006	2007	2008	2009	2010e
Inward remittance flows[a]	**99**	**153**	**201**	**218**	**283**	**278**	**253**	**280**
of which								
Workers' remittances	99	153	201	218	278	274	–	–
Compensation of employees	–	–	–	–	4	5	–	–
Migrants' transfers	–	–	–	–	–	–	–	–
Outward remittance flows	**50**	**81**	**55**	**48**	**62**	**–**	**77**	**–**
of which								
Workers' remittances	45	75	49	42	54	69	–	–
Compensation of employees	6	6	6	6	8	8	–	–
Migrants' transfers	–	–	–	–	–	–	–	–

a. For comparison: net FDI inflows US$0.2 bn, net ODA received US$0.2 bn, total international reserves US$0.4 bn, exports of goods and services US$0.8 bn in 2008.

Haiti

Population (millions, 2009)	10.0
Population growth (avg. annual %, 2000–09)	1.7
Population density (people per km², 2008)	354.9
Labor force (millions, 2008)	3.6
Unemployment rate (% of labor force, 2008)	–
Urban population (% of pop., 2009)	48.2
Surface area (1,000 km², 2008)	27.8
GNI (US$ billions, 2009)	7.0
GNI per capita, Atlas method (US$, 2008)	660
GDP growth (avg. annual %, 2004–08)	1.1
Poverty headcount ratio at national poverty line (% of pop., 2005)	58.0
Age dependency ratio (2009)	68.6

Migration

EMIGRATION, 2010

- Stock of emigrants: **1,009.4 thousands**
- Stock of emigrants as percentage of population: **9.9%**
- Top destination countries: the United States, the Dominican Republic, Canada, France, The Bahamas, Netherlands Antilles, Belgium, República Bolivariana de Venezuela, Switzerland, the Netherlands

SKILLED EMIGRATION, 2000

- Emigration rate of tertiary-educated population: **83.6%**
- Emigration of physicians: **1,142** or **36.5%** of physicians trained in the country (Source: Bhargava, Docquier, and Moullan 2010)

IMMIGRATION, 2010

- Stock of immigrants: **35.0 thousands**
- Stock of immigrants as percentage of population: **0.3%**
- Females as percentage of immigrants: **43.2%**
- Refugees as percentage of immigrants: **0.0%**
- Top source countries: the Dominican Republic, the United States, Cuba, Jamaica, Colombia, Mexico, Chile, Brazil, Peru, Argentina

Remittances

US$ millions	2003	2004	2005	2006	2007	2008	2009	2010e
Inward remittance flows[a]	**811**	**932**	**986**	**1,063**	**1,222**	**1,370**	**1,376**	**1,499**
of which								
Workers' remittances	811	932	986	1,063	1,222	1,370	1,376	–
Compensation of employees	–	–	–	–	–	–	–	–
Migrants' transfers	–	–	–	–	–	–	–	–
Outward remittance flows	**31**	**39**	**60**	**76**	**96**	**117**	**135**	**–**
of which								
Workers' remittances	31	39	60	76	96	117	135	–
Compensation of employees	–	–	–	–	–	–	–	–
Migrants' transfers	–	–	–	–	–	–	–	–

a. For comparison: net ODA received US$0.9 bn, total international reserves US$0.5 bn, exports of goods and services US$0.8 bn in 2008.

Honduras

Population (millions, 2009)	7.5
Population growth (avg. annual %, 2000–09)	2.0
Population density (people per km², 2008)	64.7
Labor force (millions, 2008)	2.6
Unemployment rate (% of labor force, 2008)	–
Urban population (% of pop., 2009)	48.3
Surface area (1,000 km², 2008)	112.1
GNI (US$ billions, 2009)	14.2
GNI per capita, Atlas method (US$, 2009)	1,820
GDP growth (avg. annual %, 2005–09)	4.2
Poverty headcount ratio at national poverty line (% of pop., 2005)	22.2
Age dependency ratio (2009)	71.4

Migration

EMIGRATION, 2010

- Stock of emigrants: **569.7 thousands**
- Stock of emigrants as percentage of population: **7.5%**
- Top destination countries: the United States, Spain, Nicaragua, El Salvador, Belize, Guatemala, Canada, Mexico, Costa Rica, Cayman Islands

SKILLED EMIGRATION, 2000

- Emigration rate of tertiary-educated population: **24.4%**
- Emigration of physicians: **164** or **3.0%** of physicians trained in the country *(Source: Bhargava, Docquier, and Moullan 2010)*

IMMIGRATION, 2010

- Stock of immigrants: **24.3 thousands**
- Stock of immigrants as percentage of population: **0.3%**
- Females as percentage of immigrants: **48.4%**
- Refugees as percentage of immigrants: **0.1%**
- Top source countries: El Salvador, Nicaragua, the United States, Guatemala, Mexico, Colombia, Costa Rica, Cuba, China, Spain

Remittances

US$ millions	2003	2004	2005	2006	2007	2008	2009	2010e
Inward remittance flows[a]	**883**	**1,175**	**1,821**	**2,391**	**2,625**	**2,869**	**2,553**	**2,662**
of which								
Workers' remittances	842	1,138	1,776	2,329	2,561	2,801	2,476	–
Compensation of employees	23	31	29	30	33	29	9	–
Migrants' transfers	18	6	16	32	31	39	35	–
Outward remittance flows	**12**	**17**	**0**	**2**	**2**	**9**	**12**	**–**
of which								
Workers' remittances	–	–	–	–	–	–	–	–
Compensation of employees	12	17	0	2	2	9	12	–
Migrants' transfers	–	–	–	–	–	–	–	–

a. For comparison: net FDI inflows US$0.9 bn, net ODA received US$0.6 bn, total international reserves US$2.5 bn, exports of goods and services US$6.5 bn in 2008.

Hong Kong SAR, China

Population (millions, 2009)	7.0
Population growth (avg. annual %, 2000–09)	0.6
Population density (people per km², 2008)	6,696.4
Labor force (millions, 2008)	3.7
Unemployment rate (% of labor force, 2008)	3.5
Urban population (% of pop., 2009)	100.0
Surface area (1,000 km², 2008)	1.1
GNI (US$ billions, 2009)	215.6
GNI per capita, Atlas method (US$, 2008)	31,420
GDP growth (avg. annual %, 2004–08)	6.3
Poverty headcount ratio at national poverty line (% of pop., 2005)	—
Age dependency ratio (2009)	32.8

Migration

EMIGRATION, 2010

- Stock of emigrants: **719.3 thousands**
- Stock of emigrants as percentage of population: **10.2%**
- Top destination countries: Canada; the United States; the United Kingdom; Australia; Macao SAR, China; the Netherlands; New Zealand; Singapore; Ireland; France

SKILLED EMIGRATION, 2000

- Emigration rate of tertiary-educated population: **28.8%**
- Emigration of physicians: **3,833** or **30.4%** of physicians trained in the country *(Source: Bhargava, Docquier, and Moullan 2010)*

IMMIGRATION, 2010

- Stock of immigrants: **2,741.8 thousands**
- Stock of immigrants as percentage of population: **38.8%**
- Females as percentage of immigrants: **57.0%**
- Refugees as percentage of immigrants: **0.0%**
- Top source countries: China; Macao SAR, China

Remittances

US$ millions	2003	2004	2005	2006	2007	2008	2009	2010e
Inward remittance flows[a]	**120**	**240**	**297**	**294**	**317**	**355**	**338**	**369**
of which								
Workers' remittances	—	—	—	—	—	—	—	—
Compensation of employees	120	240	297	294	317	355	—	—
Migrants' transfers	—	—	—	—	—	—	—	—
Outward remittance flows	**317**	**321**	**348**	**377**	**388**	**393**	**402**	—
of which								
Workers' remittances	—	—	—	—	—	—	—	—
Compensation of employees	317	321	348	377	388	393	—	—
Migrants' transfers	—	—	—	—	—	—	—	—

a. For comparison: net FDI inflows US$63.0 bn, total international reserves US$182.5 bn, exports of goods and services US$457.5 bn in 2008.

Hungary

Population (millions, 2009)	10.0
Population growth (avg. annual %, 2000–09)	-0.2
Population density (people per km², 2008)	112.0
Labor force (millions, 2008)	4.4
Unemployment rate (% of labor force, 2008)	7.8
Urban population (% of pop., 2009)	67.9
Surface area (1,000 km², 2008)	93.0
GNI (US$ billions, 2009)	121.2
GNI per capita, Atlas method (US$, 2009)	12,980
GDP growth (avg. annual %, 2005–09)	0.6
Poverty headcount ratio at national poverty line (% of pop., 2005)	0.0
Age dependency ratio (2009)	45.0

Migration

EMIGRATION, 2010

- Stock of emigrants: **462.7 thousands**
- Stock of emigrants as percentage of population: **4.6%**
- Top destination countries: Germany, the United States, Canada, Austria, the United Kingdom, Australia, Israel, Sweden, the Slovak Republic, Switzerland

SKILLED EMIGRATION, 2000

- Emigration rate of tertiary-educated population: **13.2%**
- Emigration of physicians: **3,694** or **10.9%** of physicians trained in the country *(Source: Bhargava, Docquier, and Moullan 2010)*

IMMIGRATION, 2010

- Stock of immigrants: **368.1 thousands**
- Stock of immigrants as percentage of population: **3.7%**
- Females as percentage of immigrants: **51.2%**
- Refugees as percentage of immigrants: **2.0%**
- Top source countries: Romania, Germany, Austria, China, Ukraine, the United States, the United Kingdom, Poland, France, the Slovak Republic

Remittances

US$ millions	2003	2004	2005	2006	2007	2008	2009	2010e
Inward remittance flows[a]	**295**	**1,717**	**1,931**	**2,079**	**2,280**	**2,520**	**2,277**	**2,514**
of which								
Workers' remittances	39	46	61	54	53	62	52	–
Compensation of employees	249	1,655	1,852	2,019	2,225	2,570	2,225	–
Migrants' transfers	7	16	18	6	2	–	–	–
Outward remittance flows	**114**	**814**	**915**	**986**	**1,307**	**1,467**	**1,338**	**–**
of which								
Workers' remittances	20	83	98	107	116	134	–	–
Compensation of employees	91	728	814	874	1,184	1,428	–	–
Migrants' transfers	3	3	3	5	7	–	–	–

a. **For comparison: net FDI inflows US$62.8 bn, total international reserves US$33.9 bn, exports of goods and services US$126.0 bn in 2008.**

Iceland

Population (millions, 2009)	0.3
Population growth (avg. annual %, 2000–09)	1.4
Population density (people per km², 2008)	3.2
Labor force (millions, 2008)	0.2
Unemployment rate (% of labor force, 2008)	3.0
Urban population (% of pop., 2009)	92.3
Surface area (1,000 km², 2008)	103.0
GNI (US$ billions, 2009)	10.8
GNI per capita, Atlas method (US$, 2009)	43,220
GDP growth (avg. annual %, 2005–09)	2.5
Poverty headcount ratio at national poverty line (% of pop., 2005)	–
Age dependency ratio (2009)	47.7

Migration

EMIGRATION, 2010

- Stock of emigrants: **42.7 thousands**
- Stock of emigrants as percentage of population: **13.0%**
- Top destination countries: the United States, Denmark, Norway, Sweden, Germany, the United Kingdom, Spain, Australia, Canada, the Netherlands

SKILLED EMIGRATION, 2000

- Emigration rate of tertiary-educated population: **19.7%**
- Emigration of physicians: **567** or **37.1%** of physicians trained in the country *(Source: Bhargava, Docquier, and Moullan 2010)*

IMMIGRATION, 2010

- Stock of immigrants: **37.2 thousands**
- Stock of immigrants as percentage of population: **11.3%**
- Females as percentage of immigrants: **49.4%**
- Refugees as percentage of immigrants: **0.4%**
- Top source countries: Denmark, Poland, Sweden, the United States, Germany, Norway, the Philippines, the United Kingdom, the Russian Federation, Thailand

Remittances

US$ millions	2003	2004	2005	2006	2007	2008	2009	2010e
Inward remittance flows[a]	**96**	**112**	**88**	**87**	**41**	**35**	**23**	**26**
of which								
Workers' remittances	–	–	–	–	–	–	–	–
Compensation of employees	81	80	74	72	25	19	–	–
Migrants' transfers	15	32	14	15	16	16	–	–
Outward remittance flows	**26**	**47**	**65**	**80**	**100**	**56**	**34**	**–**
of which								
Workers' remittances	–	–	–	–	–	–	–	–
Compensation of employees	6	12	24	39	54	27	–	–
Migrants' transfers	20	35	41	41	46	29	–	–

a. For comparison: net FDI inflows US$0.7 bn, total international reserves US$3.6 bn, exports of goods and services US$7.4 bn in 2008.

India

South Asia	LOWER MIDDLE INCOME
Population (millions, 2009)	1,155.3
Population growth (avg. annual %, 2000–09)	1.5
Population density (people per km², 2008)	383.4
Labor force (millions, 2008)	447.0
Unemployment rate (% of labor force, 2008)	–
Urban population (% of pop., 2009)	29.5
Surface area (1,000 km², 2008)	3,287.3
GNI (US$ billions, 2009)	1,212.6
GNI per capita, Atlas method (US$, 2009)	1,180
GDP growth (avg. annual %, 2005–09)	8.2
Poverty headcount ratio at national poverty line (% of pop., 2005)	–
Age dependency ratio (2009)	56.5

Migration

EMIGRATION, 2010

- Stock of emigrants: **11,357.5 thousands**
- Stock of emigrants as percentage of population: **0.9%**
- Top destination countries: the United Arab Emirates, the United States, Saudi Arabia, Bangladesh, Nepal, the United Kingdom, Canada, Oman, Kuwait, Sri Lanka

SKILLED EMIGRATION, 2000

- Emigration rate of tertiary-educated population: **4.3%**
- Emigration of physicians: **57,383** or **9.9%** of physicians trained in the country *(Source: Bhargava, Docquier, and Moullan 2010)*

IMMIGRATION, 2010

- Stock of immigrants: **5,436.0 thousands**
- Stock of immigrants as percentage of population: **0.4%**
- Females as percentage of immigrants: **48.7%**
- Refugees as percentage of immigrants: **2.9%**
- Top source countries: Bangladesh, Pakistan, Nepal, Sri Lanka, Myanmar, China, Malaysia, the United Arab Emirates, Afghanistan, Bhutan

Remittances

US$ millions	2003	2004	2005	2006	2007	2008	2009	2010e
Inward remittance flows[a]	**20,999**	**18,750**	**22,125**	**28,334**	**37,217**	**49,941**	**49,256**	**55,000**
of which								
Workers' remittances	20,884	18,397	21,859	28,025	36,770	49,144	–	–
Compensation of employees	115	353	266	309	447	797	–	–
Migrants' transfers	–	–	–	–	–	–	–	–
Outward remittance flows	**1,265**	**1,653**	**1,348**	**1,562**	**2,059**	**3,815**	**4,000**	**–**
of which								
Workers' remittances	487	453	361	704	1,004	2,479	–	–
Compensation of employees	778	1,200	987	858	1,055	1,336	–	–
Migrants' transfers	–	–	–	–	–	–	–	–

a. For comparison: net FDI inflows US$41.2 bn, net ODA received US$2.1 bn, total international reserves US$257.4 bn, exports of goods and services US$262.8 bn in 2008.

Indonesia

Population (millions, 2009)	230.0
Population growth (avg. annual %, 2000–09)	1.3
Population density (people per km², 2008)	126.0
Labor force (millions, 2008)	110.4
Unemployment rate (% of labor force, 2008)	8.4
Urban population (% of pop., 2009)	52.6
Surface area (1,000 km², 2008)	1,904.6
GNI (US$ billions, 2009)	521.4
GNI per capita, Atlas method (US$, 2009)	2,230
GDP growth (avg. annual %, 2005–09)	5.6
Poverty headcount ratio at national poverty line (% of pop., 2005)	–
Age dependency ratio (2009)	49.2

Migration

EMIGRATION, 2010

- Stock of emigrants: **2,502.3 thousands**
- Stock of emigrants as percentage of population: **1.1%**
- Top destination countries: Malaysia, Saudi Arabia, the Netherlands, Singapore, the United States, Jordan, Australia, Japan, Germany, the Republic of Korea

SKILLED EMIGRATION, 2000

- Emigration rate of tertiary-educated population: **2.1%**
- Emigration of physicians: **461** or **1.4%** of physicians trained in the country *(Source: Bhargava, Docquier, and Moullan 2010)*

IMMIGRATION, 2010

- Stock of immigrants: **122.9 thousands**
- Stock of immigrants as percentage of population: **0.1%**
- Females as percentage of immigrants: **44.5%**
- Refugees as percentage of immigrants: **0.3%**
- Top source countries: China, the United Kingdom

Remittances

US$ millions	2003	2004	2005	2006	2007	2008	2009	2010e
Inward remittance flows[a]	**1,489**	**1,866**	**5,420**	**5,722**	**6,174**	**6,794**	**6,793**	**7,139**
of which								
Workers' remittances	1,489	1,700	5,296	5,560	6,004	6,618	6,618	–
Compensation of employees	–	166	123	162	171	176	175	–
Migrants' transfers	–	–	–	–	–	–	–	–
Outward remittance flows	**–**	**913**	**1,179**	**1,359**	**1,654**	**1,971**	**2,702**	**–**
of which								
Workers' remittances	–	775	834	1,060	1,171	1,412	1,748	–
Compensation of employees	–	138	344	299	483	560	953	–
Migrants' transfers	–	–	–	–	–	–	–	–

a. For comparison: net FDI inflows US$9.3 bn, net ODA received US$1.2 bn, total international reserves US$51.6 bn, exports of goods and services US$152.0 bn in 2008.

Iran, Islamic Republic of

Population (millions, 2009)	72.9
Population growth (avg. annual %, 2000–09)	1.5
Population density (people per km², 2008)	44.2
Labor force (millions, 2008)	28.5
Unemployment rate (% of labor force, 2008)	–
Urban population (% of pop., 2009)	69.0
Surface area (1,000 km², 2008)	1,745.2
GNI (US$ billions, 2009)	328.6
GNI per capita, Atlas method (US$, 2009)	4,530
GDP growth (avg. annual %, 2005–09)	4.5
Poverty headcount ratio at national poverty line (% of pop., 2005)	1.5
Age dependency ratio (2009)	40.7

Migration

EMIGRATION, 2010

- Stock of emigrants: **1,295.1 thousands**
- Stock of emigrants as percentage of population: **1.7%**
- Top destination countries: the United States, Qatar, Canada, Kuwait, Germany, Israel, the United Kingdom, Sweden, the United Arab Emirates, Bahrain

SKILLED EMIGRATION, 2000

- Emigration rate of tertiary-educated population: **14.5%**
- Emigration of physicians: **6,101** or **8.4%** of physicians trained in the country *(Source: Bhargava, Docquier, and Moullan 2010)*

IMMIGRATION, 2010

- Stock of immigrants: **2,128.7 thousands**
- Stock of immigrants as percentage of population: **2.8%**
- Females as percentage of immigrants: **38.8%**
- Refugees as percentage of immigrants: **45.4%**
- Top source countries: Afghanistan, Iraq, Pakistan, Azerbaijan, Turkey, Armenia, Turkmenistan

Remittances

US$ millions	2003	2004	2005	2006	2007	2008	2009	2010e
Inward remittance flows[a]	**1,178**	**1,032**	**1,032**	**1,032**	**1,115**	**1,115**	**1,045**	**1,141**
of which								
Workers' remittances	–	–	–	–	–	–	–	–
Compensation of employees	–	–	–	–	–	–	–	–
Migrants' transfers	–	–	–	–	–	–	–	–
Outward remittance flows	–	–	–	–	–	–	–	–
of which								
Workers' remittances	–	–	–	–	–	–	–	–
Compensation of employees	–	–	–	–	–	–	–	–
Migrants' transfers	–	–	–	–	–	–	–	–

a. For comparison: net FDI inflows US$1.5 bn, net ODA received US$0.1 bn in 2008.

Iraq

Population (millions, 2009)	31.5
Population growth (avg. annual %, 2000–09)	2.6
Population density (people per km², 2008)	–
Labor force (millions, 2008)	–
Unemployment rate (% of labor force, 2008)	–
Urban population (% of pop., 2009)	66.5
Surface area (1,000 km², 2008)	438.3
GNI (US$ billions, 2009)	61.8
GNI per capita, Atlas method (US$, 2009)	2,210
GDP growth (avg. annual %, 2005–09)	4.1
Poverty headcount ratio at national poverty line (% of pop., 2005)	–
Age dependency ratio (2009)	79.7

Migration

EMIGRATION, 2010

- Stock of emigrants: **1,545.8 thousands**
- Stock of emigrants as percentage of population: **4.9%**
- Top destination countries: the Islamic Republic of Iran, Jordan, Germany, Israel, Sweden, the United States, the United Kingdom, Australia, Canada, the Netherlands

SKILLED EMIGRATION, 2000

- Emigration rate of tertiary-educated population: **11.1%**
- Emigration of physicians: **2,871** or **18.4%** of physicians trained in the country *(Source: Bhargava, Docquier, and Moullan 2010)*

IMMIGRATION, 2010

- Stock of immigrants: **83.4 thousands**
- Stock of immigrants as percentage of population: **0.3%**
- Females as percentage of immigrants: **31.1%**
- Refugees as percentage of immigrants: **52.0%**
- Top source countries: Kuwait, the Islamic Republic of Iran, the Syrian Arab Republic, West Bank and Gaza, Jordan, Sudan, the Republic of Yemen, Lebanon, the United Kingdom, Saudi Arabia

Remittances

US$ millions	2003	2004	2005	2006	2007	2008	2009	2010e
Inward remittance flows[a]	–	–	**711**	**389**	**3**	**3**	–	–
of which								
Workers' remittances	–	–	454	261	3	–	–	–
Compensation of employees	–	–	258	128	1	–	–	–
Migrants' transfers	–	–	–	–	–	–	–	–
Outward remittance flows	–	–	**83**	**781**	**17**	**17**	–	–
of which								
Workers' remittances	–	–	–	629	16	–	–	–
Compensation of employees	–	–	83	153	2	–	–	–
Migrants' transfers	–	–	–	–	–	–	–	–

a. For comparison: net ODA received US$9.9 bn, total international reserves US$50.2 bn in 2008.

Ireland

Population (millions, 2009)	4.5
Population growth (avg. annual %, 2000–09)	1.7
Population density (people per km², 2008)	64.7
Labor force (millions, 2008)	2.2
Unemployment rate (% of labor force, 2008)	6.0
Urban population (% of pop., 2009)	61.6
Surface area (1,000 km², 2008)	70.3
GNI (US$ billions, 2009)	183.2
GNI per capita, Atlas method (US$, 2009)	44,310
GDP growth (avg. annual %, 2005–09)	1.7
Poverty headcount ratio at national poverty line (% of pop., 2005)	—
Age dependency ratio (2009)	46.8

Migration

EMIGRATION, 2010

- Stock of emigrants: **737.2 thousands**
- Stock of emigrants as percentage of population: **16.1%**
- Top destination countries: the United Kingdom, the United States, Australia, Canada, Spain, Germany, New Zealand, France, the Netherlands, Belgium

SKILLED EMIGRATION, 2000

- Emigration rate of tertiary-educated population: **29.5%**
- Emigration of physicians: **11,542** or **57.8%** of physicians trained in the country *(Source: Bhargava, Docquier, and Moullan 2010)*

IMMIGRATION, 2010

- Stock of immigrants: **898.6 thousands**
- Stock of immigrants as percentage of population: **19.6%**
- Females as percentage of immigrants: **49.6%**
- Refugees as percentage of immigrants: **1.0%**
- Top source countries: the United Kingdom, Poland, the United States, Lithuania, Nigeria, Latvia, Germany, China, the Philippines, India

Remittances

US$ millions	2003	2004	2005	2006	2007	2008	2009	2010e
Inward remittance flows[a]	**337**	**414**	**513**	**531**	**590**	**646**	**581**	**618**
of which								
Workers' remittances	33	25	25	19	16	10	13	—
Compensation of employees	304	389	488	513	573	636	563	—
Migrants' transfers	—	—	—	—	—	—	—	—
Outward remittance flows	**788**	**997**	**1,535**	**1,947**	**2,625**	**2,829**	**1,988**	**—**
of which								
Workers' remittances	154	169	378	575	902	1,096	802	—
Compensation of employees	548	734	1,063	1,277	1,619	1,626	1,096	—
Migrants' transfers	86	94	95	95	104	106	89	—

a. For comparison: net FDI inflows US$19.9 bn, total international reserves US$1.0 bn in 2008.

Isle of Man

Population (thousands, 2009)	80.5
Population growth (avg. annual %, 2000–09)	0.6
Population density (people per km², 2008)	141.3
Labor force (millions, 2008)	—
Unemployment rate (% of labor force, 2008)	—
Urban population (% of pop., 2009)	50.7
Surface area (1,000 km², 2008)	0.6
GNI (US$ billions, 2009)	—
GNI per capita, Atlas method (US$, 2009)	—
GDP growth (avg. annual %, 2005–09)	—
Poverty headcount ratio at national poverty line (% of pop., 2005)	—
Age dependency ratio (2009)	—

Migration

EMIGRATION, 2010

- Stock of emigrants: **0.0 thousands**
- Stock of emigrants as percentage of population: **0.0%**

SKILLED EMIGRATION, 2000

- Skilled emigration data are currently not available for this country.

IMMIGRATION, 2010

- Stock of immigrants: **43.9 thousands**
- Stock of immigrants as percentage of population: **54.6%**
- Females as percentage of immigrants: **50.6%**
- Refugees as percentage of immigrants: **0.0%**

Remittances

Remittance data are currently not available for this country.

Israel

HIGH-INCOME NON-OECD

Population (millions, 2009)	7.4
Population growth (avg. annual %, 2000–09)	1.9
Population density (people per km², 2008)	337.7
Labor force (millions, 2008)	2.9
Unemployment rate (% of labor force, 2008)	6.2
Urban population (% of pop., 2009)	91.7
Surface area (1,000 km², 2008)	22.1
GNI (US$ billions, 2009)	190.3
GNI per capita, Atlas method (US$, 2009)	25,740
GDP growth (avg. annual %, 2005–09)	4.1
Poverty headcount ratio at national poverty line (% of pop., 2005)	–
Age dependency ratio (2009)	60.8

Migration

EMIGRATION, 2010

- Stock of emigrants: **1,019.9 thousands**
- Stock of emigrants as percentage of population: **14.0%**
- Top destination countries: West Bank and Gaza, the United States, Canada, Germany, the United Kingdom, Jordan, Australia, France, the Netherlands, Belgium

SKILLED EMIGRATION, 2000

- Emigration rate of tertiary-educated population: **7.9%**
- Emigration of physicians: **3,133** or **11.7%** of physicians trained in the country (Source: Bhargava, Docquier, and Moullan 2010)

IMMIGRATION, 2010

- Stock of immigrants: **2,940.5 thousands**
- Stock of immigrants as percentage of population: **40.4%**
- Females as percentage of immigrants: **55.9%**
- Refugees as percentage of immigrants: **0.0%**
- Top source countries: the Russian Federation, Ukraine, Morocco, Romania, Poland, Iraq, Uzbekistan, Ethiopia, Kazakhstan, the Islamic Republic of Iran

Remittances

US$ millions	2003	2004	2005	2006	2007	2008	2009	2010e
Inward remittance flows[a]	**423**	**714**	**850**	**944**	**1,042**	**1,422**	**1,267**	**1,379**
of which								
Workers' remittances	–	–	–	–	–	–	–	–
Compensation of employees	171	298	377	463	546	513	507	–
Migrants' transfers	252	417	473	481	495	909	760	–
Outward remittance flows	**2,502**	**2,218**	**2,206**	**2,334**	**2,798**	**3,550**	**3,283**	**–**
of which								
Workers' remittances	–	–	–	–	–	–	–	–
Compensation of employees	2,502	2,218	2,206	2,334	2,798	3,550	3,283	–
Migrants' transfers	–	–	–	–	–	–	–	–

a. For comparison: net FDI inflows US$9.6 bn, total international reserves US$42.5 bn, exports of goods and services US$80.8 bn in 2008.

Italy

Population (millions, 2009)	60.2
Population growth (avg. annual %, 2000–09)	0.6
Population density (people per km², 2008)	203.5
Labor force (millions, 2008)	25.2
Unemployment rate (% of labor force, 2008)	6.7
Urban population (% of pop., 2009)	68.2
Surface area (1,000 km², 2008)	301.3
GNI (US$ billions, 2009)	2,074.3
GNI per capita, Atlas method (US$, 2009)	35,080
GDP growth (avg. annual %, 2005–09)	–0.4
Poverty headcount ratio at national poverty line (% of pop., 2005)	–
Age dependency ratio (2009)	52.5

Migration

EMIGRATION, 2010

- Stock of emigrants: **3,481.6 thousands**
- Stock of emigrants as percentage of population: **5.8%**
- Top destination countries: Germany, France, the United States, Canada, Switzerland, Australia, Argentina, Belgium, the United Kingdom, Spain

SKILLED EMIGRATION, 2000

- Emigration rate of tertiary-educated population: **10.0%**
- Emigration of physicians: **8,444** or **2.4%** of physicians trained in the country *(Source: Bhargava, Docquier, and Moullan 2010)*

IMMIGRATION, 2010

- Stock of immigrants: **4,463.4 thousands**
- Stock of immigrants as percentage of population: **7.4%**
- Females as percentage of immigrants: **53.1%**
- Refugees as percentage of immigrants: **0.7%**
- Top source countries: Romania, Albania, Morocco, China, Ukraine, the Philippines, Tunisia, Poland, the former Yugoslav Republic of Macedonia, India

Remittances

US$ millions	2003	2004	2005	2006	2007	2008	2009	2010e
Inward remittance flows[a]	**2,140**	**2,174**	**2,397**	**2,624**	**3,164**	**3,139**	**2,683**	**3,393**
of which								
Workers' remittances	288	284	289	312	346	281	285	–
Compensation of employees	1,726	1,808	2,029	2,244	2,717	2,806	2,326	–
Migrants' transfers	126	82	79	68	101	52	71	–
Outward remittance flows	**4,368**	**5,512**	**7,622**	**8,440**	**11,284**	**12,716**	**12,986**	–
of which								
Workers' remittances	1,328	3,370	4,827	5,703	8,322	9,362	9,430	–
Compensation of employees	2,984	2,069	2,719	2,649	2,860	3,307	3,515	–
Migrants' transfers	57	73	77	89	102	47	41	–

a. For comparison: net FDI inflows US$15.4 bn, total international reserves US$105.6 bn, exports of goods and services US$664.2 bn in 2008.

Jamaica

Latin America and the Caribbean | **UPPER MIDDLE INCOME**

Population (millions, 2009)	2.7
Population growth (avg. annual %, 2000–09)	0.5
Population density (people per km², 2008)	248.3
Labor force (millions, 2008)	1.2
Unemployment rate (% of labor force, 2008)	10.6
Urban population (% of pop., 2009)	53.5
Surface area (1,000 km², 2008)	11.0
GNI (US$ billions, 2009)	14.1
GNI per capita, Atlas method (US$, 2009)	4,990
GDP growth (avg. annual %, 2005–09)	1.1
Poverty headcount ratio at national poverty line (% of pop., 2005)	0.3
Age dependency ratio (2009)	59.1

Migration

EMIGRATION, 2010

- Stock of emigrants: **985.5 thousands**
- Stock of emigrants as percentage of population: **36.1%**
- Top destination countries: the United States, the United Kingdom, Canada, Cayman Islands, The Bahamas, Antigua and Barbuda, Germany, Netherlands Antilles, Australia, Barbados

SKILLED EMIGRATION, 2000

- Emigration rate of tertiary-educated population: **85.1%**
- Emigration of physicians: **2,026** or **41.6%** of physicians trained in the country *(Source: Bhargava, Docquier, and Moullan 2010)*

IMMIGRATION, 2010

- Stock of immigrants: **30.0 thousands**
- Stock of immigrants as percentage of population: **1.1%**
- Females as percentage of immigrants: **49.4%**
- Refugees as percentage of immigrants: **0.0%**
- Top source countries: the United States, the United Kingdom, Canada, India

Remittances

US$ millions	2003	2004	2005	2006	2007	2008	2009	2010e
Inward remittance flows[a]	**1,398**	**1,623**	**1,784**	**1,946**	**2,144**	**2,180**	**1,924**	**2,020**
of which								
Workers' remittances	1,270	1,466	1,621	1,769	1,964	2,021	1,794	–
Compensation of employees	110	135	140	154	158	135	99	–
Migrants' transfers	19	22	22	23	21	24	19	–
Outward remittance flows	**341**	**424**	**410**	**412**	**454**	**419**	**314**	–
of which								
Workers' remittances	283	340	317	300	303	313	239	–
Compensation of employees	39	51	52	58	93	51	32	–
Migrants' transfers	19	34	41	54	58	54	43	–

a. For comparison: net FDI inflows US$1.4 bn, net ODA received US$0.1 bn, total international reserves US$1.8 bn in 2008.

Japan

Population (millions, 2009)	127.6
Population growth (avg. annual %, 2000–09)	0.1
Population density (people per km², 2008)	350.4
Labor force (millions, 2008)	65.8
Unemployment rate (% of labor force, 2008)	4.0
Urban population (% of pop., 2009)	66.6
Surface area (1,000 km², 2008)	377.9
GNI (US$ billions, 2009)	5,198.9
GNI per capita, Atlas method (US$, 2009)	37,870
GDP growth (avg. annual %, 2005–09)	0.0
Poverty headcount ratio at national poverty line (% of pop., 2005)	—
Age dependency ratio (2009)	54.5

Migration

EMIGRATION, 2010

- Stock of emigrants: **771.4 thousands**
- Stock of emigrants as percentage of population: **0.6%**
- Top destination countries: the United States, Brazil, Germany, Australia, the United Kingdom, Thailand, Canada, France, Malaysia, the Republic of Korea

SKILLED EMIGRATION, 2000

- Emigration rate of tertiary-educated population: **1.2%**
- Emigration of physicians: **2,377** or **0.9%** of physicians trained in the country (*Source: Bhargava, Docquier, and Moullan 2010*)

IMMIGRATION, 2010

- Stock of immigrants: **2,176.2 thousands**
- Stock of immigrants as percentage of population: **1.7%**
- Females as percentage of immigrants: **55.0%**
- Refugees as percentage of immigrants: **0.1%**
- Top source countries: China, the Republic of Korea, Brazil, the Philippines, Peru, the United States, Thailand, Vietnam, Indonesia, India

Remittances

US$ millions	2003	2004	2005	2006	2007	2008	2009	2010e
Inward remittance flows[a]	**1,078**	**931**	**1,080**	**1,380**	**1,577**	**1,929**	**1,776**	**1,911**
of which								
Workers' remittances	657	600	733	1,026	1,261	1,556	1,423	—
Compensation of employees	155	173	172	151	123	177	171	—
Migrants' transfers	267	157	175	203	193	196	182	—
Outward remittance flows	**1,773**	**1,411**	**1,281**	**3,476**	**4,037**	**4,743**	**4,069**	**—**
of which								
Workers' remittances	1,231	926	851	3,152	3,456	4,347	3,723	—
Compensation of employees	274	286	299	180	184	201	209	—
Migrants' transfers	269	198	131	144	398	195	136	—

a. For comparison: net FDI inflows US$24.6 bn, total international reserves US$1,030.8 bn in 2008.

Jordan

Middle East and North Africa	LOWER MIDDLE INCOME
Population (millions, 2009)	6.0
Population growth (avg. annual %, 2000–09)	2.4
Population density (people per km², 2008)	66.9
Labor force (millions, 2008)	1.6
Unemployment rate (% of labor force, 2008)	12.7
Urban population (% of pop., 2009)	78.5
Surface area (1,000 km², 2008)	88.8
GNI (US$ billions, 2009)	23.4
GNI per capita, Atlas method (US$, 2009)	3,740
GDP growth (avg. annual %, 2005–09)	7.2
Poverty headcount ratio at national poverty line (% of pop., 2005)	0.4
Age dependency ratio (2009)	61.6

Migration

EMIGRATION, 2010

- Stock of emigrants: **733.6 thousands**
- Stock of emigrants as percentage of population: **11.3%**
- Top destination countries: West Bank and Gaza, Saudi Arabia, the United States, Germany, Oman, Canada, the Arab Republic of Egypt, Australia, the United Kingdom, Italy

SKILLED EMIGRATION, 2000

- Emigration rate of tertiary-educated population: **7.2%**
- Emigration of physicians: **878** or **8.2%** of physicians trained in the country *(Source: Bhargava, Docquier, and Moullan 2010)*

IMMIGRATION, 2010

- Stock of immigrants: **2,973.0 thousands**
- Stock of immigrants as percentage of population: **45.9%**
- Females as percentage of immigrants: **49.2%**
- Refugees as percentage of immigrants: **85.0%**
- Top source countries: West Bank and Gaza, the Arab Republic of Egypt, Iraq, the Syrian Arab Republic, Sri Lanka, Indonesia, China, Bangladesh, Saudi Arabia, the Philippines

Remittances

US$ millions	2003	2004	2005	2006	2007	2008	2009	2010e
Inward remittance flows[a]	**2,201**	**2,330**	**2,500**	**2,883**	**3,434**	**3,794**	**3,597**	**3,789**
of which								
Workers' remittances	1,981	2,059	2,179	2,514	2,994	3,159	3,119	–
Compensation of employees	220	272	321	369	440	635	478	–
Migrants' transfers	–	–	–	–	–	–	–	–
Outward remittance flows	**227**	**272**	**349**	**402**	**479**	**472**	**502**	**–**
of which								
Workers' remittances	200	240	308	354	423	416	443	–
Compensation of employees	27	32	41	47	57	56	59	–
Migrants' transfers	–	–	–	–	–	–	–	–

a. For comparison: net FDI inflows US$2.0 bn, net ODA received US$0.7 bn, total international reserves US$8.9 bn, exports of goods and services US$12.4 bn in 2008.

Kazakhstan

Population (millions, 2009)	15.9
Population growth (avg. annual %, 2000–09)	0.6
Population density (people per km², 2008)	5.8
Labor force (millions, 2008)	8.2
Unemployment rate (% of labor force, 2008)	–
Urban population (% of pop., 2009)	58.2
Surface area (1,000 km², 2008)	2,724.9
GNI (US$ billions, 2009)	97.3
GNI per capita, Atlas method (US$, 2009)	6,740
GDP growth (avg. annual %, 2005–09)	6.8
Poverty headcount ratio at national poverty line (% of pop., 2005)	1.2
Age dependency ratio (2009)	44.6

Migration

EMIGRATION, 2010

- Stock of emigrants: **3,717.3 thousands**
- Stock of emigrants as percentage of population: **23.6%**
- Top destination countries: the Russian Federation, Ukraine, Uzbekistan, Israel, Germany, Turkmenistan, the United States, Latvia, Canada, the Kyrgyz Republic

SKILLED EMIGRATION, 2000

- Emigration rate of tertiary-educated population: **1.2%**
- Emigration of physicians: **124** or **0.2%** of physicians trained in the country
  (Source: Bhargava, Docquier, and Moullan 2010)

IMMIGRATION, 2010

- Stock of immigrants: **3,079.5 thousands**
- Stock of immigrants as percentage of population: **19.5%**
- Females as percentage of immigrants: **54.0%**
- Refugees as percentage of immigrants: **0.1%**
- Top source countries: the Russian Federation, Ukraine, Uzbekistan, Germany, Belarus, Azerbaijan, Turkey, Poland, Tajikistan, Moldova

Remittances

US$ millions	2003	2004	2005	2006	2007	2008	2009	2010e
Inward remittance flows[a]	**148**	**166**	**178**	**186**	**223**	**192**	**124**	**131**
of which								
Workers' remittances	38	53	56	73	132	120	56	–
Compensation of employees	4	4	6	11	11	5	5	–
Migrants' transfers	105	108	116	103	80	66	63	–
Outward remittance flows	**802**	**1,354**	**2,000**	**3,033**	**4,303**	**3,559**	**3,138**	**–**
of which								
Workers' remittances	421	806	1,158	2,000	2,998	2,004	1,704	–
Compensation of employees	230	414	735	959	1,214	1,457	1,310	–
Migrants' transfers	151	134	107	75	91	98	123	–

a. For comparison: net FDI inflows US$14.6 bn, net ODA received US$0.3 bn, total international reserves US$19.9 bn, exports of goods and services US$76.3 bn in 2008.

Kenya

Population (millions, 2009)	39.8
Population growth (avg. annual %, 2000–09)	2.6
Population density (people per km², 2008)	67.7
Labor force (millions, 2008)	17.4
Unemployment rate (% of labor force, 2008)	–
Urban population (% of pop., 2009)	21.9
Surface area (1,000 km², 2008)	580.4
GNI (US$ billions, 2009)	30.2
GNI per capita, Atlas method (US$, 2009)	770
GDP growth (avg. annual %, 2005–09)	4.6
Poverty headcount ratio at national poverty line (% of pop., 2005)	19.7
Age dependency ratio (2009)	83.3

Migration

EMIGRATION, 2010

- Stock of emigrants: **457.1 thousands**
- Stock of emigrants as percentage of population: **1.1%**
- Top destination countries: the United Kingdom, Tanzania, the United States, Uganda, Canada, Australia, Germany, India, the Netherlands, Switzerland

SKILLED EMIGRATION, 2000

- Emigration rate of tertiary-educated population: **38.4%**
- Emigration of physicians:
  - (a) **284** or **6.7%** of physicians trained in the country *(Source: Bhargava, Docquier, and Moullan 2010)*
  - (b) **3,975** or **50.8%** of physicians born in the country *(Source: Clemens and Pettersson 2006)*
- Emigration of nurses: **2,372** or **8.3%** of nurses born in the country

IMMIGRATION, 2010

- Stock of immigrants: **817.7 thousands**
- Stock of immigrants as percentage of population: **2.0%**
- Females as percentage of immigrants: **50.8%**
- Refugees as percentage of immigrants: **32.9%**
- Top source countries: Uganda, Tanzania, Sudan, Somalia, Ethiopia

Remittances

US$ millions	2003	2004	2005	2006	2007	2008	2009	2010e
Inward remittance flows[a]	**538**	**620**	**805**	**1,128**	**1,588**	**1,692**	**1,686**	**1,758**
of which								
Workers' remittances	66	376	425	570	645	667	631	–
Compensation of employees	–	–	–	–	–	–	–	–
Migrants' transfers	–	–	–	–	–	–	–	–
Outward remittance flows	**7**	**34**	**56**	**25**	**16**	**65**	**61**	–
of which								
Workers' remittances	7	34	56	25	16	64	–	–
Compensation of employees	–	–	–	–	–	–	–	–
Migrants' transfers	–	–	–	–	–	–	–	–

a. For comparison: net FDI inflows US$0.1 bn, net ODA received US$1.4 bn, total international reserves US$2.9 bn, exports of goods and services US$8.3 bn in 2008.

Kiribati

LOWER MIDDLE INCOME

Population (thousands, 2009)	98.0
Population growth (avg. annual %, 2000–09)	1.7
Population density (people per km², 2008)	119.2
Labor force (millions, 2008)	—
Unemployment rate (% of labor force, 2008)	—
Urban population (% of pop., 2009)	43.9
Surface area (1,000 km², 2008)	0.8
GNI (US$ billions, 2009)	0.2
GNI per capita, Atlas method (US$, 2009)	1,890
GDP growth (avg. annual %, 2005–09)	1.6
Poverty headcount ratio at national poverty line (% of pop., 2005)	—
Age dependency ratio (2009)	—

Migration

EMIGRATION, 2010

- Stock of emigrants: **6.4 thousands**
- Stock of emigrants as percentage of population: **6.5%**
- Top destination countries: the Solomon Islands, the United States, Germany, New Zealand, Australia, Fiji, the United Kingdom, Canada, Samoa, Japan

SKILLED EMIGRATION, 2000

- Emigration rate of tertiary-educated population: **23.1%**

IMMIGRATION, 2010

- Stock of immigrants: **2.0 thousands**
- Stock of immigrants as percentage of population: **2.0%**
- Females as percentage of immigrants: **48.8%**
- Refugees as percentage of immigrants: **0.0%**
- Top source countries: French Polynesia, Samoa, Tonga, American Samoa

Remittances

US$ millions	2003	2004	2005	2006	2007	2008	2009	2010e
Inward remittance flows	7	7	7	7	7	9	8	9
of which								
Workers' remittances	—	—	—	—	—	—	—	—
Compensation of employees	—	—	—	—	—	—	—	—
Migrants' transfers	—	—	—	—	—	—	—	—
Outward remittance flows	—	—	—	—	—	—	—	—
of which								
Workers' remittances	—	—	—	—	—	—	—	—
Compensation of employees	—	—	—	—	—	—	—	—
Migrants' transfers	—	—	—	—	—	—	—	—

Korea, Democratic People's Republic of

Population (millions, 2009)	23.9
Population growth (avg. annual %, 2000-09)	0.5
Population density (people per km², 2008)	198.1
Labor force (millions, 2008)	12.5
Unemployment rate (% of labor force, 2008)	—
Urban population (% of pop., 2009)	63.0
Surface area (1,000 km², 2008)	120.5
GNI (US$ billions, 2009)	—
GNI per capita, Atlas method (US$, 2009)	—
GDP growth (avg. annual %, 2005-09)	—
Poverty headcount ratio at national poverty line (% of pop., 2005)	—
Age dependency ratio (2009)	45.5

Migration

EMIGRATION, 2010

- Stock of emigrants: **300.8 thousands**
- Stock of emigrants as percentage of population: **1.3%**
- Top destination countries: the United States, Brazil, Germany, Paraguay, Ecuador, Greece, Denmark, Ireland, Australia, Cambodia

SKILLED EMIGRATION, 2000

- Skilled emigration data are currently not available for this country.

IMMIGRATION, 2010

- Stock of immigrants: **37.1 thousands**
- Stock of immigrants as percentage of population: **0.2%**
- Females as percentage of immigrants: **53.1%**
- Refugees as percentage of immigrants: **0.0%**

Remittances

Remittance data are currently not available for this country.

Korea, Republic of

Population (millions, 2009)	48.7
Population growth (avg. annual %, 2000–09)	0.4
Population density (people per km², 2008)	492.3
Labor force (millions, 2008)	24.2
Unemployment rate (% of labor force, 2008)	3.2
Urban population (% of pop., 2009)	81.7
Surface area (1,000 km², 2008)	99.3
GNI (US$ billions, 2009)	836.9
GNI per capita, Atlas method (US$, 2009)	19,830
GDP growth (avg. annual %, 2005–09)	3.3
Poverty headcount ratio at national poverty line (% of pop., 2005)	—
Age dependency ratio (2009)	37.9

Migration

EMIGRATION, 2010

- Stock of emigrants: **2,078.7 thousands**
- Stock of emigrants as percentage of population: **4.3%**
- Top destination countries: the United States, Japan, Canada, Australia, Germany, New Zealand, France, the United Kingdom, Denmark, Sweden

SKILLED EMIGRATION, 2000

- Emigration rate of tertiary-educated population: **5.6%**
- Emigration of physicians: **4,850** or **5.4%** of physicians trained in the country *(Source: Bhargava, Docquier, and Moullan 2010)*

IMMIGRATION, 2010

- Stock of immigrants: **534.8 thousands**
- Stock of immigrants as percentage of population: **1.1%**
- Females as percentage of immigrants: **52.7%**
- Refugees as percentage of immigrants: **0.0%**
- Top source countries: China, Vietnam, the United States, the Philippines, Thailand, Indonesia, Mongolia, Japan, Canada, Sri Lanka

Remittances

US$ millions	2003	2004	2005	2006	2007	2008	2009	2010e
Inward remittance flows[a]	**827**	**800**	**848**	**994**	**866**	**2,774**	**2,522**	**2,738**
of which								
Workers' remittances	42	30	64	138	174	372	373	—
Compensation of employees	732	713	745	685	692	745	448	—
Migrants' transfers	53	56	38	171	—	1,658	1,701	—
Outward remittance flows	**1,853**	**2,497**	**3,336**	**4,314**	**1,441**	**3,109**	**3,120**	**—**
of which								
Workers' remittances	359	559	839	982	1,255	1,419	1,426	—
Compensation of employees	97	126	119	141	186	556	646	—
Migrants' transfers	1,396	1,812	2,378	3,190	—	1,134	1,047	—

a. For comparison: net FDI inflows US$2.2 bn, total international reserves US$201.5 bn, exports of goods and services US$491.1 bn in 2008.

Kosovo

Population (millions, 2009)	1.8
Population growth (avg. annual %, 2000–09)	0.2
Population density (people per km², 2008)	–
Labor force (millions, 2008)	–
Unemployment rate (% of labor force, 2008)	–
Urban population (% of pop., 2009)	–
Surface area (1,000 km², 2008)	–
GNI (US$ billions, 2009)	5.6
GNI per capita, Atlas method (US$, 2009)	3,240
GDP growth (avg. annual %, 2005–09)	4.2
Poverty headcount ratio at national poverty line (% of pop., 2005)	–
Age dependency ratio (2009)	–

Migration

EMIGRATION, 2010

- Stock of emigrants: **25.3 thousands**
- Top destination country: the United States

SKILLED EMIGRATION, 2000

- Skilled emigration data are currently not available for this country.

IMMIGRATION, 2010

- Immigration data are currently not available for this country.

Remittances

Remittance data are currently not available for this country.

Kuwait

Population (millions, 2009)	2.8
Population growth (avg. annual %, 2000–09)	2.8
Population density (people per km², 2008)	153.1
Labor force (millions, 2008)	1.4
Unemployment rate (% of labor force, 2008)	–
Urban population (% of pop., 2009)	98.4
Surface area (1,000 km², 2008)	17.8
GNI (US$ billions, 2009)	–
GNI per capita, Atlas method (US$, 2009)	–
GDP growth (avg. annual %, 2005–09)	–
Poverty headcount ratio at national poverty line (% of pop., 2005)	–
Age dependency ratio (2009)	34.4

Migration

EMIGRATION, 2010

- Stock of emigrants: **259.4 thousands**
- Stock of emigrants as percentage of population: **8.5%**
- Top destination countries: Saudi Arabia, Iraq, the United States, Canada, the United Kingdom, India, Jordan, Australia, the Arab Republic of Egypt, Denmark

SKILLED EMIGRATION, 2000

- Emigration rate of tertiary-educated population: **7.1%**
- Emigration of physicians: **122** or **3.4%** of physicians trained in the country
  (Source: Bhargava, Docquier, and Moullan 2010)

IMMIGRATION, 2010

- Stock of immigrants: **2,097.5 thousands**
- Stock of immigrants as percentage of population: **68.8%**
- Females as percentage of immigrants: **30.0%**
- Refugees as percentage of immigrants: **1.8%**
- Top source countries: India, the Arab Republic of Egypt, Sri Lanka, Bangladesh, the Syrian Arab Republic, Pakistan, the Islamic Republic of Iran, the Philippines, Indonesia

Remittances

US$ millions	2003	2004	2005	2006	2007	2008	2009	2010e
Inward remittance flows[a]	–	–	–	–	–	–	–	–
of which								
Workers' remittances	–	–	–	–	–	–	–	–
Compensation of employees	–	–	–	–	–	–	–	–
Migrants' transfers	–	–	–	–	–	–	–	–
Outward remittance flows	**2,144**	**2,404**	**2,648**	**3,183**	**9,764**	**10,323**	**9,912**	–
of which								
Workers' remittances	2,144	2,404	2,648	3,183	9,764	10,323	9,912	–
Compensation of employees	–	–	–	–	–	–	–	–
Migrants' transfers	–	–	–	–	–	–	–	–

a. **For comparison: net FDI inflows US$0.1 bn, total international reserves US$19.3 bn, exports of goods and services US$98.3 bn in 2008.**

Kyrgyz Republic

Population (millions, 2009)	5.3
Population growth (avg. annual %, 2000–09)	0.9
Population density (people per km², 2008)	27.5
Labor force (millions, 2008)	2.3
Unemployment rate (% of labor force, 2008)	–
Urban population (% of pop., 2009)	36.4
Surface area (1,000 km², 2008)	199.9
GNI (US$ billions, 2009)	4.4
GNI per capita, Atlas method (US$, 2009)	870
GDP growth (avg. annual %, 2005–09)	4.4
Poverty headcount ratio at national poverty line (% of pop., 2005)	21.8
Age dependency ratio (2009)	52.8

Migration

EMIGRATION, 2010

- Stock of emigrants: **620.7 thousands**
- Stock of emigrants as percentage of population: **11.2%**
- Top destination countries: the Russian Federation, Ukraine, Israel, Germany, Kazakhstan, Tajikistan, the United States, Latvia, Turkey, Canada

SKILLED EMIGRATION, 2000

- Emigration rate of tertiary-educated population: **0.7%**
- Emigration of physicians: **11** or **0.1%** of physicians trained in the country
  (Source: Bhargava, Docquier, and Moullan 2010)

IMMIGRATION, 2010

- Stock of immigrants: **222.7 thousands**
- Stock of immigrants as percentage of population: **4.0%**
- Females as percentage of immigrants: **58.2%**
- Refugees as percentage of immigrants: **0.3%**
- Top source countries: Uzbekistan, the Russian Federation, Ukraine, Kazakhstan, Tajikistan, Turkey, Germany

Remittances

US$ millions	2003	2004	2005	2006	2007	2008	2009	2010e
Inward remittance flows[a]	**78**	**189**	**322**	**481**	**715**	**1,232**	**882**	**1,037**
of which								
Workers' remittances	70	179	313	473	705	1,224	–	–
Compensation of employees	–	–	–	–	–	–	–	–
Migrants' transfers	8	10	9	8	9	8	–	–
Outward remittance flows	**55**	**82**	**122**	**145**	**220**	**196**	**188**	**–**
of which								
Workers' remittances	5	15	33	44	70	77	82	–
Compensation of employees	13	14	17	19	21	22	27	–
Migrants' transfers	37	53	72	82	129	98	79	–

a. For comparison: net FDI inflows US$0.2 bn, net ODA received US$0.4 bn, total international reserves US$1.2 bn, exports of goods and services US$2.9 bn in 2008.

Lao People's Democratic Republic

East Asia and Pacific	LOW INCOME
Population (millions, 2009)	6.3
Population growth (avg. annual %, 2000–09)	1.8
Population density (people per km², 2008)	26.9
Labor force (millions, 2008)	3.0
Unemployment rate (% of labor force, 2008)	–
Urban population (% of pop., 2009)	32.0
Surface area (1,000 km², 2008)	236.8
GNI (US$ billions, 2009)	5.8
GNI per capita, Atlas method (US$, 2009)	880
GDP growth (avg. annual %, 2005–09)	7.4
Poverty headcount ratio at national poverty line (% of pop., 2005)	35.7
Age dependency ratio (2009)	70.0

Migration

EMIGRATION, 2010

- Stock of emigrants: **366.6 thousands**
- Stock of emigrants as percentage of population: **5.7%**
- Top destination countries: the United States, Thailand, France, Canada, Australia, Japan, Germany, Belgium, Cambodia, New Zealand

SKILLED EMIGRATION, 2000

- Emigration rate of tertiary-educated population: **37.4%**
- Emigration of physicians: **22** or **0.7%** of physicians trained in the country
  (*Source: Bhargava, Docquier, and Moullan 2010*)

IMMIGRATION, 2010

- Stock of immigrants: **18.9 thousands**
- Stock of immigrants as percentage of population: **0.3%**
- Females as percentage of immigrants: **48.0%**
- Refugees as percentage of immigrants: **0.0%**
- Top source countries: Vietnam, China, Thailand, Cambodia, Myanmar

Remittances

US$ millions	2003	2004	2005	2006	2007	2008	2009	2010e
Inward remittance flowsᵃ	1	1	1	1	1	1	1	1
of which								
Workers' remittances	–	–	–	–	–	–	–	–
Compensation of employees	–	–	–	–	–	–	–	–
Migrants' transfers	–	–	–	–	–	–	–	–
Outward remittance flows	–	–	–	–	–	–	–	–
of which								
Workers' remittances	–	–	–	–	–	–	–	–
Compensation of employees	–	–	–	–	–	–	–	–
Migrants' transfers	–	–	–	–	–	–	–	–

a. For comparison: net FDI inflows US$0.2 bn, net ODA received US$0.5 bn, total international reserves US$0.9 bn, exports of goods and services US$1.8 bn in 2008.

Latvia

Population (millions, 2009)	2.3
Population growth (avg. annual %, 2000–09)	-0.6
Population density (people per km², 2008)	36.4
Labor force (millions, 2008)	1.2
Unemployment rate (% of labor force, 2008)	7.5
Urban population (% of pop., 2009)	68.2
Surface area (1,000 km², 2008)	64.6
GNI (US$ billions, 2009)	28.1
GNI per capita, Atlas method (US$, 2009)	12,390
GDP growth (avg. annual %, 2005–09)	2.0
Poverty headcount ratio at national poverty line (% of pop., 2005)	0.0
Age dependency ratio (2009)	45.1

Migration

EMIGRATION, 2010

- Stock of emigrants: **272.6 thousands**
- Stock of emigrants as percentage of population: **12.2%**
- Top destination countries: the Russian Federation, the United States, the United Kingdom, Ireland, Germany, Israel, Canada, Australia, Lithuania, Sweden

SKILLED EMIGRATION, 2000

- Emigration rate of tertiary-educated population: **8.8%**
- Emigration of physicians: **235** or **3.0%** of physicians trained in the country *(Source: Bhargava, Docquier, and Moullan 2010)*

IMMIGRATION, 2010

- Stock of immigrants: **335.0 thousands**
- Stock of immigrants as percentage of population: **15.0%**
- Females as percentage of immigrants: **59.3%**
- Refugees as percentage of immigrants: **0.0%**
- Top source countries: the Russian Federation, Ukraine, Uzbekistan, Belarus, Kazakhstan, Lithuania, Azerbaijan, Georgia, Estonia, Tajikistan

Remittances

US$ millions	2003	2004	2005	2006	2007	2008	2009	2010e
Inward remittance flows[a]	**173**	**229**	**381**	**482**	**552**	**601**	**599**	**643**
of which								
Workers' remittances	2	2	2	2	2	2	2	–
Compensation of employees	172	228	379	481	551	600	589	–
Migrants' transfers	–	–	–	–	–	–	–	–
Outward remittance flows	**8**	**13**	**20**	**30**	**45**	**58**	**46**	**–**
of which								
Workers' remittances	3	4	4	4	5	4	3	–
Compensation of employees	5	10	16	25	40	54	43	–
Migrants' transfers	–	–	–	–	–	–	–	–

a. For comparison: net FDI inflows US$1.4 bn, total international reserves US$5.2 bn, exports of goods and services US$14.1 bn in 2008.

Lebanon

Population (millions, 2009)	4.2
Population growth (avg. annual %, 2000–09)	1.3
Population density (people per km², 2008)	404.6
Labor force (millions, 2008)	1.5
Unemployment rate (% of labor force, 2008)	—
Urban population (% of pop., 2009)	87.1
Surface area (1,000 km², 2008)	10.4
GNI (US$ billions, 2009)	35.2
GNI per capita, Atlas method (US$, 2009)	7,970
GDP growth (avg. annual %, 2005–09)	5.3
Poverty headcount ratio at national poverty line (% of pop., 2005)	—
Age dependency ratio (2009)	48.4

Migration

EMIGRATION, 2010

- Stock of emigrants: **664.1 thousands**
- Stock of emigrants as percentage of population: **15.6%**
- Top destination countries: the United States, Australia, Canada, Germany, Saudi Arabia, France, Sweden, Brazil, West Bank and Gaza, the United Kingdom

SKILLED EMIGRATION, 2000

- Emigration rate of tertiary-educated population: **38.6%**
- Emigration of physicians: **3,042** or **19.0%** of physicians trained in the country *(Source: Bhargava, Docquier, and Moullan 2010)*

IMMIGRATION, 2010

- Stock of immigrants: **758.2 thousands**
- Stock of immigrants as percentage of population: **17.8%**
- Females as percentage of immigrants: **49.2%**
- Refugees as percentage of immigrants: **61.0%**

Remittances

US$ millions	2003	2004	2005	2006	2007	2008	2009	2010e
Inward remittance flows[a]	**4,743**	**5,591**	**4,924**	**5,202**	**5,769**	**7,181**	**7,558**	**8,177**
of which								
Workers' remittances	3,964	5,183	4,257	4,623	5,022	5,775	6,385	—
Compensation of employees	779	409	667	579	747	1,405	1,173	—
Migrants' transfers	—	—	—	—	—	—	—	—
Outward remittance flows	**4,081**	**4,233**	**4,012**	**3,445**	**2,967**	**4,366**	**5,749**	**—**
of which								
Workers' remittances	3,694	3,573	3,281	2,783	2,370	3,576	4,715	—
Compensation of employees	387	660	731	661	597	790	1,034	—
Migrants' transfers	—	—	—	—	—	—	—	—

a. For comparison: net FDI inflows US$3.6 bn, net ODA received US$1.1 bn, total international reserves US$28.3 bn, exports of goods and services US$7.9 bn in 2008.

Lesotho

Population (millions, 2009)	2.1
Population growth (avg. annual %, 2000–09)	1.1
Population density (people per km², 2008)	66.5
Labor force (millions, 2008)	0.9
Unemployment rate (% of labor force, 2008)	–
Urban population (% of pop., 2009)	26.2
Surface area (1,000 km², 2008)	30.4
GNI (US$ billions, 2009)	2.1
GNI per capita, Atlas method (US$, 2009)	1,030
GDP growth (avg. annual %, 2005–09)	4.0
Poverty headcount ratio at national poverty line (% of pop., 2005)	38.7
Age dependency ratio (2009)	77.3

Migration

EMIGRATION, 2010

- Stock of emigrants: **427.5 thousands**
- Stock of emigrants as percentage of population: **20.5%**
- Top destination countries: South Africa, Mozambique, Tanzania, the United Kingdom, the United States, Canada, Germany, Ireland, Australia, Switzerland

SKILLED EMIGRATION, 2000

- Emigration rate of tertiary-educated population: **4.3%**
- Emigration of physicians: **57** or **33.3%** of physicians born in the country *(Source: Clemens and Pettersson 2006)*
- Emigration of nurses: **36** or **2.8%** of nurses born in the country

IMMIGRATION, 2010

- Stock of immigrants: **6.3 thousands**
- Stock of immigrants as percentage of population: **0.3%**
- Females as percentage of immigrants: **45.5%**
- Refugees as percentage of immigrants: **0.0%**
- Top source countries: South Africa, Zimbabwe, Tanzania, Botswana, Zambia, Swaziland, Malawi, Mozambique, Namibia, Angola

Remittances

US$ millions	2003	2004	2005	2006	2007	2008	2009	2010e
Inward remittance flows[a]	**288**	**355**	**327**	**361**	**451**	**439**	**450**	**525**
of which								
Workers' remittances	11	14	7	4	13	7	–	–
Compensation of employees	276	341	320	357	438	432	–	–
Migrants' transfers	–	–	–	–	–	–	–	–
Outward remittance flows	**27**	**29**	**17**	**11**	**21**	**13**	**13**	**–**
of which								
Workers' remittances	–	–	–	–	–	–	–	–
Compensation of employees	27	29	17	11	21	13	–	–
Migrants' transfers	–	–	–	–	–	–	–	–

a. For comparison: net FDI inflows US$0.2 bn, net ODA received US$0.1 bn, exports of goods and services US$0.8 bn in 2008.

Liberia

Sub-Saharan Africa **LOW INCOME**

Population (millions, 2009)	4.0
Population growth (avg. annual %, 2000–09)	4.0
Population density (people per km², 2008)	39.4
Labor force (millions, 2008)	1.4
Unemployment rate (% of labor force, 2008)	–
Urban population (% of pop., 2009)	60.8
Surface area (1,000 km², 2008)	111.4
GNI (US$ billions, 2009)	0.6
GNI per capita, Atlas method (US$, 2009)	160
GDP growth (avg. annual %, 2005–09)	6.8
Poverty headcount ratio at national poverty line (% of pop., 2005)	86.1
Age dependency ratio (2009)	84.6

Migration

EMIGRATION, 2010

- Stock of emigrants: **431.9 thousands**
- Stock of emigrants as percentage of population: **10.5%**
- Top destination countries: Guinea, Côte d'Ivoire, the United States, Sierra Leone, Nigeria, Germany, Italy, Australia, the Netherlands, the United Kingdom

SKILLED EMIGRATION, 2000

- Emigration rate of tertiary-educated population: **45.0%**
- Emigration of physicians:
  - (a) **71** or **49.8%** of physicians trained in the country *(Source: Bhargava, Docquier, and Moullan 2010)*
  - (b) **126** or **63.3%** of physicians born in the country *(Source: Clemens and Pettersson 2006)*
- Emigration of nurses: 807 or 81.4% of nurses born in the country

IMMIGRATION, 2010

- Stock of immigrants: **96.3 thousands**
- Stock of immigrants as percentage of population: **2.3%**
- Females as percentage of immigrants: **45.1%**
- Refugees as percentage of immigrants: **13.8%**
- Top source countries: Guinea, Ghana, Sierra Leone, Côte d'Ivoire, Lebanon, Nigeria, Mali, India, Togo, the United Kingdom

Remittances

US$ millions	2003	2004	2005	2006	2007	2008	2009	2010e
Inward remittance flows[a]	–	**58**	**32**	**79**	**62**	**58**	**54**	**57**
of which								
Workers' remittances	–	53	23	60	42	36	–	–
Compensation of employees	–	5	9	18	20	22	–	–
Migrants' transfers	–	–	–	–	–	–	–	–
Outward remittance flows	–	**0**	**0**	**0**	**0**	**0**	–	–
of which								
Workers' remittances	–	–	–	–	–	–	–	–
Compensation of employees	–	0	0	0	0	0	–	–
Migrants' transfers	–	–	–	–	–	–	–	–

a. For comparison: net FDI inflows US$0.1 bn, net ODA received US$1.3 bn, total international reserves US$0.2 bn, exports of goods and services US$0.3 bn in 2008.

Libya

Population (millions, 2009)	6.4
Population growth (avg. annual %, 2000–09)	2.0
Population density (people per km², 2008)	3.6
Labor force (millions, 2008)	2.3
Unemployment rate (% of labor force, 2008)	–
Urban population (% of pop., 2009)	77.7
Surface area (1,000 km², 2008)	1,759.5
GNI (US$ billions, 2009)	62.0
GNI per capita, Atlas method (US$, 2009)	12,020
GDP growth (avg. annual %, 2005–09)	5.5
Poverty headcount ratio at national poverty line (% of pop., 2005)	–
Age dependency ratio (2009)	52.4

Migration

EMIGRATION, 2010

- Stock of emigrants: **110.1 thousands**
- Stock of emigrants as percentage of population: **1.7%**
- Top destination countries: Israel, the United Kingdom, Chad, the United States, Jordan, the Arab Republic of Egypt, Germany, Turkey, Canada, Italy

SKILLED EMIGRATION, 2000

- Emigration rate of tertiary-educated population: **2.4%**
- Emigration of physicians:
  - (a) **800** or **10.6%** of physicians trained in the country *(Source: Bhargava, Docquier, and Moullan 2010)*
  - (b) **585** or **8.4%** of physicians born in the country *(Source: Clemens and Pettersson 2006)*
- Emigration of nurses: **391** or **2.2%** of nurses born in the country

IMMIGRATION, 2010

- Stock of immigrants: **682.5 thousands**
- Stock of immigrants as percentage of population: **10.4%**
- Females as percentage of immigrants: **35.5%**
- Refugees as percentage of immigrants: **0.5%**
- Top source countries: the Arab Republic of Egypt, Tunisia, West Bank and Gaza, the Syrian Arab Republic

Remittances

US$ millions	2003	2004	2005	2006	2007	2008	2009	2010e
Inward remittance flows[a]	8	10	15	16	16	16	14	16
of which								
Workers' remittances	3	5	7	6	–	–	–	–
Compensation of employees	5	5	8	10	–	–	–	–
Migrants' transfers	–	–	–	–	–	–	–	–
Outward remittance flows	676	975	914	945	762	964	1,000	–
of which								
Workers' remittances	644	940	854	880	762	964	–	–
Compensation of employees	32	35	60	65	–	–	–	–
Migrants' transfers	–	–	–	–	–	–	–	–

a. For comparison: net FDI inflows US$4.1 bn, net ODA received US$0.1 bn, total international reserves US$96.3 bn, exports of goods and services US$62.8 bn in 2008.

Liechtenstein

Population (thousands, 2009)	36.0
Population growth (avg. annual %, 2000–09)	1.0
Population density (people per km², 2008)	222.0
Labor force (millions, 2008)	–
Unemployment rate (% of labor force, 2008)	–
Urban population (% of pop., 2009)	14.3
Surface area (1,000 km², 2008)	0.2
GNI (US$ billions, 2009)	–
GNI per capita, Atlas method (US$, 2009)	–
GDP growth (avg. annual %, 2005–09)	–
Poverty headcount ratio at national poverty line (% of pop., 2005)	–
Age dependency ratio (2009)	–

Migration

EMIGRATION, 2010

- Stock of emigrants: **6.2 thousands**
- Stock of emigrants as percentage of population: **17.1%**
- Top destination countries: Switzerland, Greece, Austria, Germany, Spain, France, the United States, Canada, Italy, the United Kingdom

SKILLED EMIGRATION, 2000

- Emigration rate of tertiary-educated population: **17.0**

IMMIGRATION, 2010

- Stock of immigrants: **12.5 thousands**
- Stock of immigrants as percentage of population: **34.6%**
- Females as percentage of immigrants: **48.3%**
- Refugees as percentage of immigrants: **2.2%**
- Top source countries: Switzerland, Austria, Germany, Italy, Turkey, Portugal, Spain, Bosnia and Herzegovina, Croatia, the former Yugoslav Republic of Macedonia

Remittances

Remittance data are currently not available for this country.

Lithuania

Europe and Central Asia	UPPER MIDDLE INCOME

Population (millions, 2009)	3.3
Population growth (avg. annual %, 2000–09)	-0.6
Population density (people per km², 2008)	53.6
Labor force (millions, 2008)	1.6
Unemployment rate (% of labor force, 2008)	5.8
Urban population (% of pop., 2009)	67.0
Surface area (1,000 km², 2008)	65.3
GNI (US$ billions, 2009)	37.2
GNI per capita, Atlas method (US$, 2009)	11,410
GDP growth (avg. annual %, 2005–09)	2.6
Poverty headcount ratio at national poverty line (% of pop., 2005)	0.4
Age dependency ratio (2009)	45.1

Migration

EMIGRATION, 2010

- Stock of emigrants: **440.4 thousands**
- Stock of emigrants as percentage of population: **13.5%**
- Top destination countries: the Russian Federation, Poland, the United Kingdom, Ireland, the United States, Spain, Israel, Germany, Latvia, Canada

SKILLED EMIGRATION, 2000

- Emigration rate of tertiary-educated population: **8.6%**
- Emigration of physicians: **318** or **2.2%** of physicians trained in the country *(Source: Bhargava, Docquier, and Moullan 2010)*

IMMIGRATION, 2010

- Stock of immigrants: **128.9 thousands**
- Stock of immigrants as percentage of population: **4.0%**
- Females as percentage of immigrants: **56.6%**
- Refugees as percentage of immigrants: **0.5%**
- Top source countries: the Russian Federation, Belarus, Ukraine, Latvia, Kazakhstan, Poland, Uzbekistan, Germany, Azerbaijan, Estonia

Remittances

US$ millions	2003	2004	2005	2006	2007	2008	2009	2010e
Inward remittance flows[a]	**115**	**324**	**534**	**994**	**1,433**	**1,460**	**1,168**	**1,210**
of which								
Workers' remittances	33	162	310	746	1,177	1,263	982	–
Compensation of employees	82	163	224	248	256	197	186	–
Migrants' transfers	–	–	–	–	–	–	–	–
Outward remittance flows	**42**	**28**	**47**	**426**	**567**	**615**	**620**	**–**
of which								
Workers' remittances	6	2	2	375	481	536	492	–
Compensation of employees	36	26	45	51	85	79	127	–
Migrants' transfers	–	–	–	–	–	–	–	–

a. For comparison: net FDI inflows US$1.8 bn, total international reserves US$6.4 bn, exports of goods and services US$28.0 bn in 2008.

Luxembourg

Population (millions, 2009)	0.5
Population growth (avg. annual %, 2000–09)	1.5
Population density (people per km², 2008)	188.3
Labor force (millions, 2008)	0.2
Unemployment rate (% of labor force, 2008)	5.1
Urban population (% of pop., 2009)	82.3
Surface area (1,000 km², 2008)	2.6
GNI (US$ billions, 2009)	36.0
GNI per capita, Atlas method (US$, 2009)	74,430
GDP growth (avg. annual %, 2005–09)	2.8
Poverty headcount ratio at national poverty line (% of pop., 2005)	—
Age dependency ratio (2009)	46.7

Migration

EMIGRATION, 2010

- Stock of emigrants: **57.8 thousands**
- Stock of emigrants as percentage of population: **11.8%**
- Top destination countries: Germany, Belgium, France, Portugal, the United States, Spain, the United Kingdom, Switzerland, the Netherlands, Canada

SKILLED EMIGRATION, 2000

- Emigration rate of tertiary-educated population: **8.0%**
- Emigration of physicians: **22** or **2.0%** of physicians trained in the country
  (Source: Bhargava, Docquier, and Moullan 2010)

IMMIGRATION, 2010

- Stock of immigrants: **173.2 thousands**
- Stock of immigrants as percentage of population: **35.2%**
- Females as percentage of immigrants: **50.2%**
- Refugees as percentage of immigrants: **1.4%**
- Top source countries: Portugal, France, Belgium, Germany, Italy, the Netherlands, the United Kingdom, Cape Verde, Spain, Bosnia and Herzegovina

Remittances

US$ millions	2003	2004	2005	2006	2007	2008	2009	2010e
Inward remittance flows[a]	**1,022**	**1,130**	**1,269**	**1,361**	**1,554**	**1,723**	**1,718**	**1,724**
of which								
Workers' remittances	1	4	4	4	5	3	–	–
Compensation of employees	994	1,115	1,259	1,345	1,525	1,701	–	–
Migrants' transfers	28	11	5	12	23	19	–	–
Outward remittance flows	**5,011**	**6,000**	**6,627**	**7,414**	**9,068**	**10,832**	**10,556**	**–**
of which								
Workers' remittances	53	65	68	81	92	101	–	–
Compensation of employees	4,930	5,928	6,542	7,302	8,963	10,698	–	–
Migrants' transfers	27	7	17	30	13	32	–	–

a. For comparison: net FDI inflows US$115.8 bn, total international reserves US$0.4 bn, exports of goods and services US$96.3 bn in 2008.

Macao SAR, China

Population (millions, 2009)	0.5
Population growth (avg. annual %, 2000–09)	2.1
Population density (people per km², 2008)	18,658.8
Labor force (millions, 2008)	0.3
Unemployment rate (% of labor force, 2008)	2.9
Urban population (% of pop., 2009)	100.0
Surface area (1,000 km², 2008)	0.0
GNI (US$ billions, 2009)	—
GNI per capita, Atlas method (US$, 2009)	—
GDP growth (avg. annual %, 2005–09)	—
Poverty headcount ratio at national poverty line (% of pop., 2005)	—
Age dependency ratio (2009)	25.2

Migration

EMIGRATION, 2010

- Stock of emigrants: **97.9 thousands**
- Stock of emigrants as percentage of population: **17.9%**
- Top destination countries: Hong Kong SAR, China; the United States; Canada; Portugal; Australia; the United Kingdom; New Zealand; Ireland; France; the Netherlands

SKILLED EMIGRATION, 2000

- Emigration rate of tertiary-educated population: **14.4%**

IMMIGRATION, 2010

- Stock of immigrants: **299.7 thousands**
- Stock of immigrants as percentage of population: **54.7%**
- Females as percentage of immigrants: **51.7%**
- Refugees as percentage of immigrants: **0.0%**
- Top source countries: China; Hong Kong SAR, China; the Philippines; Portugal; Thailand

Remittances

US$ millions	2003	2004	2005	2006	2007	2008	2009	2010e
Inward remittance flows[a]	**161**	**355**	**588**	**511**	**399**	**507**	**488**	**571**
of which								
Workers' remittances	48	53	53	55	60	63	—	—
Compensation of employees	—	—	—	—	—	—	—	—
Migrants' transfers	113	302	534	456	339	444	—	—
Outward remittance flows	**119**	**160**	**229**	**494**	**838**	**961**	**707**	**—**
of which								
Workers' remittances	83	106	156	326	655	741	—	—
Compensation of employees	11	26	54	151	168	196	—	—
Migrants' transfers	25	28	20	17	15	23	—	—

a. For comparison: net FDI inflows US$3.4 bn, total international reserves US$15.9 bn in 2008.

Macedonia, Former Yugoslav Republic of

Population (millions, 2009)	2.0
Population growth (avg. annual %, 2000–09)	0.2
Population density (people per km², 2008)	80.1
Labor force (millions, 2008)	0.9
Unemployment rate (% of labor force, 2008)	33.8
Urban population (% of pop., 2009)	67.4
Surface area (1,000 km², 2008)	25.7
GNI (US$ billions, 2009)	9.4
GNI per capita, Atlas method (US$, 2009)	4,400
GDP growth (avg. annual %, 2005–09)	3.6
Poverty headcount ratio at national poverty line (% of pop., 2005)	0.3
Age dependency ratio (2009)	42.4

Migration

EMIGRATION, 2010

- Stock of emigrants: **447.1 thousands**
- Stock of emigrants as percentage of population: **21.9%**
- Top destination countries: Italy, Germany, Australia, Switzerland, Turkey, Austria, Slovenia, Croatia, France, Canada

SKILLED EMIGRATION, 2000

- Emigration rate of tertiary-educated population: **29.1%**
- Emigration of physicians: **91** or **2.0%** of physicians trained in the country
  (Source: Bhargava, Docquier, and Moullan 2010)

IMMIGRATION, 2010

- Stock of immigrants: **129.7 thousands**
- Stock of immigrants as percentage of population: **6.3%**
- Females as percentage of immigrants: **58.3%**
- Refugees as percentage of immigrants: **1.0%**
- Top source countries: Albania, Turkey, Serbia, Bosnia and Herzegovina

Remittances

US$ millions	2003	2004	2005	2006	2007	2008	2009	2010e
Inward remittance flows[a]	**174**	**213**	**227**	**267**	**345**	**407**	**401**	**414**
of which								
Workers' remittances	146	161	169	198	239	266	260	–
Compensation of employees	28	52	57	69	106	140	121	–
Migrants' transfers	–	–	–	–	–	–	–	–
Outward remittance flows	**16**	**16**	**16**	**18**	**25**	**33**	**26**	–
of which								
Workers' remittances	15	15	14	16	22	28	22	–
Compensation of employees	1	1	2	2	3	5	4	–
Migrants' transfers	–	–	–	–	–	–	–	–

a. For comparison: net FDI inflows US$0.6 bn, net ODA received US$0.2 bn, total international reserves US$2.1 bn, exports of goods and services US$5.0 bn in 2008.

Madagascar

Population (millions, 2009)	19.6
Population growth (avg. annual %, 2000–09)	2.8
Population density (people per km², 2008)	32.9
Labor force (millions, 2008)	8.9
Unemployment rate (% of labor force, 2008)	–
Urban population (% of pop., 2009)	29.9
Surface area (1,000 km², 2008)	587.0
GNI (US$ billions, 2009)	8.9
GNI per capita, Atlas method (US$, 2008)	410
GDP growth (avg. annual %, 2004–08)	5.6
Poverty headcount ratio at national poverty line (% of pop., 2005)	67.8
Age dependency ratio (2009)	85.0

Migration

EMIGRATION, 2010

- Stock of emigrants: **79.8 thousands**
- Stock of emigrants as percentage of population: **0.4%**
- Top destination countries: France, the Comoros, Canada, Belgium, the United States, Italy, Mauritius, Switzerland, the United Kingdom, Germany

SKILLED EMIGRATION, 2000

- Emigration rate of tertiary-educated population: **7.6%**
- Emigration of physicians:
  - (a) **34** or **2.1%** of physicians trained in the country *(Source: Bhargava, Docquier, and Moullan 2010)*
  - (b) **920** or **39.2%** of physicians born in the country *(Source: Clemens and Pettersson 2006)*
- Emigration of nurses: **1,171** or **27.5%** of nurses born in the country

IMMIGRATION, 2010

- Stock of immigrants: **37.8 thousands**
- Stock of immigrants as percentage of population: **0.2%**
- Females as percentage of immigrants: **46.1%**
- Refugees as percentage of immigrants: **0.0%**
- Top source countries: France, the Comoros, India, Algeria, China, Pakistan, Mauritius, Germany, Italy, the United States

Remittances

US$ millions	2003	2004	2005	2006	2007	2008	2009	2010e
Inward remittance flows[a]	**16**	**12**	**11**	**11**	**11**	**11**	**10**	**10**
of which								
Workers' remittances	8	4	1	–	–	–	–	–
Compensation of employees	8	7	10	–	–	–	–	–
Migrants' transfers	–	–	–	–	–	–	–	–
Outward remittance flows	**18**	**9**	**21**	**–**	**–**	**–**	**–**	**–**
of which								
Workers' remittances	13	3	8	–	–	–	–	–
Compensation of employees	5	6	13	–	–	–	–	–
Migrants' transfers	–	–	–	–	–	–	–	–

a. For comparison: net FDI inflows US$1.5 bn, net ODA received US$0.8 bn, total international reserves US$1.0 bn, exports of goods and services US$2.5 bn in 2008.

Malawi

Sub-Saharan Africa — **LOW INCOME**

Population (millions, 2009)	15.3
Population growth (avg. annual %, 2000–09)	2.9
Population density (people per km², 2008)	151.8
Labor force (millions, 2008)	5.8
Unemployment rate (% of labor force, 2008)	–
Urban population (% of pop., 2009)	19.3
Surface area (1,000 km², 2008)	118.5
GNI (US$ billions, 2009)	4.4
GNI per capita, Atlas method (US$, 2009)	280
GDP growth (avg. annual %, 2005–09)	7.4
Poverty headcount ratio at national poverty line (% of pop., 2005)	73.9
Age dependency ratio (2009)	97.2

Migration

EMIGRATION, 2010

- Stock of emigrants: **212.6 thousands**
- Stock of emigrants as percentage of population: **1.4%**
- Top destination countries: Zimbabwe, Tanzania, the United Kingdom, South Africa, Zambia, Mozambique, the United States, Australia, Canada, Portugal

SKILLED EMIGRATION, 2000

- Emigration rate of tertiary-educated population: **18.7%**
- Emigration of physicians:
  - (a) **36** or **11.2%** of physicians trained in the country *(Source: Bhargava, Docquier, and Moullan 2010)*
  - (b) **293** or **59.4%** of physicians born in the country *(Source: Clemens and Pettersson 2006)*
- Emigration of nurses: **377** or **16.8%** of nurses born in the country

IMMIGRATION, 2010

- Stock of immigrants: **275.9 thousands**
- Stock of immigrants as percentage of population: **1.8%**
- Females as percentage of immigrants: **51.6%**
- Refugees as percentage of immigrants: **1.2%**
- Top source countries: Mozambique, Zambia, Zimbabwe, Tanzania, India, South Africa

Remittances

US$ millions	2003	2004	2005	2006	2007	2008	2009	2010e
Inward remittance flows[a]	1	1	1	1	1	1	1	1
of which								
Workers' remittances	–	–	–	–	–	–	–	–
Compensation of employees	–	–	–	–	–	–	–	–
Migrants' transfers	–	–	–	–	–	–	–	–
Outward remittance flows	–	–	–	–	–	–	–	–
of which								
Workers' remittances	–	–	–	–	–	–	–	–
Compensation of employees	–	–	–	–	–	–	–	–
Migrants' transfers	–	–	–	–	–	–	–	–

a. **For comparison: net ODA received US$0.9 bn, total international reserves US$0.3 bn, exports of goods and services US$1.0 bn in 2008.**

Malaysia

East Asia and Pacific — UPPER MIDDLE INCOME

Population (millions, 2009)	27.5
Population growth (avg. annual %, 2000–09)	1.9
Population density (people per km², 2008)	82.2
Labor force (millions, 2008)	11.6
Unemployment rate (% of labor force, 2008)	–
Urban population (% of pop., 2009)	71.3
Surface area (1,000 km², 2008)	329.7
GNI (US$ billions, 2009)	185.5
GNI per capita, Atlas method (US$, 2009)	7,230
GDP growth (avg. annual %, 2005–09)	4.1
Poverty headcount ratio at national poverty line (% of pop., 2005)	0.5
Age dependency ratio (2009)	52.0

Migration

EMIGRATION, 2010

- Stock of emigrants: **1,481.2 thousands**
- Stock of emigrants as percentage of population: **5.3%**
- Top destination countries: Singapore, Australia, Brunei Darussalam, the United Kingdom, the United States, Canada, New Zealand, India, Japan, Germany

SKILLED EMIGRATION, 2000

- Emigration rate of tertiary-educated population: **11.1%**
- Emigration of physicians: **1,727** or **9.6%** of physicians trained in the country *(Source: Bhargava, Docquier, and Moullan 2010)*

IMMIGRATION, 2010

- Stock of immigrants: **2,357.6 thousands**
- Stock of immigrants as percentage of population: **8.4%**
- Females as percentage of immigrants: **45.2%**
- Refugees as percentage of immigrants: **1.5%**
- Top source countries: Indonesia, the Philippines, China, Bangladesh, India, Singapore, Thailand, Japan, Myanmar, Pakistan

Remittances

US$ millions	2003	2004	2005	2006	2007	2008	2009	2010e
Inward remittance flows[a]	**571**	**802**	**1,117**	**1,365**	**1,570**	**1,329**	**1,110**	**1,576**
of which								
Workers' remittances	–	–	–	–	–	–	–	–
Compensation of employees	571	802	1,117	1,365	1,563	1,329	–	–
Migrants' transfers	–	–	–	–	–	7	–	–
Outward remittance flows	**3,464**	**5,064**	**5,679**	**5,597**	**6,412**	**6,786**	**6,800**	**–**
of which								
Workers' remittances	2,643	4,001	4,435	4,147	4,644	5,238	–	–
Compensation of employees	821	1,064	1,244	1,449	1,738	1,547	–	–
Migrants' transfers	–	–	–	–	29	–	–	–

a. For comparison: net FDI inflows US$7.4 bn, net ODA received US$0.2 bn, total international reserves US$92.2 bn in 2008.

Maldives

Population (millions, 2009)	0.3
Population growth (avg. annual %, 2000–09)	1.4
Population density (people per km², 2008)	1,034.9
Labor force (millions, 2008)	0.1
Unemployment rate (% of labor force, 2008)	—
Urban population (% of pop., 2009)	39.2
Surface area (1,000 km², 2008)	0.3
GNI (US$ billions, 2009)	1.3
GNI per capita, Atlas method (US$, 2009)	3,870
GDP growth (avg. annual %, 2005–09)	4.7
Poverty headcount ratio at national poverty line (% of pop., 2005)	—
Age dependency ratio (2009)	47.8

Migration

EMIGRATION, 2010

- Stock of emigrants: **2.0 thousands**
- Stock of emigrants as percentage of population: **0.6%**
- Top destination countries: Nepal, Australia, the United Kingdom, India, New Zealand, Germany, the United States, Switzerland, Japan, Italy

SKILLED EMIGRATION, 2000

- Emigration rate of tertiary-educated population: **1.2%**

IMMIGRATION, 2010

- Stock of immigrants: **3.3 thousands**
- Stock of immigrants as percentage of population: **1.0%**
- Females as percentage of immigrants: **44.7%**
- Refugees as percentage of immigrants: **0.0%**

Remittances

US$ millions	2003	2004	2005	2006	2007	2008	2009	2010e
Inward remittance flows[a]	**2**	**3**	**2**	**3**	**3**	**3**	**3**	**3**
of which								
Workers' remittances	—	—	—	—	—	—	—	—
Compensation of employees	2	3	2	3	3	3	4	—
Migrants' transfers	—	—	—	—	—	—	—	—
Outward remittance flows	**55**	**62**	**70**	**84**	**106**	**129**	**116**	—
of which								
Workers' remittances	55	61	70	83	105	128	—	—
Compensation of employees	0	0	0	0	0	0	—	—
Migrants' transfers	—	—	—	—	—	—	—	—

a. For comparison: net ODA received US$0.1 bn, total international reserves US$0.2 bn, exports of goods and services US$1.1 bn in 2008.

Mali

Sub-Saharan Africa | **LOW INCOME**

Population (millions, 2009)	13.0
Population growth (avg. annual %, 2000–09)	2.3
Population density (people per km², 2008)	10.4
Labor force (millions, 2008)	3.4
Unemployment rate (% of labor force, 2008)	—
Urban population (% of pop., 2009)	32.7
Surface area (1,000 km², 2008)	1,240.2
GNI (US$ billions, 2009)	9.0
GNI per capita, Atlas method (US$, 2009)	680
GDP growth (avg. annual %, 2005–09)	5.0
Poverty headcount ratio at national poverty line (% of pop., 2005)	51.4
Age dependency ratio (2009)	86.8

Migration

EMIGRATION, 2010

- Stock of emigrants: **1,012.7 thousands**
- Stock of emigrants as percentage of population: **7.6%**
- Top destination countries: Côte d'Ivoire, Nigeria, Niger, France, Burkina Faso, Gabon, Spain, Senegal, Guinea, The Gambia

SKILLED EMIGRATION, 2000

- Emigration rate of tertiary-educated population: **15.0%**
- Emigration of physicians:
  (a) **6** or **1.2%** of physicians trained in the country *(Source: Bhargava, Docquier, and Moullan 2010)*
  (b) **157** or **22.9%** of physicians born in the country *(Source: Clemens and Pettersson 2006)*
- Emigration of nurses: **265** or **15.0%** of nurses born in the country

IMMIGRATION, 2010

- Stock of immigrants: **162.7 thousands**
- Stock of immigrants as percentage of population: **1.2%**
- Females as percentage of immigrants: **47.6%**
- Refugees as percentage of immigrants: **6.1%**
- Top source countries: Côte d'Ivoire, Burkina Faso, Guinea, Senegal, Mauritania, Niger, Gabon, the Republic of Congo, Ghana, France

Remittances

US$ millions	2003	2004	2005	2006	2007	2008	2009	2010e
Inward remittance flows[a]	**154**	**155**	**177**	**212**	**344**	**431**	**405**	—
of which								
Workers' remittances	139	138	153	193	323	406	—	—
Compensation of employees	15	17	24	19	21	25	—	—
Migrants' transfers	—	—	—	—.	—	—	—	—
Outward remittance flows	**58**	**64**	**69**	**57**	**83**	**105**	**105**	—
of which								
Workers' remittances	48	5 2	51	47	69	—	—	—
Compensation of employees	10	12	19	10	13	—	—	—
Migrants' transfers	—	—	—	—	—	—	—	—

a. For comparison: net FDI inflows US$0.1 bn, net ODA received US$1.0 bn, total international reserves US$1.1 bn in 2008.

Malta

Population (millions, 2009)	0.4
Population growth (avg. annual %, 2000–09)	0.7
Population density (people per km², 2008)	1,285.8
Labor force (millions, 2008)	0.2
Unemployment rate (% of labor force, 2008)	6.0
Urban population (% of pop., 2009)	94.5
Surface area (1,000 km², 2008)	0.3
GNI (US$ billions, 2009)	—
GNI per capita, Atlas method (US$, 2009)	—
GDP growth (avg. annual %, 2005–09)	—
Poverty headcount ratio at national poverty line (% of pop., 2005)	—
Age dependency ratio (2009)	42.8

Migration

EMIGRATION, 2010

- Stock of emigrants: **107.5 thousands**
- Stock of emigrants as percentage of population: **26.2%**
- Top destination countries: Australia, the United Kingdom, the United States, Canada, Italy, France, Germany, New Zealand, Ireland, Greece

SKILLED EMIGRATION, 2000

- Emigration rate of tertiary-educated population: **57.6%**
- Emigration of physicians: **412** or **28.5%** of physicians trained in the country *(Source: Bhargava, Docquier, and Moullan 2010)*

IMMIGRATION, 2010

- Stock of immigrants: **15.5 thousands**
- Stock of immigrants as percentage of population: **3.8%**
- Females as percentage of immigrants: **51.6%**
- Refugees as percentage of immigrants: **17.5%**
- Top source countries: the United Kingdom, Australia, Canada, Italy, the United States, Libya, Germany, France

Remittances

US$ millions	2003	2004	2005	2006	2007	2008	2009	2010e
Inward remittance flows[a]	**27**	**31**	**34**	**36**	**48**	**48**	**45**	**50**
of which								
Workers' remittances	1	0	0	0	0	0	—	—
Compensation of employees	25	31	33	35	43	49	—	—
Migrants' transfers	1	0	0	0	0	0	—	—
Outward remittance flows	**13**	**21**	**33**	**46**	**54**	**65**	**53**	**—**
of which								
Workers' remittances	1	2	7	4	4	5	—	—
Compensation of employees	10	16	22	39	46	56	—	—
Migrants' transfers	1	3	4	3	4	4	—	—

a. For comparison: net FDI inflows US$0.9 bn, total international reserves US$0.4 bn in 2008.

Marshall Islands

East Asia and Pacific | LOWER MIDDLE INCOME

Population (thousands, 2009)	61.0
Population growth (avg. annual %, 2000–09)	1.8
Population density (people per km², 2008)	331.5
Labor force (millions, 2008)	–
Unemployment rate (% of labor force, 2008)	–
Urban population (% of pop., 2009)	71.4
Surface area (1,000 km², 2008)	0.2
GNI (US$ billions, 2009)	0.2
GNI per capita, Atlas method (US$, 2009)	3,060
GDP growth (avg. annual %, 2005–09)	0.9
Poverty headcount ratio at national poverty line (% of pop., 2005)	–
Age dependency ratio (2009)	–

Migration

EMIGRATION, 2010

- Stock of emigrants: **10.5 thousands**
- Stock of emigrants as percentage of population: **16.6%**
- Top destination countries: the United States, the Philippines, Guam, Fiji, Northern Mariana Islands, Canada, Australia, New Zealand, Japan, Switzerland

SKILLED EMIGRATION, 2000

- Emigration rate of tertiary-educated population: **39.4%**

IMMIGRATION, 2010

- Stock of immigrants: **1.7 thousands**
- Stock of immigrants as percentage of population: **2.7%**
- Females as percentage of immigrants: **41.0%**
- Refugees as percentage of immigrants: **0.0%**
- Top source countries: Australia, Japan, China, the Philippines, the United States, New Zealand

Remittances

Remittance data are currently not available for this country.

Mauritania

Sub-Saharan Africa **LOW INCOME**

Population (millions, 2009)	3.3
Population growth (avg. annual %, 2000–09)	2.6
Population density (people per km², 2008)	3.1
Labor force (millions, 2008)	1.3
Unemployment rate (% of labor force, 2008)	–
Urban population (% of pop., 2009)	41.2
Surface area (1,000 km², 2008)	1,030.7
GNI (US$ billions, 2009)	3.0
GNI per capita, Atlas method (US$, 2009)	960
GDP growth (avg. annual %, 2005–09)	4.3
Poverty headcount ratio at national poverty line (% of pop., 2005)	13.4
Age dependency ratio (2009)	72.9

Migration

EMIGRATION, 2010

- Stock of emigrants: **118.0 thousands**
- Stock of emigrants as percentage of population: **3.5%**
- Top destination countries: Senegal, Nigeria, Côte d'Ivoire, France, Spain, Mali, The Gambia, the United States, the Republic of Congo, Germany

SKILLED EMIGRATION, 2000

- Emigration rate of tertiary-educated population: **11.8%**
- Emigration of physicians: **43** or **11.4%** of physicians born in the country *(Source: Clemens and Pettersson 2006)*
- Emigration of nurses: **117** or **6.9%** of nurses born in the country

IMMIGRATION, 2010

- Stock of immigrants: **99.2 thousands**
- Stock of immigrants as percentage of population: **2.9%**
- Females as percentage of immigrants: **42.2%**
- Refugees as percentage of immigrants: **30.6%**
- Top source countries: Senegal, Mali, Guinea, Algeria, France, Guinea-Bissau, Benin, Cameroon, Morocco, Saudi Arabia

Remittances

US$ millions	2003	2004	2005	2006	2007	2008	2009	2010e
Inward remittance flows[a]	2	2	2	2	2	2	2	2
of which								
Workers' remittances	–	–	–	–	–	–	–	–
Compensation of employees	–	–	–	–	–	–	–	–
Migrants' transfers	–	–	–	–	–	–	–	–
Outward remittance flows	–	–	–	–	–	–	–	–
of which								
Workers' remittances	–	–	–	–	–	–	–	–
Compensation of employees	–	–	–	–	–	–	–	–
Migrants' transfers	–	–	–	–	–	–	–	–

a. For comparison: net FDI inflows US$0.1 bn, net ODA received US$0.3 bn in 2008.

Mauritius

|

Population (millions, 2009)	1.3
Population growth (avg. annual %, 2000–09)	0.8
Population density (people per km², 2008)	625.0
Labor force (millions, 2008)	0.6
Unemployment rate (% of labor force, 2008)	7.3
Urban population (% of pop., 2009)	42.5
Surface area (1,000 km², 2008)	2.0
GNI (US$ billions, 2009)	8.9
GNI per capita, Atlas method (US$, 2009)	7,240
GDP growth (avg. annual %, 2005–09)	3.6
Poverty headcount ratio at national poverty line (% of pop., 2005)	—
Age dependency ratio (2009)	42.7

Migration

EMIGRATION, 2010

- Stock of emigrants: **140.7 thousands**
- Stock of emigrants as percentage of population: **10.9%**
- Top destination countries: the United Kingdom, France, Australia, Italy, Canada, Belgium, Switzerland, the United States, Germany, Tanzania

SKILLED EMIGRATION, 2000

- Emigration rate of tertiary-educated population: **56.2%**
- Emigration of physicians:
  - (a) **6** or **0.6%** of physicians trained in the country *(Source: Bhargava, Docquier, and Moullan 2010)*
  - (b) **822** or **46.1%** of physicians born in the country *(Source: Clemens and Pettersson 2006)*
- Emigration of nurses: **4,531** or **63.3%** of nurses born in the country

IMMIGRATION, 2010

- Stock of immigrants: **42.9 thousands**
- Stock of immigrants as percentage of population: **3.3%**
- Females as percentage of immigrants: **63.3%**
- Refugees as percentage of immigrants: **0.0%**
- Top source countries: China, India, France, the United Kingdom, South Africa, Germany, Madagascar, Italy, Australia, the United States

Remittances

US$ millions	2003	2004	2005	2006	2007	2008	2009	2010e
Inward remittance flows[a]	**215**	**215**	**215**	**215**	**215**	**215**	**211**	**220**
of which								
Workers' remittances	–	–	–	–	–	–	–	–
Compensation of employees	1	1	1	1	1	1	–	–
Migrants' transfers	–	–	–	–	–	–	–	–
Outward remittance flows	**10**	**11**	**11**	**13**	**12**	**14**	**12**	**–**
of which								
Workers' remittances	–	–	–	–	–	–	–	–
Compensation of employees	9	9	9	10	10	13	–	–
Migrants' transfers	1	2	2	3	2	1	–	–

a. For comparison: net FDI inflows US$0.4 bn, net ODA received US$0.1 bn, total international reserves US$1.8 bn, exports of goods and services US$4.9 bn in 2008.

Mayotte

     UPPER MIDDLE INCOME

Population (millions, 2009)	0.2
Population growth (avg. annual %, 2000–09)	2.9
Population density (people per km², 2008)	511.2
Labor force (millions, 2008)	—
Unemployment rate (% of labor force, 2008)	—
Urban population (% of pop., 2009)	—
Surface area (1,000 km², 2008)	0.4
GNI (US$ billions, 2009)	—
GNI per capita, Atlas method (US$, 2009)	—
GDP growth (avg. annual %, 2005–09)	—
Poverty headcount ratio at national poverty line (% of pop., 2005)	—
Age dependency ratio (2009)	72.4

Migration

EMIGRATION, 2010

- Stock of emigrants: **1.0 thousand**
- Stock of emigrants as percentage of population: **0.5%**
- Top destination countries: the Comoros, the Netherlands, Chile

SKILLED EMIGRATION, 2000

- Skilled emigration data are currently not available for this country.

IMMIGRATION, 2010

- Stock of immigrants: **71.7 thousands**
- Stock of immigrants as percentage of population: **36.0%**
- Females as percentage of immigrants: **49.9%**
- Refugees as percentage of immigrants: **0.0%**

Remittances

Remittance data are currently not available for this country.

Mexico

Population (millions, 2009)	107.4
Population growth (avg. annual %, 2000–09)	1.1
Population density (people per km², 2008)	54.7
Labor force (millions, 2008)	44.4
Unemployment rate (% of labor force, 2008)	4.0
Urban population (% of pop., 2009)	77.5
Surface area (1,000 km², 2008)	1,964.4
GNI (US$ billions, 2009)	860.8
GNI per capita, Atlas method (US$, 2009)	8,920
GDP growth (avg. annual %, 2005–09)	1.3
Poverty headcount ratio at national poverty line (% of pop., 2005)	1.7
Age dependency ratio (2009)	53.6

Migration

EMIGRATION, 2010

- Stock of emigrants: **11,859.2 thousands**
- Stock of emigrants as percentage of population: **10.7%**
- Top destination countries: the United States, Canada, Spain, Bolivia, Germany, Guatemala, France, the United Kingdom, Italy, Panama

SKILLED EMIGRATION, 2000

- Emigration rate of tertiary-educated population: **15.3%**
- Emigration of physicians: **12,081** or **8.5%** of physicians trained in the country *(Source: Bhargava, Docquier, and Moullan 2010)*

IMMIGRATION, 2010

- Stock of immigrants: **725.7 thousands**
- Stock of immigrants as percentage of population: **0.7%**
- Females as percentage of immigrants: **49.4%**
- Refugees as percentage of immigrants: **0.3%**
- Top source countries: the United States, Guatemala, Spain, Cuba, Argentina, Colombia, Canada, France, Germany, El Salvador

Remittances

US$ millions	2003	2004	2005	2006	2007	2008	2009	2010e
Inward remittance flows[a]	**16,556**	**19,861**	**23,062**	**26,877**	**27,136**	**26,304**	**22,153**	**22,572**
of which								
Workers' remittances	15,041	18,331	21,689	25,567	26,069	25,137	21,181	–
Compensation of employees	1,515	1,530	1,054	1,000	1,000	813	884	–
Migrants' transfers	–	–	–	–	–	–	–	–
Outward remittance flows	–	–	–	–	–	–	–	–
of which								
Workers' remittances	–	–	–	–	–	–	–	–
Compensation of employees	–	–	–	–	–	–	–	–
Migrants' transfers	–	–	–	–	–	–	–	–

a. For comparison: net FDI inflows US$22.5 bn, net ODA received US$0.1 bn, total international reserves US$95.3 bn, exports of goods and services US$307.7 bn in 2008.

Micronesia, Federated States of

Population (millions, 2009)	0.1
Population growth (avg. annual %, 2000–09)	0.3
Population density (people per km², 2008)	159.0
Labor force (millions, 2008)	—
Unemployment rate (% of labor force, 2008)	—
Urban population (% of pop., 2009)	22.6
Surface area (1,000 km², 2008)	0.7
GNI (US$ billions, 2009)	0.3
GNI per capita, Atlas method (US$, 2009)	2,220
GDP growth (avg. annual %, 2005–09)	-3.0
Poverty headcount ratio at national poverty line (% of pop., 2005)	—
Age dependency ratio (2009)	68.4

Migration

EMIGRATION, 2010

- Stock of emigrants: **21.9 thousands**
- Stock of emigrants as percentage of population: **19.7%**
- Top destination countries: the United States, Guam, Northern Mariana Islands, the Philippines, Fiji, Palau, Spain, New Zealand, Japan, Canada

SKILLED EMIGRATION, 2000

- Emigration rate of tertiary-educated population: **37.8%**

IMMIGRATION, 2010

- Stock of immigrants: **2.7 thousands**
- Stock of immigrants as percentage of population: **2.4%**
- Females as percentage of immigrants: **46.4%**
- Refugees as percentage of immigrants: **0.1%**
- Top source country: the United States

Remittances

Remittance data are currently not available for this country.

Moldova

Population (millions, 2009)	3.6
Population growth (avg. annual %, 2000–09)	-1.4
Population density (people per km², 2008)	110.5
Labor force (millions, 2008)	1.4
Unemployment rate (% of labor force, 2008)	4.0
Urban population (% of pop., 2009)	41.5
Surface area (1,000 km², 2008)	33.8
GNI (US$ billions, 2009)	5.8
GNI per capita, Atlas method (US$, 2009)	1,590
GDP growth (avg. annual %, 2005–09)	3.3
Poverty headcount ratio at national poverty line (% of pop., 2005)	8.1
Age dependency ratio (2009)	38.8

Migration

EMIGRATION, 2010

- Stock of emigrants: **770.3 thousands**
- Stock of emigrants as percentage of population: **21.5%**
- Top destination countries: the Russian Federation, Ukraine, Italy, Romania, the United States, Israel, Spain, Germany, Kazakhstan, Greece

SKILLED EMIGRATION, 2000

- Emigration rate of tertiary-educated population: **3.4%**
- Emigration of physicians: **127** or **0.9%** of physicians trained in the country
  (Source: Bhargava, Docquier, and Moullan 2010)

IMMIGRATION, 2010

- Stock of immigrants: **408.3 thousands**
- Stock of immigrants as percentage of population: **11.4%**
- Females as percentage of immigrants: **56.0%**
- Refugees as percentage of immigrants: **0.0%**
- Top source countries: Ukraine, the Russian Federation, Bulgaria, Belarus

Remittances

US$ millions	2003	2004	2005	2006	2007	2008	2009	2010e
Inward remittance flows[a]	**487**	**705**	**920**	**1,182**	**1,498**	**1,897**	**1,211**	**1,316**
of which								
Workers' remittances	152	221	395	603	842	1,046	635	–
Compensation of employees	332	480	520	573	649	842	563	–
Migrants' transfers	3	4	5	6	7	9	12	–
Outward remittance flows	**67**	**67**	**68**	**86**	**87**	**115**	**103**	**–**
of which								
Workers' remittances	1	1	3	6	16	13	–	–
Compensation of employees	43	41	43	50	56	79	–	–
Migrants' transfers	24	25	22	29	15	23	–	–

a. For comparison: net FDI inflows US$0.7 bn, net ODA received US$0.3 bn, total international reserves US$1.7 bn, exports of goods and services US$2.5 bn in 2008.

Monaco

HIGH-INCOME NON-OECD

Population (thousands, 2009)	32.8
Population growth (avg. annual %, 2000–09)	0.3
Population density (people per km², 2008)	16,820.5
Labor force (millions, 2008)	–
Unemployment rate (% of labor force, 2008)	–
Urban population (% of pop., 2009)	100.0
Surface area (1,000 km², 2008)	0.0
GNI (US$ billions, 2009)	–
GNI per capita, Atlas method (US$, 2009)	–
GDP growth (avg. annual %, 2005–09)	–
Poverty headcount ratio at national poverty line (% of pop., 2005)	–
Age dependency ratio (2009)	–

Migration

EMIGRATION, 2010

- Stock of emigrants: **18.5 thousands**
- Stock of emigrants as percentage of population: **56.4%**
- Top destination countries: France, the United States, Spain, the United Kingdom, the Philippines, Switzerland, Canada, Belgium, Australia, the Netherlands

SKILLED EMIGRATION, 2000

- Emigration rate of tertiary-educated population: **15.9%**

IMMIGRATION, 2010

- Stock of immigrants: **23.6 thousands**
- Stock of immigrants as percentage of population: **71.6%**
- Females as percentage of immigrants: **50.6%**
- Refugees as percentage of immigrants: **0.0%**
- Top source countries: France, Italy, the United Kingdom, Belgium, the United States

Remittances

Remittance data are currently not available for this country.

Mongolia

East Asia and Pacific **LOWER MIDDLE INCOME**

Population (millions, 2009)	2.7
Population growth (avg. annual %, 2000-09)	1.2
Population density (people per km², 2008)	1.7
Labor force (millions, 2008)	1.1
Unemployment rate (% of labor force, 2008)	2.8
Urban population (% of pop., 2009)	57.3
Surface area (1,000 km², 2008)	1,566.5
GNI (US$ billions, 2009)	4.0
GNI per capita, Atlas method (US$, 2009)	1,630
GDP growth (avg. annual %, 2005-09)	6.7
Poverty headcount ratio at national poverty line (% of pop., 2005)	22.4
Age dependency ratio (2009)	42.9

Migration

EMIGRATION, 2010

- Stock of emigrants: **32.1 thousands**
- Stock of emigrants as percentage of population: **1.2%**
- Top destination countries: the Republic of Korea, Germany, Japan, the United States, the Czech Republic, Hungary, Poland, the United Kingdom, the Netherlands, Australia

SKILLED EMIGRATION, 2000

- Emigration rate of tertiary-educated population: **1.1%**
- Emigration of physicians: **16** or **0.3%** of physicians trained in the country
  (Source: Bhargava, Docquier, and Moullan 2010)

IMMIGRATION, 2010

- Stock of immigrants: **10.0 thousands**
- Stock of immigrants as percentage of population: **0.4%**
- Females as percentage of immigrants: **54.0%**
- Refugees as percentage of immigrants: **0.0%**
- Top source countries: the Russian Federation, China, Kazakhstan, the Republic of Korea

Remittances

US$ millions	2003	2004	2005	2006	2007	2008	2009	2010e
Inward remittance flows[a]	**129**	**203**	**180**	**181**	**194**	**200**	**194**	**211**
of which								
Workers' remittances	129	195	178	180	–	–	–	–
Compensation of employees	–	7	3	2	–	–	–	–
Migrants' transfers	–	–	–	–	–	–	–	–
Outward remittance flows	**54**	**49**	**40**	**77**	**–**	**–**	**–**	**–**
of which								
Workers' remittances	54	49	40	77	–	–	–	–
Compensation of employees	–	–	–	–	–	–	–	–
Migrants' transfers	–	–	–	–	–	–	–	–

a. For comparison: net FDI inflows US$0.7 bn, net ODA received US$0.2 bn, exports of goods and services US$3.0 bn in 2008.

Migration and Remittances Factbook 2011

Montenegro

Population (millions, 2009)	0.6
Population growth (avg. annual %, 2000–09)	-0.5
Population density (people per km², 2008)	45.1
Labor force (millions, 2008)	–
Unemployment rate (% of labor force, 2008)	–
Urban population (% of pop., 2009)	59.8
Surface area (1,000 km², 2008)	14.0
GNI (US$ billions, 2009)	4.1
GNI per capita, Atlas method (US$, 2009)	6,550
GDP growth (avg. annual %, 2005–09)	4.7
Poverty headcount ratio at national poverty line (% of pop., 2005)	–
Age dependency ratio (2009)	47.4

Migration

EMIGRATION, 2010

- Stock of emigrants: **0.0 thousands**
- Stock of emigrants as percentage of population: **0.0%**
- Top destination countries: Denmark, Japan, Hungary

SKILLED EMIGRATION, 2000

- Emigration of nurses: **5,176** or **14.9%** of nurses born in the country

IMMIGRATION, 2010

- Stock of immigrants: **42.5 thousands**
- Stock of immigrants as percentage of population: **6.8%**
- Femalesas percentage of immigrants: **61.5%**
- Refugees as percentage of immigrants: **18.2%**

Remittances

Remittance data are currently not available for this country.

Morocco

Middle East and North Africa	LOWER MIDDLE INCOME

Population (millions, 2009)	32.0
Population growth (avg. annual %, 2000–09)	1.2
Population density (people per km², 2008)	70.0
Labor force (millions, 2008)	11.2
Unemployment rate (% of labor force, 2008)	9.6
Urban population (% of pop., 2009)	56.4
Surface area (1,000 km², 2008)	446.6
GNI (US$ billions, 2009)	89.9
GNI per capita, Atlas method (US$, 2009)	2,790
GDP growth (avg. annual %, 2005–09)	4.8
Poverty headcount ratio at national poverty line (% of pop., 2005)	3.0
Age dependency ratio (2009)	50.9

Migration

EMIGRATION, 2010

- Stock of emigrants: **3,016.6 thousands**
- Stock of emigrants as percentage of population: **9.3%**
- Top destination countries: France, Spain, Italy, Israel, Belgium, the Netherlands, Germany, the United States, Canada, Saudi Arabia

SKILLED EMIGRATION, 2000

- Emigration rate of tertiary-educated population: **17.0%**
- Emigration of physicians:
  - (a) **654** or **4.7%** of physicians trained in the country (*Source: Bhargava, Docquier, and Moullan 2010*)
  - (b) **6,506** or **31.3%** of physicians born in the country *(Source: Clemens and Pettersson 2006)*

IMMIGRATION, 2010

- Stock of immigrants: **49.1 thousands**
- Stock of immigrants as percentage of population: **0.2%**
- Females as percentage of immigrants: **49.7%**
- Refugees as percentage of immigrants: **1.3%**

Remittances

US$ millions	2003	2004	2005	2006	2007	2008	2009	2010e
Inward remittance flows[a]	**3,614**	**4,221**	**4,590**	**5,451**	**6,730**	**6,895**	**6,271**	**6,447**
of which								
Workers' remittances	3,614	4,221	4,589	5,451	6,730	6,894	6,271	–
Compensation of employees	–	–	–	–	–	–	–	–
Migrants' transfers	–	–	0	–	–	1	–	–
Outward remittance flows	**44**	**42**	**40**	**41**	**52**	**58**	**61**	–
of which								
Workers' remittances	34	34	35	38	49	54	60	–
Compensation of employees	–	–	–	–	–	–	–	–
Migrants' transfers	10	8	5	3	3	3	1	–

a. For comparison: net FDI inflows US$2.5 bn, net ODA received US$1.2 bn, total international reserves US$22.7 bn, exports of goods and services US$32.6 bn in 2008.

Mozambique

Population (millions, 2009)	22.9
Population growth (avg. annual %, 2000–09)	2.5
Population density (people per km², 2008)	27.7
Labor force (millions, 2008)	9.9
Unemployment rate (% of labor force, 2008)	–
Urban population (% of pop., 2009)	37.6
Surface area (1,000 km², 2008)	799.4
GNI (US$ billions, 2009)	9.7
GNI per capita, Atlas method (US$, 2009)	440
GDP growth (avg. annual %, 2005–09)	7.5
Poverty headcount ratio at national poverty line (% of pop., 2005)	68.2
Age dependency ratio (2009)	89.6

Migration

EMIGRATION, 2010

- Stock of emigrants: **1,178.5 thousands**
- Stock of emigrants as percentage of population: **5.0%**
- Top destination countries: South Africa, Malawi, Zimbabwe, Tanzania, Portugal, Swaziland, the United Kingdom, Germany, the United States, Spain

SKILLED EMIGRATION, 2000

- Emigration rate of tertiary-educated population: **45.1%**
- Emigration of physicians:
  (a) **31** or **6.6%** of physicians trained in the country *(Source: Bhargava, Docquier, and Moullan 2010)*
  (b) **1,334** or **75.4%** of physicians born in the country *(Source: Clemens and Pettersson 2006)*
- Emigration of nurses: **853** or **18.9%** of nurses born in the country

IMMIGRATION, 2010

- Stock of immigrants: **450.0 thousands**
- Stock of immigrants as percentage of population: **1.9%**
- Females as percentage of immigrants: **52.1%**
- Refugees as percentage of immigrants: **0.6%**
- Top source countries: South Africa, Portugal, Zimbabwe, Lesotho, Cape Verde, Tanzania, India, Malawi, Pakistan, Zambia

Remittances

US$ millions	2003	2004	2005	2006	2007	2008	2009	2010e
Inward remittance flows[a]	69	58	57	80	99	116	111	117
of which								
Workers' remittances	30	3	6	16	31	34	–	–
Compensation of employees	40	55	51	64	68	82	–	–
Migrants' transferss	0	–	–	–	–	–	–	–
Outward remittance flows	30	20	21	26	45	57	63	–
of which								
Workers' remittances	20	11	11	12	26	38	–	–
Compensation of employees	9	9	10	14	19	19	–	–
Migrants' transfer	0	–	–	–	–	–	–	–

a. For comparison: net FDI inflows US$0.6 bn, net ODA received US$2.0 bn, total international reserves US$1.7 bn, exports of goods and services US$3.3 bn in 2008.

Myanmar

Population (millions, 2009)	50.0
Population growth (avg. annual %, 2000–09)	0.8
Population density (people per km², 2008)	74.8
Labor force (millions, 2008)	27.5
Unemployment rate (% of labor force, 2008)	–
Urban population (% of pop., 2009)	33.2
Surface area (1,000 km², 2008)	676.6
GNI (US$ billions, 2009)	–
GNI per capita, Atlas method (US$, 2009)	–
GDP growth (avg. annual %, 2005–09)	–
Poverty headcount ratio at national poverty line (% of pop., 2005)	–
Age dependency ratio (2009)	47.6

Migration

EMIGRATION, 2010

- Stock of emigrants: **514.2 thousands**
- Stock of emigrants as percentage of population: **1.0%**
- Top destination countries: Thailand, the United States, India, Malaysia, Australia, the United Kingdom, Japan, Canada, the Republic of Korea, Germany

SKILLED EMIGRATION, 2000

- Emigration rate of tertiary-educated population: **4.0%**
- Emigration of physicians: **1,662** or **10.4%** of physicians trained in the country (Source: Bhargava, Docquier, and Moullan 2010)

IMMIGRATION, 2010

- Stock of immigrants: **88.7 thousands**
- Stock of immigrants as percentage of population: **0.2%**
- Females as percentage of immigrants: **48.7%**
- Refugees as percentage of immigrants: **0.0%**
- Top source countries: China, India, Pakistan, Bangladesh

Remittances

US$ millions	2003	2004	2005	2006	2007	2008	2009	2020e
Inward remittance flows[a]	**85**	**118**	**131**	**116**	**125**	**150**	**137**	**154**
of which								
Workers' remittances	59	81	87	66	–	–	–	–
Compensation of employees	26	36	44	51	–	–	–	–
Migrants' transfers	–	–	–	–	–	–	–	–
Outward remittance flows	**23**	**25**	**19**	**32**	**–**	**–**	**–**	**–**
of which								
Workers' remittances	23	25	19	32	–	–	–	–
Compensation of employees	–	–	–	–	–	–	–	–
Migrants' transfers	–	–	–	–	–	–	–	–

a. For comparison: net FDI inflows US$0.3 bn, net ODA received US$0.5 bn in 2008.

Namibia

Population (millions, 2009)	2.2
Population growth (avg. annual %, 2000–09)	2.0
Population density (people per km², 2008)	2.6
Labor force (millions, 2008)	0.7
Unemployment rate (% of labor force, 2008)	—
Urban population (% of pop., 2009)	37.4
Surface area (1,000 km², 2008)	824.3
GNI (US$ billions, 2009)	9.3
GNI per capita, Atlas method (US$, 2009)	4,290
GDP growth (avg. annual %, 2005–09)	3.8
Poverty headcount ratio at national poverty line (% of pop., 2005)	43.8
Age dependency ratio (2009)	68.0

Migration

EMIGRATION, 2010

- Stock of emigrants: **16.5 thousands**
- Stock of emigrants as percentage of population: **0.7%**
- Top destination countries: Mozambique, Tanzania, the United Kingdom, the United States, Australia, Germany, Canada, New Zealand, Zambia, the Netherlands

SKILLED EMIGRATION, 2000

- Emigration rate of tertiary-educated population: **3.5%**
- Emigration of physicians: **382** or **45.0%** of physicians born in the country *(Source: Clemens and Pettersson 2006)*
- Emigration of nurses: **152** or **5.4%** of nurses born in the country

IMMIGRATION, 2010

- Stock of immigrants: **138.9 thousands**
- Stock of immigrants as percentage of population: **6.3%**
- Females as percentage of immigrants: **47.6%**
- Refugees as percentage of immigrants: **4.3%**
- Top source countries: Angola, South Africa, Zambia, Botswana

Remittances

US$ millions	2003	2004	2005	2006	2007	2008	2009	2010e
Inward remittance flows[a]	**12**	**15**	**18**	**17**	**16**	**14**	**14**	**14**
of which								
Workers' remittances	5	6	7	7	6	5	–	–
Compensation of employees	7	9	11	10	9	8	–	–
Migrants' transfers	0	1	1	0	0	0	–	–
Outward remittance flows	**15**	**18**	**19**	**20**	**16**	**43**	**16**	**–**
of which								
Workers' remittances	4	4	4	4	4	3	–	–
Compensation of employees	11	13	14	16	12	39	–	–
Migrants' transfers	0	0	1	1	0	0	–	–

a. For comparison: net FDI inflows US$0.5 bn, net ODA received US$0.2 bn, total international reserves US$1.3 bn, exports of goods and services US$3.7 bn in 2008.

Nepal

Population (millions, 2009)	29.3
Population growth (avg. annual %, 2000–09)	2.1
Population density (people per km², 2008)	199.9
Labor force (millions, 2008)	11.8
Unemployment rate (% of labor force, 2008)	–
Urban population (% of pop., 2009)	17.7
Surface area (1,000 km², 2008)	147.2
GNI (US$ billions, 2009)	12.8
GNI per capita, Atlas method (US$, 2009)	440
GDP growth (avg. annual %, 2005–09)	4.0
Poverty headcount ratio at national poverty line (% of pop., 2005)	54.7
Age dependency ratio (2009)	68.3

Migration

EMIGRATION, 2010

- Stock of emigrants: **982.2 thousands**
- Stock of emigrants as percentage of population: **3.3%**
- Top destination countries: India, Qatar, the United States, Thailand, the United Kingdom, Saudi Arabia, Japan, Brunei Darussalam, Australia, Canada

SKILLED EMIGRATION, 2000

- Emigration rate of tertiary-educated population: **5.3%**
- Emigration of physicians: **40** or **3.3%** of physicians trained in the country *(Source: Bhargava, Docquier, and Moullan 2010)*

IMMIGRATION, 2010

- Stock of immigrants: **945.9 thousands**
- Stock of immigrants as percentage of population: **3.2%**
- Females as percentage of immigrants: **68.2%**
- Refugees as percentage of immigrants: **13.8%**
- Top source countries: India, Bhutan, Pakistan, China, Australia, Sri Lanka, Bangladesh, Maldives, New Zealand

Remittances

US$ millions	2003	2004	2005	2006	2007	2008	2009	2010e
Inward remittance flows[a]	**771**	**823**	**1,212**	**1,453**	**1,734**	**2,727**	**2,986**	**3,513**
of which								
Workers' remittances	744	793	1,126	1,373	1,647	2,581	2,858	–
Compensation of employees	27	30	85	80	87	146	127	–
Migrants' transfers	–	–	–	–	–	–	1	–
Outward remittance flows	**26**	**64**	**66**	**79**	**4**	**5**	**12**	**–**
of which								
Workers' remittances	25	63	60	69	–	–	–	–
Compensation of employees	1	1	5	10	4	5	12	–
Migrants' transfers	–	–	–	–	–	–	–	–

a. For comparison: net ODA received US$0.7 bn, exports of goods and services US$1.5 bn in 2008.

Netherlands, The

Population (millions, 2009)	16.5
Population growth (avg. annual %, 2000–09)	0.4
Population density (people per km², 2008)	485.3
Labor force (millions, 2008)	8.5
Unemployment rate (% of labor force, 2008)	2.8
Urban population (% of pop., 2009)	82.4
Surface area (1,000 km², 2008)	41.5
GNI (US$ billions, 2009)	788.1
GNI per capita, Atlas method (US$, 2009)	49,350
GDP growth (avg. annual %, 2005–09)	1.4
Poverty headcount ratio at national poverty line (% of pop., 2005)	—
Age dependency ratio (2009)	48.8

Migration

EMIGRATION, 2010

- Stock of emigrants: **993.4 thousands**
- Stock of emigrants as percentage of population: **6.0%**
- Top destination countries: Germany, Canada, Belgium, Australia, the United States, Spain, the United Kingdom, France, Turkey, New Zealand

SKILLED EMIGRATION, 2000

- Emigration rate of tertiary-educated population: **9.6%**
- Emigration of physicians: **3,718** or **6.8%** of physicians trained in the country *(Source: Bhargava, Docquier, and Moullan 2010)*

IMMIGRATION, 2010

- Stock of immigrants: **1,752.9 thousands**
- Stock of immigrants as percentage of population: **10.5%**
- Females as percentage of immigrants: **51.9%**
- Refugees as percentage of immigrants: **5.3%**
- Top source countries: Turkey, Suriname, Morocco, Indonesia, Germany, Netherlands Antilles, Belgium, the United Kingdom, Poland, China

Remittances

US$ millions	2003	2004	2005	2006	2007	2008	2009	2010e
Inward remittance flows[a]	**2,024**	**2,164**	**2,197**	**2,785**	**2,860**	**3,299**	**3,657**	**4,079**
of which								
Workers' remittances	—	—	—	310	312	265	—	—
Compensation of employees	1,120	1,251	1,203	1,186	1,319	1,387	—	—
Migrants' transfers	904	913	994	1,289	1,229	1,647	—	—
Outward remittance flows	**4,239**	**5,032**	**5,928**	**6,610**	**7,843**	**8,280**	**8,142**	**—**
of which								
Workers' remittances	656	644	849	783	921	1,077	—	—
Compensation of employees	1,812	2,290	2,670	2,972	3,002	3,410	—	—
Migrants' transfers	1,770	2,098	2,409	2,855	3,920	3,794	—	—

a. For comparison: net FDI inflows US$2.4 bn, total international reserves US$28.6 bn, exports of goods and services US$669.4 bn in 2008.

Netherlands Antilles

Population (millions, 2009)	0.2
Population growth (avg. annual %, 2000–09)	0.9
Population density (people per km², 2008)	242.3
Labor force (millions, 2008)	0.1
Unemployment rate (% of labor force, 2008)	–
Urban population (% of pop., 2009)	92.9
Surface area (1,000 km², 2008)	0.8
GNI (US$ billions, 2009)	–
GNI per capita, Atlas method (US$, 2009)	–
GDP growth (avg. annual %, 2005–09)	–
Poverty headcount ratio at national poverty line (% of pop., 2005)	–
Age dependency ratio (2009)	45.2

Migration

EMIGRATION, 2010

- Stock of emigrants: **101.9 thousands**
- Stock of emigrants as percentage of population: **50.8%**
- Top destination countries: the Netherlands, the United States, the United Kingdom, República Bolivariana de Venezuela, Canada, St. Lucia, Belgium, Bolivia, Panama, Portugal

SKILLED EMIGRATION, 2000

- Skilled emigration data are currently not available for this country.

IMMIGRATION, 2010

- Stock of immigrants: **53.0 thousands**
- Stock of immigrants as percentage of population: **26.4%**
- Females as percentage of immigrants: **56.8%**
- Refugees as percentage of immigrants: **0.0%**
- Top source countries: the Dominican Republic, the Netherlands, Aruba, Haiti, Colombia, Suriname, Cuba, República Bolivariana de Venezuela, Jamaica, Guyana

Remittances

US$ millions	2003	2004	2005	2006	2007	2008	2009	2010e
Inward remittance flows[a]	**8**	**5**	**8**	**19**	**32**	**32**	**32**	**32**
of which								
Workers' remittances	1	1	1	0	1	–	–	–
Compensation of employees	6	4	7	17	29	–	–	–
Migrants' transfers	2	1	–	1	3	–	–	–
Outward remittance flows	**59**	**52**	**59**	**61**	**72**	**94**	**106**	**–**
of which								
Workers' remittances	18	17	17	21	24	–	–	–
Compensation of employees	34	35	42	38	44	–	–	–
Migrants' transfers	6	1	0	2	5	–	–	–

a. For comparison: total international reserves US$1.2 bn in 2008.

New Caledonia

Population (millions, 2009)	0.3
Population growth (avg. annual %, 2000–09)	1.8
Population density (people per km², 2008)	13.5
Labor force (millions, 2008)	0.1
Unemployment rate (% of labor force, 2008)	—
Urban population (% of pop., 2009)	65.1
Surface area (1,000 km², 2008)	18.6
GNI (US$ billions, 2009)	—
GNI per capita, Atlas method (US$, 2009)	—
GDP growth (avg. annual %, 2005–09)	—
Poverty headcount ratio at national poverty line (% of pop., 2005)	—
Age dependency ratio (2009)	49.2

Migration

EMIGRATION, 2010

- Stock of emigrants: **2.3 thousands**
- Stock of emigrants as percentage of population: **0.9%**
- Top destination countries: Australia, New Zealand, the Solomon Islands, French Polynesia, Fiji, Vanuatu, the Dominican Republic, the Netherlands, Chile, Ecuador

SKILLED EMIGRATION, 2000

- Skilled emigration data are currently not available for this country.

IMMIGRATION, 2010

- Stock of immigrants: **59.8 thousands**
- Stock of immigrants as percentage of population: **23.6%**
- Females as percentage of immigrants: **46.6%**
- Refugees as percentage of immigrants: **0.0%**
- Top source countries: Papua New Guinea, Fiji, the Solomon Islands, French Polynesia, Indonesia, Vietnam, Vanuatu

Remittances

US$ millions	2003	2004	2005	2006	2007	2008	2009	2010e
Inward remittance flows[a]	**448**	**493**	**512**	**537**	**585**	**624**	**581**	**659**
of which								
Workers' remittances	5	8	5	4	3	6	—	—
Compensation of employees	444	485	507	533	582	618	—	—
Migrants' transfers	—	—	—	—	—	—	—	—
Outward remittance flows	**21**	**21**	**28**	**50**	**56**	**66**	**66**	**—**
of which								
Workers' remittances	6	7	10	18	18	18	—	—
Compensation of employees	15	15	17	32	37	48	—	—
Migrants' transfers	—	—	—	—	—	—	—	—

a. **For comparison: net FDI inflows US$1.6 bn in 2008.**

New Zealand

Population (millions, 2009)	4.3
Population growth (avg. annual %, 2000–09)	1.2
Population density (people per km², 2008)	15.9
Labor force (millions, 2008)	2.3
Unemployment rate (% of labor force, 2008)	4.1
Urban population (% of pop., 2009)	86.7
Surface area (1,000 km², 2008)	267.7
GNI (US$ billions, 2008)	121.3
GNI per capita, Atlas method (US$, 2008)	27,940
GDP growth (avg. annual %, 2004–08)	1.9
Poverty headcount ratio at national poverty line (% of pop., 2005)	–
Age dependency ratio (2009)	49.6

Migration

EMIGRATION, 2010

- Stock of emigrants: **624.9 thousands**
- Stock of emigrants as percentage of population: **14.5%**
- Top destination countries: Australia, the United Kingdom, the United States, Canada, Thailand, Japan, the Netherlands, Ireland, Samoa, Malaysia

SKILLED EMIGRATION, 2000

- Emigration rate of tertiary-educated population: **20.7%**
- Emigration of physicians: **2,386** or **21.9%** of physicians trained in the country (Source: Bhargava, Docquier, and Moullan 2010)

IMMIGRATION, 2010

- Stock of immigrants: **962.1 thousands**
- Stock of immigrants as percentage of population: **22.4%**
- Females as percentage of immigrants: **52.4%**
- Refugees as percentage of immigrants: **0.4%**
- Top source countries: the United Kingdom, China, Australia, Samoa, India, South Africa, Fiji, the Republic of Korea, the Netherlands, Tonga

Remittances

US$ millions	2003	2004	2005	2006	2007	2008	2009	2010e
Inward remittance flows[a]	**1,065**	**958**	**739**	**650**	**650**	**626**	**611**	**685**
of which								
Workers' remittances	–	–	–	–	–	–	–	–
Compensation of employees	–	–	–	–	–	–	–	–
Migrants' transfers	1,065	958	739	650	650	626	–	–
Outward remittance flows	**561**	**806**	**936**	**865**	**1,207**	**1,202**	**871**	**–**
of which								
Workers' remittances	–	–	–	–	–	–	–	–
Compensation of employees	–	–	–	–	–	–	–	–
Migrants' transfers	561	806	936	865	1,207	1,202	–	–

a. For comparison: net FDI inflows US$5.5 bn, total international reserves US$11.1 bn in 2008.

Nicaragua

Population (millions, 2009)	5.7
Population growth (avg. annual %, 2000–09)	1.3
Population density (people per km², 2008)	46.8
Labor force (millions, 2008)	2.2
Unemployment rate (% of labor force, 2008)	–
Urban population (% of pop., 2009)	57.0
Surface area (1,000 km², 2008)	130.0
GNI (US$ billions, 2009)	5.8
GNI per capita, Atlas method (US$, 2009)	1,000
GDP growth (avg. annual %, 2005–09)	2.7
Poverty headcount ratio at national poverty line (% of pop., 2005)	15.8
Age dependency ratio (2009)	65.7

Migration

EMIGRATION, 2010

- Stock of emigrants: **728.7 thousands**
- Stock of emigrants as percentage of population: **12.5%**
- Top destination countries: Costa Rica, the United States, Spain, Canada, El Salvador, Panama, Guatemala, Honduras, Mexico, República Bolivariana de Venezuela

SKILLED EMIGRATION, 2000

- Emigration rate of tertiary-educated population: **29.6%**
- Emigration of physicians: **304** or **5.2%** of physicians trained in the country *(Source: Bhargava, Docquier, and Moullan 2010)*

IMMIGRATION, 2010

- Stock of immigrants: **40.1 thousands**
- Stock of immigrants as percentage of population: **0.7%**
- Females as percentage of immigrants: **48.3%**
- Refugees as percentage of immigrants: **0.5%**
- Top source countries: Honduras, Costa Rica, the United States, El Salvador, Guatemala, Mexico, Cuba, Spain, Panama, the Russian Federation

Remittances

US$ millions	2003	2004	2005	2006	2007	2008	2009	2010e
Inward remittance flowsᵃ	**439**	**519**	**616**	**698**	**740**	**818**	**768**	**803**
of which								
Workers' remittances	439	519	616	698	740	818	768	–
Compensation of employees	–	–	–	–	–	–	–	–
Migrants' transfers	–	–	–	–	–	–	–	–
Outward remittance flows	–	–	–	–	–	–	–	–
of which								
Workers' remittances	–	–	–	–	–	–	–	–
Compensation of employees	–	–	–	–	–	–	–	–
Migrants' transfers	–	–	–	–	–	–	–	–

a. For comparison: net FDI inflows US$0.6 bn, net ODA received US$0.7 bn, total international reserves US$1.1 bn in 2008.

Niger

Population (millions, 2009)	15.3
Population growth (avg. annual %, 2000–09)	3.6
Population density (people per km², 2008)	11.6
Labor force (millions, 2008)	4.6
Unemployment rate (% of labor force, 2008)	–
Urban population (% of pop., 2009)	16.6
Surface area (1,000 km², 2008)	1,267.0
GNI (US$ billions, 2009)	5.3
GNI per capita, Atlas method (US$, 2009)	340
GDP growth (avg. annual %, 2005–09)	5.4
Poverty headcount ratio at national poverty line (% of pop., 2005)	65.9
Age dependency ratio (2009)	108.0

Migration

EMIGRATION, 2010

- Stock of emigrants: **386.9 thousands**
- Stock of emigrants as percentage of population: **2.4%**
- Top destination countries: Nigeria, Côte d'Ivoire, Benin, Chad, Burkina Faso, Togo, Mali, France, Guinea, the United States

SKILLED EMIGRATION, 2000

- Emigration rate of tertiary-educated population: **6.0%**
- Emigration of physicians: **37** or **8.7%** of physicians born in the country *(Source: Clemens and Pettersson 2006)*
- Emigration of nurses: **66** or **2.4%** of nurses born in the country

IMMIGRATION, 2010

- Stock of immigrants: **202.2 thousands**
- Stock of immigrants as percentage of population: **1.3%**
- Females as percentage of immigrants: **53.9%**
- Refugees as percentage of immigrants: **0.2%**
- Top source countries: Mali, Nigeria, Burkina Faso, Benin, Togo, Ghana, Côte d'Ivoire

Remittances

US$ millions	2003	2004	2005	2006	2007	2008	2009	2010e
Inward remittance flows[a]	**25**	**60**	**66**	**78**	**79**	**79**	**75**	**70**
of which								
Workers' remittances	12	43	46	49	43	–	–	–
Compensation of employees	14	17	21	29	37	–	–	–
Migrants' transfers	–	–	–	–	–	–	–	–
Outward remittance flows	**9**	**25**	**29**	**29**	**18**	**18**	**22**	**–**
of which								
Workers' remittances	7	22	27	27	12	–	–	–
Compensation of employees	2	3	2	2	6	–	–	–
Migrants' transfers	–	–	–	–	–	–	–	–

a. **For comparison: net FDI inflows US$0.1 bn, net ODA received US$0.6 bn, total international reserves US$0.7 bn in 2008.**

Nigeria

Sub-Saharan Africa **LOWER MIDDLE INCOME**

Population (millions, 2009)	154.7
Population growth (avg. annual %, 2000–09)	2.4
Population density (people per km², 2008)	166.1
Labor force (millions, 2008)	46.1
Unemployment rate (% of labor force, 2008)	—
Urban population (% of pop., 2009)	49.1
Surface area (1,000 km², 2008)	923.8
GNI (US$ billions, 2009)	155.3
GNI per capita, Atlas method (US$, 2009)	1,140
GDP growth (avg. annual %, 2005-09)	5.4
Poverty headcount ratio at national poverty line (% of pop., 2005)	62.4
Age dependency ratio (2009)	84.0

Migration

EMIGRATION, 2010

- Stock of emigrants: **1,000.0 thousands**
- Stock of emigrants as percentage of population: **0.6%**
- Top destination countries: the United States, the United Kingdom, Chad, Cameroon, Italy, Benin, Côte d'Ivoire, Spain, Sudan, Niger

SKILLED EMIGRATION, 2000

- Emigration rate of tertiary-educated population: **10.7%**
- Emigration of physicians:
  - (a) **4,127** or **10.8%** of physicians trained in the country *(Source: Bhargava, Docquier, and Moullan 2010)*
  - (b) **4,856** or **13.6%** of physicians born in the country *(Source: Clemens and Pettersson 2006)*
- Emigration of nurses: **12,579** or **11.7%** of nurses born in the country

IMMIGRATION, 2010

- Stock of immigrants: **1,127.7 thousands**
- Stock of immigrants as percentage of population: **0.7%**
- Females as percentage of immigrants: **47.4%**
- Refugees as percentage of immigrants: **0.8%**
- Top source countries: Benin, Ghana, Mali, Togo, Niger, Chad, Cameroon, Liberia, Mauritania, the Arab Republic of Egypt

Remittances

US$ millions	2003	2004	2005	2006	2007	2008	2009	2010e
Inward remittance flows[a]	1,063	2,273	3,329	5,435	9,221	9,980	9,585	9,975
of which								
Workers' remittances	1,063	2,273	14,485	16,740	17,796	17,880	—	—
Compensation of employees	—	—	155	192	218	171	—	—
Migrants' transfers	—	—	—	—	—	—	—	—
Outward remittance flows	12	21	68	102	54	58	66	—
of which								
Workers' remittances	12	21	14	35	26	22	—	—
Compensation of employees	—	—	54	66	28	33	—	—
Migrants' transfers	—	—	—	—	—	—	—	—

a. For comparison: net FDI inflows US$3.6 bn, net ODA received US$1.3 bn, total international reserves US$53.6 bn, exports of goods and services US$86.1 bn in 2008.

Northern Mariana Islands

HIGH-INCOME NON-OECD

Population (thousands, 2009)	86.9
Population growth (avg. annual %, 2000–09)	2.6
Population density (people per km², 2008)	185.7
Labor force (millions, 2008)	–
Unemployment rate (% of labor force, 2008)	–
Urban population (% of pop., 2009)	91.2
Surface area (1,000 km², 2008)	0.5
GNI (US$ billions, 2009)	–
GNI per capita, Atlas method (US$, 2009)	–
GDP growth (avg. annual %, 2005–09)	–
Poverty headcount ratio at national poverty line (% of pop., 2005)	–
Age dependency ratio (2009)	–

Migration

EMIGRATION, 2010

- Stock of emigrants: **8.9 thousands**
- Stock of emigrants as percentage of population: **10.1%**
- Top destination countries: the United States, Guam, the Philippines, Palau, Fiji, Greece, Australia, the Czech Republic, New Zealand, Turkey

SKILLED EMIGRATION, 2000

- Skilled emigration data are currently not available for this country.

IMMIGRATION, 2010

- Stock of immigrants: **54.8 thousands**
- Stock of immigrants as percentage of population: **62.0%**
- Females as percentage of immigrants: **47.4%**
- Refugees as percentage of immigrants: **0.0%**
- Top source countries: the Philippines, China, the United States, the Federated States of Micronesia, the Republic of Korea, Guam, Palau, Bangladesh, Japan, Nepal

Remittances

Remittance data are currently not available for this country.

Norway

Population (millions, 2009)	4.8
Population growth (avg. annual %, 2000–09)	0.8
Population density (people per km², 2008)	15.7
Labor force (millions, 2008)	2.5
Unemployment rate (% of labor force, 2008)	2.6
Urban population (% of pop., 2009)	77.5
Surface area (1,000 km², 2008)	323.8
GNI (US$ billions, 2009)	384.4
GNI per capita, Atlas method (US$, 2009)	86,440
GDP growth (avg. annual %, 2005–09)	1.6
Poverty headcount ratio at national poverty line (% of pop., 2005)	–
Age dependency ratio (2009)	51.0

Migration

EMIGRATION, 2010

- Stock of emigrants: **184.0 thousands**
- Stock of emigrants as percentage of population: **3.8%**
- Top destination countries: Sweden, the United States, Spain, Denmark, the United Kingdom, Germany, Canada, Australia, Turkey, France

SKILLED EMIGRATION, 2000

- Emigration rate of tertiary-educated population: **6.5%**
- Emigration of physicians: **460** or **2.9%** of physicians trained in the country *(Source: Bhargava, Docquier, and Moullan 2010)*

IMMIGRATION, 2010

- Stock of immigrants: **485.4 thousands**
- Stock of immigrants as percentage of population: **10.0%**
- Females as percentage of immigrants: **47.4%**
- Refugees as percentage of immigrants: **7.4%**
- Top source countries: Sweden, Denmark, the United States, Iraq, Pakistan, the United Kingdom, Germany, Bosnia and Herzegovina, Vietnam, the Islamic Republic of Iran

Remittances

US$ millions	2003	2004	2005	2006	2007	2008	2009	2010e
Inward remittance flows[a]	**392**	**465**	**505**	**524**	**613**	**685**	**631**	**657**
of which								
Workers' remittances	–	–	–	–	–	–	–	–
Compensation of employees	392	465	505	524	613	685	631	–
Migrants' transfers	–	–	–	–	–	–	–	–
Outward remittance flows	**1,430**	**1,749**	**2,174**	**2,620**	**3,642**	**4,776**	**4,147**	**–**
of which								
Workers' remittances	–	–	–	–	–	–	–	–
Compensation of employees	1,430	1,749	2,174	2,620	3,642	4,776	4,147	–
Migrants' transfers	–	–	–	–	–	–	–	–

a. For comparison: net FDI inflows US$1.5 bn, total international reserves US$50.9 bn, exports of goods and services US$217.3 bn in 2008.

Oman

Population (millions, 2009)	2.8
Population growth (avg. annual %, 2000–09)	1.9
Population density (people per km², 2008)	9.0
Labor force (millions, 2008)	1.0
Unemployment rate (% of labor force, 2008)	–
Urban population (% of pop., 2009)	71.7
Surface area (1,000 km², 2008)	309.5
GNI (US$ billions, 2009)	–
GNI per capita, Atlas method (US$, 2009)	–
GDP growth (avg. annual %, 2005–09)	–
Poverty headcount ratio at national poverty line (% of pop., 2005)	–
Age dependency ratio (2009)	52.5

Migration

EMIGRATION, 2010

- Stock of emigrants: **15.3 thousands**
- Stock of emigrants as percentage of population: **0.5%**
- Top destination countries: Jordan, the United Kingdom, the United States, Australia, Canada, Bahrain, the Arab Republic of Egypt, the Netherlands, New Zealand, Germany

SKILLED EMIGRATION, 2000

- Emigration rate of tertiary-educated population: **0.6%**
- Emigration of physicians: **12** or **0.4%** of physicians trained in the country (*Source: Bhargava, Docquier, and Moullan 2010*)

IMMIGRATION, 2010

- Stock of immigrants: **826.1 thousands**
- Stock of immigrants as percentage of population: **28.4%**
- Females as percentage of immigrants: **20.8%**
- Refugees as percentage of immigrants: **0.0%**
- Top source countries: India, Bangladesh, Pakistan, the Arab Republic of Egypt, Sri Lanka, the Philippines, Sudan, Jordan, the United Kingdom, the Netherlands

Remittances

US$ millions	2003	2004	2005	2006	2007	2008	2009	2010e
Inward remittance flows[a]	**39**	**39**	**39**	**39**	**39**	**39**	**38**	**40**
of which								
Workers' remittances	–	–	–	–	–	–	–	–
Compensation of employees	39	39	39	39	39	39	–	–
Migrants' transfers	–	–	–	–	–	–	–	–
Outward remittance flows	**1,672**	**1,826**	**2,257**	**2,788**	**3,670**	**5,181**	**5,313**	**–**
of which								
Workers' remittances	1,672	1,826	2,257	2,788	3,670	5,181	5,313	–
Compensation of employees	–	–	–	–	–	–	–	–
Migrants' transfers	–	–	–	–	–	–	–	–

a. **For comparison: net FDI inflows US$2.9 bn, total international reserves US$11.6 bn in 2008.**

Pakistan

Population (millions, 2009)	169.7
Population growth (avg. annual %, 2000–09)	2.3
Population density (people per km², 2008)	215.4
Labor force (millions, 2008)	54.5
Unemployment rate (% of labor force, 2008)	–
Urban population (% of pop., 2009)	36.6
Surface area (1,000 km², 2008)	796.1
GNI (US$ billions, 2009)	171.7
GNI per capita, Atlas method (US$, 2009)	1,020
GDP growth (avg. annual %, 2005–09)	5.1
Poverty headcount ratio at national poverty line (% of pop., 2005)	22.6
Age dependency ratio (2009)	69.4

Migration

EMIGRATION, 2010

- Stock of emigrants: **4,677.0 thousands**
- Stock of emigrants as percentage of population: **2.5%**
- Top destination countries: India, Saudi Arabia, the United Arab Emirates, the United Kingdom, the United States, Qatar, Canada, Kuwait, Oman, Italy

SKILLED EMIGRATION, 2000

- Emigration rate of tertiary-educated population: **12.6%**
- Emigration of physicians: **12,727** or **13.3%** of physicians trained in the country *(Source: Bhargava, Docquier, and Moullan 2010)*

IMMIGRATION, 2010

- Stock of immigrants: **4,233.6 thousands**
- Stock of immigrants as percentage of population: **2.3%**
- Females as percentage of immigrants: **44.7%**
- Refugees as percentage of immigrants: **49.9%**

Remittances

US$ millions	2003	2004	2005	2006	2007	2008	2009	2010e
Inward remittance flows[a]	**3,964**	**3,945**	**4,280**	**5,121**	**5,998**	**7,039**	**8,720**	**9,407**
of which								
Workers' remittances	3,963	3,943	4,277	5,113	5,992	7,025	8,701	–
Compensation of employees	1	2	3	8	6	14	16	–
Migrants' transfers	–	–	–	–	–	–	–	–
Outward remittance flows	**5**	**10**	**3**	**3**	**2**	**2**	**8**	–
of which								
Workers' remittances	5	9	2	1	2	–	–	–
Compensation of employees	–	–	1	1	2	–	–	–
Migrants' transfers	–	–	–	–	–	–	–	–

a. For comparison: net FDI inflows US$5.4 bn, net ODA received US$1.5 bn, total international reserves US$9.0 bn, exports of goods and services US$21.1 bn in 2008.

Palau

UPPER MIDDLE INCOME

Population (thousands, 2009)	20.4
Population growth (avg. annual %, 2000–09)	0.8
Population density (people per km², 2008)	44.1
Labor force (millions, 2008)	—
Unemployment rate (% of labor force, 2008)	—
Urban population (% of pop., 2009)	81.6
Surface area (1,000 km², 2008)	0.5
GNI (US$ billions, 2009)	0.2
GNI per capita, Atlas method (US$, 2009)	8,940
GDP growth (avg. annual %, 2005–09)	1.5
Poverty headcount ratio at national poverty line (% of pop., 2005)	—
Age dependency ratio (2009)	—

Migration

EMIGRATION, 2010

- Stock of emigrants: **8.0 thousands**
- Stock of emigrants as percentage of population: **38.8%**
- Top destination countries: the United States, the Philippines, Northern Mariana Islands, Guam, Mexico, Fiji, Japan, Australia, Greece, New Zealand

SKILLED EMIGRATION, 2000

- Emigration rate of tertiary-educated population: **26.1%**

IMMIGRATION, 2010

- Stock of immigrants: **5.8 thousands**
- Stock of immigrants as percentage of population: **28.1%**
- Females as percentage of immigrants: **40.2%**
- Refugees as percentage of immigrants: **0.0%**
- Top source countries: the Philippines, the United States, the Federated States of Micronesia, Japan, Guam, Northern Mariana Islands, the Republic of Korea

Remittances

Remittance data are currently not available for this country.

Panama

Population (millions, 2009)	3.5
Population growth (avg. annual %, 2000–09)	1.8
Population density (people per km², 2008)	45.6
Labor force (millions, 2008)	1.5
Unemployment rate (% of labor force, 2008)	–
Urban population (% of pop., 2009)	74.0
Surface area (1,000 km², 2008)	75.5
GNI (US$ billions, 2009)	23.7
GNI per capita, Atlas method (US$, 2009)	6,710
GDP growth (avg. annual %, 2005–09)	8.2
Poverty headcount ratio at national poverty line (% of pop., 2005)	9.2
Age dependency ratio (2009)	55.7

Migration

EMIGRATION, 2010

- Stock of emigrants: **141.1 thousands**
- Stock of emigrants as percentage of population: **4.0%**
- Top destination countries: the United States, Costa Rica, Spain, Canada, Mexico, Colombia, Ecuador, the Dominican Republic, República Bolivariana de Venezuela, Chile

SKILLED EMIGRATION, 2000

- Emigration rate of tertiary-educated population: **16.0%**
- Emigration of physicians: **283** or **5.6%** of physicians trained in the country
  (Source: Bhargava, Docquier, and Moullan 2010)

IMMIGRATION, 2010

- Stock of immigrants: **121.0 thousands**
- Stock of immigrants as percentage of population: **3.4%**
- Females as percentage of immigrants: **51.3%**
- Refugees as percentage of immigrants: **13.9%**
- Top source countries: Colombia, China, the Dominican Republic, the United States, Nicaragua, Costa Rica, Peru, Spain, Mexico, India

Remittances

US$ millions	2003	2004	2005	2006	2007	2008	2009	2010e
Inward remittance flows[a]	**107**	**109**	**130**	**157**	**180**	**196**	**175**	**198**
of which								
Workers' remittances	94	105	124	149	173	187	167	–
Compensation of employees	13	4	5	8	7	9	8	–
Migrants' transfers	–	–	–	–	–	–	–	–
Outward remittance flows	**57**	**72**	**88**	**121**	**151**	**198**	**229**	–
of which								
Workers' remittances	57	72	88	121	151	198	229	–
Compensation of employees	–	–	–	–	–	–	–	–
Migrants' transfers	–	–	–	–	–	–	–	–

a. For comparison: net FDI inflows US$2.4 bn, exports of goods and services US$17.3 bn in 2008.

Papua New Guinea

East Asia and Pacific	LOWER MIDDLE INCOME
Population (millions, 2009)	6.7
Population growth (avg. annual %, 2000–09)	2.5
Population density (people per km², 2008)	14.2
Labor force (millions, 2008)	2.7
Unemployment rate (% of labor force, 2008)	–
Urban population (% of pop., 2009)	12.5
Surface area (1,000 km², 2008)	462.8
GNI (US$ billions, 2009)	7.8
GNI per capita, Atlas method (US$, 2009)	1,180
GDP growth (avg. annual %, 2005–09)	4.9
Poverty headcount ratio at national poverty line (% of pop., 2005)	29.7
Age dependency ratio (2009)	73.1

Migration

EMIGRATION, 2010

- Stock of emigrants: **61.2 thousands**
- Stock of emigrants as percentage of population: **0.9%**
- Top destination countries: Australia, New Caledonia, the United States, the Solomon Islands, the United Kingdom, New Zealand, Fiji, Canada, the Philippines, Switzerland

SKILLED EMIGRATION, 2000

- Emigration rate of tertiary-educated population: **28.5%**
- Emigration of physicians: **85** or **24.2%** of physicians trained in the country *(Source: Bhargava, Docquier, and Moullan 2010)*

IMMIGRATION, 2010

- Stock of immigrants: **24.5 thousands**
- Stock of immigrants as percentage of population: **0.4%**
- Females as percentage of immigrants: **37.4%**
- Refugees as percentage of immigrants: **41.1%**
- Top source countries: Australia, the United Kingdom, New Zealand, the United States, Germany, Indonesia, the Netherlands, China, India, Japan

Remittances

US$ millions	2003	2004	2005	2006	2007	2008	2009	2010e
Inward remittance flows[a]	**13**	**16**	**13**	**13**	**13**	**13**	**12**	**14**
of which								
Workers' remittances	4	8	6	–	–	–	–	–
Compensation of employees	3	2	1	–	–	–	–	–
Migrants' transfers	6	6	6	–	–	–	–	–
Outward remittance flows	**97**	**123**	**135**	**–**	**–**	**–**	**–**	**–**
of which								
Workers' remittances	41	61	75	–	–	–	–	–
Compensation of employees	50	56	54	–	–	–	–	–
Migrants' transfers	6	6	6	–	–	–	–	–

a. For comparison: net ODA received US$0.3 bn, total international reserves US$2.0 bn, exports of goods and services US$6.0 bn in 2008.

Paraguay

Population (millions, 2009)	6.3
Population growth (avg. annual %, 2000–09)	1.9
Population density (people per km², 2008)	15.7
Labor force (millions, 2008)	3.1
Unemployment rate (% of labor force, 2008)	5.7
Urban population (% of pop., 2009)	60.9
Surface area (1,000 km², 2008)	406.8
GNI (US$ billions, 2009)	14.7
GNI per capita, Atlas method (US$, 2009)	2,270
GDP growth (avg. annual %, 2005–09)	3.2
Poverty headcount ratio at national poverty line (% of pop., 2005)	9.3
Age dependency ratio (2009)	64.1

Migration

EMIGRATION, 2010

- Stock of emigrants: **510.4 thousands**
- Stock of emigrants as percentage of population: **7.9%**
- Top destination countries: Argentina, Spain, Brazil, the United States, Canada, Bolivia, Japan, Chile, Uruguay, Germany

SKILLED EMIGRATION, 2000

- Emigration rate of tertiary-educated population: **3.9%**
- Emigration of physicians: **243** or **3.8%** of physicians trained in the country
  (*Source: Bhargava, Docquier, and Moullan 2010*)

IMMIGRATION, 2010

- Stock of immigrants: **161.3 thousands**
- Stock of immigrants as percentage of population: **2.5%**
- Females as percentage of immigrants: **48.3%**
- Refugees as percentage of immigrants: **0.0%**
- Top source countries: Brazil, Argentina, Uruguay, Chile, Japan, the Republic of Korea, Germany, Mexico, the United States, Peru

Remittances

US$ millions	2003	2004	2005	2006	2007	2008	2009	2010e
Inward remittance flows[a]	**222**	**238**	**269**	**463**	**484**	**579**	**555**	**573**
of which								
Workers' remittances	110	132	161	336	341	363	366	–
Compensation of employees	113	106	108	127	143	225	214	–
Migrants' transfers	–	–	–	–	–	–	–	–
Outward remittance flows	–	–	–	–	–	–	–	–
of which								
Workers' remittances	–	–	–	–	–	–	–	–
Compensation of employees	–	–	–	–	–	–	–	–
Migrants' transfers	–	–	–	–	–	–	–	–

a. For comparison: net FDI inflows US$0.3 bn, net ODA received US$0.1 bn, total international reserves US$2.9 bn, exports of goods and services US$8.5 bn in 2008.

Peru

Latin America and the Caribbean	UPPER MIDDLE INCOME
Population (millions, 2009)	29.2
Population growth (avg. annual %, 2000–09)	1.3
Population density (people per km², 2008)	22.5
Labor force (millions, 2008)	14.3
Unemployment rate (% of labor force, 2008)	–
Urban population (% of pop., 2009)	71.5
Surface area (1,000 km², 2008)	1,285.2
GNI (US$ billions, 2009)	119.4
GNI per capita, Atlas method (US$, 2009)	4,150
GDP growth (avg. annual %, 2005–09)	6.8
Poverty headcount ratio at national poverty line (% of pop., 2005)	8.2
Age dependency ratio (2009)	56.7

Migration

EMIGRATION, 2010

- Stock of emigrants: **1,090.8 thousands**
- Stock of emigrants as percentage of population: **3.7%**
- Top destination countries: the United States, Spain, Italy, Argentina, Chile, Japan, República Bolivariana de Venezuela, Canada, Ecuador, Bolivia

SKILLED EMIGRATION, 2000

- Emigration rate of tertiary-educated population: **5.8%**
- Emigration of physicians: **1,830** or **5.7%** of physicians trained in the country *(Source: Bhargava, Docquier, and Moullan 2010)*

IMMIGRATION, 2010

- Stock of immigrants: **37.6 thousands**
- Stock of immigrants as percentage of population: **0.1%**
- Females as percentage of immigrants: **52.4%**
- Refugees as percentage of immigrants: **2.5%**
- Top source countries: the United States, Chile, Argentina, China, Spain, Bolivia, Italy, Brazil, Colombia, Japan

Remittances

US$ millions	2003	2004	2005	2006	2007	2008	2009	2010e
Inward remittance flows[a]	**869**	**1,133**	**1,440**	**1,837**	**2,131**	**2,444**	**2,378**	**2,494**
of which								
Workers' remittances	869	1,133	1,440	1,837	2,131	2,444	2,378	–
Compensation of employees	–	–	–	–	–	–	–	–
Migrants' transfers	–	–	–	–	–	–	–	–
Outward remittance flows	**116**	**113**	**129**	**133**	**137**	**133**	**85**	–
of which								
Workers' remittances	–	–	–	–	–	–	–	–
Compensation of employees	–	–	–	–	–	–	–	–
Migrants' transfers	116	113	129	133	137	133	85	–

a. For comparison: net FDI inflows US$4.1 bn, net ODA received US$0.5 bn, total international reserves US$31.2 bn, exports of goods and services US$35.0 bn in 2008.

Philippines, The

East Asia and Pacific — LOWER MIDDLE INCOME

Population (millions, 2009)	92.0
Population growth (avg. annual %, 2000–09)	1.9
Population density (people per km², 2008)	303.0
Labor force (millions, 2008)	37.7
Unemployment rate (% of labor force, 2008)	7.4
Urban population (% of pop., 2009)	65.7
Surface area (1,000 km², 2008)	300.0
GNI (US$ billions, 2009)	160.4
GNI per capita, Atlas method (US$, 2009)	1,790
GDP growth (avg. annual %, 2005–09)	4.4
Poverty headcount ratio at national poverty line (% of pop., 2005)	22.6
Age dependency ratio (2009)	61.5

Migration

EMIGRATION, 2010

- Stock of emigrants: **4,275.2 thousands**
- Stock of emigrants as percentage of population: **4.6%**
- Top destination countries: the United States, Saudi Arabia, Canada, Malaysia, Japan, Australia, Italy, Qatar, the United Arab Emirates, the United Kingdom

SKILLED EMIGRATION, 2000

- Emigration rate of tertiary-educated population: **13.7%**
- Emigration of physicians: **20,149** or **17.5%** of physicians trained in the country *(Source: Bhargava, Docquier, and Moullan 2010)*

IMMIGRATION, 2010

- Stock of immigrants: **435.4 thousands**
- Stock of immigrants as percentage of population: **0.5%**
- Females as percentage of immigrants: **51.1%**
- Refugees as percentage of immigrants: **0.0%**
- Top source countries: the United States, China, the United Kingdom, Bahrain, Japan, Antigua and Barbuda, Indonesia, India, Brazil, Angola

Remittances

US$ millions	2003	2004	2005	2006	2007	2008	2009	2010e
Inward remittance flows[a]	**10,243**	**11,471**	**13,566**	**15,251**	**16,302**	**18,642**	**19,766**	**21,311**
of which								
Workers' remittances	7,681	8,617	10,668	12,481	13,255	14,536	15,141	–
Compensation of employees	2,558	2,851	2,893	2,758	3,030	4,092	4,585	–
Migrants' transfers	4	3	5	12	17	14	40	–
Outward remittance flows	**18**	**17**	**15**	**20**	**35**	**44**	**58**	**–**
of which								
Workers' remittances	–	–	–	–	–	–	–	–
Compensation of employees	–	–	–	–	–	–	–	–
Migrants' transfers	18	17	15	20	35	44	58	–

a. For comparison: net FDI inflows US$1.4 bn, net ODA received US$0.1 bn, total international reserves US$37.5 bn, exports of goods and services US$61.5 bn in 2008.

Poland

Population (millions, 2009)	38.1
Population growth (avg. annual %, 2000–09)	-0.1
Population density (people per km², 2008)	124.5
Labor force (millions, 2008)	17.3
Unemployment rate (% of labor force, 2008)	7.1
Urban population (% of pop., 2009)	61.3
Surface area (1,000 km², 2008)	312.7
GNI (US$ billions, 2009)	416.1
GNI per capita, Atlas method (US$, 2009)	12,260
GDP growth (avg. annual %, 2005–09)	4.7
Poverty headcount ratio at national poverty line (% of pop., 2005)	0.1
Age dependency ratio (2009)	39.5

Migration

EMIGRATION, 2010

- Stock of emigrants: **3,102.6 thousands**
- Stock of emigrants as percentage of population: **8.2%**
- Top destination countries: Germany, the United Kingdom, the United States, Belarus, Canada, France, Italy, Israel, Ireland, Spain

SKILLED EMIGRATION, 2000

- Emigration rate of tertiary-educated population: **14.1%**
- Emigration of physicians: **8,553** or **9.1%** of physicians trained in the country *(Source: Bhargava, Docquier, and Moullan 2010)*

IMMIGRATION, 2010

- Stock of immigrants: **827.5 thousands**
- Stock of immigrants as percentage of population: **2.2%**
- Females as percentage of immigrants: **59.0%**
- Refugees as percentage of immigrants: **1.0%**
- Top source countries: Ukraine, Belarus, Germany, Lithuania, the Russian Federation, France, the United States, the Czech Republic, Austria, Kazakhstan

Remittances

US$ millions	2003	2004	2005	2006	2007	2008	2009	2010e
Inward remittance flows[a]	**2,284**	**4,728**	**6,482**	**8,496**	**10,496**	**10,447**	**8,816**	**9,080**
of which								
Workers' remittances	741	1,124	1,822	2,955	4,242	4,700	3,788	–
Compensation of employees	1,543	3,600	4,649	5,531	6,226	5,708	4,996	–
Migrants' transfers	–	4	11	10	28	39	32	–
Outward remittance flows	**325**	**460**	**602**	**802**	**1,278**	**1,717**	**1,328**	**–**
of which								
Workers' remittances	33	16	13	13	16	32	9	–
Compensation of employees	292	438	571	776	1,238	1,651	1,309	–
Migrants' transfers	–	6	18	13	24	34	10	–

a. **For comparison: net FDI inflows US$14.8 bn, total international reserves US$62.2 bn, exports of goods and services US$209.9 bn in 2008.**

Portugal

Population (millions, 2009)	10.6
Population growth (avg. annual %, 2000–09)	0.4
Population density (people per km², 2008)	116.1
Labor force (millions, 2008)	5.6
Unemployment rate (% of labor force, 2008)	7.6
Urban population (% of pop., 2009)	60.1
Surface area (1,000 km², 2008)	92.1
GNI (US$ billions, 2009)	216.7
GNI per capita, Atlas method (US$, 2009)	20,940
GDP growth (avg. annual %, 2005–09)	0.3
Poverty headcount ratio at national poverty line (% of pop., 2005)	—
Age dependency ratio (2009)	49.1

Migration

EMIGRATION, 2010

- Stock of emigrants: **2,230.0 thousands**
- Stock of emigrants as percentage of population: **20.8%**
- Top destination countries: France, Brazil, Germany, the United States, Canada, Spain, Switzerland, the United Kingdom, Mozambique, República Bolivariana de Venezuela

SKILLED EMIGRATION, 2000

- Emigration rate of tertiary-educated population: **19.5%**
- Emigration of physicians: **807** or **2.4%** of physicians trained in the country *(Source: Bhargava, Docquier, and Moullan 2010)*

IMMIGRATION, 2010

- Stock of immigrants: **918.6 thousands**
- Stock of immigrants as percentage of population: **8.6%**
- Females as percentage of immigrants: **50.3%**
- Refugees as percentage of immigrants: **0.0%**
- Top source countries: Angola, France, Mozambique, Brazil, Cape Verde, Germany, República Bolivariana de Venezuela, Guinea-Bissau, Spain, Switzerland

Remittances

US$ millions	2003	2004	2005	2006	2007	2008	2009	2010e
Inward remittance flows[a]	**3,042**	**3,304**	**3,101**	**3,334**	**3,941**	**4,057**	**3,585**	**3,664**
of which								
Workers' remittances	2,752	3,032	2,826	3,045	3,551	3,647	3,190	—
Compensation of employees	237	230	235	265	340	343	333	—
Migrants' transfers	53	43	41	24	50	67	61	—
Outward remittance flows	**935**	**1,163**	**1,306**	**1,377**	**1,284**	**1,410**	**1,460**	**—**
of which								
Workers' remittances	529	604	695	766	783	847	781	—
Compensation of employees	259	378	436	445	346	388	516	—
Migrants' transfers	148	182	175	166	155	176	162	—

a. For comparison: net FDI inflows US$3.6 bn, total international reserves US$12.0 bn, exports of goods and services US$80.1 bn in 2008.

Puerto Rico

Population (millions, 2009)	4.0
Population growth (avg. annual %, 2000–09)	0.4
Population density (people per km², 2008)	445.8
Labor force (millions, 2008)	1.5
Unemployment rate (% of labor force, 2008)	11.6
Urban population (% of pop., 2009)	98.6
Surface area (1,000 km², 2008)	9.0
GNI (US$ billions, 2009)	—
GNI per capita, Atlas method (US$, 2009)	—
GDP growth (avg. annual %, 2005–09)	—
Poverty headcount ratio at national poverty line (% of pop., 2005)	—
Age dependency ratio (2009)	51.5

Migration

EMIGRATION, 2010

- Stock of emigrants: **1,706.0 thousands**
- Stock of emigrants as percentage of population: **42.7%**
- Top destination countries: the United States, the Dominican Republic, Mexico, Ecuador, República Bolivariana de Venezuela, Panama, Colombia, the United Kingdom, Canada, Chile

SKILLED EMIGRATION, 2000

- Skilled emigration data are currently not available for this country.

IMMIGRATION, 2010

- Stock of immigrants: **324.0 thousands**
- Stock of immigrants as percentage of population: **8.1%**
- Females as percentage of immigrants: **52.7%**
- Refugees as percentage of immigrants: **0.0%**
- Top source country: the United States

Remittances

Remittance data are currently not available for this country.

Qatar

Population (millions, 2009)	1.4
Population growth (avg. annual %, 2000–09)	8.7
Population density (people per km², 2008)	116.4
Labor force (millions, 2008)	0.7
Unemployment rate (% of labor force, 2008)	–
Urban population (% of pop., 2009)	95.7
Surface area (1,000 km², 2008)	11.0
GNI (US$ billions, 2009)	–
GNI per capita, Atlas method (US$, 2009)	–
GDP growth (avg. annual %, 2005–09)	–
Poverty headcount ratio at national poverty line (% of pop., 2005)	–
Age dependency ratio (2009)	20.6

Migration

EMIGRATION, 2010

- Stock of emigrants: **9.9 thousands**
- Stock of emigrants as percentage of population: **0.7%**
- Top destination countries: the United States, Jordan, Canada, the United Kingdom, Australia, the Arab Republic of Egypt, France, Bahrain, Ireland, Germany

SKILLED EMIGRATION, 2000

- Emigration rate of tertiary-educated population: **2.5%**

IMMIGRATION, 2010

- Stock of immigrants: **1,305.4 thousands**
- Stock of immigrants as percentage of population: **86.5%**
- Females as percentage of immigrants: **25.8%**
- Refugees as percentage of immigrants: **0.0%**
- Top source countries: Pakistan, India, Nepal, the Islamic Republic of Iran, the Philippines, the Arab Republic of Egypt, Sri Lanka

Remittances

Remittance data are currently not available for this country.

Romania

Population (millions, 2009)	21.5
Population growth (avg. annual %, 2000–09)	-0.4
Population density (people per km², 2008)	93.5
Labor force (millions, 2008)	9.7
Unemployment rate (% of labor force, 2008)	5.8
Urban population (% of pop., 2009)	54.4
Surface area (1,000 km², 2008)	238.4
GNI (US$ billions, 2009)	164.1
GNI per capita, Atlas method (US$, 2009)	8,330
GDP growth (avg. annual %, 2005–09)	3.8
Poverty headcount ratio at national poverty line (% of pop., 2005)	0.8
Age dependency ratio (2009)	43.0

Migration

EMIGRATION, 2010

- Stock of emigrants: **2,769.4 thousands**
- Stock of emigrants as percentage of population: **13.1%**
- Top destination countries: Italy, Spain, Hungary, Israel, the United States, Germany, Canada, Austria, France, the United Kingdom

SKILLED EMIGRATION, 2000

- Emigration rate of tertiary-educated population: **11.8%**
- Emigration of physicians: **3,119** or **6.9%** of physicians trained in the country *(Source: Bhargava, Docquier, and Moullan 2010)*

IMMIGRATION, 2010

- Stock of immigrants: **132.8 thousands**
- Stock of immigrants as percentage of population: **0.6%**
- Females as percentage of immigrants: **51.3%**
- Refugees as percentage of immigrants: **1.3%**
- Top source countries: Moldova, Bulgaria, Ukraine, the Russian Federation, the Syrian Arab Republic, Hungary, Greece, Turkey, Italy, Germany

Remittances

US$ millions	2003	2004	2005	2006	2007	2008	2009	2010e
Inward remittance flows[a]	**124**	**132**	**4,733**	**6,718**	**8,542**	**9,381**	**4,928**	**4,517**
of which								
Workers' remittances	14	18	3,754	5,509	6,835	7,580	4,207	–
Compensation of employees	110	113	954	1,165	1,626	1,705	651	–
Migrants' transfers	–	1	25	44	81	96	71	–
Outward remittance flows	**8**	**8**	**33**	**57**	**353**	**664**	**310**	**–**
of which								
Workers' remittances	1	1	4	6	289	482	243	–
Compensation of employees	7	5	24	42	55	169	61	–
Migrants' transfers	–	2	6	8	9	13	6	–

a. For comparison: net FDI inflows US$13.9 bn, total international reserves US$39.8 bn, exports of goods and services US$59.8 bn in 2008.

Russian Federation

Europe and Central Asia	UPPER MIDDLE INCOME
Population (millions, 2009)	141.9
Population growth (avg. annual %, 2000–09)	–0.3
Population density (people per km², 2008)	8.7
Labor force (millions, 2008)	75.9
Unemployment rate (% of labor force, 2008)	6.2
Urban population (% of pop., 2009)	72.8
Surface area (1,000 km², 2008)	17,098.2
GNI (US$ billions, 2009)	1,194.9
GNI per capita, Atlas method (US$, 2009)	9,370
GDP growth (avg. annual %, 2005–09)	4.0
Poverty headcount ratio at national poverty line (% of pop., 2005)	0.2
Age dependency ratio (2009)	38.6

Migration

EMIGRATION, 2010

- Stock of emigrants: **11,055.6 thousands**
- Stock of emigrants as percentage of population: **7.9%**
- Top destination countries: Ukraine, Kazakhstan, Israel, Belarus, the United States, Uzbekistan, Germany, Latvia, Tajikistan, Moldova

SKILLED EMIGRATION, 2000

- Emigration rate of tertiary-educated population: **1.5%**
- Emigration of physicians: **3,922** or **0.6%** of physicians trained in the country *(Source: Bhargava, Docquier, and Moullan 2010)*

IMMIGRATION, 2010

- Stock of immigrants: **12,270.4 thousands**
- Stock of immigrants as percentage of population: **8.7%**
- Females as percentage of immigrants: **57.8%**
- Refugees as percentage of immigrants: **0.0%**
- Top source countries: Ukraine, Kazakhstan, Belarus, Uzbekistan, Azerbaijan, Georgia, Armenia, the Kyrgyz Republic, Tajikistan, Moldova

Remittances

US$ millions	2003	2004	2005	2006	2007	2008	2009	2010e
Inward remittance flows[a]	**1,453**	**2,495**	**3,012**	**3,344**	**4,713**	**6,033**	**5,359**	**5,590**
of which								
Workers' remittances	300	925	621	766	852	802	775	–
Compensation of employees	814	1,206	1,807	1,899	2,613	3,792	3,326	–
Migrants' transfers	339	364	583	678	1,249	1,439	1,258	–
Outward remittance flows	**3,233**	**5,188**	**7,008**	**11,467**	**17,763**	**26,145**	**18,613**	**–**
of which								
Workers' remittances	1,306	2,672	3,051	4,587	6,942	7,264	5,927	–
Compensation of employees	958	1,464	2,940	6,067	9,931	17,971	12,027	–
Migrants' transfers	969	1,052	1,017	813	890	910	659	–

a. For comparison: net FDI inflows US$72.9 bn, total international reserves US$427.1 bn, exports of goods and services US$517.7 bn in 2008.

Rwanda

Sub-Saharan Africa	LOW INCOME
Population (millions, 2009)	10.0
Population growth (avg. annual %, 2000–09)	3.0
Population density (people per km², 2008)	394.0
Labor force (millions, 2008)	4.4
Unemployment rate (% of labor force, 2008)	–
Urban population (% of pop., 2009)	18.6
Surface area (1,000 km², 2008)	26.3
GNI (US$ billions, 2009)	5.0
GNI per capita, Atlas method (US$, 2009)	460
GDP growth (avg. annual %, 2005–09)	7.8
Poverty headcount ratio at national poverty line (% of pop., 2005)	74.4
Age dependency ratio (2009)	81.0

Migration

EMIGRATION, 2010

- Stock of emigrants: **263.4 thousands**
- Stock of emigrants as percentage of population: **2.6%**
- Top destination countries: Uganda, Tanzania, Burundi, Belgium, Canada, the United Kingdom, France, the United States, Italy, Germany

SKILLED EMIGRATION, 2000

- Emigration rate of tertiary-educated population: **26.0%**
- Emigration of physicians:
  - (a) **23** or **12.7%** of physicians trained in the country *(Source: Bhargava, Docquier, and Moullan 2010)*
  - (b) **118** or **43.2%** of physicians born in the country *(Source: Clemens and Pettersson 2006)*
- Emigration of nurses: **292** or **13.9%** of nurses born in the country

IMMIGRATION, 2010

- Stock of immigrants: **465.5 thousands**
- Stock of immigrants as percentage of population: **4.5%**
- Females as percentage of immigrants: **53.9%**
- Refugees as percentage of immigrants: **11.0%**
- Top source countries: the Democratic Republic of Congo, Burundi, Uganda, Tanzania, India, Belgium

Remittances

US$ millions	2003	2004	2005	2006	2007	2008	2009	2010e
Inward remittance flows[a]	**10**	**10**	**21**	**21**	**51**	**68**	**93**	**91**
of which								
Workers' remittances	9	10	9	17	28	63	–	–
Compensation of employees		0	12	4	23	4	–	–
Migrants' transfers	–	–	–	–	–	–	–	–
Outward remittance flows	**30**	**31**	**35**	**47**	**68**	**70**	**71**	**–**
of which								
Workers' remittances	15	15	14	17	20	32	35	–
Compensation of employees	14	16	21	30	48	38	36	–
Migrants' transfers	–	–	–	–	–	–	–	–

a. For comparison: net FDI inflows US$0.1 bn, net ODA received US$0.9 bn, total international reserves US$0.6 bn, exports of goods and services US$0.7 bn in 2008.

Samoa

Population (millions, 2009)	0.2
Population growth (avg. annual %, 2000–09)	0.2
Population density (people per km², 2008)	64.1
Labor force (millions, 2008)	0.1
Unemployment rate (% of labor force, 2008)	–
Urban population (% of pop., 2009)	23.2
Surface area (1,000 km², 2008)	2.8
GNI (US$ billions, 2009)	0.5
GNI per capita, Atlas method (US$, 2009)	2,840
GDP growth (avg. annual %, 2005–09)	1.6
Poverty headcount ratio at national poverty line (% of pop., 2005)	–
Age dependency ratio (2009)	79.4

Migration

EMIGRATION, 2010

- Stock of emigrants: **120.4 thousands**
- Stock of emigrants as percentage of population: **67.3%**
- Top destination countries: New Zealand, the United States, American Samoa, Australia, Fiji, Kiribati, the United Kingdom, Canada, Italy, Japan

SKILLED EMIGRATION, 2000

- Emigration rate of tertiary-educated population: **76.4%**

IMMIGRATION, 2010

- Stock of immigrants: **9.0 thousands**
- Stock of immigrants as percentage of population: **5.0%**
- Females as percentage of immigrants: **44.7%**
- Refugees as percentage of immigrants: **0.0%**
- Top source countries: American Samoa, New Zealand, the United States, Australia, Fiji, Tonga, China, Japan, Papua New Guinea, Germany

Remittances

US$ millions	2003	2004	2005	2006	2007	2008	2009	2010e
Inward remittance flows[a]	45	88	110	108	120	135	124	142
of which								
Workers' remittances	–	–	–	–	–	–	–	–
Compensation of employees	–	1	1	1	1	–	–	–
Migrants' transfers	–	–	–	–	–	–	–	–
Outward remittance flows	–	11	11	2	13	–	–	–
of which								
Workers' remittances	–	–	–	–	–	–	–	–
Compensation of employees	–	11	11	2	13	–	–	–
Migrants' transfers	–	–	–	–	–	–	–	–

a. For comparison: total international reserves US$0.1 bn, exports of goods and services US$0.2 bn in 2008.

San Marino

HIGH-INCOME NON-OECD

Population (thousands, 2009)	31.4
Population growth (avg. annual %, 2000–09)	1.3
Population density (people per km², 2008)	516.8
Labor force (millions, 2008)	—
Unemployment rate (% of labor force, 2008)	—
Urban population (% of pop., 2009)	94.3
Surface area (1,000 km², 2008)	0.1
GNI (US$ billions, 2009)	—
GNI per capita, Atlas method (US$, 2009)	—
GDP growth (avg. annual %, 2005–09)	—
Poverty headcount ratio at national poverty line (% of pop., 2005)	—
Age dependency ratio (2009)	—

Migration

EMIGRATION, 2010

- Stock of emigrants: **3.1 thousands**
- Stock of emigrants as percentage of population: **9.9%**
- Top destination countries: Italy, the United States, France, Germany, Belgium, Spain, Canada, Switzerland, the United Kingdom, Greece

SKILLED EMIGRATION, 2000

- Emigration rate of tertiary-educated population: **17.1%**

IMMIGRATION, 2010

- Stock of immigrants: **11.7 thousands**
- Stock of immigrants as percentage of population: **37.0%**
- Females as percentage of immigrants: **53.5%**
- Refugees as percentage of immigrants: **0.0%**
- Top source country: Italy

Remittances

Remittance data are currently not available for this country.

São Tomé and Principe

Population (millions, 2009)	0.2
Population growth (avg. annual %, 2000–09)	1.7
Population density (people per km², 2008)	167.7
Labor force (millions, 2008)	0.1
Unemployment rate (% of labor force, 2008)	–
Urban population (% of pop., 2009)	61.4
Surface area (1,000 km², 2008)	1.0
GNI (US$ billions, 2009)	0.2
GNI per capita, Atlas method (US$, 2009)	1,140
GDP growth (avg. annual %, 2005–09)	5.6
Poverty headcount ratio at national poverty line (% of pop., 2005)	–
Age dependency ratio (2009)	80.6

Migration

EMIGRATION, 2010

- Stock of emigrants: **36.2 thousands**
- Stock of emigrants as percentage of population: **21.9%**
- Top destination countries: Portugal, Angola, Cape Verde, Spain, France, the United Kingdom, the Netherlands, the United States, Germany, Italy

SKILLED EMIGRATION, 2000

- Emigration rate of tertiary-educated population: **22.0%**
- Emigration of physicians: **97** or **60.6%** of physicians born in the country
  (Source: Clemens and Pettersson 2006)
- Emigration of nurses: **149** or **46.4%** of nurses born in the country

IMMIGRATION, 2010

- Stock of immigrants: **5.3 thousands**
- Stock of immigrants as percentage of population: **3.2%**
- Females as percentage of immigrants: **48.0%**
- Refugees as percentage of immigrants: **0.0%**
- Top source countries: Angola, Cape Verde, Portugal, Gabon, Equatorial Guinea, Mozambique, Guinea-Bissau, the Russian Federation, the Republic of Congo, France

Remittances

US$ millions	2003	2004	2005	2006	2007	2008	2009	2010e
Inward remittance flows	2	1	2	2	2	3	2	2
of which								
Workers' remittances	2	1	2	2	2	–	–	–
Compensation of employees	–	–	–	–	–	–	–	–
Migrants' transfers	–	–	–	–	–	–	–	–
Outward remittance flows	1	1	0	1	1	1	1	–
of which								
Workers' remittances	–	–	–	–	–	–	–	–
Compensation of employees	1	1	0	1	1	–	–	–
Migrants' transfers	–	–	–	–	–	–	–	–

Saudi Arabia

Population (millions, 2009)	25.4
Population growth (avg. annual %, 2000-09)	2.3
Population density (people per km², 2008)	11.5
Labor force (millions, 2008)	8.7
Unemployment rate (% of labor force, 2008)	–
Urban population (% of pop., 2009)	82.3
Surface area (1,000 km², 2008)	2,149.7
GNI (US$ billions, 2009)	–
GNI per capita, Atlas method (US$, 2009)	–
GDP growth (avg. annual %, 2005–09)	–
Poverty headcount ratio at national poverty line (% of pop., 2005)	–
Age dependency ratio (2009)	54.6

Migration

EMIGRATION, 2010

- Stock of emigrants: **178.7 thousands**
- Stock of emigrants as percentage of population: **0.7%**
- Top destination countries: Jordan, the United States, the United Kingdom, Canada, the Arab Republic of Egypt, Bahrain, Australia, Turkey, India, France

SKILLED EMIGRATION, 2000

- Emigration rate of tertiary-educated population: **0.9%**
- Emigration of physicians: **359** or **1.2%** of physicians trained in the country
  (Source: Bhargava, Docquier, and Moullan 2010)

IMMIGRATION, 2010

- Stock of immigrants: **7,288.9 thousands**
- Stock of immigrants as percentage of population: **27.8%**
- Females as percentage of immigrants: **30.1%**
- Refugees as percentage of immigrants: **3.3%**
- Top source countries: India, the Arab Republic of Egypt, Pakistan, the Republic of Yemen, the Philippines, Bangladesh, Sri Lanka, Indonesia, Sudan, Jordan

Remittances

US$ millions	2003	2004	2005	2006	2007	2008	2009	2010e
Inward remittance flows[a]	–	–	94	106	124	216	217	233
of which								
Workers' remittances	–	–	–	–	–	–	–	–
Compensation of employees	–	–	94	106	124	216	217	–
Migrants' transfers	–	–	–	–	–	–	–	–
Outward remittance flows	14,783	13,555	14,315	15,964	16,447	21,696	25,969	–
of which								
Workers' remittances	14,783	13,555	13,716	15,299	15,746	20,946	25,187	–
Compensation of employees	–	–	599	665	701	751	782	–
Migrants' transfers	–	–	–	–	–	–	–	–

a. **For comparison: net FDI inflows US$22.5 bn, total international reserves US$34.3 bn, exports of goods and services US$323.1 bn in 2008.**

Senegal

Population (millions, 2009)	12.5
Population growth (avg. annual %, 2000–09)	2.6
Population density (people per km², 2008)	63.4
Labor force (millions, 2008)	4.9
Unemployment rate (% of labor force, 2008)	–
Urban population (% of pop., 2009)	42.6
Surface area (1,000 km², 2008)	196.7
GNI (US$ billions, 2009)	12.9
GNI per capita, Atlas method (US$, 2009)	1,030
GDP growth (avg. annual %, 2005–09)	3.6
Poverty headcount ratio at national poverty line (% of pop., 2005)	33.5
Age dependency ratio (2009)	85.0

Migration

EMIGRATION, 2010

- Stock of emigrants: **636.2 thousands**
- Stock of emigrants as percentage of population: **4.9%**
- Top destination countries: The Gambia, France, Italy, Mauritania, Spain, Côte d'Ivoire, Gabon, the United States, Mali, Guinea-Bissau

SKILLED EMIGRATION, 2000

- Emigration rate of tertiary-educated population: **17.7%**
- Emigration of physicians:
  - (a) **27** or **2.9%** of physicians trained in the country *(Source: Bhargava, Docquier, and Moullan 2010)*
  - (b) **678** or **51.4%** of physicians born in the country *(Source: Clemens and Pettersson 2006)*
- Emigration of nurses: **695** or **26.9%** of nurses born in the country

IMMIGRATION, 2010

- Stock of immigrants: **210.1 thousands**
- Stock of immigrants as percentage of population: **1.6%**
- Females as percentage of immigrants: **51.2%**
- Refugees as percentage of immigrants: **9.8%**
- Top source countries: Guinea, Mauritania, Guinea-Bissau, Mali, France, Cape Verde, The Gambia, Morocco, the Syrian Arab Republic, the United States

Remittances

US$ millions	2003	2004	2005	2006	2007	2008	2009	2010e
Inward remittance flows[a]	**511**	**633**	**789**	**925**	**1,192**	**1,288**	**1,191**	**1,164**
of which								
Workers' remittances	448	563	717	851	1,107	–	–	–
Compensation of employees	63	70	72	75	85	–	–	–
Migrants' transfers	–	–	–	–	–	–	–	–
Outward remittance flows	**57**	**77**	**98**	**96**	**143**	**–**	**–**	**–**
of which								
Workers' remittances	48	67	87	87	130	–	–	–
Compensation of employees	9	10	11	10	13	–	–	–
Migrants' transfers	–	–	–	–	–	–	–	–

a. For comparison: net FDI inflows US$0.7 bn, net ODA received US$1.1 bn, total international reserves US$1.6 bn, exports of goods and services US$3.3 bn in 2008.

Serbia

Population (millions, 2009)	7.3
Population growth (avg. annual %, 2000-09)	-0.3
Population density (people per km², 2008)	83.2
Labor force (millions, 2008)	3.1
Unemployment rate (% of labor force, 2008)	13.6
Urban population (% of pop., 2009)	52.2
Surface area (1,000 km², 2008)	88.4
GNI (US$ billions, 2009)	41.9
GNI per capita, Atlas method (US$, 2009)	5,990
GDP growth (avg. annual %, 2005-09)	4.1
Poverty headcount ratio at national poverty line (% of pop., 2005)	—
Age dependency ratio (2009)	47.3

Migration

EMIGRATION, 2010

- Stock of emigrants: **196.0 thousands**
- Stock of emigrants as percentage of population: **2.0%**
- Top destination countries: Austria, the United States, France, the former Yugoslav Republic of Macedonia, Denmark, Japan

SKILLED EMIGRATION, 2000

- Emigration of physicians: **1,466** or **6.1%** of physicians trained in the country (Source: Bhargava, Docquier, and Moullan 2010)

IMMIGRATION, 2010

- Stock of immigrants: **525.4 thousands**
- Stock of immigrants as percentage of population: **5.3%**
- Females as percentage of immigrants: **56.7%**
- Refugees as percentage of immigrants: **18.7%**

Remittances

US$ millions	2003	2004	2005	2006	2007	2008	2009	2010e
Inward remittance flows[a]	**2,661**	**4,129**	**4,650**	**4,703**	**5,377**	**5,538**	**5,406**	**558**
of which								
Workers' remittances	—	—	—	—	2,948	2,913	3,755	—
Compensation of employees	—	—	—	—	148	191	184	—
Migrants' transfers	—	—	—	—	2	2	3	—
Outward remittance flows	—	—	—	—	**114**	**138**	**91**	—
of which								
Workers' remittances	—	—	—	—	95	114	70	—
Compensation of employees	—	—	—	—	17	23	20	—
Migrants' transfers	—	—	—	—	2	1	1	—

a. For comparison: net FDI inflows US$3.0 bn, net ODA received US$1.0 bn, total international reserves US$11.5 bn, exports of goods and services US$14.8 bn in 2008.

Seychelles

Sub-Saharan Africa **UPPER MIDDLE INCOME**

Population (thousands, 2009)	88.0
Population growth (avg. annual %, 2000–09)	0.9
Population density (people per km², 2008)	187.7
Labor force (millions, 2008)	–
Unemployment rate (% of labor force, 2008)	–
Urban population (% of pop., 2009)	54.8
Surface area (1,000 km², 2008)	0.5
GNI (US$ billions, 2009)	0.7
GNI per capita, Atlas method (US$, 2009)	8,480
GDP growth (avg. annual %, 2005–09)	3,4
Poverty headcount ratio at national poverty line (% of pop., 2005)	–
Age dependency ratio (2009)	–

Migration

EMIGRATION, 2010

- Stock of emigrants: **12.3 thousands**
- Stock of emigrants as percentage of population: **14.6%**
- Top destination countries: the United Kingdom, Australia, Canada, Italy, the United States, Tanzania, France, Germany, Switzerland, Mauritius

SKILLED EMIGRATION, 2000

- Emigration rate of tertiary-educated population: **55.9%**
- Emigration of physicians:
  (a) **4** or **3.5%** of physicians trained in the country *(Source: Bhargava, Docquier, and Moullan 2010)*
  (b) **50** or **29.4%** of physicians born in the country *(Source: Clemens and Pettersson 2006)*
- Emigration of nurses: **175** or **29.3%** of nurses born in the country

IMMIGRATION, 2010

- Stock of immigrants: **10.8 thousands**
- Stock of immigrants as percentage of population: **12.8%**
- Females as percentage of immigrants: **42.5%**
- Refugees as percentage of immigrants: **0.0%**

Remittances

US$ millions	2003	2004	2005	2006	2007	2008	2009	2010e
Inward remittance flows[a]	5	7	12	13	11	12	12	13
of which								
Workers' remittances	5	7	12	13	11	–	–	–
Compensation of employees	0	0	0	0	0	–	–	–
Migrants' transfers	–	–	–	–	–	–	–	–
Outward remittance flows	7	8	10	17	21	24	24	–
of which								
Workers' remittances	2	3	4	10	10	11	9	–
Compensation of employees	5	5	6	8	11	13	14	–
Migrants' transfers	–	–	–	–	–	–	–	–

a. For comparison: net FDI inflows US$0.4 bn, total international reserves US$0.1 bn, exports of goods and services US$1.1 bn in 2008.

Sierra Leone

Sub-Saharan Africa	LOW INCOME
Population (millions, 2009)	5.7
Population growth (avg. annual %, 2000–09)	3.2
Population density (people per km², 2008)	77.6
Labor force (millions, 2008)	2.0
Unemployment rate (% of labor force, 2008)	–
Urban population (% of pop., 2009)	38.1
Surface area (1,000 km², 2008)	71.7
GNI (US$ billions, 2009)	1.9
GNI per capita, Atlas method (US$, 2009)	340
GDP growth (avg. annual %, 2005–09)	6.1
Poverty headcount ratio at national poverty line (% of pop., 2005)	49.9
Age dependency ratio (2009)	82.6

Migration

EMIGRATION, 2010

- Stock of emigrants: **267.0 thousands**
- Stock of emigrants as percentage of population: **4.6%**
- Top destination countries: Guinea, the United Kingdom, the United States, Liberia, Germany, the Netherlands, Nigeria, The Gambia, Canada, Australia

SKILLED EMIGRATION, 2000

- Emigration rate of tertiary-educated population: **52.5%**
- Emigration of physicians:
  - (a) **23** or **5.8%** of physicians trained in the country *(Source: Bhargava, Docquier, and Moullan 2010)*
  - (b) **249** or **42.4%** of physicians born in the country *(Source: Clemens and Pettersson 2006)*
- Emigration of nurses: **1,457** or **48.9%** of nurses born in the country

IMMIGRATION, 2010

- Stock of immigrants: **106.8 thousands**
- Stock of immigrants as percentage of population: **1.8%**
- Females as percentage of immigrants: **45.7%**
- Refugees as percentage of immigrants: **16.9%**
- Top source countries: Guinea, Liberia, The Gambia, Nigeria, Ghana, Lebanon, Mali, Senegal, India, Côte d'Ivoire

Remittances

US$ millions	2003	2004	2005	2006	2007	2008	2009	2010e
Inward remittance flows[a]	**26**	**25**	**2**	**16**	**42**	**28**	**47**	**48**
of which								
Workers' remittances	26	25	2	12	40	20	–	–
Compensation of employees	0	0	0	4	2	2	–	–
Migrants' transfers	–	–	–	–	–	–	–	–
Outward remittance flows	**3**	**3**	**2**	**4**	**4**	**3**	**3**	**–**
of which								
Workers' remittances	1	0	0	2	1	2	–	–
Compensation of employees	2	2	2	2	3	1	–	–
Migrants' transfers	–	–	–	–	–	–	–	–

a. **For comparison: net ODA received US$0.4 bn, total international reserves US$0.2 bn, exports of goods and services US$0.3 bn in 2008.**

Singapore

Population (millions, 2009)	5.0
Population growth (avg. annual %, 2000–09)	2.3
Population density (people per km², 2008)	7,023.8
Labor force (millions, 2008)	2.4
Unemployment rate (% of labor force, 2008)	3.2
Urban population (% of pop., 2009)	100.0
Surface area (1,000 km², 2008)	0.7
GNI (US$ billions, 2009)	179.2
GNI per capita, Atlas method (US$, 2009)	37,220
GDP growth (avg. annual %, 2005–09)	6.2
Poverty headcount ratio at national poverty line (% of pop., 2005)	—
Age dependency ratio (2009)	35.3

Migration

EMIGRATION, 2010

- Stock of emigrants: **297.2 thousands**
- Stock of emigrants as percentage of population: **6.1%**
- Top destination countries: Malaysia, Australia, the United Kingdom, the United States, Canada, New Zealand, India, Brunei Darussalam, the Netherlands, Japan

SKILLED EMIGRATION, 2000

- Emigration rate of tertiary-educated population: **15.2%**
- Emigration of physicians: **1,030** or **15.5%** of physicians trained in the country (*Source: Bhargava, Docquier, and Moullan 2010*)

IMMIGRATION, 2010

- Stock of immigrants: **1,966.9 thousands**
- Stock of immigrants as percentage of population: **40.7%**
- Females as percentage of immigrants: **56.0%**
- Refugees as percentage of immigrants: **0.0%**
- Top source countries: Malaysia; China; India; Indonesia; Pakistan; Bangladesh; the United States; Sri Lanka; Hong Kong SAR, China; Canada

Remittances

Remittance data are currently not available for this country.

Slovak Republic

Population (millions, 2009)	5.4
Population growth (avg. annual %, 2000–09)	0.0
Population density (people per km², 2008)	112.4
Labor force (millions, 2008)	2.7
Unemployment rate (% of labor force, 2008)	9.5
Urban population (% of pop., 2009)	56.7
Surface area (1,000 km², 2008)	49.0
GNI (US$ billions, 2009)	84.7
GNI per capita, Atlas method (US$, 2009)	16,130
GDP growth (avg. annual %, 2005–09)	5.1
Poverty headcount ratio at national poverty line (% of pop., 2005)	0.0
Age dependency ratio (2009)	37.9

Migration

EMIGRATION, 2010

- Stock of emigrants: **520.1 thousands**
- Stock of emigrants as percentage of population: **9.6%**
- Top destination countries: the Czech Republic, the United Kingdom, Germany, the United States, Austria, Canada, Ireland, Italy, Israel, Spain

SKILLED EMIGRATION, 2000

- Emigration rate of tertiary-educated population: **16.7%**
- Emigration of physicians: **1,895** or **9.8%** of physicians trained in the country *(Source: Bhargava, Docquier, and Moullan 2010)*

IMMIGRATION, 2010

- Stock of immigrants: **130.7 thousands**
- Stock of immigrants as percentage of population: **2.4%**
- Females as percentage of immigrants: **56.0%**
- Refugees as percentage of immigrants: **0.2%**
- Top source countries: the Czech Republic, Hungary, Ukraine, Poland, the Russian Federation, Germany, the former Yugoslav Republic of Macedonia, Romania, Austria, the United States

Remittances

US$ millions	2003	2004	2005	2006	2007	2008	2009	2010e
Inward remittance flows[a]	**425**	**529**	**946**	**1,088**	**1,483**	**1,973**	**1,671**	**1,651**
of which								
Workers' remittances	–	–	–	–	–	–	–	–
Compensation of employees	425	529	946	1,088	1,483	1,973	1,671	–
Migrants' transfers	–1	–	–	–	–	–	–	–
Outward remittance flows	**16**	**22**	**39**	**48**	**73**	**144**	**134**	**–**
of which								
Workers' remittances	–	–	–	–	–	–	–	–
Compensation of employees	16	22	39	48	73	144	134	–
Migrants' transfers	0	–	–	–	–	–	–	–

a. For comparison: net FDI inflows US$3.2 bn, total international reserves US$18.8 bn, exports of goods and services US$81.8 bn in 2008.

Migration and Remittances Factbook 2011

Slovenia

Population (millions, 2009)	2.0
Population growth (avg. annual %, 2000–09)	0.3
Population density (people per km², 2008)	101.3
Labor force (millions, 2008)	1.0
Unemployment rate (% of labor force, 2008)	4.4
Urban population (% of pop., 2009)	48.3
Surface area (1,000 km², 2008)	20.3
GNI (US$ billions, 2009)	47.3
GNI per capita, Atlas method (US$, 2009)	23,520
GDP growth (avg. annual %, 2005–09)	2.6
Poverty headcount ratio at national poverty line (% of pop., 2005)	0.0
Age dependency ratio (2009)	42.9

Migration

EMIGRATION, 2010

- Stock of emigrants: **132.0 thousands**
- Stock of emigrants as percentage of population: **6.5%**
- Top destination countries: Germany, Croatia, Austria, Canada, France, Australia, the United States, Switzerland, Italy, the United Kingdom

SKILLED EMIGRATION, 2000

- Emigration rate of tertiary-educated population: **11.5%**
- Emigration of physicians: **107** or **2.4%** of physicians trained in the country
  (Source: Bhargava, Docquier, and Moullan 2010)

IMMIGRATION, 2010

- Stock of immigrants: **163.9 thousands**
- Stock of immigrants as percentage of population: **8.1%**
- Females as percentage of immigrants: **46.6%**
- Refugees as percentage of immigrants: **0.2%**
- Top source countries: Bosnia and Herzegovina, Croatia, the former Yugoslav Republic of Macedonia, Ukraine, Germany, the Russian Federation, Italy, Austria, Romania, France

Remittances

US$ millions	2003	2004	2005	2006	2007	2008	2009	2010e
Inward remittance flows[a]	**238**	**266**	**264**	**282**	**323**	**347**	**279**	**297**
of which								
Workers' remittances	13	12	7	6	5	–	–	–
Compensation of employees	217	249	254	274	315	347	279	–
Migrants' transfers	8	5	3	3	2	–	–	–
Outward remittance flows	**66**	**80**	**94**	**129**	**250**	**380**	**191**	**–**
of which								
Workers' remittances	0	1	1	1	1	40	34	–
Compensation of employees	65	78	90	127	247	339	158	–
Migrants' transfers	1	2	4	1	2	–	–	–

a. For comparison: net FDI inflows US$1.9 bn, total international reserves US$1.0 bn in 2008.

Solomon Islands

Population (millions, 2009)	0.5
Population growth (avg. annual %, 2000–09)	2.6
Population density (people per km², 2008)	18.1
Labor force (millions, 2008)	0.2
Unemployment rate (% of labor force, 2008)	–
Urban population (% of pop., 2009)	18.3
Surface area (1,000 km², 2008)	28.9
GNI (US$ billions, 2009)	0.5
GNI per capita, Atlas method (US$, 2009)	910
GDP growth (avg. annual %, 2005–09)	5.6
Poverty headcount ratio at national poverty line (% of pop., 2005)	–
Age dependency ratio (2009)	72.9

Migration

EMIGRATION, 2010

- Stock of emigrants: **5.4 thousands**
- Stock of emigrants as percentage of population: **1.0%**
- Top destination countries: Australia, New Caledonia, New Zealand, the United Kingdom, the United States, Fiji, Canada, Japan, Samoa, Switzerland

SKILLED EMIGRATION, 2000

- Emigration rate of tertiary-educated population: **6.4%**

IMMIGRATION, 2010

- Stock of immigrants: **7.0 thousands**
- Stock of immigrants as percentage of population: **1.3%**
- Females as percentage of immigrants: **43.9%**
- Refugees as percentage of immigrants: **0.0%**
- Top source countries: Papua New Guinea, Kiribati, Australia, China, Fiji, the Philippines, New Zealand, the United States, Malaysia, New Caledonia

Remittances

US$ millions	2003	2004	2005	2006	2007	2008	2009	2010e
Inward remittance flows[a]	**4**	**9**	**7**	**20**	**20**	**20**	**2**	**3**
of which								
Workers' remittances	1	2	3	10	–	–	–	–
Compensation of employees	3	7	4	9	–	–	–	–
Migrants' transfers	–	–	–	2	–	–	–	–
Outward remittance flows	**2**	**2**	**2**	**3**	**3**	**3**	**4**	**–**
of which								
Workers' remittances	0	0	0	1	–	–	–	–
Compensation of employees	1	2	2	2	–	–	–	–
Migrants' transfers	0	0	0	0	–	–	–	–

a. For comparison: net FDI inflows US$0.1 bn, net ODA received US$0.2 bn, total international reserves US$0.1 bn in 2008.

Somalia

Sub-Saharan Africa **LOW INCOME**

Population (millions, 2009)	9.1
Population growth (avg. annual %, 2000–09)	2.4
Population density (people per km², 2008)	14.3
Labor force (millions, 2008)	3.4
Unemployment rate (% of labor force, 2008)	–
Urban population (% of pop., 2009)	37.0
Surface area (1,000 km², 2008)	637.7
GNI (US$ billions, 2009)	–
GNI per capita, Atlas method (US$, 2009)	–
GDP growth (avg. annual %, 2005–09)	–
Poverty headcount ratio at national poverty line (% of pop., 2005)	–
Age dependency ratio (2009)	90.9

Migration

EMIGRATION, 2010

- Stock of emigrants: **812.7 thousands**
- Stock of emigrants as percentage of population: **8.7%**
- Top destination countries: Ethiopia, the United Kingdom, the United States, the Republic of Yemen, Djibouti, Kenya, the Arab Republic of Egypt, Saudi Arabia, Canada, Sweden

SKILLED EMIGRATION, 2000

- Emigration rate of tertiary-educated population: **32.7%**
- Emigration of physicians:
  - (a) **98** or **21.9%** of physicians trained in the country *(Source: Bhargava, Docquier, and Moullan 2010)*
  - (b) **151** or **32.8%** of physicians born in the country *(Source: Clemens and Pettersson 2006)*
- Emigration of nurses: **164** or **9.9%** of nurses born in the country

IMMIGRATION, 2010

- Stock of immigrants: **22.8 thousands**
- Stock of immigrants as percentage of population: **0.2%**
- Females as percentage of immigrants: **45.9%**
- Refugees as percentage of immigrants: **3.4%**

Remittances

Remittance data are currently not available for this country.

South Africa

Population (millions, 2009)	49.3
Population growth (avg. annual %, 2000–09)	1.4
Population density (people per km², 2008)	40.1
Labor force (millions, 2008)	17.6
Unemployment rate (% of labor force, 2008)	22.9
Urban population (% of pop., 2009)	61.2
Surface area (1,000 km², 2008)	1,219.1
GNI (US$ billions, 2009)	279.7
GNI per capita, Atlas method (US$, 2009)	5,770
GDP growth (avg. annual %, 2005–09)	3.7
Poverty headcount ratio at national poverty line (% of pop., 2005)	20.6
Age dependency ratio (2009)	53.8

Migration

EMIGRATION, 2010

- Stock of emigrants: **878.1 thousands**
- Stock of emigrants as percentage of population: **1.7%**
- Top destination countries: the United Kingdom, Mozambique, Australia, the United States, Canada, New Zealand, Namibia, Zimbabwe, Portugal, the Netherlands

SKILLED EMIGRATION, 2000

- Emigration rate of tertiary-educated population: **7.5%**
- Emigration of physicians:
  - (a) **12,108** or **29.4%** of physicians trained in the country *(Source: Bhargava, Docquier, and Moullan 2010)*
  - (b) **7,363** or **21.1%** of physicians born in the country *(Source: Clemens and Pettersson 2006)*
- Emigration of nurses: **4,844** or **5.1%** of nurses born in the country

IMMIGRATION, 2010

- Stock of immigrants: **1,862.9 thousands**
- Stock of immigrants as percentage of population: **3.7%**
- Females as percentage of immigrants: **42.7%**
- Refugees as percentage of immigrants: **1.9%**
- Top source countries: Zimbabwe, Mozambique, Lesotho, Swaziland, Botswana, Malawi, Australia, New Zealand

Remittances

US$ million	2003	2004	2005	2006	2007	2008	2009	2010e
Inward remittance flows[a]	**434**	**523**	**658**	**734**	**834**	**823**	**902**	**1,008**
of which								
Workers' remittances	–	–	–	–	–	–	–	–
Compensation of employees	391	468	614	692	792	783	862	–
Migrants' transfers	44	55	44	43	41	39	40	–
Outward remittance flows	**706**	**937**	**1,055**	**1,068**	**1,186**	**1,133**	**1,158**	**–**
of which								
Workers' remittances	–	–	–	–	–	–	–	–
Compensation of employees	706	935	1,041	1,055	1,172	1,119	1,144	–
Migrants' transfers	–	2	14	12	13	14	14	–

a. For comparison: net FDI inflows US$9.6 bn, net ODA received US$1.1 bn, total international reserves US$34.1 bn, exports of goods and services US$97.8 bn in 2008.

Spain

Population (millions, 2009)	46.0
Population growth (avg. annual %, 2000–09)	1.4
Population density (people per km², 2008)	91.3
Labor force (millions, 2008)	22.0
Unemployment rate (% of labor force, 2008)	11.3
Urban population (% of pop., 2009)	77.3
Surface area (1,000 km², 2008)	505.4
GNI (US$ billions, 2009)	1,419.2
GNI per capita, Atlas method (US$, 2009)	31,870
GDP growth (avg. annual %, 2005–09)	1.7
Poverty headcount ratio at national poverty line (% of pop., 2005)	—
Age dependency ratio (2009)	46.8

Migration

EMIGRATION, 2010

- Stock of emigrants: **1,373.1 thousands**
- Stock of emigrants as percentage of population: **3.0%**
- Top destination countries: France, Germany, Argentina, the United States, República Bolivariana de Venezuela, the United Kingdom, Switzerland, Brazil, Belgium, Andorra

SKILLED EMIGRATION, 2000

- Emigration rate of tertiary-educated population: **4.3%**
- Emigration of physicians: **7,780** or **5.7%** of physicians trained in the country (Source: Bhargava, Docquier, and Moullan 2010)

IMMIGRATION, 2010

- Stock of immigrants: **6,900.5 thousands**
- Stock of immigrants as percentage of population: **15.2%**
- Females as percentage of immigrants: **44.3%**
- Refugees as percentage of immigrants: **0.1%**
- Top source countries: Romania, Morocco, Ecuador, the United Kingdom, Colombia, Argentina, Bolivia, Germany, France, Peru

Remittances

US$ millions	2003	2004	2005	2006	2007	2008	2009	2010e
Inward remittance flows[a]	**6,568**	**7,528**	**7,961**	**8,890**	**10,739**	**11,807**	**9,904**	**10,245**
of which								
Workers' remittances	4,718	5,196	5,343	6,071	7,286	7,878	6,733	—
Compensation of employees	1,013	1,157	1,318	1,513	2,012	2,242	1,883	—
Migrants' transfers	838	1,175	1,299	1,306	1,441	1,687	1,289	—
Outward remittance flows	**5,140**	**6,977**	**8,136**	**11,326**	**15,191**	**14,755**	**12,646**	—
of which								
Workers' remittances	3,939	5,211	6,123	8,888	11,605	11,630	9,985	—
Compensation of employees	925	1,341	1,545	1,867	2,388	2,321	2,059	—
Migrants' transfers	275	425	468	571	1,190	804	602	—

a. For comparison: net FDI inflows US$71.2 bn, total international reserves US$20.3 bn, exports of goods and services US$423.8 bn in 2008.

Sri Lanka

South Asia	LOWER MIDDLE INCOME
Population (millions, 2009)	20.3
Population growth (avg. annual %, 2000–09)	0.9
Population density (people per km², 2008)	311.9
Labor force (millions, 2008)	8.9
Unemployment rate (% of labor force, 2008)	5.2
Urban population (% of pop., 2009)	15.1
Surface area (1,000 km², 2008)	65.6
GNI (US$ billions, 2009)	41.5
GNI per capita, Atlas method (US$, 2009)	1,990
GDP growth (avg. annual %, 2005–09)	6.0
Poverty headcount ratio at national poverty line (% of pop., 2005)	10.3
Age dependency ratio (2009)	46.5

Migration

EMIGRATION, 2010

- Stock of emigrants: **1,847.5 thousands**
- Stock of emigrants as percentage of population: **9.1%**
- Top destination countries: Saudi Arabia, Kuwait, India, the United Arab Emirates, Canada, the United Kingdom, Jordan, Qatar, Italy, Australia

SKILLED EMIGRATION, 2000

- Emigration rate of tertiary-educated population: **29.7%**
- Emigration of physicians: **4,006** or **33.6%** of physicians trained in the country (Source: Bhargava, Docquier, and Moullan 2010)

IMMIGRATION, 2010

- Stock of immigrants: **339.9 thousands**
- Stock of immigrants as percentage of population: **1.7%**
- Females as percentage of immigrants: **49.8%**
- Refugees as percentage of immigrants: **0.1%**
- Top source countries: India, Australia, France, the United Kingdom, China, Sweden, Malaysia, Germany, the United States, Pakistan

Remittances

US$ millions	2003	2004	2005	2006	2007	2008	2009	2010e
Inward remittance flows[a]	**1,438**	**1,590**	**1,991**	**2,185**	**2,527**	**2,947**	**3,363**	**3,612**
of which								
Workers' remittances	1,414	1,564	1,968	2,161	2,502	2,918	3,330	—
Compensation of employees	10	10	7	6	6	7	7	—
Migrants' transfers	14	16	15	18	19	23	26	—
Outward remittance flows	**230**	**236**	**257**	**283**	**314**	**385**	**435**	—
of which								
Workers' remittances	209	214	233	258	288	353	403	—
Compensation of employees	15	16	16	17	17	20	17	—
Migrants' transfers	6	7	8	8	10	12	14	—

a. For comparison: net FDI inflows US$0.8 bn, net ODA received US$0.7 bn, total international reserves US$2.6 bn, exports of goods and services US$10.1 bn in 2008.

St. Kitts and Nevis

Population (thousands, 2009)	50.0
Population growth (avg. annual %, 2000–09)	1.6
Population density (people per km², 2008)	189.2
Labor force (millions, 2008)	–
Unemployment rate (% of labor force, 2008)	–
Urban population (% of pop., 2009)	32.4
Surface area (1,000 km², 2008)	0.3
GNI (US$ billions, 2009)	0.5
GNI per capita, Atlas method (US$, 2009)	10,100
GDP growth (avg. annual %, 2005–09)	1.9
Poverty headcount ratio at national poverty line (% of pop., 2005)	–
Age dependency ratio (2009)	–

Migration

EMIGRATION, 2010

- Stock of emigrants: **31.9 thousands**
- Stock of emigrants as percentage of population: **61.0%**
- Top destination countries: the United States, the United Kingdom, Virgin Islands (U.S.), Canada, Netherlands Antilles, Antigua and Barbuda, the Dominican Republic, the Netherlands, Australia, St. Lucia

SKILLED EMIGRATION, 2000

- Emigration rate of tertiary-educated population: **78.5%**
- Emigration of physicians: **28** or **34.9%** of physicians trained in the country *(Source: Bhargava, Docquier, and Moullan 2010)*

IMMIGRATION, 2010

- Stock of immigrants: **5.0 thousands**
- Stock of immigrants as percentage of population: **9.6%**
- Females as percentage of immigrants: **46.3%**
- Refugees as percentage of immigrants: **0.0%**
- Top source countries: the United States, Guyana, the Dominican Republic, Virgin Islands (U.S.), the United Kingdom, Antigua and Barbuda, Jamaica, Dominica, Trinidad and Tobago

Remittances

US$ millions	2003	2004	2005	2006	2007	2008	2009	2010e
Inward remittance flows[a]	**30**	**31**	**34**	**36**	**40**	**44**	**41**	**44**
of which								
Workers' remittances	–	–	–	–	–	–	–	–
Compensation of employees	–	–	–	–	–	–	–	–
Migrants' transfers	–	–	–	–	–	–	–	–
Outward remittance flows	**4**	**8**	**8**	**6**	**6**	**6**	**6**	**–**
of which								
Workers' remittances	4	5	5	4	5	5	5	–
Compensation of employees	4	3	3	1	1	1	1	–
Migrants' transfers	0	0	0	0	0	0	0	–

a. For comparison: net FDI inflows US$0.1 bn, total international reserves US$0.1 bn, exports of goods and services US$0.2 bn in 2008.

St. Lucia

Latin America and the Caribbean	UPPER MIDDLE INCOME
Population (millions, 2009)	0.2
Population growth (avg. annual %, 2000–09)	1.1
Population density (people per km², 2008)	278.6
Labor force (millions, 2008)	0.1
Unemployment rate (% of labor force, 2008)	–
Urban population (% of pop., 2009)	27.9
Surface area (1,000 km², 2008)	0.6
GNI (US$ billions, 2009)	0.9
GNI per capita, Atlas method (US$, 2009)	5,170
GDP growth (avg. annual %, 2005–09)	1.9
Poverty headcount ratio at national poverty line (% of pop., 2005)	17.8
Age dependency ratio (2009)	49.4

Migration

EMIGRATION, 2010

- Stock of emigrants: **40.4 thousands**
- Stock of emigrants as percentage of population: **23.2%**
- Top destination countries: the United States, the United Kingdom, Barbados, Canada, Virgin Islands (U.S.), Trinidad and Tobago, Antigua and Barbuda, Spain, the Dominican Republic, Guyana

SKILLED EMIGRATION, 2000

- Emigration rate of tertiary-educated population: **71.1%**
- Emigration of physicians: **293** or **78.4%** of physicians trained in the country *(Source: Bhargava, Docquier, and Moullan 2010)*

IMMIGRATION, 2010

- Stock of immigrants: **10.2 thousands**
- Stock of immigrants as percentage of population: **5.9%**
- Females as percentage of immigrants: **51.3%**
- Refugees as percentage of immigrants: **0.0%**
- Top source countries: the United Kingdom, Barbados, the United States, Canada, Virgin Islands (U.S.), Guyana, Trinidad and Tobago, Netherlands Antilles, Antigua and Barbuda, St. Vincent and the Grenadines

Remittances

US$ millions	2003	2004	2005	2006	2007	2008	2009	2010e
Inward remittance flows[a]	27	29	29	30	31	31	28	30
of which								
Workers' remittances	–	–	–	–	–	–	–	–
Compensation of employees	–	–	–	–	–	–	–	–
Migrants' transfers	–	–	–	–	–	–	–	–
Outward remittance flows	4	4	4	4	4	4	4	–
of which								
Workers' remittances	3	3	3	3	.3	3	3	–
Compensation of employees	–	–	–	–	–	–	–	–
Migrants' transfers	1	1	1	1	1	1	1	–

a. For comparison: net FDI inflows US$0.1 bn, total international reserves US$0.1 bn, exports of goods and services US$0.5 bn in 2008.

St. Vincent and the Grenadines

Latin America and the Caribbean	UPPER MIDDLE INCOME
Population (millions, 2009)	0.1
Population growth (avg. annual %, 2000–09)	0.1
Population density (people per km², 2008)	279.8
Labor force (millions, 2008)	0.1
Unemployment rate (% of labor force, 2008)	–
Urban population (% of pop., 2009)	47.4
Surface area (1,000 km², 2008)	0.4
GNI (US$ billions, 2009)	0.6
GNI per capita, Atlas method (US$, 2009)	5,110
GDP growth (avg. annual %, 2005–09)	3.7
Poverty headcount ratio at national poverty line (% of pop., 2005)	–
Age dependency ratio (2009)	50.8

Migration

EMIGRATION, 2010

- Stock of emigrants: **41.1 thousands**
- Stock of emigrants as percentage of population: **37.6%**
- Top destination countries: Canada, the United Kingdom, the United States, Trinidad and Tobago, Barbados, Antigua and Barbuda, Netherlands Antilles, St. Lucia, República Bolivariana de Venezuela, Greece

SKILLED EMIGRATION, 2000

- Emigration rate of tertiary-educated population: **84.5%**

IMMIGRATION, 2010

- Stock of immigrants: **8.6 thousands**
- Stock of immigrants as percentage of population: **7.9%**
- Females as percentage of immigrants: **51.9%**
- Refugees as percentage of immigrants: **0.0%**
- Top source countries: Trinidad and Tobago, Guyana, the United Kingdom, the United States, Grenada, Barbados, Canada, St. Lucia, Jamaica, Dominica

Remittances

US$ millions	2003	2004	2005	2006	2007	2008	2009	2101e
Inward remittance flowsª	24	26	26	30	33	31	30	33
of which								
Workers' remittances	–	–	–	–	–	–	–	–
Compensation of employees	–	–	–	–	–	–	–	–
Migrants' transfers	–	–	–	–	–	–	–	–
Outward remittance flows	5	5	6	7	7	7	7	–
of which								
Workers' remittances	4	4	4	5	5	5	5	–
Compensation of employees	–	–	1	1	1	0	0	–
Migrants' transfers	1	1	1	2	2	2	2	–

a. For comparison: net FDI inflows US$0.1 bn, total international reserves US$0.1 bn, exports of goods and services US$0.3 bn in 2008.

Sudan

LOWER MIDDLE INCOME

Population (millions, 2009)	42.3
Population growth (avg. annual %, 2000–09)	2.1
Population density (people per km², 2008)	17.4
Labor force (millions, 2008)	12.5
Unemployment rate (% of labor force, 2008)	–
Urban population (% of pop., 2009)	44.3
Surface area (1,000 km², 2008)	2,505.8
GNI (US$ billions, 2009)	49.7
GNI per capita, Atlas method (US$, 2009)	1,220
GDP growth (avg. annual %, 2005–09)	7.7
Poverty headcount ratio at national poverty line (% of pop., 2005)	–
Age dependency ratio (2009)	74.6

Migration

EMIGRATION, 2010

- Stock of emigrants: **967.5 thousands**
- Stock of emigrants as percentage of population: **2.2%**
- Top destination countries: Saudi Arabia, Uganda, the Republic of Yemen, Kenya, the United States, Chad, the United Arab Emirates, Australia, Jordan, Canada

SKILLED EMIGRATION, 2000

- Emigration rate of tertiary-educated population: **6.9%**
- Emigration of physicians:
  - (a) **1,083** or **17.9%** of physicians trained in the country *(Source: Bhargava, Docquier, and Moullan 2010)*
  - (b) **758** or **13.2%** of physicians born in the country *(Source: Clemens and Pettersson 2006)*
- Emigration of nurses: **166** or **0.6%** of nurses born in the country

IMMIGRATION, 2010

- Stock of immigrants: **753.4 thousands**
- Stock of immigrants as percentage of population: **1.7%**
- Females as percentage of immigrants: **48.2%**
- Refugees as percentage of immigrants: **27.8%**
- Top source countries: Eritrea, Ethiopia, Chad, Nigeria, the Arab Republic of Egypt, the Republic of Yemen, India, West Bank and Gaza, the Democratic Republic of Congo, Somalia

Remittances

US$ millions	2003	2004	2005	2006	2007	2008	2009	2010e
Inward remittance flows[a]	**1,224**	**1,403**	**1,016**	**1,179**	**1,769**	**3,100**	**2,993**	**3,178**
of which								
Workers' remittances	1,218	1,401	1,014	1,177	1,767	3,100	–	–
Compensation of employees	5	2	2	2	2	–	–	–
Migrants' transfers	–	–	–	–	–	–	–	–
Outward remittance flows	**1**	**2**	**2**	**2**	**2**	**2**	–	–
of which								
Workers' remittances	–	–	–	–	–	–	–	–
Compensation of employees	1	2	2	2	2	–	–.	–
Migrants' transfers	–	–	–	–	–	–	–	–

a. For comparison: net FDI inflows US$2.6 bn, net ODA received US$2.4 bn, total international reserves US$1.4 bn, exports of goods and services US$13.3 bn in 2008.

Suriname

Population (millions, 2009)	0.5
Population growth (avg. annual %, 2000–09)	1.2
Population density (people per km², 2008)	3.3
Labor force (millions, 2008)	0.2
Unemployment rate (% of labor force, 2008)	–
Urban population (% of pop., 2009)	75.3
Surface area (1,000 km², 2008)	163.3
GNI (US$ billions, 2008)	2.7
GNI per capita, Atlas method (US$, 2008)	4,990
GDP growth (avg. annual %, 2004–08)	5.8
Poverty headcount ratio at national poverty line (% of pop., 2005)	14.2
Age dependency ratio (2009)	55.0

Migration

EMIGRATION, 2010

- Stock of emigrants: **204.4 thousands**
- Stock of emigrants as percentage of population: **39.0%**
- Top destination countries: the Netherlands, the United States, Guyana, Netherlands Antilles, Canada, Belgium, the United Kingdom, France, Brazil, Spain

SKILLED EMIGRATION, 2000

- Emigration rate of tertiary-educated population: **47.9%**
- Emigration of physicians: **15** or **7.2%** of physicians trained in the country *(Source: Bhargava, Docquier, and Moullan 2010)*

IMMIGRATION, 2010

- Stock of immigrants: **39.5 thousands**
- Stock of immigrants as percentage of population: **7.5%**
- Females as percentage of immigrants: **45.4%**
- Refugees as percentage of immigrants: **0.0%**
- Top source countries: Guyana, the Netherlands, Brazil, China, France, Haiti, the United States

Remittances

US$ millions	2003	2004	2005	2006	2007	2008	2009	2010e
Inward remittance flows[a]	**24**	**9**	**4**	**2**	**140**	**2**	**2**	**2**
of which								
Workers' remittances	21	7	2	0	138	0	–	–
Compensation of employees	2	2	2	2	2	2	–	–
Migrants' transfers	0	–	–	–	–	–	–	–
Outward remittance flows	**28**	**14**	**10**	**4**	**65**	**8**	**8**	**–**
of which								
Workers' remittances	23	9	5	2	60	2	–	–
Compensation of employees	5	5	4	3	4	7	–	–
Migrants' transfers	0	–	–	–	–	–	–	–

a. For comparison: net FDI inflows US$−0.2 bn, net ODA received US$0.1 bn, total international reserves US$0.5 bn in 2008.

Swaziland

Population (millions, 2009)	1.2
Population growth (avg. annual %, 2000-09)	1.1
Population density (people per km², 2008)	67.9
Labor force (millions, 2008)	0.4
Unemployment rate (% of labor force, 2008)	28.2
Urban population (% of pop., 2009)	25.2
Surface area (1,000 km², 2008)	17.4
GNI (US$ billions, 2009)	2.7
GNI per capita, Atlas method (US$, 2009)	2,350
GDP growth (avg. annual %, 2005-09)	2.3
Poverty headcount ratio at national poverty line (% of pop., 2005)	62.4
Age dependency ratio (2009)	74.5

Migration

EMIGRATION, 2010

- Stock of emigrants: **160.3 thousands**
- Stock of emigrants as percentage of population: **13.3%**
- Top destination countries: South Africa, Mozambique, the United Kingdom, the United States, Australia, Canada, Portugal, Tanzania, Germany, Turkey

SKILLED EMIGRATION, 2000

- Emigration rate of tertiary-educated population: **0.5%**
- Emigration of physicians: **53** or **28.5%** of physicians born in the country *(Source: Clemens and Pettersson 2006)*
- Emigration of nurses: **96** or **2.8%** of nurses born in the country

IMMIGRATION, 2010

- Stock of immigrants: **40.4 thousands**
- Stock of immigrants as percentage of population: **3.4%**
- Females as percentage of immigrants: **47.7%**
- Refugees as percentage of immigrants: **1.9%**
- Top source countries: Mozambique, South Africa

Remittances

US$ millions	2003	2004	2005	2006	2007	2008	2009	2010e
Inward remittance flows[a]	**65**	**83**	**95**	**99**	**100**	**100**	**102**	**118**
of which								
Workers' remittances	–	1	1	1	1	–	–	–
Compensation of employees	65	82	94	94	94	–	–	–
Migrants' transfers	–	–	0	3	5	–	–	–
Outward remittance flows	**39**	**5**	**8**	**17**	**8**	**–**	**–**	**–**
of which								
Workers' remittances	37	0	3	1	1	–	–	–
Compensation of employees	2	4	5	15	7	–	–	–
Migrants' transfers	–	1	0	0	0	–	–	–

a. For comparison: net ODA received US$0.1 bn, total international reserves US$0.8 bn, exports of goods and services US$1.9 bn in 2008.

Sweden

Population (millions, 2009)	9.3
Population growth (avg. annual %, 2000–09)	0.5
Population density (people per km², 2008)	22.5
Labor force (millions, 2008)	4.9
Unemployment rate (% of labor force, 2008)	6.2
Urban population (% of pop., 2009)	84.6
Surface area (1,000 km², 2008)	450.3
GNI (US$ billions, 2009)	413.1
GNI per capita, Atlas method (US$, 2009)	48,930
GDP growth (avg. annual %, 2005–09)	1.0
Poverty headcount ratio at national poverty line (% of pop., 2005)	—
Age dependency ratio (2009)	52.8

Migration

EMIGRATION, 2010

- Stock of emigrants: **317.9 thousands**
- Stock of emigrants as percentage of population: **3.4%**
- Top destination countries: Norway, the United States, Finland, Germany, Spain, the United Kingdom, Denmark, Italy, Australia, France

SKILLED EMIGRATION, 2000

- Emigration rate of tertiary-educated population: **4.3%**
- Emigration of physicians: **1,552** or **5.4%** of physicians trained in the country *(Source: Bhargava, Docquier, and Moullan 2010)*

IMMIGRATION, 2010

- Stock of immigrants: **1,306.0 thousands**
- Stock of immigrants as percentage of population: **14.1%**
- Females as percentage of immigrants: **50.5%**
- Refugees as percentage of immigrants: **5.7%**
- Top source countries: Finland, Iraq, Poland, the Islamic Republic of Iran, Bosnia and Herzegovina, Denmark, Germany, Norway, Turkey, Chile

Remittances

US$ millions	2003	2004	2005	2006	2007	2008	2009	2010e
Inward remittance flows[a]	**578**	**420**	**612**	**595**	**738**	**780**	**703**	**796**
of which								
Workers' remittances	203	—	222	222	146	167	168	—
Compensation of employees	336	377	346	372	592	613	535	—
Migrants' transfers	39	43	43	—	—	—	—	—
Outward remittance flows	**600**	**646**	**814**	**553**	**741**	**742**	**757**	**—**
of which								
Workers' remittances	24	—	255	26	—	—	7	—
Compensation of employees	554	621	534	579	741	742	750	—
Migrants' transfers	22	25	25	—	—	—	—	—

a. For comparison: net FDI inflows US$41.9 bn, total international reserves US$29.7 bn, exports of goods and services US$259.7 bn in 2008.

Switzerland

Population (millions, 2009)	7.7
Population growth (avg. annual %, 2000–09)	0.8
Population density (people per km², 2008)	190.8
Labor force (millions, 2008)	4.3
Unemployment rate (% of labor force, 2008)	3.4
Urban population (% of pop., 2009)	73.5
Surface area (1,000 km², 2008)	41.3
GNI (US$ billions, 2008)	533.5
GNI per capita, Atlas method (US$, 2008)	65,330
GDP growth (avg. annual %, 2004–08)	2.6
Poverty headcount ratio at national poverty line (% of pop., 2005)	—
Age dependency ratio (2009)	47.7

Migration

EMIGRATION, 2010

- Stock of emigrants: **407.8 thousands**
- Stock of emigrants as percentage of population: **5.4%**
- Top destination countries: Spain, France, Germany, the United States, Canada, Portugal, the United Kingdom, Austria, Australia, Turkey

SKILLED EMIGRATION, 2000

- Emigration rate of tertiary-educated population: **8.9%**
- Emigration of physicians: **2,607** or **9.4%** of physicians trained in the country *(Source: Bhargava, Docquier, and Moullan 2010)*

IMMIGRATION, 2010

- Stock of immigrants: **1,762.8 thousands**
- Stock of immigrants as percentage of population: **23.2%**
- Females as percentage of immigrants: **49.7%**
- Refugees as percentage of immigrants: **2.7%**
- Top source countries: Italy, Germany, Portugal, France, Spain, Turkey, Austria, Bosnia and Herzegovina, the former Yugoslav Republic of Macedonia, the United Kingdom

Remittances

US$ millions	2003	2004	2005	2006	2007	2008	2009	2010e
Inward remittance flows[a]	**1,706**	**1,889**	**1,828**	**1,903**	**1,979**	**2,200**	**2,119**	**2,096**
of which								
Workers' remittances	173	194	202	209	292	330	314	—
Compensation of employees	1,533	1,695	1,626	1,695	1,687	1,871	2,211	—
Migrants' transfers	—	—	—	—	—	—	—	—
Outward remittance flows	**11,451**	**12,921**	**13,324**	**14,377**	**16,292**	**19,022**	**19,562**	—
of which								
Workers' remittances	2,741	3,139	3,341	3,718	4,160	4,693	5,047	—
Compensation of employees	8,711	9,782	9,983	10,658	12,133	14,329	14,514	—
Migrants' transfers	—	—	—	—	—	—	—	—

a. For comparison: net FDI inflows US$6.5 bn, total international reserves US$74.1 bn in 2008.

Syrian Arab Republic

Middle East and North Africa	LOWER MIDDLE INCOME
Population (millions, 2009)	21.1
Population growth (avg. annual %, 2000–09)	2.7
Population density (people per km², 2008)	115.5
Labor force (millions, 2008)	6.6
Unemployment rate (% of labor force, 2008)	–
Urban population (% of pop., 2009)	54.6
Surface area (1,000 km², 2008)	185.2
GNI (US$ billions, 2009)	50.9
GNI per capita, Atlas method (US$, 2009)	2,410
GDP growth (avg. annual %, 2005–09)	4.6
Poverty headcount ratio at national poverty line (% of pop., 2005)	–
Age dependency ratio (2009)	61.8

Migration

EMIGRATION, 2010

- Stock of emigrants: **944.6 thousands**
- Stock of emigrants as percentage of population: **4.2%**
- Top destination countries: Jordan, Kuwait, Saudi Arabia, the United States, Germany, West Bank and Gaza, Libya, Canada, Sweden, France

SKILLED EMIGRATION, 2000

- Emigration rate of tertiary-educated population: **6.1%**
- Emigration of physicians: **3,966** or **15.4%** of physicians trained in the country *(Source: Bhargava, Docquier, and Moullan 2010)*

IMMIGRATION, 2010

- Stock of immigrants: **2,205.8 thousands**
- Stock of immigrants as percentage of population: **9.8%**
- Females as percentage of immigrants: **49.0%**
- Refugees as percentage of immigrants: **71.7%**
- Top source country: West Bank and Gaza

Remittances

US$ millions	2003	2004	2005	2006	2007	2008	2009	2010e
Inward remittance flows[a]	**889**	**855**	**823**	**795**	**1,150**	**1,400**	**1,332**	**1,407**
of which								
Workers' remittances	743	690	763	770	1,000	1,250	–	–
Compensation of employees	146	165	60	25	30	75	–	–
Migrants' transfers	–	–	–	–	120	75	–	–
Outward remittance flows	**40**	**42**	**40**	**235**	**252**	**212**	**212**	**–**
of which								
Workers' remittances	–	1	2	160	170	–	–	–
Compensation of employees	40	41	38	75	80	–	–	–
Migrants' transfers	–	–	–	–	2	–	–	–

a. For comparison: net ODA received US$0.1 bn, exports of goods and services US$17.3 bn in 2008.

Tajikistan

Europe and Central Asia	LOW INCOME

Population (millions, 2009)	7.0
Population growth (avg. annual %, 2000–09)	1.3
Population density (people per km², 2008)	48.8
Labor force (millions, 2008)	2.6
Unemployment rate (% of labor force, 2008)	–
Urban population (% of pop., 2009)	26.5
Surface area (1,000 km², 2008)	142.6
GNI (US$ billions, 2009)	4.9
GNI per capita, Atlas method (US$, 2009)	700
GDP growth (avg. annual %, 2005–09)	6.6
Poverty headcount ratio at national poverty line (% of pop., 2005)	21.5
Age dependency ratio (2009)	68.3

Migration

EMIGRATION, 2010

- Stock of emigrants: **791.1 thousands**
- Stock of emigrants as percentage of population: **11.2%**
- Top destination countries: the Russian Federation, Uzbekistan, Ukraine, Israel, Kazakhstan, the Kyrgyz Republic, the United States, Latvia, Germany, Canada

SKILLED EMIGRATION, 2000

- Emigration rate of tertiary-educated population: **0.4%**
- Emigration of physicians: **41** or **0.3%** of physicians trained in the country
  (Source: Bhargava, Docquier, and Moullan 2010)

IMMIGRATION, 2010

- Stock of immigrants: **284.3 thousands**
- Stock of immigrants as percentage of population: **4.0%**
- Females as percentage of immigrants: **57.1%**
- Refugees as percentage of immigrants: **0.4%**
- Top source countries: the Russian Federation, Afghanistan, Uzbekistan, the Kyrgyz Republic

Remittances

US$ millions	2003	2004	2005	2006	2007	2008	2009	2010e
Inward remittance flows[a]	**146**	**252**	**467**	**1,019**	**1,691**	**2,544**	**1,748**	**2,065**
of which								
Workers' remittances	146	252	465	1,015	1,685	2,537	1,742	–
Compensation of employees	0	0	1	4	5	7	6	–
Migrants' transfers	–	–	–	–	–	–	–	–
Outward remittance flows	**64**	**119**	**145**	**395**	**184**	**199**	**124**	**–**
of which								
Workers' remittances	64	119	144	393	180	194	120	–
Compensation of employees	0	0	1	2	4	5	4	–
Migrants' transfers	–	–	–	–	–	–	–	–

a. For comparison: net FDI inflows US$0.4 bn, net ODA received US$0.3 bn, exports of goods and services US$0.9 bn in 2008.

Tanzania

Population (millions, 2009)	43.7
Population growth (avg. annual %, 2000–09)	2.7
Population density (people per km², 2008)	48.0
Labor force (millions, 2008)	20.2
Unemployment rate (% of labor force, 2008)	–
Urban population (% of pop., 2009)	26.0
Surface area (1,000 km², 2008)	947.3
GNI (US$ billions, 2009)	21.5
GNI per capita, Atlas method (US$, 2009)	500
GDP growth (avg. annual %, 2005–09)	6.8
Poverty headcount ratio at national poverty line (% of pop., 2005)	82.4
Age dependency ratio (2009)	91.6

Migration

EMIGRATION, 2010

- Stock of emigrants: **316.9 thousands**
- Stock of emigrants as percentage of population: **0.7%**
- Top destination countries: Kenya, Uganda, the United Kingdom, Canada, Mozambique, Malawi, the United States, Burundi, Rwanda, Australia

SKILLED EMIGRATION, 2000

- Emigration rate of tertiary-educated population: **12.4%**
- Emigration of physicians:
  - (a) **119** or **12.4%** of physicians trained in the country *(Source: Bhargava, Docquier, and Moullan 2010)*
  - (b) **1,356** or **51.8%** of physicians born in the country *(Source: Clemens and Pettersson 2006)*
- Emigration of nurses: **953** or **3.5%** of nurses born in the country

IMMIGRATION, 2010

- Stock of immigrants: **659.2 thousands**
- Stock of immigrants as percentage of population: **1.5%**
- Females as percentage of immigrants: **50.4%**
- Refugees as percentage of immigrants: **69.9%**
- Top source countries: Burundi, Mozambique, Kenya, the Republic of Congo, Rwanda, Zambia, Uganda, Malawi, India, the United States

Remittances

US$ millions	2003	2004	2005	2006	2007	2008	2009	2010e
Inward remittance flows[a]	9	14	19	15	14	19	16	17
of which								
Workers' remittances	2	6	9	9	8	9	–	–
Compensation of employees	7	8	10	6	6	9	–	–
Migrants' transfers	–	–	–	–	–	–	–	–
Outward remittance flows	27	34	33	30	46	54	54	–
of which								
Workers' remittances	5	6	8	6	–	–	–	–
Compensation of employees	22	28	25	23	46	54	–	–
Migrants' transfers	–	–	–	–	–	–	–	–

a. For comparison: net FDI inflows US$0.7 bn, net ODA received US$2.3 bn, total international reserves US$2.9 bn in 2008.

Thailand

| **LOWER MIDDLE INCOME**

Population (millions, 2009)	67.8
Population growth (avg. annual %, 2000-09)	0.9
Population density (people per km², 2008)	131.9
Labor force (millions, 2008)	37.9
Unemployment rate (% of labor force, 2008)	1.4
Urban population (% of pop., 2009)	33.7
Surface area (1,000 km², 2008)	513.1
GNI (US$ billions, 2009)	252.0
GNI per capita, Atlas method (US$, 2009)	3,760
GDP growth (avg. annual %, 2005-09)	3.0
Poverty headcount ratio at national poverty line (% of pop., 2005)	0.4
Age dependency ratio (2009)	41.4

Migration

EMIGRATION, 2010

- Stock of emigrants: **810.8 thousands**
- Stock of emigrants as percentage of population: **1.2%**
- Top destination countries: the United States, Cambodia, Malaysia, Germany, Japan, Australia, the United Kingdom, Sweden, Saudi Arabia, the Republic of Korea

SKILLED EMIGRATION, 2000

- Emigration rate of tertiary-educated population: **2.4%**
- Emigration of physicians: **2,390** or **11.6%** of physicians trained in the country (Source: Bhargava, Docquier, and Moullan 2010)

IMMIGRATION, 2010

- Stock of immigrants: **1,157.3 thousands**
- Stock of immigrants as percentage of population: **1.7%**
- Females as percentage of immigrants: **48.4%**
- Refugees as percentage of immigrants: **11.2%**
- Top source countries: China, Myanmar, the Lao People's Democratic Republic, Cambodia, Nepal, Sri Lanka, Japan, India, Vietnam, the United States

Remittances

US$ millions	2003	2004	2005	2006	2007	2008	2009	2010e
Inward remittance flows[a]	**1,607**	**1,622**	**1,187**	**1,333**	**1,635**	**1,898**	**1,637**	**1,788**
of which								
Workers' remittances	–	–	–	–	–	–	–	–
Compensation of employees	1,607	1,622	1,187	1,333	1,635	1,898	1,637	–
Migrants' transfers	–	–	–	–	–	–	–	–
Outward remittance flows	–	–	–	–	–	–	–	–
of which								
Workers' remittances	–	–	–	–	–	–	–	–
Compensation of employees	–	–	–	–	–	–	–	–
Migrants' transfers	–	–	–	–	–	–	–	–

a. For comparison: net FDI inflows US$9.8 bn, net ODA received US$-0.6 bn, total international reserves US$111.0 bn, exports of goods and services US$208.8 bn in 2008.

Timor-Leste

Population (millions, 2009)	1.1
Population growth (avg. annual %, 2000–09)	3.3
Population density (people per km², 2008)	73.9
Labor force (millions, 2008)	0.4
Unemployment rate (% of labor force, 2008)	–
Urban population (% of pop., 2009)	27.7
Surface area (1,000 km², 2008)	14.9
GNI (US$ billions, 2008)	2.9
GNI per capita, Atlas method (US$, 2008)	2,460
GDP growth (avg. annual %, 2004–08)	5.1
Poverty headcount ratio at national poverty line (% of pop., 2005)	43.6
Age dependency ratio (2009)	92.1

Migration

EMIGRATION, 2010

- Stock of emigrants: **16.8 thousands**
- Stock of emigrants as percentage of population: **1.4%**
- Top destination countries: Australia, Portugal, the Philippines, Canada, New Zealand, the Netherlands, Japan, República Bolivariana de Venezuela, the Czech Republic, Norway

SKILLED EMIGRATION, 2000

- Emigration rate of tertiary-educated population: **15.5%**
- Emigration of physicians: **14** or **26.4%** of physicians trained in the country *(Source: Bhargava, Docquier, and Moullan 2010)*

IMMIGRATION, 2010

- Stock of immigrants: **13.8 thousands**
- Stock of immigrants as percentage of population: **1.2%**
- Females as percentage of immigrants: **52.6%**
- Refugees as percentage of immigrants: **0.0%**
- Top source countries: Indonesia, the Philippines, Australia

Remittances

Remittance data are currently not available for this country.

Togo

Population (millions, 2009)	6.6
Population growth (avg. annual %, 2000–09)	2.6
Population density (people per km², 2008)	118.7
Labor force (millions, 2008)	2.6
Unemployment rate (% of labor force, 2008)	–
Urban population (% of pop., 2009)	42.7
Surface area (1,000 km², 2008)	56.8
GNI (US$ billions, 2009)	2.8
GNI per capita, Atlas method (US$, 2009)	440
GDP growth (avg. annual %, 2005–09)	2.3
Poverty headcount ratio at national poverty line (% of pop., 2005)	38.7
Age dependency ratio (2009)	76.7

Migration

EMIGRATION, 2010

- Stock of emigrants: **368.7 thousands**
- Stock of emigrants as percentage of population: **5.4%**
- Top destination countries: Nigeria, Côte d'Ivoire, Benin, Burkina Faso, France, Germany, Niger, Gabon, Italy, the United States

SKILLED EMIGRATION, 2000

- Emigration rate of tertiary-educated population: **18.7%**
- Emigration of physicians:
  - (a) **31** or **10.1%** of physicians trained in the country *(Source: Bhargava, Docquier, and Moullan 2010)*
  - (b) **180** or **40.4%** of physicians born in the country *(Source: Clemens and Pettersson 2006)*
- Emigration of nurses: **186** or **19.2%** of nurses born in the country

IMMIGRATION, 2010

- Stock of immigrants: **185.4 thousands**
- Stock of immigrants as percentage of population: **2.7%**
- Females as percentage of immigrants: **50.2%**
- Refugees as percentage of immigrants: **2.1%**
- Top source countries: Benin, Ghana, Nigeria, Niger, France, Mali, Lebanon, Germany, the United States

Remittances

US$ millions	2003	2004	2005	2006	2007	2008	2009	2010e
Inward remittance flows[a]	**149**	**179**	**193**	**232**	**284**	**337**	**307**	**302**
of which								
Workers' remittances	128	153	164	203	252	301	–	–
Compensation of employees	20	26	28	29	32	36	–	–
Migrants' transfers	–	–	–	–	–	–	–	–
Outward remittance flows	**28**	**34**	**35**	**39**	**47**	**58**	**58**	**–**
of which								
Workers' remittances	27	33	35	38	46	56	–	–
Compensation of employees	1	1	1	1	1	2	–	–
Migrants' transfers	–	–	–	–	–	–	–	–

a. For comparison: net FDI inflows US$0.1 bn, net ODA received US$0.3 bn, total international reserves US$0.6 bn in 2008.

Tonga

LOWER MIDDLE INCOME

Population (millions, 2009)	0.1
Population growth (avg. annual %, 2000–09)	0.6
Population density (people per km², 2008)	143.8
Labor force (millions, 2008)	0.0
Unemployment rate (% of labor force, 2008)	–
Urban population (% of pop., 2009)	25.0
Surface area (1,000 km², 2008)	0.8
GNI (US$ billions, 2009)	0.3
GNI per capita, Atlas method (US$, 2009)	3,260
GDP growth (avg. annual %, 2005–09)	0.0
Poverty headcount ratio at national poverty line (% of pop., 2005)	–
Age dependency ratio (2009)	76.3

Migration

EMIGRATION, 2010

- Stock of emigrants: **47.4 thousands**
- Stock of emigrants as percentage of population: **45.4%**
- Top destination countries: New Zealand, the United States, Australia, American Samoa, Chile, Fiji, France, Kiribati, the United Kingdom, Samoa

SKILLED EMIGRATION, 2000

- Emigration rate of tertiary-educated population: **75.2%**

IMMIGRATION, 2010

- Stock of immigrants: **0.8 thousand**
- Stock of immigrants as percentage of population: **0.8%**
- Females as percentage of immigrants: **48.7%**
- Refugees as percentage of immigrants: **0.0%**
- Top source countries: Fiji, Samoa, India, China, Japan

Remittances

US$ millions	2003	2004	2005	2006	2007	2008	2009	2010e
Inward remittance flows[a]	60	69	69	79	101	94	87	99
of which								
Workers' remittances	–	–	–	–	–	–	–	–
Compensation of employees	–	–	–	–	–	–	–	–
Migrants' transfers	–	–	–	–	–	–	–	–
Outward remittance flows	9	11	12	12	12	14	14	–
of which								
Workers' remittances	8	10	12	12	12	12	–	–
Compensation of employees	1	0	–	–	0	0	–	–
Migrants' transfers	0	0	0	0	0	2	–	–

a. For comparison: total international reserves US$0.1 bn in 2008.

Trinidad and Tobago

Population (millions, 2009)	1.3
Population growth (avg. annual %, 2000–09)	0.4
Population density (people per km², 2008)	260.8
Labor force (millions, 2008)	0.7
Unemployment rate (% of labor force, 2008)	–
Urban population (% of pop., 2009)	13.6
Surface area (1,000 km², 2008)	5.1
GNI (US$ billions, 2009)	20.6
GNI per capita, Atlas method (US$, 2009)	16,490
GDP growth (avg. annual %, 2005–09)	4.7
Poverty headcount ratio at national poverty line (% of pop., 2005)	0.5
Age dependency ratio (2009)	37.8

Migration

EMIGRATION, 2010

- Stock of emigrants: **358.6 thousands**
- Stock of emigrants as percentage of population: **26.7%**
- Top destination countries: the United States, Canada, the United Kingdom, St. Vincent and the Grenadines, República Bolivariana de Venezuela, Virgin Islands (U.S.), Barbados, Australia, Germany, Guyana

SKILLED EMIGRATION, 2000

- Emigration rate of tertiary-educated population: **79.3%**
- Emigration of physicians: 50 or 4.7% of physicians trained in the country *(Source: Bhargava, Docquier, and Moullan 2010)*

IMMIGRATION, 2010

- Stock of immigrants: **34.3 thousands**
- Stock of immigrants as percentage of population: **2.6%**
- Females as percentage of immigrants: **54.0%**
- Refugees as percentage of immigrants: 0.0%
- Top source countries: Grenada, St. Vincent and the Grenadines, Guyana, the United States, the United Kingdom, Barbados, República Bolivariana de Venezuela, St. Lucia, India

Remittances

US$ millions	2003	2004	2005	2006	2007	2008	2009	2010e
Inward remittance flows[a]	87	87	92	91	109	109	99	109
of which								
Workers' remittances	87	87	92	91	109	–	–	–
Compensation of employees	–	–	–	–	–	–	–	–
Migrants' transfers	–	–	–	–	–	–	–	–
Outward remittance flows	–	–	–	–	–	–	–	–
of which								
Workers' remittances	–	–	–	–	–	–	–	–
Compensation of employees	–	–	–	–	–	–	–	–
Migrants' transfers	–	–	–	–	–	–	–	–

a. For comparison: total international reserves US$9.5 bn, exports of goods and services US$17.7 bn in 2008.

Tunisia

Population (millions, 2009)	10.4
Population growth (avg. annual %, 2000–09)	1.0
Population density (people per km², 2008)	66.5
Labor force (millions, 2008)	3.7
Unemployment rate (% of labor force, 2008)	–
Urban population (% of pop., 2009)	66.9
Surface area (1,000 km², 2008)	163.6
GNI (US$ billions, 2009)	37.3
GNI per capita, Atlas method (US$, 2009)	3,720
GDP growth (avg. annual %, 2005–09)	4.7
Poverty headcount ratio at national poverty line (% of pop., 2005)	1.0
Age dependency ratio (2009)	42.8

Migration

EMIGRATION, 2010

- Stock of emigrants: **651.6 thousands**
- Stock of emigrants as percentage of population: **6.3%**
- Top destination countries: France, Italy, Libya, Germany, Israel, Saudi Arabia, Belgium, Canada, the United States, Switzerland

SKILLED EMIGRATION, 2000

- Emigration rate of tertiary-educated population: **12.5%**
- Emigration of physicians:
  - (a) **222** or **3.2%** of physicians trained in the country (Source: Bhargava, Docquier, and Moullan 2010)
  - (b) **3,192** or **33.1%** of physicians born in the country (Source: Clemens and Pettersson 2006)
- Emigration of nurses: **1,478** or **5.3%** of nurses born in the country

IMMIGRATION, 2010

- Stock of immigrants: **33.6 thousands**
- Stock of immigrants as percentage of population: **0.3%**
- Females as percentage of immigrants: **49.3%**
- Refugees as percentage of immigrants: **0.3%**
- Top source countries: Algeria, Morocco, France, Italy, Libya

Remittances

US$ millions	2003	2004	2005	2006	2007	2008	2009	2010e
Inward remittance flows[a]	**1,250**	**1,431**	**1,393**	**1,510**	**1,716**	**1,977**	**1,966**	**1,960**
of which								
Workers' remittances	1,107	1,268	1,195	1,304	1,446	1,725	1,727	–
Compensation of employees	143	163	198	206	269	252	238	–
Migrants' transfers	–	–	–	–	–	–	–	–
Outward remittance flows	**17**	**13**	**16**	**16**	**15**	**16**	**13**	–
of which								
Workers' remittances	11	7	7	7	7	6	–	–
Compensation of employees	7	6	8	10	8	10	–	–
Migrants' transfers	–	–	–	–	–	–	–	–

a. For comparison: net FDI inflows US$2.6 bn, net ODA received US$0.5 bn, total international reserves US$9.0 bn, exports of goods and services US$24.6 bn in 2008.

Turkey

Population (millions, 2009)	74.8
Population growth (avg. annual %, 2000–09)	1.3
Population density (people per km², 2008)	96.0
Labor force (millions, 2008)	25.1
Unemployment rate (% of labor force, 2008)	9.4
Urban population (% of pop., 2009)	69.1
Surface area (1,000 km², 2008)	783.6
GNI (US$ billions, 2009)	609.4
GNI per capita, Atlas method (US$, 2009)	8,730
GDP growth (avg. annual %, 2005–09)	3.2
Poverty headcount ratio at national poverty line (% of pop., 2005)	2.7
Age dependency ratio (2009)	48.6

Migration

EMIGRATION, 2010

- Stock of emigrants: **4,261.6 thousands**
- Stock of emigrants as percentage of population: **5.6%**
- Top destination countries: Germany, France, the Netherlands, Austria, the United States, Bulgaria, Belgium, Saudi Arabia, the United Kingdom, Switzerland

SKILLED EMIGRATION, 2000

- Emigration rate of tertiary-educated population: **5.8%**
- Emigration of physicians: **2,742** or **3.2%** of physicians trained in the country (Source: Bhargava, Docquier, and Moullan 2010)

IMMIGRATION, 2010

- Stock of immigrants: **1,410.9 thousands**
- Stock of immigrants as percentage of population: **1.9%**
- Females as percentage of immigrants: **52.0%**
- Refugees as percentage of immigrants: **0.3%**
- Top source countries: Bulgaria, Germany, Greece, the former Yugoslav Republic of Macedonia, the Netherlands, Romania, the Russian Federation, the United Kingdom, Azerbaijan, France

Remittances

US$ millions	2003	2004	2005	2006	2007	2008	2009	2010e
Inward remittance flows[a]	**729**	**804**	**887**	**1,146**	**1,248**	**1,476**	**970**	**950**
of which								
Workers' remittances	729	804	887	1,111	1,209	1,431	934	–
Compensation of employees	–	–	36	35	39	45	36	–
Migrants' transfers	–	–	–	–	–	–	–	–
Outward remittance flows	**–**	**–**	**96**	**107**	**106**	**111**	**141**	**–**
of which								
Workers' remittances	–	–	–	–	–	–	–	–
Compensation of employees	–	–	96	107	106	111	141	–
Migrants' transfers	–	–	–	–	–	–	–	–

a. For comparison: net FDI inflows US$18.3 bn, net ODA received US$2.0 bn, total international reserves US$73.7 bn, exports of goods and services US$175.8 bn in 2008.

Turkmenistan

LOWER MIDDLE INCOME

Population (millions, 2009)	5.1
Population growth (avg. annual %, 2000–09)	1.4
Population density (people per km², 2008)	10.7
Labor force (millions, 2008)	2.2
Unemployment rate (% of labor force, 2008)	–
Urban population (% of pop., 2009)	49.1
Surface area (1,000 km², 2008)	488.1
GNI (US$ billions, 2009)	19.2
GNI per capita, Atlas method (US$, 2009)	3,420
GDP growth (avg. annual %, 2005–09)	10.9
Poverty headcount ratio at national poverty line (% of pop., 2005)	11.7
Age dependency ratio (2009)	50.9

Migration

EMIGRATION, 2010

- Stock of emigrants: **261.0 thousands**
- Stock of emigrants as percentage of population: **5.0%**
- Top destination countries: the Russian Federation, Ukraine, Israel, Latvia, Turkey, Germany, Armenia, the United States, Kazakhstan, the Islamic Republic of Iran

SKILLED EMIGRATION, 2000

- Emigration rate of tertiary-educated population: **0.2%**

IMMIGRATION, 2010

- Stock of immigrants: **207.7 thousands**
- Stock of immigrants as percentage of population: **4.0%**
- Females as percentage of immigrants: **57.1%**
- Refugees as percentage of immigrants: **0.2%**
- Top source countries: Uzbekistan, the Russian Federation, Kazakhstan, Azerbaijan, Armenia, Ukraine

Remittances

Remittance data are currently not available for this country.

Uganda

Sub-Saharan Africa   **LOW INCOME**

Population (millions, 2009)	32.7
Population growth (avg. annual %, 2000–09)	3.2
Population density (people per km², 2008)	160.6
Labor force (millions, 2008)	13.4
Unemployment rate (% of labor force, 2008)	–
Urban population (% of pop., 2009)	13.0
Surface area (1,000 km², 2008)	241.0
GNI (US$ billions, 2009)	15.4
GNI per capita, Atlas method (US$, 2009)	460
GDP growth (avg. annual %, 2005–09)	8.3
Poverty headcount ratio at national poverty line (% of pop., 2005)	51.5
Age dependency ratio (2009)	105.8

Migration

EMIGRATION, 2010

- Stock of emigrants: **757.5 thousands**
- Stock of emigrants as percentage of population: **2.2%**
- Top destination countries: Kenya, the United Kingdom, Tanzania, the United States, Rwanda, Canada, Sweden, Australia, Germany, Denmark

SKILLED EMIGRATION, 2000

- Emigration rate of tertiary-educated population: **35.6%**
- Emigration of physicians:
  - (a) **532** or **36.4%** of physicians trained in the country *(Source: Bhargava, Docquier, and Moullan 2010)*
  - (b) **1,837** or **43.1%** of physicians born in the country *(Source: Clemens and Pettersson 2006)*
- Emigration of nurses: **1,122** or **10.2%** of nurses born in the country

IMMIGRATION, 2010

- Stock of immigrants: **646.5 thousands**
- Stock of immigrants as percentage of population: **1.9%**
- Females as percentage of immigrants: **49.9%**
- Refugees as percentage of immigrants: **38.7%**
- Top source countries: Sudan, Rwanda, Burundi, the Democratic Republic of Congo, Tanzania, Kenya, the United Kingdom, the United States, Canada, Australia

Remittances

US$ millions	2003	2004	2005	2006	2007	2008	2009	2010e
Inward remittance flows[a]	**299**	**311**	**322**	**411**	**452**	**724**	**694**	**773**
of which								
Workers' remittances	299	311	322	411	452	724	–	–
Compensation of employees	–	–	–	–	–	–	–	–
Migrants' transfers	–	–	–	–	–	–	–	–
Outward remittance flows	**182**	**194**	**197**	**206**	**236**	**381**	**463**	**–**
of which								
Workers' remittances	134	140	145	185	203	–	–	–
Compensation of employees	47	54	52	21	33	–	–	–
Migrants' transfers	–	–	–	–	–	–	–	–

a. For comparison: net FDI inflows US$0.8b n, net ODA received US$1.7 bn, total international reserves US$2.3 bn, exports of goods and services US$2.2 bn in 2008.

Ukraine

Population (millions, 2009)	46.0
Population growth (avg. annual %, 2000–09)	-0.8
Population density (people per km², 2008)	79.8
Labor force (millions, 2008)	23.3
Unemployment rate (% of labor force, 2008)	6.4
Urban population (% of pop., 2009)	68.0
Surface area (1,000 km², 2008)	603.6
GNI (US$ billions, 2009)	111.1
GNI per capita, Atlas method (US$, 2009)	2,800
GDP growth (avg. annual %, 2005–09)	1.0
Poverty headcount ratio at national poverty line (% of pop., 2005)	0.1
Age dependency ratio (2009)	42.0

Migration

EMIGRATION, 2010

- Stock of emigrants: **6,563.1 thousands**
- Stock of emigrants as percentage of population: **14.4%**
- Top destination countries: the Russian Federation, Poland, the United States, Kazakhstan, Israel, Germany, Moldova, Italy, Belarus, Spain

SKILLED EMIGRATION, 2000

- Emigration rate of tertiary-educated population: **3.5%**
- Emigration of physicians: **1,350** or **0.9%** of physicians trained in the country *(Source: Bhargava, Docquier, and Moullan 2010)*

IMMIGRATION, 2010

- Stock of immigrants: **5,257.5 thousands**
- Stock of immigrants as percentage of population: **11.6%**
- Females as percentage of immigrants: **57.2%**
- Refugees as percentage of immigrants: **0.1%**
- Top source countries: the Russian Federation, Belarus, Kazakhstan, Uzbekistan, Moldova, Azerbaijan, Georgia, Armenia, Tajikistan, the Kyrgyz Republic

Remittances

US$ millions	2003	2004	2005	2006	2007	2008	2009	2010e
Inward remittance flows[a]	**330**	**411**	**595**	**829**	**4,503**	**5,769**	**5,073**	**5,289**
of which								
Workers' remittances	185	193	236	289	2,292	2,140	1,643	–
Compensation of employees	145	218	359	540	2,210	3,629	3,426	–
Migrants' transfers	2	–	–	–	–	1	4	–
Outward remittance flows	**29**	**20**	**34**	**30**	**42**	**54**	**25**	**–**
of which								
Workers' remittances	–	–	2	2	7	13	4	–
Compensation of employees	4	6	10	9	11	18	15	–
Migrants' transfers	25	14	22	19	24	23	6	–

a. For comparison: net FDI inflows US$10.9 bn, net ODA received US$0.6 bn, total international reserves US$31.5 bn, exports of goods and services US$75.3 bn in 2008.

United Arab Emirates

Population (millions, 2009)	4.6
Population growth (avg. annual %, 2000–09)	4.1
Population density (people per km², 2008)	53.6
Labor force (millions, 2008)	2.7
Unemployment rate (% of labor force, 2008)	–
Urban population (% of pop., 2009)	77.9
Surface area (1,000 km², 2008)	83.6
GNI (US$ billions, 2009)	–
GNI per capita, Atlas method (US$, 2009)	–
GDP growth (avg. annual %, 2005–09)	–
Poverty headcount ratio at national poverty line (% of pop., 2005)	–
Age dependency ratio (2009)	25.2

Migration

EMIGRATION, 2010

- Stock of emigrants: **55.9 thousands**
- Stock of emigrants as percentage of population: **1.2%**
- Top destination countries: India, Canada, the United States, the United Kingdom, Australia, Jordan, Germany, New Zealand, Bahrain, France

SKILLED EMIGRATION, 2000

- Emigration rate of tertiary-educated population: **1.0%**
- Emigration of physicians: **258** or **3.8%** of physicians trained in the country *(Source: Bhargava, Docquier, and Moullan 2010)*

IMMIGRATION, 2010

- Stock of immigrants: **3,293.3 thousands**
- Stock of immigrants as percentage of population: **70.0%**
- Females as percentage of immigrants: **27.4%**
- Refugees as percentage of immigrants: **0.0%**
- Top source countries: India, Pakistan, Sri Lanka, the Arab Republic of Egypt, the Philippines, Bangladesh, the Republic of Yemen, the Islamic Republic of Iran, Sudan

Remittances

Remittance data are currently not available for this country.

United Kingdom

Population (millions, 2009)	61.8
Population growth (avg. annual %, 2000–09)	0.5
Population density (people per km², 2008)	253.8
Labor force (millions, 2008)	31.4
Unemployment rate (% of labor force, 2008)	5.6
Urban population (% of pop., 2009)	90.0
Surface area (1,000 km², 2008)	243.6
GNI (US$ billions, 2009)	2,226.2
GNI per capita, Atlas method (US$, 2009)	41,520
GDP growth (avg. annual %, 2005–09)	0.6
Poverty headcount ratio at national poverty line (% of pop., 2005)	–
Age dependency ratio (2009)	51.2

Migration

EMIGRATION, 2010

- Stock of emigrants: **4,668.3 thousands**
- Stock of emigrants as percentage of population: **7.5%**
- Top destination countries: Australia, the United States, Canada, Spain, Ireland, New Zealand, France, Germany, the Netherlands, the Philippines

SKILLED EMIGRATION, 2000

- Emigration rate of tertiary-educated population: **16.7%**
- Emigration of physicians: **16,710** or **12.4%** of physicians trained in the country (Source: Bhargava, Docquier, and Moullan 2010)

IMMIGRATION, 2010

- Stock of immigrants: **6,955.7 thousands**
- Stock of immigrants as percentage of population: **11.2%**
- Females as percentage of immigrants: **49.7%**
- Refugees as percentage of immigrants: **4.3%**
- Top source countries: India, Poland, Pakistan, Ireland, Germany, South Africa, Bangladesh, the United States, Jamaica, Kenya

Remittances

US$ millions	2003	2004	2005	2006	2007	2008	2009	2010e
Inward remittance flows[a]	**5,029**	**5,915**	**6,302**	**6,754**	**7,877**	**7,861**	**6,847**	**7,433**
of which								
Workers' remittances	–	–	–	–	–	–	–	–
Compensation of employees	1,825	1,706	1,772	1,730	1,965	1,939	1,425	–
Migrants' transfers	3,204	4,208	4,530	5,023	5,913	5,922	5,422	–
Outward remittance flows	**2,624**	**3,552**	**3,877**	**4,732**	**4,834**	**4,637**	**3,670**	**–**
of which								
Workers' remittances	–	–	–	–	–	–	–	–
Compensation of employees	1,728	2,610	2,876	3,501	3,440	3,255	2,511	–
Migrants' transfers	896	942	1,001	1,231	1,394	1,382	1,160	–

a. For comparison: net FDI inflows US$93.5 bn, total international reserves US$53.0 bn, exports of goods and services US$772.9 bn in 2008.

United States

Population (millions, 2009)	307.0
Population growth (avg. annual %, 2000–09)	1.0
Population density (people per km², 2008)	33.2
Labor force (millions, 2008)	156.3
Unemployment rate (% of labor force, 2008)	5.8
Urban population (% of pop., 2009)	82.0
Surface area (1,000 km², 2008)	9,632.0
GNI (US$ billions, 2009)	14,345.3
GNI per capita, Atlas method (US$, 2009)	47,240
GDP growth (avg. annual %, 2005–09)	1.2
Poverty headcount ratio at national poverty line (% of pop., 2005)	–
Age dependency ratio (2009)	49.5

Migration

EMIGRATION, 2010

- Stock of emigrants: **2,423.6 thousands**
- Stock of emigrants as percentage of population: **0.8%**
- Top destination countries: Mexico, Canada, Puerto Rico, the United Kingdom, Germany, Australia, West Bank and Gaza, Japan, France, the Philippines

SKILLED EMIGRATION, 2000

- Emigration rate of tertiary-educated population: **0.5%**
- Emigration of physicians: **1,664** or **0.2%** of physicians trained in the country (*Source: Bhargava, Docquier, and Moullan 2010*)

IMMIGRATION, 2010

- Stock of immigrants: **42,813.3 thousands**
- Stock of immigrants as percentage of population: **13.5%**
- Females as percentage of immigrants: **49.9%**
- Refugees as percentage of immigrants: **1.3%**
- Top source countries: Mexico, China, the Philippines, India, Puerto Rico, Vietnam, El Salvador, the Republic of Korea, Cuba, Canada

Remittances

US$ *millions*	2003	2004	2005	2006	2007	2008	2009	2010e
Inward remittance flows[a]	**2,813**	**2,822**	**2,890**	**2,883**	**2,970**	**3,045**	**2,947**	**3,122**
of which								
Workers' remittances	–	–	–	–	–	–	–	–
Compensation of employees	2,813	2,822	2,890	2,883	2,970	3,045	2,947	–
Migrants' transfers	–	–	–	–	–	–	–	–
Outward remittance flows	**36,545**	**39,347**	**40,635**	**43,620**	**46,995**	**48,829**	**48,304**	–
of which								
Workers' remittances	28,033	30,384	31,345	34,130	36,929	38,465	37,552	–
Compensation of employees	8,512	8,963	9,290	9,490	10,066	10,364	10,756	–
Migrants' transfers	–	–	–	–	–	–	–	–

a. For comparison: net FDI inflows US$319.7 bn, total international reserves US$294.0 bn in 2008.

Uruguay

Population (millions, 2009)	3.3
Population growth (avg. annual %, 2000–09)	0.2
Population density (people per km², 2008)	19.0
Labor force (millions, 2008)	1.6
Unemployment rate (% of labor force, 2008)	7.6
Urban population (% of pop., 2009)	92.4
Surface area (1,000 km², 2008)	176.2
GNI (US$ billions, 2009)	35.3
GNI per capita, Atlas method (US$, 2009)	9,360
GDP growth (avg. annual %, 2005-09)	6.0
Poverty headcount ratio at national poverty line (% of pop., 2005)	—
Age dependency ratio (2009)	57.7

Migration

EMIGRATION, 2010

- Stock of emigrants: **353.4 thousands**
- Stock of emigrants as percentage of population: **10.5%**
- Top destination countries: Argentina, Spain, the United States, Brazil, Australia, Canada, República Bolivariana de Venezuela, Chile, Paraguay, Sweden

SKILLED EMIGRATION, 2000

- Emigration rate of tertiary-educated population: **8.1%**
- Emigration of physicians: **298** or **2.4%** of physicians trained in the country
  (Source: Bhargava, Docquier, and Moullan 2010)

IMMIGRATION, 2010

- Stock of immigrants: **79.9 thousands**
- Stock of immigrants as percentage of population: **2.4%**
- Females as percentage of immigrants: **54.0%**
- Refugees as percentage of immigrants: **0.2%**
- Top source countries: Argentina, Spain, Brazil, Italy, Chile, Germany, Paraguay, Poland, the United States, France

Remittances

US$ millions	2003	2004	2005	2006	2007	2008	2009	2010e
Inward remittance flows[a]	**62**	**70**	**77**	**89**	**96**	**108**	**101**	**104**
of which								
Workers' remittances	62	70	77	89	96	108	—	—
Compensation of employees	—	0	0	0	—	—	—	—
Migrants' transfers	—	—	—	—	—	—	—	—
Outward remittance flows	**1**	**2**	**2**	**3**	**4**	**5**	**6**	—
of which								
Workers' remittances	1	2	2	3	4	5	—	—
Compensation of employees	—	—	—	—	—	—	—	—
Migrants' transfers	—	—	—	—	—	—	—	—

a. For comparison: net FDI inflows US$2.2 bn, total international reserves US$6.4 bn, exports of goods and services US$9.1 bn in 2008.

Uzbekistan

LOWER MIDDLE INCOME

Population (millions, 2009)	27.8
Population growth (avg. annual %, 2000–09)	1.3
Population density (people per km², 2008)	64.2
Labor force (millions, 2008)	11.9
Unemployment rate (% of labor force, 2008)	—
Urban population (% of pop., 2009)	36.9
Surface area (1,000 km², 2008)	447.4
GNI (US$ billions, 2009)	32.9
GNI per capita, Atlas method (US$, 2009)	1,100
GDP growth (avg. annual %, 2005–09)	8.2
Poverty headcount ratio at national poverty line (% of pop., 2005)	38.8
Age dependency ratio (2009)	51.0

Migration

EMIGRATION, 2010

- Stock of emigrants: **1,955.1 thousands**
- Stock of emigrants as percentage of population: **7.0%**
- Top destination countries: the Russian Federation, Ukraine, Kazakhstan, Israel, the Kyrgyz Republic, Turkmenistan, Latvia, the United States, Tajikistan, Germany

SKILLED EMIGRATION, 2000

- Emigration rate of tertiary-educated population: **0.7%**
- Emigration of physicians: **214** or **0.3%** of physicians trained in the country *(Source: Bhargava, Docquier, and Moullan 2010)*

IMMIGRATION, 2010

- Stock of immigrants: **1,175.9 thousands**
- Stock of immigrants as percentage of population: **4.2%**
- Females as percentage of immigrants: **57.1%**
- Refugees as percentage of immigrants: **0.1%**
- Top source countries: the Russian Federation, Tajikistan, Kazakhstan

Remittances

Remittance data are currently not available for this country.

Vanuatu

LOWER MIDDLE INCOME

Population (millions, 2009)	0.2
Population growth (avg. annual %, 2000–09)	2.6
Population density (people per km², 2008)	19.0
Labor force (millions, 2008)	0.1
Unemployment rate (% of labor force, 2008)	–
Urban population (% of pop., 2009)	25.2
Surface area (1,000 km², 2008)	12.2
GNI (US$ billions, 2009)	0.6
GNI per capita, Atlas method (US$, 2009)	2,620
GDP growth (avg. annual %, 2005–09)	5.9
Poverty headcount ratio at national poverty line (% of pop., 2005)	–
Age dependency ratio (2009)	72.1

Migration

EMIGRATION, 2010

- Stock of emigrants: **3.9 thousands**
- Stock of emigrants as percentage of population: **1.6%**
- Top destination countries: Australia, New Caledonia, France, New Zealand, the United Kingdom, Colombia, the United States, Spain, Fiji, Samoa

SKILLED EMIGRATION, 2000

- Emigration rate of tertiary-educated population: **8.2%**

IMMIGRATION, 2010

- Stock of immigrants: **0.8 thousand**
- Stock of immigrants as percentage of population: **0.3%**
- Females as percentage of immigrants: **46.8%**
- Refugees as percentage of immigrants: **0.1%**
- Top source countries: Australia, France, New Zealand, the United Kingdom, Fiji, New Caledonia, Papua New Guinea, the Solomon Islands

Remittances

US$ millions	2003	2004	2005	2006	2007	2008	2009	2010e
Inward remittance flows[a]	4	5	5	5	6	7	6	7
of which								
Workers' remittances	0	0	0	0	1	–	–	–
Compensation of employees	4	5	5	5	4	–	–	–
Migrants' transfers	–	–	–	–	–	–	–	–
Outward remittance flows	3	3	3	3	3	–	–	–
of which								
Workers' remittances	0	0	0	0	0	–	–	–
Compensation of employees	3	3	3	3	2	–	–	–
Migrants' transfers	–	–	–	–	–	–	–	–

a. For comparison: net ODA received US$0.1 bn, total international reserves US$0.1 bn, exports of goods and services US$0.3 bn in 2008.

Venezuela, República Bolivariana de

Population (millions, 2009)	28.4
Population growth (avg. annual %, 2000–09)	1.7
Population density (people per km², 2008)	31.7
Labor force (millions, 2008)	12.7
Unemployment rate (% of labor force, 2008)	7.4
Urban population (% of pop., 2009)	93.7
Surface area (1,000 km², 2008)	912.1
GNI (US$ billions, 2009)	327.2
GNI per capita, Atlas method (US$, 2009)	10,150
GDP growth (avg. annual %, 2005–09)	6.0
Poverty headcount ratio at national poverty line (% of pop., 2005)	10.0
Age dependency ratio (2009)	54.5

Migration

EMIGRATION, 2010

- Stock of emigrants: **521.5 thousands**
- Stock of emigrants as percentage of population: **1.8%**
- Top destination countries: the United States, Spain, Colombia, Portugal, the Dominican Republic, Ecuador, Canada, Chile, Italy, the United Kingdom

SKILLED EMIGRATION, 2000

- Emigration rate of tertiary-educated population: **3.4%**
- Emigration of physicians: **1,136** or **2.4%** of physicians trained in the country *(Source: Bhargava, Docquier, and Moullan 2010)*

IMMIGRATION, 2010

- Stock of immigrants: **1,007.4 thousands**
- Stock of immigrants as percentage of population: **3.5%**
- Females as percentage of immigrants: **50.1%**
- Refugees as percentage of immigrants: **19.9%**
- Top source countries: Colombia, Spain, Portugal, Italy, Peru, Ecuador, Chile, the Dominican Republic, the Syrian Arab Republic, Cuba

Remittances

US$ millions	2003	2004	2005	2006	2007	2008	2009	2010e
Inward remittance flows[a]	**208**	**143**	**148**	**165**	**151**	**137**	**131**	**129**
of which								
Workers' remittances	187	123	128	145	131	117	109	—
Compensation of employees	21	20	20	20	20	20	22	—
Migrants' transfers	—	—	—	—	—	—	—	—
Outward remittance flows	**209**	**214**	**211**	**257**	**649**	**860**	**581**	—
of which								
Workers' remittances	179	186	183	225	622	832	550	—
Compensation of employees	30	28	28	32	27	28	31	—
Migrants' transfers	—	—	—	—	—	—	—	—

a. For comparison: net FDI inflows US$0.3 bn, net ODA received US$0.1 bn, total international reserves US$43.1 bn, exports of goods and services US$95.4 bn in 2008.

Vietnam

Population (millions, 2009)	87.3
Population growth (avg. annual %, 2000–09)	1.2
Population density (people per km², 2008)	278.0
Labor force (millions, 2008)	44.9
Unemployment rate (% of labor force, 2008)	–
Urban population (% of pop., 2009)	28.3
Surface area (1,000 km², 2008)	329.3
GNI (US$ billions, 2009)	88.6
GNI per capita, Atlas method (US$, 2009)	1,010
GDP growth (avg. annual %, 2005–09)	7.4
Poverty headcount ratio at national poverty line (% of pop., 2005)	22.8
Age dependency ratio (2009)	47.2

Migration

EMIGRATION, 2010

- Stock of emigrants: **2,226.4 thousands**
- Stock of emigrants as percentage of population: **2.5%**
- Top destination countries: the United States, Australia, Canada, Cambodia, Germany, France, the Republic of Korea, Japan, the United Kingdom, Thailand

SKILLED EMIGRATION, 2000

- Emigration rate of tertiary-educated population: **27.1%**
- Emigration of physicians: **1,933** or **4.5%** of physicians trained in the country (*Source: Bhargava, Docquier, and Moullan 2010*)

IMMIGRATION, 2010

- Stock of immigrants: **69.3 thousands**
- Stock of immigrants as percentage of population: **0.1%**
- Females as percentage of immigrants: **36.6%**
- Refugees as percentage of immigrants: **3.4%**

Remittances

US$ millions	2003	2004	2005	2006	2007	2008	2009	2010e
Inward remittance flows[a]	**2,700**	**3,200**	**4,000**	**4,800**	**5,500**	**7,200**	**6,626**	**7,215**
of which								
Workers' remittances	–	–	–	–	–	–	–	–
Compensation of employees	–	–	–	–	–	–	–	–
Migrants' transfers	–	–	–	–	–	–	–	–
Outward remittance flows	–	–	–	–	–	–	–	–
of which								
Workers' remittances	–	–	–	–	–	–	–	–
Compensation of employees	–	–	–	–	–	–	–	–
Migrants' transfers	–	–	–	–	–	–	–	–

a. For comparison: net FDI inflows US$9.6 bn, net ODA received US$2.6 bn, total international reserves US$23.9 bn, exports of goods and services US$70.9 bn in 2008.

Virgin Islands (U.S.)

Population (millions, 2009)	0.1
Population growth (avg. annual %, 2000–09)	0.1
Population density (people per km², 2008)	313.8
Labor force (millions, 2008)	0.1
Unemployment rate (% of labor force, 2008)	—
Urban population (% of pop., 2009)	95.1
Surface area (1,000 km², 2008)	0.4
GNI (US$ billions, 2009)	—
GNI per capita, Atlas method (US$, 2009)	—
GDP growth (avg. annual %, 2005–09)	—
Poverty headcount ratio at national poverty line (% of pop., 2005)	—
Age dependency ratio (2009)	52.8

Migration

EMIGRATION, 2010

- Stock of emigrants: **51.1 thousands**
- Stock of emigrants as percentage of population: **46.7%**
- Top destination countries: the United States, the Dominican Republic, St. Lucia, Antigua and Barbuda, St. Kitts and Nevis, Netherlands Antilles, the United Kingdom, Canada, Panama, Greece

SKILLED EMIGRATION, 2000

- Skilled emigration data are currently not available for this country.

IMMIGRATION, 2010

- Stock of immigrants: **61.8 thousands**
- Stock of immigrants as percentage of population: **56.5%**
- Females as percentage of immigrants: **53.3%**
- Refugees as percentage of immigrants: **0.0%**
- Top source countries: the United States, St. Kitts and Nevis, Dominica, Antigua and Barbuda, St. Lucia, the Dominican Republic, Trinidad and Tobago, Haiti, Jamaica, Cayman Islands

Remittances

Remittance data are currently not available for this country.

West Bank and Gaza

Population (millions, 2009)	4.0
Population growth (avg. annual %, 2000–09)	3.3
Population density (people per km², 2008)	637.5
Labor force (millions, 2008)	0.8
Unemployment rate (% of labor force, 2008)	26.0
Urban population (% of pop., 2009)	72.0
Surface area (1,000 km², 2008)	6.0
GNI (US$ billions, 2009)	–
GNI per capita, Atlas method (US$, 2009)	–
GDP growth (avg. annual %, 2005–09)	–
Poverty headcount ratio at national poverty line (% of pop., 2005)	–
Age dependency ratio (2009)	91.5

Migration

EMIGRATION, 2010

- Stock of emigrants: **3,013.7 thousands**
- Stock of emigrants as percentage of population: **68.3%**
- Top destination countries: the Syrian Arab Republic, Jordan, Saudi Arabia, the Arab Republic of Egypt, Libya, the Republic of Yemen, Canada, Iraq, the United Kingdom, Australia

SKILLED EMIGRATION, 2000

- Emigration rate of tertiary-educated population: **7.2%**
- Emigration of physicians: **15** or **0.7%** of physicians trained in the country
  (Source: Bhargava, Docquier, and Moullan 2010)

IMMIGRATION, 2010

- Stock of immigrants: **1,923.8 thousands**
- Stock of immigrants as percentage of population: **43.6%**
- Females as percentage of immigrants: **49.2%**
- Refugees as percentage of immigrants: **100.0%**
- Top source countries: Israel, Jordan, the Arab Republic of Egypt, the United States, the Syrian Arab Republic, Lebanon, the Republic of Yemen, Tunisia

Remittances

US$ millions	2003	2004	2005	2006	2007	2008	2009	2010e
Inward remittance flows[a]	**572**	**638**	**705**	**928**	**1,085**	**1,220**	**1,261**	**1,307**
of which								
Workers' remittances	115	199	156	346	475	468	–	–
Compensation of employees	428	421	487	579	599	738	–	–
Migrants' transfers	29	17	62	3	12	14	–	–
Outward remittance flows	**22**	**13**	**8**	**9**	**9**	**9**	**9**	–
of which								
Workers' remittances	21	12	7	8	8	9	–	–
Compensation of employees	1	1	1	1	1	1	–	–
Migrants' transfers	–	–	–	–	–	–	–	–

a. For comparison: net ODA received US$2.6 bn in 2008.

Yemen, Republic of

Population (millions, 2009)	23.6
Population growth (avg. annual %, 2000–09)	2.9
Population density (people per km², 2008)	43.7
Labor force (millions, 2008)	5.4
Unemployment rate (% of labor force, 2008)	–
Urban population (% of pop., 2009)	31.2
Surface area (1,000 km², 2008)	528.0
GNI (US$ billions, 2009)	24.9
GNI per capita, Atlas method (US$, 2009)	1,060
GDP growth (avg. annual %, 2005–09)	3.9
Poverty headcount ratio at national poverty line (% of pop., 2005)	17.5
Age dependency ratio (2009)	85.7

Migration

EMIGRATION, 2010

- Stock of emigrants: **1,134.7 thousands**
- Stock of emigrants as percentage of population: **4.7%**
- Top destination countries: Saudi Arabia, the United Arab Emirates, the United States, Israel, Jordan, the United Kingdom, West Bank and Gaza, Sudan, Germany, France

SKILLED EMIGRATION, 2000

- Emigration rate of tertiary-educated population: **6.0%**
- Emigration of physicians: **47** or **1.3%** of physicians trained in the country *(Source: Bhargava, Docquier, and Moullan 2010)*

IMMIGRATION, 2010

- Stock of immigrants: **517.9 thousands**
- Stock of immigrants as percentage of population: **2.1%**
- Females as percentage of immigrants: **38.3%**
- Refugees as percentage of immigrants: **20.6%**
- Top source countries: Sudan, Somalia, the Arab Republic of Egypt, Iraq, West Bank and Gaza, the Syrian Arab Republic

Remittances

US$ millions	2003	2004	2005	2006	2007	2008	2009	2010e
Inward remittance flow[aa]	**1,270**	**1,283**	**1,283**	**1,283**	**1,322**	**1,411**	**1,378**	**1,471**
of which								
Workers' remittances	1,270	1,283	1,283	1,283	1,322	1,411	–	–
Compensation of employees	–	–	–	–	–	–	–	–
Migrants' transfers	–	–	–	–	–	–	–	–
Outward remittance flows	**60**	**108**	**109**	**120**	**319**	**337**	**337**	**–**
of which								
Workers' remittances	60	36	37	41	41	48	–	–
Compensation of employees	–	72	72	80	278	289	–	–
Migrants' transfers	–	–	–	–	–	–	–	–

a. For comparison: net FDI inflows US$1.6 bn, net ODA received US$0.3 bn, total international reserves US$8.2 bn in 2008.

Zambia

Sub-Saharan Africa **LOW INCOME**

Population (millions, 2009)	12.9
Population growth (avg. annual %, 2000–09)	2.4
Population density (people per km², 2008)	17.0
Labor force (millions, 2008)	4.6
Unemployment rate (% of labor force, 2008)	–
Urban population (% of pop., 2009)	35.6
Surface area (1,000 km², 2008)	752.6
GNI (US$ billions, 2009)	11.4
GNI per capita, Atlas method (US$, 2009)	970
GDP growth (avg. annual %, 2005–09)	5.9
Poverty headcount ratio at national poverty line (% of pop., 2005)	64.3
Age dependency ratio (2009)	97.1

Migration

EMIGRATION, 2010

- Stock of emigrants: **185.8 thousands**
- Stock of emigrants as percentage of population: **1.4%**
- Top destination countries: Tanzania, the United Kingdom, Zimbabwe, Malawi, Namibia, the United States, Mozambique, Australia, Canada, New Zealand

SKILLED EMIGRATION, 2000

- Emigration rate of tertiary-educated population: **16.8%**
- Emigration of physicians:
  - (a) **224** or **24.7%** of physicians trained in the country *(Source: Bhargava, Docquier, and Moullan 2010)*
  - (b) **883** or **56.9%** of physicians born in the country *(Source: Clemens and Pettersson 2006)*
- Emigration of nurses: **1,110** or **9.2%** of nurses born in the country

IMMIGRATION, 2010

- Stock of immigrants: **233.1 thousands**
- Stock of immigrants as percentage of population: **1.8%**
- Females as percentage of immigrants: **49.6%**
- Refugees as percentage of immigrants: **50.0%**
- Top source countries: Angola, the Democratic Republic of Congo, Zimbabwe, Malawi, India, the Republic of Congo, South Africa, the United Kingdom, Mozambique, the United States

Remittances

US$ million	2003	2004	2005	2006	2007	2008	2009	2010e
Inward remittance flows[a]	**36**	**48**	**53**	**58**	**59**	**68**	**68**	**71**
of which								
Workers' remittances	36	48	53	58	59	68	–	–
Compensation of employees	–	–	–	–	–	–	–	–
Migrants' transfers	–	–	–	–	–	–	–	–
Outward remittance flows	**72**	**76**	**94**	**115**	**124**	**139**	**66**	**–**
of which								
Workers' remittances	55	64	77	93	96	110	37	–
Compensation of employees	17	12	17	23	28	29	29	–
Migrants' transfers	–	–	–	–	–	–	–	–

a. For comparison: net FDI inflows US$0.9 bn, net ODA received US$1.1 bn, total international reserves US$1.1 bn, exports of goods and services US$5.3 bn in 2008.

Zimbabwe

Sub-Saharan Africa — **LOW INCOME**

Population (millions, 2009)	12.5
Population growth (avg. annual %, 2000–09)	0.1
Population density (people per km², 2008)	32.2
Labor force (millions, 2008)	5.2
Unemployment rate (% of labor force, 2008)	—
Urban population (% of pop., 2009)	37.8
Surface area (1,000 km², 2008)	390.8
GNI (US$ billions, 2009)	—
GNI per capita, Atlas method (US$, 2009)	—
GDP growth (avg. annual %, 2005–09)	—
Poverty headcount ratio at national poverty line (% of pop., 2005)	—
Age dependency ratio (2009)	78.5

Migration

EMIGRATION, 2010

- Stock of emigrants: **1,253.1 thousands**
- Stock of emigrants as percentage of population: **9.9%**
- Top destination countries: South Africa, the United Kingdom, Mozambique, Australia, Zambia, the United States, Malawi, New Zealand, Canada, Ireland

SKILLED EMIGRATION, 2000

- Emigration rate of tertiary-educated population: **12.7%**
- Emigration of physicians:
  - (a) **449** or **30.7%** of physicians trained in the country *(Source: Bhargava, Docquier, and Moullan 2010)*
  - (b) **1,602** or **51.1%** of physicians born in the country *(Source: Clemens and Pettersson 2006)*
- Emigration of nurses: **3,723** or **24.2%** of nurses born in the country

IMMIGRATION, 2010

- Stock of immigrants: **372.3 thousands**
- Stock of immigrants as percentage of population: **2.9%**
- Females as percentage of immigrants: **37.8%**
- Refugees as percentage of immigrants: **1.0%**
- Top source countries: Mozambique, Malawi, Zambia, the United Kingdom, South Africa, Botswana

Remittances

Remittance data are currently not available for this country.

Glossary

Age dependency ratio (dependents to working-age population) is the ratio of dependents—people younger than age 15 or older than age 64—to the working-age population. For example, 70 means there are 70 dependents for every 100 working-age people (World Bank).

Compensation of employees comprises wages, salaries, and other benefits (in cash or in kind) earned by individuals—in countries other than those in which they are residents—for work performed for and paid for by residents of those countries. Employees, in this context, include seasonal or other short-term workers (less than one year) and border workers who have centers of economic interest in their own countries (IMF 2010b).

Emigration rate of tertiary-educated population is the stock of emigrants with at least tertiary education as a fraction of the total tertiary-educated population in the country. Tertiary education refers to more than secondary education—more than high school or 13 years of education (Docquier and Marfouk 2006).

Labor force comprises people who meet the International Labour Organization (ILO) definition of the economically active population: all people who supply labor for the production of goods and services during a specified period. It includes both the employed and the unemployed. Although national practices vary in the treatment of such groups as the armed forces and seasonal or part-time workers, in general the labor force includes the armed forces, the unemployed, and first-time job seekers, but excludes homemakers and other unpaid caregivers and workers in the informal sector (ILO, using World Bank population estimates).

Migrants are persons who move to a country other than that of their usual residence for a period of at least one year, so that the country of destination effectively becomes their new country of usual residence (UNPD).

Migrants' transfers are contra-entries to flows of goods and changes in financial items that arise from migration (change of residence for at least one year) of individuals from one country to another. The transfers to be recorded are thus equal to the net worth of the migrants (IMF 2010a).

Poverty headcount ratio at national poverty line is the percentage of the population living below the national poverty line. Since its *World Development Report 1990* (World Bank 1990), the World Bank's "global" poverty measures have usually been based on an international poverty line of about US$1 a day; more precisely, the line is US$32.74 per month, at 1993 international purchasing power parity (World Bank).

Refugees are individuals who owing to a well-founded fear of being persecuted for reasons of race, religion, nationality, membership of a particular social group or political opinion, are outside the country of their nationality and are unable or, owing to such fear, are unwilling to avail themselves of the protection of that country; or who, not having a nationality and being outside the country of their former habitual residence as a result of such events, are unable or, owing to such fear, are unwilling to return to it. The estimates of refugee populations as of mid-2005 were prepared by the UN Population Division. (UNPD)

Remittances are the sum of workers' remittances, compensation of employees, and migrants' transfers (World Bank).

Workers' remittances are current transfers by migrants who are considered residents in the destination country (IMF 2010a).

green
press
INITIATIVE

www.ingramcontent.com/pod-product-compliance
Lightning Source LLC
Chambersburg PA
CBHW071845270326
41929CB00013B/2107